Chicago Blues

Music in American Life

A list of books in the series
appears at the end of this book.

Chicago
Blues

PORTRAITS
AND STORIES

David Whiteis

UNIVERSITY OF ILLINOIS PRESS
URBANA AND CHICAGO

Library of Congress Cataloging-in-Publication Data
Whiteis, David. Chicago blues : portraits
and stories / David Whiteis.
p.   cm. — (Music in American life)
Includes bibliographical references (p.) and index.
ISBN-13: 978-0-252-03068-0 (cloth : alk. paper)
ISBN-10: 0-252-03068-0 (cloth : alk. paper)
ISBN-13: 978-0-252-7309-0 (pbk. : alk. paper)
ISBN-10: 0-252-07309-6 (pbk. : alk. paper)
1. Blues musicians—Illinois—Chicago—Biography.
2. African Americans—Illinois—Chicago—Music—
History and criticism. 3. Blues (Music)—Illinois—
Chicago—History and criticism.
I. Title. II. Series.
ML394.W5   2006
781.643'09773'11—dc22   2005021528

Dedicated to the memories of Corrina and Elijah Bell-Greenberg

Come away, O human child!
To the waters and the wild
With a faery, hand in hand,
For the world's more full of weeping
than you can understand.
　　—W. B. Yeats

Contents

Part 3: Torchbearers

Part 4: "The Soul Side of Town"

Acknowledgments

Without the kindness and resourcefulness of Scott Barretta, former editor of *Living Blues* magazine, this project would never have gotten off the ground. Without the ongoing support and professional dedication of Judy McCulloh, Cope Cumpston, and the rest of the dedicated crew at the University of Illinois Press, it would have crashed. I offer my sincere thanks and gratitude toward these friends and colleagues.

Dick Shurman and Steve Wisner generously shared their recordings from the early careers of Jody Williams, Bonnie Lee, Cicero Blake, and Artie "Blues Boy" White. Jim Themelis allowed me to peruse his Big Walter Horton archives. Carolyn "the Blues Lady" Alexander lent me items from her extensive collection of videos that she had taped in clubs and at other Chicago blues venues over the years. Jim O'Neal was always ready to field questions and prod my thinking in new directions. Cilla Huggins contributed her extensive knowledge of Memphis blues recording history. Both Bob Pruter and Bill Dahl provided historical and discographical information, as well as fact-checking rigor and scholarly assistance. Dr. John O'Connor, a former professor at the University of Illinois in Urbana, kindly shared his memories of Harmonica Khan's participation in the university-sponsored prisoners' music program; he also allowed me to borrow a copy of the rare LP on which Khan appeared.

People whose expertise, friendship, support, and encouragement over the years helped inspire and facilitate this project include Gaye Adegbalola, Alice the Drum Diva, Jillina Arrigo, Steve Balkin, Eddie Berner (Chicago's no. 1 blues fan), Brett Bonner, John Brisbin, Mark Brumbach, Holly Bullamore, Sam Burckhardt, the late Bill Burke, Dayna Calderon, Barbara Campbell,

Eddie C. Campbell, Jerry Chodkowski, Quinton Claunch, Nadine Cohodas, Bob Corritore, Pete Crawford, Steve Cushing, Clark Dean, Jim DeJong, Scott Dirks, Steve Ditzell, Barry Dolins, Mot Dutko, Deb Ellis, Deitra Farr, Bill Fitzgerald, Jim Fraher, Michael Frank, Niles Frantz, Steve Freund, Shelley Fu, Paul Garon, Ann Gibson, Lacy Gibson, Bill Gilmore, Lea Gilmore, Martin Goggin, Robert Gordon, Maggie Green, Leola Grey, Ray Grey, Peter Guralnick, Jeff Hannusch (aka "Almost Slim"), Hannah Hayes, Rob Hecko, Erwin Helfer, Dave Helland, Dave Hoekstra, Larry Hoffman, Marguerite Horberg, Abby Hotchkiss, Jody Houldcroft, Bruce Iglauer, Incense Tony, Fruteland Jackson, the late Willie James, the late Susan Jeffries, Patty Johnson, Bob Jones, the late Floyd Jones, Harrel Jones (H. J. the D.J.), Kay Jones, Letha Jones, Willie Kent, Bob Koester, Sue Koester, Jon Lathrop, Mike Lipsey, Andria Lisle, Jennifer Littleton, John Litweiler, Mama Rosa, Tony Mangiullo, Peter Margasak, Ewa Matysik, Ralph Metcalfe Jr., Mike Miner, Blythe Modrowski, Tom Morris ("Illinois Slim"), Mr. A., Paul Natkin, Theresa Needham, David Nelson, Yoko Noge, Justin O'Brien, Sterling Plumpp, Sandra Pointer-Jones, Marc PoKempner, John Primer, Ann Rabson, Wes Race, Karen Risinger, the late Gail Sacks, Ben Sandmel, Delores Scott, the late Elaine "Cookie" Shmura, Rosalie Sorrels, Pervis Spann, Robert Stroger, Kenny Tams, Neil Tesser, Carmella Tomaso, Alison True, Twist Turner, the late Lois Ulry, Amy Van Singel, the late Tenner "Playboy" Venson, Steve Wagner, Dick Waterman, Liz Weinstein, Kirk Whiting, Felix Wohrstein, Lynn Wohrstein, Carl Wright, Kiki Yablon, Little Rich Yescalis, Christine Zoodeedoo—and of course, all the artists and everyone else who gave their time to talk to me and put up with my pestering questions over the course of interviews and follow-ups for this book.

Chicago **Blues**

Introduction

"Mister Blues, How Do You Do?" / "Can I Change My Mind?"

Someone Done Hoodoo'd the Hoodoo Man

"How do you like the snow?"

Junior Wells, looking knife-sharp and dapper in a gray fedora and pinstriped suit, sat on a barstool near the entrance of Theresa's Lounge and broke into an impish grin. I had just told him how thrilled I was to meet him, only a week or so after I'd arrived in town, in the legendary little basement tavern that served as his Chicago home base. I'm not sure what I expected his reaction to be. Like many enthusiasts, I had no doubt constructed a heroic image of myself as a lone traveler on the blues highway, seeking "authenticity" in places where few white men had gone before. Maybe I anticipated gratitude or even astonishment from this man who had helped create the sound known as Chicago blues, the sound that had brought me from Connecticut in hopes of experiencing it on its home turf. But his hip nonchalance and offhand comment about the weather weren't among the possibilities I had considered. For the first of what would be innumerable occasions, I found my preconceived notions about Chicago blues—the music, the people, the culture—confounded. Such confound-

The Hoodoo Man: Junior Wells, November 24, 1995. Photo by Joeff Davis/www
.Joeff.com

ings eventually spawned new and unexpected perspectives, angles of vision,
and—I hope—understandings, some of which eventually gave rise to this
book.

In this book I focus on the blues as a living element of a vital and ever-
changing diasporan culture rooted in African American experience but with
a universality that speaks to diverse audiences and listeners. As befits the
music of an uprooted people, the blues casts travel as one of its archetypal
themes—travel away from oppression, toward horizons real and metaphorical,
in search of a better day. In that spirit, this book, too, chronicles a journey:
my own journey of discovery, which I've found myself undertaking over the
course of twenty-five years on the Chicago scene. Junior, in other words, did
his job well. Like Eshu-Eleggua, the Yoruba trickster god who resides at the
crossroads and controls the portal between this realm and the spirit world,[1]
he jolted me out of complacency and into a state of uncertainty and confu-

sion—the better to prepare me for insight as I began to immerse myself more deeply into the world at whose periphery I encountered him on that cold January night in 1979.

Further on up the Road

The Great Migration of the early and middle twentieth century saw the up-rooting of a predominately rural and southern African American culture rich with elements extending back to antebellum times and to African tradition before that. Along with gospel, jazz, and (later) R&B and soul music, the blues served as an impetus for, a soundtrack to, and a commentary on this migratory phenomenon. As people moved north, southern folkways—famil-ial, religious, musical, social, even culinary and recreational—were adapted to an urban industrial environment. The music changed too, of course, as migrants adjusted to life in communities that were in many ways freer than the South had been yet also presented new challenges, new forms of racial and economic disfranchisement, and new threats to both individual and cultural survival.

The lives of the musicians profiled here illustrate these concerns. Most Chicago-based blues artists who are middle-aged or older were born in the South. Even many of the younger proponents, including those whose styles are strongly influenced by soul, R&B, and contemporary pop as well as "tra-ditional" blues forms, are well aware of the heritage their music represents. Lurrie Bell, for example, spent some of his formative years living with relatives in Mississippi and Alabama. Billy Branch, the scion of a middle-class family, was born in Chicago, moved to California, and then returned to the city of his birth, yet he considers the time he spent sitting at the feet of southern-born elders like Big Walter Horton and pianist Jimmy Walker to have been among the most formative and inspirational of his life.[2]

Yet to call the blues nothing but "roots music" is to perpetrate a misnomer and, worse yet, to perpetuate a stereotype. The tension between traditional values and modernist challenges to these values represents a common theme, repeated across succeeding generations, in the development of the blues. It's also reflected in these narratives. Older musicians such as Sunnyland Slim, Big Walter Horton, and Junior Wells, who found their styles becoming passé in their own communities during the 1950s and 1960s, were "rediscovered" by (predominantly white) intellectuals and aficionados a few years later. Many settled somewhat uneasily into the role of "elder statesmen" to a generation of music lovers whose cultural and social frameworks were far removed from their own. More recently, younger performers such as Sharon Lewis and Billy Branch have similarly attempted to balance their music and even their public personas to remain both "contemporary" and sufficiently rooted in tradition to be considered legitimate blues artists; they wrestle daily with the contradiction of carrying an aesthetic torch that many members of their own community have chosen to abandon.

That's Why They Call It the Blues

The definition of the blues in the African American community, though, has never been static, and it has evolved and broadened through the years. In fact, perhaps what has been "abandoned" is less the music than an imposed folkloric paradigm that the community had never really embraced to begin with. I intend this book to be something of a corrective to the pessimistic conclusion on the future (or even the present) of Chicago blues that Mike Rowe draws in his landmark 1973 study *Chicago Breakdown*.[3] Rather than prophesy the music's death or bemoan its annihilation by assimilation, I want to use the words and life stories of some of the artists themselves, as well as vignettes from venues where the music is performed, to show the current status of the blues as a living presence in Chicago's African American community. In so doing, I also want to raise some suggestions about the music's possible future directions.

Normally such an endeavor would entail determining or at least proposing a precise definition of what it is we're trying to look at and predict. In direct opposition to the reductionist approach of conventional Western scholarship—and, I believe, in the spirit of Eshu himself—I strongly resist pinning the blues under definitions of this nature. Many or even most contemporary artists are similarly reluctant to cast paradigms in stone. Some of today's most important performers specialize in what has come to be called "soulblues," a stylistic amalgam drawn from such diverse influences as the smooth, swing-influenced twelve-bar blues pioneered by artists like T-Bone Walker, B. B. King, and Bobby "Blue" Bland; 1960s-era deep soul; R&B; and—increasingly—rap and hip-hop. Even Artie White, who proudly considers himself one of the last of the true blues singers, works in a style not radically different from that of many soul-blues vocalists who just as proudly refuse to pigeonhole themselves as "blues" artists, although they appear regularly on blues shows and their fan base consists of the same people who pay to see and hear more traditionally labeled blues stars, such as King and Bland.

Things get even more complex when one notes that many of these performers—like Cicero Blake and, at least marginally, Little Scotty—were labeled "soul" artists in the 1960s and 1970s yet now carry on in "blues" by singing much the same kind of material as before. As they moved into the blues arena, they brought their aesthetic perspectives with them, and in doing so they widened the entire landscape, making room for younger artists to widen it still more. In 2003 black-oriented blues stations began to program R. Kelly's ballad "You Made Me Love You." A few oldheads grumbled, but listeners responded favorably, and no less an authority than Cicero Blake averred, "That's blues! There's no way that's not a blues record!"[4]

In fact, it appears that the term *blues,* if presented in the right context, can now encompass nearly any secular music that tells its story in a way that reflects unencumbered emotional honesty from an adult perspective and at least somewhat echoes the diasporan voice (i.e., "soul" in the broader sense of the term). This definitional flexibility isn't necessarily new, either: Al Green, a soul singer turned minister, has publicly referred to his 1977 hit "Love and Happiness" as "a blues song," and he has also affirmed that it's a "good song" that he can (and does) include in his gospel performances.[5] Memphis songwriter Roosevelt Jamison, after implying that he saw the blues as reflecting an earlier, oppressive era (he emphasized that his creations, unlike "the gutbucket stuff," are uplifting and literate), praised soul legend James Carr, his own protégé and the primary purveyor of his songs, as "one of the greatest blues singers of all time."[6]

When pressed, some of the artists profiled here responded with their own opinions on what the blues means to them, and in most cases, despite their best efforts, they ended up sounding almost as ambiguous as Green and Jamison (to say nothing of the various scholars and musicologists who have weighed in over the years). Lurrie Bell maintains that the shuffle-based, twelve-bar Chicago style he used to play alongside his father, harpist Carey Bell, represents the blues closest to his heart, but when it came time for him to bond with his newborn babies as they lay weak and unwell in a hospital ICU, he strapped on his acoustic guitar and sang them songs by the Temptations and Sam Cooke.[7] Sharon Lewis is more adamant on insisting on what the blues *isn't* ("one-four-five, dump-de-dump, dump-de-dump") than on trying to codify what it *is;*[8] Cicero Blake, who started out in street-corner doo-wop, passed through jump blues and soul, and finally made his mark in soul-blues with a pop-tinged twelve-bar ballad in the 1970s, uses almost identical terminology in disparaging that "old lump-de-bump-de-bump 'Sweet Home Chicago' stuff"—and then goes on to praise R. Kelly's hip-hop–influenced crooning.[9]

In the end the blues is revealed to be a malleable concept, rooted in deeply shared cultural and aesthetic values ("cultural memory," to use Samuel Floyd's preferred phrase)[10] but continuously adaptable to shifting conditions and realities. It is this meld of common heritage, individual and collective lived experience, and commercially influenced popular tastes that represents the musical, social, and cultural expression known as "the blues." Seen in this light, the impossibility of pinning down specifics is part of the definition. The music defines itself as it is created and as its audience reacts to it; it evolves in an ongoing dialogic process that ultimately has little to do with labels imposed by record companies, intellectuals, or critics.

This process, moreover, continues to be misunderstood. Francis Davis, for instance, has suggested that promoters reveal their desperation when they include acts like the Staple Singers in blues festivals, that they are stretching definitions past a point of meaninglessness.[11] I suggest the opposite: such eclecticism on the part of (mostly white) festival program committees represents a belated awareness of what the black community has known all along: the blues is not "just a feeling," "just notes," "just a style," or "just" anything else. It is an evolving and growing concept, philosophical—even existential—as much as it is an ideology or even an aesthetic, and it is always understood and responded to within the historical, cultural, and social context of which it is inextricably a part.

Star Time

Within this context many of the dualisms taken for granted in the Western cultural worldview—individual versus collective, serious versus playful, supernatural versus worldly, or for that matter blues versus nonblues—are not necessarily drawn sharply.[12] In its deepest essence, the blues is rooted in a venerable tradition in which spirit and flesh mingle closely, with dance, rhythm, melody, and prayer woven together into a single celebration. In this tradition a singer or storyteller (or in pre–Middle Passage days, a shaman) would spin fables or perform rituals as a member of a group—an exalted member, perhaps, but not an authority presiding from behind a podium or a pulpit or on a stage. Today this heritage survives in the well-known "call-and-response" pattern found in music, dance, oratory, and even everyday conversation, with the preacher, performer, or speaker being only one component of an ongoing communal dynamic. The audience, congregation, or listeners are vital participants; their responses—really, their half of the dialogue—are essential for the song or message to succeed.[13]

In blues performance this cultural context is usually implied or tacitly understood rather than proclaimed. Nonetheless, it touches virtually every aspect of the way the music is presented and the way people react to it. Take the notion of celebrity itself: in a milieu where respondents share the public "stage" with performers and where the in-the-moment ability to summon the celebratory spirit may be more valued than official credentials or permission to do so, the delineation between star and local favorite can be elusive and not necessarily determined by objective criteria like record sales. In fact, as Guralnick has pointed out, virtually everyone "is a celebrity in one way or another."[14] Every active artist has a "following," whether that following consists of a handful of Saturday night locals, a few thousand record-buying fans, or tens of thousands of admirers.

When a vocalist like Little Scotty takes the stage at the New Excuse Lounge on South Halsted draped in hipster finery, he's introduced with the same fanfare as if he were headlining an all-star show at the old Regal Theater on Forty-seventh Street on the South Side or at the Chicago Theatre downtown: "Ladies and gentlemen! It's *star time!* Put your hands together! . . ." This isn't disingenuous; it's a legitimate representation of the status Scotty and

Cyrus Hayes, with tip bucket, performing at Wallace's Catfish Corner, September 15, 2004. Photo by Joeff Davis/www.Joeff.com

similar artists enjoy in the community. Offstage, Scotty—or any of a dozen others, such as Bobby Too Tough, Willie D., Foxy Lady, Pamela Zachery, Little Al, and Leon McNeal—may be recognized on the street, feted at local awards ceremonies, and admired publicly by men and women alike. The walls of their dens and home studios will be adorned with publicity photos and posters from past gigs; they'll cherish the handful of 45s or CDs they may have recorded over the years for small labels. In their everyday lives, as well as on Saturday night, they'll carry themselves, think of themselves, and be regarded by others as blues stars.

Conversely, even world-famous artists usually maintain a local base—or more precisely, a network of local bases—that they must continually reaffirm if they want to remain true to the aesthetic and cultural norms of their communities. Junior Wells eschewed suburban isolation, preferring to live on Chicago's South Side, where he held down his fabled residency at Theresa's and the Checkerboard even after he attained international acclaim. Billy Branch continues in this same tradition today with his regular Monday night gigs at Artis's Lounge. Soul-blues stars like Artie White and Cicero Blake make it their business to be as prominently recognizable in the audiences at local shows, bantering at the bar or seated regally at a table near the front of the room, as they are when they take the stage. Even B. B. King returns annually to Indianola, Mississippi, to play a benefit concert that reunites him with old friends and reaffirms his connection to his roots.

The blues "community," then, still consists largely of the people who reside in the neighborhoods from which the artists themselves arose and where local performers continue to ply their trade, as well as the intricately networked series of local and regionally based clubs, theaters, and lounges that provide an important outlet for even some of the best-known performers. The link between the local and the national is represented in the overlapping histories, experiences, and stories related by the musicians in this compilation, most of whom continue to have a foot in each camp. Chicago's ongoing role as a vital nexus in this network also emerges through these stories.

A Dollar Goes from Hand to Hand

None of this means, however, that blues artists are content with mere local celebrity or don't want bigger things, brighter lights, or fatter paychecks. Quite the contrary: one of the many preconceptions I found upended when I began to explore the Chicago blues world was my romantic concept of the blues musician as a heroic troubadour of the soul, a pure "folk" artist somehow removed from crass day-to-day concerns such as remuneration.

It didn't take more than one or two Sunday afternoons in the presence of Bob the Pig-Ear Man, the raconteur/hustler who sold soul food out of a cart in front of Florence's Lounge near the corner of Fifty-fifth and Shields, to disabuse me of that notion. "He ain't makin' no *money*" was Bob's usual scornful indictment of most of the "living legends" who showed up there regularly to jam, and to my initial surprise, the musicians gathered around his cart would nod in solemn agreement when he delivered his verdict.

It's not that these "legends" weren't respected. Some had made undeniable and even historic contributions to Chicago blues in the past. In fact, most were still recognized as celebrities, at least in the sense outlined previously. But along with this recognition was an almost universal insistence, among musicians at least, on a cold, real-world truth: a musician who "ain't making no money" *today* is not a successful bluesman, no matter how many history books he's in, no matter how many tourists venture into the ghetto to ask for his autograph, and even no matter how many women scream his name when he sits in at a South Side juke on Sunday afternoon.

I was confounded by this at first, for I had heard enough musicians talk about the blues as "a feeling" and about their own feelings of release and liberation when they played the blues to know that music wasn't simply a job to most of them. I also knew that most of the local stars I encountered were paid little and either held day jobs or depended on a spouse or companion who did. Yet once I got out into the clubs, I found that money or the lack thereof dominated musicians' awareness and conversations probably more than anything else associated with their work. Even guest artists sitting in for a song or two might place a tip bucket or an upturned hat at their feet. Some of the more popular didn't even have to do that: revelers would come up to them and thrust dollar bills directly into their hands as they performed.

I shouldn't have been so surprised. It has always been that way, even back in the days of "folk" blues, when musicians hoboed around the South and scraped out a living in jukes, at picnics and barbecues, and on street corners. This component of the bluesman's profession, however, has until recently been seriously downplayed by most folklorists.

"It is customary to regard the 'folk singer' as an amateur outside 'the commercial side' of blues singing," bristled Stephen Calt and Gayle Dean Wardlow in *King of the Delta Blues*, their 1988 biography of Delta blues pioneer Charlie Patton. They added that "one would infer from [a particular folklorist's] writings that Mississippi bluesmen sang from the purest of motives" even though Ishman Bracey, a contemporary and sometime accompanist of revered "folk" bluesman Tommy Johnson, expressed a habitual sentiment when he gloated: "Me and old Tommy would play. . . . We'd be *make some money!*"[15]

Getting the house: Z. Z. Hill Jr. at Bossman Blues Center, June 2004. Photo by Andrzej Matysik/*Twoj Blues* magazine

Sam Chatmon, a founding member of the Mississippi Sheiks, expressed much the same sentiment. Despite their latter-day lionization as "authentic" carriers of the Delta blues torch, the Sheiks were a string band that specialized in novelty and pop tunes, which during their 1930s-era heyday they played mostly for whites because, as Chatmon put it, "the colored . . . didn't have nothing to hire you with."[16]

If a more contemporary voice is needed, consider Sharon Lewis, who speaks with near reverence about the way the blues came to her in her darkest hour and virtually saved her life (if not her soul). Lewis is no less adamant than are Bracey and Chatmon about day-to-day economic essentials and no less caustic than are Calt and Wardlow about the way some aficionados still seem unable to get the point. "With laypeople," she told me, "one of the things you can't talk about is the money. They'll say, 'Isn't it nice to get paid?'

Wouldn't it be nice to be able to make a living off something that you love? I don't—the club owners are gonna line their pockets first."[17]

In fact, as she implies, the code is honored more in the breach than in the practice. Almost every artist seems to have a ready phrase to rationalize a free gig or to save face over an engagement that pays a fraction of what he or she insists is the usual, nonnegotiable price: "I'm just doing the promoter a favor," "This is publicity for my *real* show coming up," or "I'm rehearsing the band." This does not alter the core truth, however. These musicians work in a world where scarcity remains a way of life and where benefits to help musicians and their families pay for hospital bills, recover from losses and tragedies such as home fires or accidents, and bury their dead are almost as common as in-club birthday parties. In this world the folk saying (and oft-repeated blues lyric) "a dollar goes from hand to hand"[18] reflects not just a philosophical verity but an everyday reality, and the determination to grab that dollar and "hold on to it till them eagles grin"[19] represents not penuriousness but a simple tool for survival.

None of which in any way compromises the sincerity of the blues musician's art—or for that matter, the sincerity of anyone else's art. There isn't sufficient space here to postulate why Anglo-European culture has traditionally held so-called folk artists to higher standards of artistic purity than, for instance, Renaissance painters or classical composers (Bach composed some of his most-noted works for his "day job" as a church choirmaster); suffice it to say that for most blues performers, their desire to make music of integrity and honesty is no more compromised by an equally fervent desire to get paid than Bach's was—a truism that seems so banal I almost cringe to write it but that somehow eludes too many observers who still idealize the bluesman as the romantic hero incarnate.[20]

(Not So) Strange Things Happening

Nonetheless, one of the most alluring elements of the urban blues scene continues to be the ease with which "professionals" and "amateurs" interact, share stages, and in general approach their music as a living communal celebration. Even today, neighborhood clubs may have the barmaid's latest CD on the jukebox; the band can include the electrician who fixes the lighting system and the proprietor of the catfish joint down the block, and they may be joined onstage for a guest set by a woman who lives around the corner and has shown up that Sunday evening still dressed for church. The guitarist, however, has just returned from an out-of-state tour, and next week's headliner is an internationally known recording star who still lives nearby or who has come back to the old neighborhood as a favor to the clubowner—a buddy of his or maybe a former sideman.

Moreover, as noted previously, when the music starts, the audience's response will be as important as what's going on onstage. In fact, many neighborhood blues venues don't even have a stage as such: the musicians stand literally on the same footing as their fellow celebrants. Constant back-and-forth exchange, often eye to eye, is an inextricable component of their evening's work. Yet again, the milieu unifies elements (performer/audience and professional/amateur) that mainstream Western culture tends to view as contraries.

Add to this mix the exuberant sexual energy that literally throbs in the air when things get rocking, and it's no wonder that a Saturday night in a blues lounge or a juke can seem impossibly exotic to someone coming in from the outside. And yes, even today, seekers from the world over arrive at America's blues meccas on weekend evenings, searching for the blues experience as if they were pilgrims questing for a piece of the True Cross. And yes, I was initially one of those seekers—but here again I return to my theme of shattered preconceptions and altered expectations. Because for all the exultant carnality and lusty fellowship that permeates the ritual bacchanal of the blues party, when Saturday night is over, most of the revelers—as well as most of the musicians on the bandstand—leave the club and go home to sober families and tight-knit communities.

Again, this is a prosaic point but one that's too often missed. The misunderstanding in this case may have as much to do with social class as with ethnicity. Many if not most musicologists and folklorists come from middle-class backgrounds, and judging from what gets written in travelogues and roots-music fanzines, most will approach an Appalachian honky-tonk or a Cajun roadhouse with the same wide-eyed sense of wonder with which they enter a backstreet gin mill on Chicago's West Side. But regardless of the reason, too many observers and commentators have conflated what occurs in a juke on Saturday night with a romanticized cultural constant.[21] Thus the mythical "blues experience" gets reified as a state of ecstatic fury that no human being—let alone any human community—could sustain for long and remain sane. This isn't a new phenomenon, of course. Norman Mailer did pretty much the same thing in his notorious essay "The White Negro" in 1957,[22] and he was merely slogging through territory that earlier Holy Primitivists like Carl Van Vechten and even white jazz musicians such as Mezz Mezzrow had by then pretty much tapped dry.[23]

The lived reality is both more quotidian and more profound. Again reflecting what might be called a working-class social dynamic as much as anything associated with ethnicity or race, taverns in communities like Chicago's West and South Sides have traditionally been not merely nightspots or places to hear music but extensions of their neighborhoods. They're places where people gather to relax after a hard week's work, where birthdays are celebrated, where social clubs and fraternal organizations have parties, where young soldiers receive send-offs and welcomes home, where neighbors and friends toast the everyday events of life. And even today all this often takes place against a hard-driving blues or soul-blues soundtrack.

One need only pay a daytime visit to a blues club such as the Starlite at the corner of Fifth and Pulaski on the West Side, or even the notoriously tourist-hungry Checkerboard Lounge on Forty-third Street,[24] to get a better feel for what these institutions really represent. In a corner of the Checkerboard a game of bid whist may be in progress. The men slap their cards down with flamboyant gestures and expressions of mock combat, and they punctuate their talk with throaty guffaws and ribald asides as friends drop by. A group of women sit at a table in the middle of the room, sip tonic water out of tall glasses, and discuss plans for their church group's upcoming weekend bus excursion. Guitarists John Primer and Johnny Dollar hang near the bar and trade road stories; Artie "Blues Boy" White holds court at another table across the room.

At the Starlite a group of sinewy men who have just gotten off from work lean on the bar, toss back a few shots, and trade tall tales about fishing and hunting back home in Mississippi. A haggard-looking fellow in a torn windbreaker sits in a booth alongside a woman who appears to be at least in her sixties; they discreetly spike their soda water with whiskey from a half-pint she carries in her purse as they discuss the acting genius of Lee J. Cobb. At a table near the bandstand, which serves as the Sunday evening site for the neighborhood's floating poker game while the weekly blues show is in progress, bluesman Jumpin' Willie Cobbs engages the owner in a raucous game of verbal sparring that stops just short of the dozens.

If the jukebox is on, it's probably playing something by the late Little Milton, Tyrone Davis, a local celebrity like Leon McNeal, or a classic soulster such as James Brown—but that's almost beside the point. The cadences, tones, rhythms, accents, and inflections of the conversation in the air are themselves a blues concert, as resonant and as vital to an understanding of what "the blues" is truly about as anything that will emanate from the bandstand later on.

Yet again, I fear some readers will think I'm belaboring the obvious. Nevertheless, there remains a powerful strain of something similar to what Said has labeled "orientalism" in much contemporary blues writing,[25] especially in regard to the atmosphere and social milieu of the juke joint, so that it is appropriate to suggest an alternative. I'm hardly the first to do so: W. E. B. Du Bois, in his scathing review of Van Vechten's *Nigger Heaven* in 1926, emphasized much the same point:

> The average colored man in Harlem is an everyday laborer, attending church, lodge and movie, and is as conservative and as conventional as ordinary working folk everywhere. Something they have which is racial, something distinctively Negroid can be found; but it is expressed by subtle, almost delicate nuance, and not by the wildly barbaric drunken orgy in whose details Van Vechten revels . . . so overlaid and enwrapped with cheaper stuff that no one but a fool could mistake it for the genuine exhibition of the spirit of the people.[26]

Ancient to the Future

Yet that's not the entire picture, either. There *is* something exotic (for want of a better term) about a rite of ecstatic abandon, which is what the blues party represents at its core. Its own participants are as aware of this as is anyone else. Willie Dixon's classic "Wang Dang Doodle," with its flamboyant cast of characters, its funk-drenched aura ("fish scent fill the air / there be snuff juice everywhere"), and its promise to "break out all the windows / and kick down all the doors," might be the best-known example, but one could point to the current spate of soul-blues songs extolling the heady atmosphere of all-night hole-in-the-wall joints and offerings like "47th Street," the Chicago-based jazz trumpeter and composer Malachi Thompson's vivid vignette of bebop-era nightlife ("If you wanna go to heaven, just go down to forty-seven"), with its equally telling observation that "the culture [was] big business" along that fabled South Side stroll.

Where the "orientalists" fall short is not in their praise of the subversive power of a blues party, laced as it is with open carnality and implicit defiance of social norms. Rather, too many have forgotten that the liberating role and social function of the Trickster—the Lord of Misrule—in the African-based cultures from which the blues derived was largely *ritual* in nature. It is this ritual of rebellion, recreation, and affirmation, enacted and lived publicly within the context of everyday community life, that lies at the heart of blues expression.

Traditionally the blues has drawn its strength from courageously confronting paradox: the best blues transcends everyday reality by acknowledging and even celebrating it in all its flawed, horrific intensity. This is one reason the still-popular notion of the blues as music of nascent revolution, like most absolutist stereotypes, captures only part of the truth. The blues, to paraphrase John Clellon Holmes,[27] is the music of an oppressed people who dare to *feel* free, if only for the moment ("One of these mornings the chain is gonna break / But up until that day, I'm gonna take all I can take," as Aretha Franklin sings in "Chain of Fools"). The music constitutes act of resistance, to be sure, but one that does not necessarily require the physical or political transformation of the external environment.

All this goes some distance toward explaining the complex and usually nonideological vision of freedom illuminated by the stories in this book. Time and again my informants return to the theme of the blues as a force of liberation in their lives. In the paradigm-melding, shape-shifting spirit of Eshu-Eleggua, however, they conflate personal, political, social, and existential liberation—along with other, more worldly considerations, such as financial security and emotional stability—into an ideal whole that, while still distant, probably seems at least a little more attainable than it did previously. In virtually every case, the lesson that both propels and derives from these tales of struggle and perseverance is that if you just hang on long enough, with stout heart and good faith, the best is—*must* be—yet to come. If that sounds like the exegesis of a parable, it probably should. As Francis Davis has suggested, the blues arose from a theology-infused cultural environment in which prophecy was accepted as everyday fact and in which this world, not the next, was often interpreted as metaphor.[28]

The Key to the Highway

This book illustrates these themes by documenting the stories and lives of selected Chicago-based artists and by providing slice-of-life vignettes drawn from clubs and public performance spaces. Despite the cultural specificity of much blues expression, the blues, like any viable art form, expresses universal human concerns in a language accessible to listeners from diverse backgrounds. This dual quality of specificity and universality comprises another ongoing theme in these portraits. Some of the artists profiled here perform primarily for African American audiences, both locally and on the southern-based "chitlin circuit"; others ply their trade mostly in white clubs, although with one exception, all maintain at least some connection to the neighborhood circuits of the South and West Sides, even if it's limited to a handful of guest appearances at outdoor parties or informal weeknight jam sessions. And they all "speak," musically, in the diasporan language that remains the lingua franca of the blues.

In the spirit of the invocation of ancestors that often signals the initiation of a traditional African ritual, I begin with "Elder Spirits," biographical sketches of three bluesmen—Junior Wells, pianist Sunnyland Slim, and harpist Big Walter Horton—who were instrumental in developing the postwar Chicago sound. I selected these three men because they are all historically important but also because each in his own way was a mentor to me. Through getting to know them and listening to their music and their words—and sometimes, through learning to negotiate through the Trickster-like obfuscations and barriers they liked to throw up to keep newcomers off balance—I gained a richer understanding of the music and the ongoing historical, social, and cultural reality in which it thrived. As the proverb tells us, we all stand on the shoulders of giants. These three giants lent me their shoulders, and I'm still humbled and gratified by the gift.

Empowered by their presence, in the next section ("We Gon' Pitch a Boo-gie-Woogie") I visit some Chicago blues venues past and present. Florence's Lounge and Maxwell Street both helped initiate me into the world of Chicago blues. My journey from "orientalist" awe to, I hope, an honest appreciation and understanding of the milieu and meaning of the blues should be evident as I describe my initial impression of the scene at Florence's, an impression that was challenged, altered, and eventually deepened immeasurably as I learned to better understand the venue and what went on there in its cultural and social context. The Maxwell Street Market, the long-running open-air market on Chicago's Near West Side, was and always will be the city's great and irreplaceable carnival of the soul. I hope my travelogue of the market as it looked, sounded, smelled, and felt on its last day of existence conveys at least some of the wonderment and delight it never failed to serve up.

From the now-defunct Delta Fish Market to Wallace's Catfish Corner, I trace the trajectory of an eccentric but long-running West Side tradition: fried fish and southern-fried blues, both served up on Friday and Saturday afternoons. Also on the West Side is the Starlite Lounge, where artists like Jumpin' Willie Cobbs, Willie D., and the brooding and world-wounded but still undefeated Harmonica Khan hold forth on Sunday nights. The stories told here are those of struggle and sometimes defeat, along with courage and faith. There is no guarantee that endings will be happy or that dreams will be fulfilled—an existential truth as valid in the blues as in the "real life" the music and the celebration both invoke and attempt to transcend. It's the enactment of belief that matters, and that's what I have tried to show.

From there I shift gears a bit to visit East of the Ryan, a South Side show lounge where nationally feted soul-blues artists like Denise LaSalle usually perform when they're in town. East of the Ryan represents yet another challenge to a stereotype, that of the blues venue (and its habitués) as necessarily disheveled, drunken, and poor. The elegance of the atmosphere there, juxtaposed against the earthy carnality of the show itself, again reveals the indigenous genius of the blues as a force for unity and the rectification of contradictions.

"Torchbearers" is the heart of the book: in it I provide portraits of still-active artists, each of whom, in his or her own way, carries on the tradition of elders such as those profiled in the first section. Not all these musicians would be considered major stylists in terms of widespread influence or popularity. Each, however, is representative of the music that remains prevalent on the contemporary scene, and each one's story exemplifies important facets of the "blues life" as it is lived and experienced by contemporary artists, regardless of their chosen style. Again, expectations may be challenged: the blues life is revealed to encompass everything from Jody Williams's gentlemanly reserve to the combination of rootsy passion and scholarly sophistication that characterizes Billy Branch in both his music and his offstage demeanor, from Bonnie Lee's demure passivity in the wake of life's travails to the harrowing encounters with turmoil, dissolution, and worse that survivors like Sharon Lewis and Lurrie Bell have endured.

In "The Soul Side of Town" I present three purveyors of the modern soul-blues style, the blues form preferred among most contemporary African American listeners. Cicero Blake got his start in the doo-wop era in Chicago, cut his first soul sides in the early 1960s, and then gravitated to a bluesier style. His records are perennial favorites on black-oriented blues radio. Artie "Blues Boy" White, born in Vicksburg, Mississippi, was influenced by sophisticates like B. B. King and Bobby Bland, but he purveys a somewhat rootsier meld of gospel, soul, and twelve-bar blues. Little Scotty has spent most of his life on the periphery of the scene, but on the South Side he is respected as both a community leader and an entertainer who epitomizes the local star phenomenon I described previously.

In the final section I consider the state of the blues and its possible future in our increasingly cosmopolitan world, where the desire to celebrate cultural diversity exists alongside an apparently unstoppable corporate-driven cultural homogenization. To address some of these possible directions, I will continue to consider the blues in two general senses. On the one hand, it is a musical form defined not only by identifiable melodic, harmonic, and structural characteristics but also by performance practices (e.g., delivery style) and lyric content, which may resist formal description but which are nonetheless vital if we are to understand what blues and blues expression mean in the African American community. On the other hand, it is a cultural expression based on traditions and mores that are rooted in specific historic conditions and that have evolved and been adapted as the repositories of this culture have dispersed from the rural South to urbanized northern areas and across the United States. This final section will thus revisit considerations—musical, aesthetic, cultural—that have been raised in the previous chapters.

A word about format: a time-honored tradition in blues performance is to allow the band to play a song or two to "warm up the stage," creating an environment and a context for the fronting performer. In that spirit, I've placed my comments—historical overviews, stage-setting thoughts, and notes—directly before artists' profiles and my dispatches from venues. The only exceptions occur in the "Elder Spirits" section. Because these individuals constitute living history, they require no such introductions: they themselves are the context. Finally, some quotations from my interviews have been slightly modified for the sake of coherence and clarity. All the words and the meanings expressed, however, are the respondents' own.

Part 1

Elder Spirits

1

Junior Wells
"Come On in This House"

Junior Wells relished and cultivated his role as bluesman incarnate with as much dedication as he tended his
hard-earned reputation as one of the premier architects
of the fabled postwar Chicago harmonica style. Offstage,
even his simplest movements—repositioning his arm,
straightening his collar, lighting a cigarette—were stylized and above all cool. His eyes shone with an ineffable
combination of street-tough glint and comradely warmth
or, if you were a woman, a flirtatious twinkle. He spoke in
brusque, clipped phrases, sometimes skewing his mouth
into a brief sneer, as if to signify a simmering inner defiance that could erupt into combat at any time. Then he
would bare his teeth in a tight-lipped smile, often accompanied by one of his patented vocal effects—a falsetto
whoop, a theatrical gasp, a rim-shot tongue click—as he
met your gaze, finally letting you in on the joke.

I always thought of him as a bantam rooster, a tough
little guy strutting around, plumage on display, ready
to take on the world. I never met another man who
could wear clothes the way Junior could, with never a
thread out of place or the slightest smudge or smear on
his shoes, no matter how sweaty the room or chaotic
the situation. Even on those rare occasions when he
deigned to wear something as pedestrian as jeans, they

Styling: Junior Wells in 1987. Photo by Paul Natkin/Photo Reserve

would be pressed so perfectly that it looked as if you could cut your finger on the crease. He'd step off the bandstand after a set—and I'm talking about *torrid* sets, back when he had the energy and the chops to set a stage on fire just by getting near it—and he would look as clean and unruffled as if he had just left home. I don't think anyone ever figured out exactly how he did it.

But then, Junior spent most of his life confounding others' expectations. He was born Amos Wells Blakemore in West Memphis, Arkansas, on December 9, 1931. Flamboyance seems to have run in the family: his mother, Lena Blakemore, used to regale visitors with tales of his childhood escapades, and as she spoke she would high-step around the room and act out her stories, bringing the old days back to life through the sheer force of her personality. Here was little Junior, draped in improvised preacher's robes, holding a solemn funeral in the backyard for a deceased house pet. Here he was again, sitting on a bed that had suddenly collapsed with a house-rattling crash, looking tearfully into his mother's eyes.

"Mama!" he sobbed. "I was just playing 'Captain Marvel'! I said, 'Shazaam!' and the bed said, 'Wham!'"[1]

Later in life Junior reveled in his image as a street-hardened bluesman who had been on his own almost from the beginning. But in fact he spent his earliest years in relatively staid, if impoverished, circumstances. Miss Lena, as his mother was known throughout her life, worked as a maid in motels and hotels, including the famous Peabody Hotel in Memphis, before she left her family behind and headed north to Chicago. For a full day's labor she might bring home three dollars. Junior's father, Sylvester "Champ" Wells, was a hard-working country man with a reputation as one of the most proficient cotton pickers in the area around Marion, Arkansas, a rural hamlet about seven miles north of Memphis. On a good year he would clear five or six hundred dollars after he paid off his expenses to the man who owned the plantation.

Champ Wells wanted the best for his son. One day Junior found his father lying on the porch of his sharecroppers' shack, "just shakin' and cryin'," fighting off the effects of "a bad chill." "Now here's what I want you to do," he told Junior between gasps. "Your mom is in Chicago. This is no life for you. So I want you to go and stay with your mom, see if you can go to school and get you an education. I don't want you to be like me." Not long afterward Junior was riding a northbound bus on U.S. Highway 61. He was about nine years old.[2]

Junior was devoted to his family. He always spoke of his father with respect, he often visited southern relatives after he moved north, and in Chicago he lived with his mother until she died. Nonetheless, it's clear that there was little chance he would grow up to be quite "like" anyone else. From the beginning, music was never far from his life. He heard blues records on the radio, and he eventually befriended harpist Junior Parker, who lived in West Memphis. He wasn't a regular churchgoer, but he did attend some services, and he was transported by the exultation of the gospel music he heard there. (He once claimed that the first time he entered a "sanctified" church, he thought it was a juke joint because of the spirited music emanating from it. Before the night was over, he found himself baptized.) His mother frequented jukes around the Memphis area; she and Sunnyland Slim even operated a bootleg liquor business for a while.[3]

Junior's first harmonica lesson, if you could call it that, came from Rice Miller (Sonny Boy Williamson no. 2). Junior had moved to Chicago by then, and Miller was still based in the South. During one of his visits home Junior found the legendary harp man and began to follow him around. Miller, hardened by the blues life, didn't want to fool with a kid, but he finally showed the boy a few licks. He then grabbed Junior's harp, threw it to the ground, and stomped on it. Pulling out his knife, he fixed Junior with a hawk-eyed glare and rasped: "You ain't never gonna learn how to play no harmonica, you dumb sum bitch! Now get out of my face!"[4]

"I cried," Junior related years later. "Nothing ever hurt me before like that before in my life. That hurt me to my soul." His response to that hurt, though, was that of a bluesman: "I was more determined then—I was gonna do it!"[5]

Back in Chicago, he listened carefully to established figures like John Lee Williamson, the original "Sonny Boy" and the blues' leading harp innovator until his death in 1948 (Little Walter came along soon after and proceeded to revolutionize the instrument all over again). His first onstage appearance, alongside guitarist Tampa Red and pianist Johnnie Jones, was at a South Side club called Miss Tifford's, on the corner of Twenty-second and Prairie. Before long Junior was sharing stages with Sunnyland, Robert Jr. Lockwood, Muddy Waters, and other members of Chicago's burgeoning blues elite. He would play harp, dance, put on a show—do whatever it took to get over with the audience and collect his tips.

By his own admission Junior was a rather hot-blooded young man. He fought to defend his honor against the taunts and threats of schoolkids who dubbed him "Country" and ridiculed the cheap "brogans" his mother bought him. Eventually he became the leader of what he called his "gang," the Calumet Aces. They would rumble with boys from outside the neighborhood and look out for one another at school. As Junior explained, "If you didn't have somebody to help you out, you were liable to get your butt whooped!"[6]

Junior never became much of a criminal, although on one memorable occasion he did get a bit overzealous trying to secure a harp for himself. He recalled,

> I went to this pawnshop downtown and the man had a harmonica priced at $2.00. I got a job on a soda truck, . . . played hookey from school, . . . worked all week and on Saturday the man gave me a dollar-and-a-half. A dollar-and-a-half! For a whole week of work. I went to the pawnshop and the man said the price was $2.00. I told him I *had* to have that harp. He walked away from the counter—left the harp there. So I laid my dollar-and-a-half on the counter and picked up the harp.
> When my trial came up the judge asked me why I did it. I told him I had to have that harp. The judge asked me to play it and when I did he gave the man the 50 cents and hollered, "Case Dismissed!"[7]

Eventually, though, as he and his Calumet Aces began to develop a reputation for brawling, Junior found himself in front of less sympathetic judges. One threatened to send him to a juvenile facility or even jail. Lena, desperate not to lose her son a second time, recruited Muddy, Sunnyland, Tampa Red, and pianist Big Maceo to testify on his behalf. The judge responded by naming the hard-bitten crew his legal guardians. "Whatever Junior does," he warned them, "you *all* did it! Now you all got to keep him straight."

Junior initially balked at cooperating in this unlikely social-work project, but when he tried to slip away, Muddy responded with a tough-love approach not too different from Rice Miller's. "When he pulled me," Junior said, "I snatched away from him. When I snatched away he say boom, and knocked me down. He always carried a little old .25 automatic, like I do. He said, 'You know what? I'll kill you. You ain't no good to your own self, your Mama, me or nobody else, the way you're actin'.' He said, 'Now get in the car.' And I did."[8] "If it hadn't been for all the older musicians taking up so much time with me," he mused toward the end of his life, "I'd probably be in the penitentiary or dead."[9]

By 1950 music had become his primary focus. He hooked up with guitarists Louis and Dave Myers, and billed as the Three Deuces (later the Three Aces), they began to establish themselves as one of the hottest young bands on the competitive South Side scene. When drummer Fred Below joined them, they became the Four Aces and then finally just the Aces. Graced by Below's swing and Louis Myers's sophisticated fretboard technique (Dave mostly played "guitar bass," using the bottom strings of his instrument as a makeshift electric bass), they fused Chicago blues' primal Delta roots with a forward-looking, jazz-influenced emphasis.

In 1952 Junior left the Aces when Little Walter, emboldened by the success of his hit single "Juke," quit his post as Muddy Water's harp man and joined forces with the Myers brothers and Below. Walter's saxlike improvisations made him the perfect harpist for the Aces, who were rechristened the Jukes to capitalize on his hit. Junior, with his somewhat more down-home style, joined Muddy. The following year he was drafted into the army and shipped west to California, where he was ensconced in Camp Roberts, a mammoth 42,784-acre spread located along U.S. Highway 101 about halfway between Los Angeles and San Francisco.[10]

It didn't take long for the harsh discipline of army life to chafe on Junior. "I stood up," he remembered, "and I said, 'No, you're not talkin' to me if you're tellin' me that I gotta get on my knees and pick up some cigarette butts! I'm not gon' do that!'"[11]

That kind of attitude pretty quickly got him put on restriction. But one payday, having finally secured a pass, he ventured out into the hot California evening. He stopped off in San Francisco and then continued to Oakland, where he found a nightclub, sat in with the band (an organ trio), and enjoyed several more drinks. Things got pretty hazy after a while. When he woke up, his head still spinning, he was on a bus headed back to Chicago.

Despite his AWOL "wanted man" status, Junior boldly began to sit in at various places on the South Side. Guitarist Jody Williams gleefully recalled the cat-and-mouse antics that ensued between Junior and the authorities, who were by then hot on his trail:

> They knew how he was about music. They knew it was only a matter of time before he'd show up, so they'd just come down there and they'd wait on him. And sure enough—when he'd run off from the army and go AWOL he would come down to the 708 Club [on Forty-seventh Street]. They'd just come down there, he'd come off the stage, and they'd take him. Two FBI agents come in, one sit by the door there, one stood up, so when they got Junior's attention, they go [gestures with his hand]. They let him finish it out, but when he came on down, they took him off. Yeah, he was determined! He just wanted to play his music![12]

Junior eventually spent time in the stockade at Ft. Sheridan, north of Chicago in Highwood, Illinois. But even the stockade couldn't hold him. After chasing him down in Chicago for the third or fourth time, the army finally mustered him out on a medical discharge.

In June 1953, perhaps during one of his AWOL excursions, Junior began his tenure at Leonard Allen's States label, an association that resulted in such Wells classics as "Hoodoo Man" (with its slow-grinding twelve-bar groove and archetypal backwoods voodoo imagery) and "Tomorrow Night." In 1957 Mel London recorded him for Profile, Chief, and U.S.A., among other labels.

In 1960 Junior hit the national R&B charts with "Little by Little" on Profile (featuring none other than London himself, along with Junior and Willie Dixon, on the tune's three-part harmony). During this period he also cut such classics as "Come On in This House" and the protofunk "Messin' with the Kid," which became his signature tune.[13]

As much as anyone else did, Junior carried the Chicago blues harp tradition into the 1960s and beyond. His style was heavily influenced by Little Walter's jazz-tinged inventions, but he couched it in a tone more clearly drawn from the squalling, bent-note down-home style. His persona, both on record and in performance, was an updating of the timeless bluesman's pose as a hard-living, hard-loving street man, tough yet emotionally vulnerable, ready to surrender his heart to a good woman but also prepared to use any means necessary to protect it from being broken or betrayed.

By the mid-1960s twelve-bar Chicago blues had fallen out of favor with most younger black listeners, but the folk-blues "revival" and the blues-rockers who followed made it popular among young white aficionados. In 1965 Junior entered the studio of Delmark Records, a white-run jazz and blues label, and recorded *Hoodoo Man Blues*, which turned out to be one of the decade's most important blues albums. Buttressed by the unerring guitar accompaniment of Buddy Guy (waggishly credited as "Friendly Chap" because of contractual conflicts), he gave his new audience an uncompromising dose of the same music that he and his colleagues had been laying down in Chicago for the better part of fifteen years.

Junior was no museum piece, however; unlike some of his peers, he never hesitated to change with the times. *Hoodoo Man Blues* kicks off with "Snatch It Back and Hold It," a soulful groove laid over a fatback funk beat. In 1966 Junior signed with the West Side entrepreneur Willie Barney, who owned the Four Brothers label along with the subsidiaries Bright Star and Hit Sound. Barney and producer Jack Daniels released a series of steaming sides with Junior, including horns playing charts by Monk Higgins. These cuts included "I'm Losing You" (a remake of "Little by Little"), "Up in Heah" (featuring a funked-up reincarnation of the classic "Messin' with the Kid" intro), and "I'm Gonna Cramp Your Style," all on Bright Star. Another cooker, "It's All Soul," appeared on the Hit Sound label. In 1968 Junior hit the national R&B charts for a second time with "You're Tuff Enough" on Blue Rock, a Mercury subsidiary for which Daniels was A&R man.[14]

Some purists have tended to downplay this period of Junior's career. They've criticized him for selling out to pop tastes, accusing him of becoming mired in a James Brown fixation from which he never fully escaped. In fact, however, Junior's 1960s fusions of the blues with contemporary rhythms and arrangements constitute an important landmark in the music's development. As the Chicago R&B historian Robert Pruter has written: "By the standards of the mid-1960s Wells's Bright Star sides were genuinely downhome, and for Wells to come out with the records featuring his harmonica was extraordinary. The Monk Higgins horn arrangements were superb in updating Wells yet keeping to the downhome approach and staying true to the esthetic considerations of the black working-class audience."[15] In other words, Junior was playing soul-blues before soul-blues had a name.

Despite the criticism, Junior savored his newfound success with the white audience, and he soon became an international blues celebrity. He first toured Europe in 1966; the following year he performed in Africa under the aegis of the U.S. State Department—not bad for a former AWOL renegade. By the 1970s he and his teammate Buddy Guy had won a place among the most in-demand blues acts in the world. They opened shows for the Rolling Stones; they recorded, both together and as solo artists, for Vanguard; and they cut an all-star session on Atco, *Buddy Guy and Junior Wells Play the Blues*, supported by such pop stars as Eric Clapton and Dr. John. *Buddy and the Juniors*, released on Blue Thumb in the early 1970s, added jazz keyboardist Junior Mance to Buddy and Junior's volatile Chicago blues mix. In 1974 Buddy (who by now usually got top billing) and Junior played the prestigious Montreaux Jazz Festival. The show was recorded, and the results came out on Blind Pig some years later.[16]

Eventually the team broke up, but Junior continued to tour steadily, fronting his own group. When he wasn't on the road, he could usually be found performing or sitting in somewhere in Chicago. For years he held down simultaneous weekend gigs at Theresa's and the Checkerboard Lounge, on the South Side; he would travel back and forth between the clubs, keeping the spirit of Chicago blues alive in the neighborhoods where that spirit had first been summoned forth.

Junior, raised in the hard-drinking blues tradition, was never exactly easy on himself, and by the 1980s he had begun to show signs of age. He could still stoke the old fires when the occasion demanded it, but he chose his spots carefully. His wind was no longer as strong as it had been (he is said to have suffered a collapsed lung in a domestic dispute years earlier), and on some nights he mostly sang, leaving the strenuous instrumental work to the band. It didn't help that they sometimes sounded a bit ragged around the edges, with out-of-tune horns, overlong guitar solos, and uncertain communication among the rhythm section marring Junior's usual tight show.

He continued to tour, however, and on a good night he could still be among the blues' most riveting performers. Resplendent in his color-coor-

Still styling: Junior Wells in 1993. Photo by Paul Natkin/Photo Reserve

dinated suits and glittering jewelry, he barked commands at his sidemen, coaxed intricate if increasingly brief filigrees out of his harp, and took total command of the stage and the crowd. His voice combined the lonesome graininess of his down-home blues lineage with a blunt-edged rhythmic snap that showed his debt to 1960s soul men like James Brown—musicians whose styles he resolutely continued to replicate in his performances, whether the purists liked it or not. Not for nothing did his longtime admirers call him the "Godfather of the Blues."

In 1990 he appeared on *Harp Attack*, Alligator Records' all-star harmonica summit featuring Junior, Carey Bell, Billy Branch, and James Cotton. He followed that up with four discs for Telarc, most of which captured him at medium-boil—not exactly disappointing but short of vintage form. Perhaps the best of the lot was 1996's mostly acoustic *Come On in This House*, an intimate affair that showcased some of the most heartfelt playing and singing he had put on record in years.

Yet no matter how famous or successful he became, Junior never abandoned the community that gave him his start. Until the end he resided in the South Side home he had bought for his mother, who passed away in 1995. He continued to make periodic treks to clubs like the Checkerboard, where he would hang out, share a few drinks, and sometimes sit in with the band. He had friends and confidants from all walks of life, and he could certainly have afforded to move to the suburbs if he had wanted to, but he chose to remain close to his roots.

He also savored his tough-guy image. He loved to regale listeners with stories of how, back in the 1960s, he had faced down some of the South Side's most notorious street-gang members when they tried to muscle in on the scene at Pepper's Lounge and Theresa's, where young white fans were beginning to explore the fabled neighborhood blues world of Chicago. He claimed to have fathered upward of thirty-four children,[17] and the bevy of girlfriends and ex-girlfriends who showed up at his gigs (as well as some of the stories they told) indicated that his reputation as a player was well deserved.

Junior's songs were full of signifying and sexual boasting, and his onstage demeanor was self-confident to the point of arrogance. Even his legendary trick of augmenting lyrics with vocal sound effects—moans, whoops, tongue clicks, gargles, and gasps—bespoke a fiercely independent spirit, a determination to shape things to his own ends and defy the expected. Sometimes he would forgo words entirely and ascend into realms of aural abstraction so unearthly it almost sounded as if he were speaking in tongues.

Nevertheless, beneath that cock-of-the-walk strut lay a tender spirit he would reveal through spontaneous, almost prosaic acts of kindness. He once visited a fast-food restaurant after a gig, spotted a hungry-looking dog in the parking lot, and ended up buying the pooch a chicken dinner. If someone making the scene struck him as vulnerable in some way, he would try to make sure that the person was safe. "Got your money in your pocket?" he once asked a friend of mine at Theresa's. When my friend nodded, Junior shot a quick look toward a scruffy character lurking nearby: "Keep it there." He remained seated at his post near the end of the bar, keeping a sharp eye on all who entered, until he was sure the coast was clear.

He showed a similar loyalty to his companions and mentors in music. He never made a big deal of it, but he was always ready with support and assistance for musicians in need. He didn't limit his assistance to the musicians, either: he would give their children presents, maybe slip some money to their wives, and help their families any way he could. His loyalty extended to death and beyond: in 1994, after Louis Myers died, Junior purchased a headstone for him.[18]

Despite his penchant for clowning, Junior believed fiercely in the blues as an art form deserving dignity and respect. He reacted with deep resentment when a veteran Chicago bluesman who had scored mainstream success showed up to collect a Grammy decked out in bib overalls instead of a respectable suit. After Muddy Waters's funeral on May 4, 1983, Junior took the stage at the Checkerboard and berated a touristy crowd (most of whom were there in response to a rumor that the Rolling Stones might show up) for turning Muddy's tribute into a "circus." He then stalked off, to the consternation of the tourists and the admiration of everyone else.[19]

Some of us who were privileged to know him personally got to witness a more profound manifestation of his benevolence: for years he quietly and devotedly tended to a friend who was slowly dying from a terminal illness, not a musician or anyone famous, simply a person to whom he had been close for a long time and whom he refused to abandon when things got tough. Even when it became so painful for him that he would break into tears, he never gave up. He would send cards from the road, sometimes with inspirational messages painstakingly handwritten inside. He even made it a point to educate himself as much as he could about his friend's condition, so he could lend a more understanding ear and provide the most appropriate type of help.

As the 1990s wore on, Junior became thin to the point of gauntness. He kept up with his touring schedule in the wake of the success of his Telarc releases, but it was obvious that he was no longer in the best of health. There were also personal losses. The 1992 death of Theresa Needham, owner of Theresa's and one of his closest friends, was heartbreaking; within a few years Needham's death was followed by those of his mother and his long-suffering friend. Never one to reveal his vulnerable side in public, Junior clenched his teeth and struggled on, but the toll it took was obvious to anyone who knew him well. His diagnosis of lymphoma in 1997, his ensuing heart attack and coma, and his death on January 15, 1998, seemed to confirm what a lot of people had known in their hearts but scarcely dared to talk about for quite some time.

Over six hundred people packed A. A. Rayner and Sons Funeral Home, on Seventy-first Street, where Junior lay in a silver casket, dressed in a bright blue suit with matching fedora, on Friday, January 23, 1998.[20] Next to him stood a tray of harmonicas and, courtesy of his nephew, Michael Blakemore, a pint of Tanqueray gin to ease him along his journey home. Wreaths sent by John Lee Hooker, Robert Cray, and Van Morrison (who sent a card that read, "Respected friend, be at peace") adorned the chapel. Friends and fellow musicians shared reminiscences both tender and ribald, although Buddy Guy, overcome with emotion, bowed out of the opportunity to give a final salute to his longtime musical companion.

After the service the funeral procession, extending for nearly six blocks, snaked its way through Junior's beloved South Side blues turf, past the building that had once housed Theresa's Lounge, at 4801 South Indiana, and the Checkerboard, on Forty-third Street. It ended up at Oak Woods Cemetery, at Sixty-seventh and Cottage Grove, not far from the neighborhood where young Amos Blakemore had once run the streets with his Calumet Aces, snatching harmonicas, charming judges, and daring the world to take him on any terms but his own.

At the gravesite some of the mourners reached over to touch his coffin one last time. A harmonica was bolted to its silver lid. Finally, after a few more prayers and words of remembrance, Junior's body was lowered into the earth, and the crowd began to disperse. Harpist Sugar Blue, solitary against the gray winter landscape, stood over the grave and played "Taps." The clarion tone of his harmonica filled the cold January air. It was the last sound most of the people heard in the cemetery that day.

Epilogue

In the days and weeks after Junior's death, a lot of people felt the need to pay tribute to this man who had been one of the last living links to the glory days of Chicago blues. Driving back to Chicago from Indiana the day after he died, I heard a radio station play an excerpt from one of Junior's recorded versions of Tampa Red's "It Hurts Me Too," probably the one released on the Chief label back in 1961. I doubt that anyone at the station knew it, but "It

Hurts Me Too" had for years been a coded message Junior would sing at gigs for his treasured, doomed friend, first as a warning and then, when her death was imminent, as something close to a prayer:

> You lovin' him more, when you should love him less
> Why stand behind him, and take his mess
> When things go wrong, so wrong with you,
> It hurts me too . . .

Tears stung my eyes as I listened. This can't be a coincidence, I thought. Junior, you sly motherfucker, still signifying and preaching to us in blues-tongues, still conveying your oracular wisdom and life lessons from the other side.

I knew then, if there had ever been any doubt, that Junior was all right.

2

Sunnyland Slim
"It Given Me a Tender Heart"

Even as an old man Sunnyland Slim cut a commanding figure. His massive head looked as if it could have been sculpted from the Mississippi earth itself; his shoulders seemed almost as wide and strong as the yokes that held the mules he had once driven on plantations and in Delta labor camps. He stood well over six feet tall and in his prime probably weighed over 225 pounds; his voice alternated between a raspy growl when he was talking and a flat-out roar when he sat down at a piano and tore into one of his ribald blues classics. As he spoke, he would wave his gnarled hands for emphasis and lean forward to stress a point, eyes widening in wonderment or going soft with melancholy as the memories and lessons of his life came rushing back almost too fast for words.

Late in the autumn of 1987, though, it looked as if the mighty Sunnyland might finally have met defeat. Ensconced in Mercy Hospital, on the city's Near South Side, he spent weeks curled up in a bed, trembling and shivering, coughing until it seemed he was going to pass out, and unable to communicate in anything stronger than a rattling whisper. Some of us who knew him were beginning to fear the worst. But then one day, when I entered his room, my heart leapt with gladness: he was reclining comfortably, his gigantic frame propped

Sunnyland Slim at the home of guitarist Hubert Sumlin and Willie Bea Sumlin, Milwaukee, 1988. Photo by Cathrine Burckhardt

up against a pillow, reading a church bulletin. Sunnyland, the great survivor, had pulled through again.

Images like that—of his strength, his resilience, and his uncanny ability to spread inspiration and joy even during the bleakest times—were what first came rushing back to me when I learned of Sunnyland's death in March 1995. I had gotten to know him in the early 1980s when I interviewed him for a biographical feature for the *Chicago Reader*. After telling me his life story, he felt a bond, and after that, when I showed up at his gigs, we always greeted each other warmly, bought each other drinks, and hung out together. A few times I visited him at his home on South Halsted Street.

We weren't what you might call blood brothers. I don't claim to have been his intimate confidant. Nonetheless, I honestly believe that no one else ever taught me more about life than Sunnyland Slim did. To hear that voice growl through the octaves, build into a leonine roar, and then soar into high-tenor declamations of freedom-bound blues passion—or just to spend time in the presence of this tender-hearted giant of a man—was to learn life lessons of the most profound and lasting kind. A West African proverb tells us that "when an old man dies, a library burns to the ground." In Sunnyland's case, it was an ancestral treasury.

Sunnyland Slim's story traces the history of the blues, from Mississippi to Chicago and beyond. He was born Albert Luandrew in the country near Vance, Mississippi, on September 5, 1907, the grandson of slaves and son of the Reverend T. W. and Martha Luandrew. The family owned the property they lived on ("It was my grandfather's farm; Ol' Master was his daddy, back in slavery times"), but the racist southern political machinery eventually stripped them of their control of most of it.

Growing up, the boy heard music all around him—work songs in the fields and spirituals and hymns in church—and it didn't take him long to get the urge to play and sing himself. A neighbor had a pump organ on which young Albert learned to plunk out standards ("Tramp, Tramp, Tramp, the Boys Are Marching") and spirituals ("If I Could Hear My Mother Pray" and "When the Trumpets Sound"). He drew diagrams on a shoebox to help him remember the fingerings. Then he would run home and practice on the box until he had another chance at the keyboard.

Albert's mother died before he was ten years old. His father soon remarried, but his stepmother, Mary, was harsh in her discipline, and the boy began to steal away and hide out until his father or another relative came to get him. Finally, when he was about thirteen or fourteen, he left home for good. Life on his own was a dangerous proposition, and the youngster rapidly learned to live by his wits. There were no child-labor laws for young African American runaways in the South: he picked cotton, toiled under near-slavery conditions in work gangs, drove mule teams, and worked as a cook.

Music became a more important part of his life. By the early 1920s Albert was playing for his fellow workers in labor camps and on plantations, and he found performance opportunities in the towns, too. The Hot Shot Lounge in Lambert, Mississippi, was the site of one early gig: "That was a dollar fifty," he remembered, adding, "Hey, man, you didn't get but sixty-five, seventy-five cents a day [in the fields] from sunup to sundown. That makes you *interested*."

He also played piano in a movie theater, entertaining the audience while the projectionist changed reels.

One evening in 1923 Luandrew and a running buddy named Rover Brown were driving along a gravel road near Canton, Mississippi. Years later he would remember Brown as "a big-time hustler out in that area—you know, cards, dice, whiskey." But on this night luck hadn't been running their way: they had spent the previous night in jail; the women they had been traveling with had departed; and now, just outside of Canton, their car had broken down. But there was a sawmill nearby, and on the mill's land was a two-story juke where a Saturday night blow-out was in full roar. Smelling opportunity, the pair entered and made their way to a card table, and soon they were deeply involved in a game of Georgia skin. After a while Luandrew left the gamblers to their own devices and went upstairs to the music. There he met the man who was to become both his mentor and his closest friend: pianist Eurreal "Little Brother" Montgomery, who had been born in Louisiana in 1906 and was already among the most popular pianists on the backwoods southern circuit.[1]

Brother was getting tired (in those days juke-joint entertainers played all night long), and he was more than happy to let the young newcomer sing a few numbers while he played behind him. After a while Luandrew sat down at the keyboard and tore into "Rollin' and Tumblin'"—a bold move, since Montgomery had his own signature version of the tune, which he had adapted from a previous variation known as "The Forty-Fours" and retitled "Vicksburg Blues" and which was destined to become a Delta keyboard standard.

Sunnyland never forgot what happened that night: "Them niggers were clappin' till you'd get scared!" he related with relish almost sixty years later. "Every motherfucker in that place was standin' up—I made nine dollars from [one] song!" He ended up taking over the rest of the night from Little Brother. Emboldened by that experience and prodded by Brother's sophisticated two-handed meld of jazz, ragtime, and barrelhouse blues, he began to perform and travel more extensively, although unlike some others, he had the foresight to augment his musical income with day jobs and hustles. Along with pursuing manual labor, he expanded his activities into such sidelines as moonshining, gambling, and cheating with loaded dice—the usual sporting-life occupations.

He moved to Memphis and made the wide-open city his base. He remembered working for a short time with Ma Rainey in her Arkansas Swift Foots Revue, and he also played in the area's teeming jukes and gambling clubs, where rural field hands and big-city hustlers congregated on weekends or when the cotton fields lay fallow. The parties were raucous, the liquor and cocaine flowed freely, and death was always in the air—early in the twentieth century Memphis was known as the "murder capital of America," registering nearly ninety murders per 100,000 citizens each year.[2]

Things weren't much safer out in the country. Sometime around 1928 or 1929, along the tracks of the old Frisco Road outside Memphis, Luandrew witnessed the tragedy that gave him his stagename. "The Sunnyland Train killed my aunt's husband," he told writer Robert Palmer,[3] but later in life he reflected mostly on the children whom he saw destroyed by the fast-moving train in two accidents within one week. "Seein' those little white kids and black kids killed," he recalled, "that rested on my mind, and it given me a tender heart."

"Sunnyland Train" became his theme song; the train's name, his own. He may have had other names as well. Lena Blakemore, Junior Wells's mother, knew Sunnyland well in those days. She remembered calling him "Dudlow," a popular nickname for pianists at the time, probably because the style we now call "boogie-woogie" was then sometimes known as "Dudlow" or "Dudlow Joe."[4]

Sunnyland recalled visiting Chicago as early as the 1930s. Before he moved there permanently, however, he settled for a time in the southern Illinois city of Cairo, where he played music and helped run a gambling joint: "That was back there in Al Capone days[,] and I got up there, got in with his group." Another itinerant Mississippi bluesman, guitarist Honeyboy Edwards, sometimes dropped by the club to use its craps table as a makeshift bed.

He finally made the move to Chicago in the early 1940s, by which time he had assimilated a wide range of musical influences, both urban and rural. He sang in the high, lonesome tones of the field hollers and work songs he had heard in Mississippi as a boy, but he seasoned his raw yell with a vibrato-rich timbre reminiscent of the Chicago-based vocalist Peter "Doctor" Clayton (whom B. B. King, too, has cited as a major inspiration).[5] On piano Sunnyland was capable of a wide range of variations on blues and blues-related themes, ranging from boogie flag wavers and mournful twelve-bar ballads through a sparse, Basie-like swing. His most readily identifiable trademark was a shimmering cascade. He would begin with a chiming two-handed treble flurry and then ease back into the melody with a complex descent through the octaves. His versatility was a point of pride for him throughout his life, and along with his ability to hustle indefatigably, it helps explain why he eventually became one of Chicago's most in-demand blues session men.

But he had to scuffle to make a name for himself, especially in the beginning. It helped, of course, that Chicago was a major blues recording center and that many of the nation's most popular artists lived and worked in the city. The era's blues elite—guitarists Big Bill Broonzy and Tampa Red, harpist John Lee "Sonny Boy" Williamson, and pianist Memphis Slim—soon accepted the gregarious Sunnyland into their circle. He began to play the rough-and-tumble circuit of house socials and after-hours rent parties. It was a hard and often dangerous living, but for a lifelong hustler like Sunnyland, the rewards were worth it. In fact, he often made more money this way than an established professional might earn playing legitimate gigs.

"Me and Sonny Boy played for these parties," he remembered later. "We'd leave there with ten or twelve dollars apiece and go on to another place—union scale was $8.50 for sidemen. Sometimes I'd be so drunk I couldn't get up the stairs, but we played all of 'em. I stayed up here two or three years before I done anything else but just run up and down the road with Sonny Boy. Then they put my ass in the union."

He cut some sides for Opera (the exact date of these sessions has been a matter of some dispute) under the name "Delta Joe." It's possible he used the fake moniker to disguise his nonunion status. In 1947 he recorded for RCA Victor under another pseudonym, "Doctor Clayton's Buddy." That same year he also landed a recording session for Phil and Leonard Chess of Aristocrat Records, this time under his own name. He invited an eager young guitarist named Muddy Waters, with whom he had played some gigs around town, to join him. With Muddy backing him, Sunnyland recorded "Johnson Machine Gun" and "Fly Right, Little Girl"; Muddy took the lead on "Gypsy Woman" and "Little Anna Mae." Within a few years the label would be called Chess, Muddy Waters would be its biggest star, and American popular music would be revolutionized.

For some reason, however, fame was elusive. Perhaps because his reputation as a sideman eclipsed his own work as a leader, or maybe because his instrument didn't lend itself to the kind of flamboyant displays increasingly favored by guitarists and harp blowers as the Chicago blues style developed—whatever the reason, Sunnyland never achieved the renown that contemporaries like Muddy, Howlin' Wolf, Little Walter, and Elmore James eventually garnered. He nonetheless performed steadily, occasionally on the road but mostly in town; he also kept himself busy with occupations ranging from gambling and running after-hours joints to barbering (Wolf was one of his customers). Most of his recording sessions were for small labels, including Tempo-Tone, Apollo, and J.O.B. Some accounts suggest he was part-owner of J.O.B., along with Joe Brown and St. Louis Jimmy Oden (the composer of the standard "Going Down Slow," among others). Then as now it was hard to get blues records distributed; Sunnyland sometimes sold them himself out of the trunk of his car.

The general public may have been somewhat unaware of his gifts, but Sunnyland's fellow musicians held him in high esteem. He worked with artists as diverse as saxophonists Red Holloway and King Curtis and the Chicago-based drummer and bandleader Jump Jackson. He also remained in demand as a straight blues session man. His driving accompaniment on J. B. Lenoir's "The Mojo," to cite only one example, is a classic of postwar Chicago blues piano.

It wasn't until the folk-blues "revival" of the late 1950s and early 1960s that Sunnyland Slim achieved anything approaching fame. He was one of the first U.S. blues musicians to tour Canada, and around this time he began to appear regularly on LPs both as a solo artist and with other "rediscovered" Chicago greats, such as Big Walter Horton, Hubert Sumlin, and Johnny Shines. In 1964, as a member of European promoters Horst Lippmann and Fritz Rau's American Folk Blues Festival package tour, Sunnyland participated in the first American blues revue to perform behind the Iron Curtain.[6]

In the mid-1970s, determined as ever to remain independent and in control of his own destiny, Sunnyland initiated his own label, Airway, using it to reissue some of his earlier sides as well as newer and previously unheard material. Airway releases also featured Big Time Sarah, Bonnie Lee, and others he was helping to groom for success. The lists of band members on some of those sessions read like a blues lover's dream: on one cut the Aces—the Myers brothers and drummer Fred Below—are joined by harpist Walter Horton, saxophonist Marcus Johnson, and Sunnyland himself. Other sides featured the likes of Eddie Taylor, Hubert Sumlin, or Byther "Smitty" Smith on guitar and drummers such as Clifton James or Sam Lay. The Earwig label now owns the Airway catalog; an anthology, *Be Careful How You Vote,* was released in 1989. In 1991 a live recording from a mid-1970s European tour was also released under Airway's auspices.

Sunnyland also recorded for independent labels like Red Beans in Chicago; Evidence has subsequently reissued the Red Beans disks and added a few bonus tracks. Mapleshade has reissued a live 1987 recording Sunnyland made in Washington, D.C., that had originally been released around 1989. In the years before he died, Sunnyland expressed the desire to cut a gospel album (tentatively to be titled *God Can Do It All,* one of his favorite aphorisms), but failing health prevented him from accomplishing that project.

During the final decade of his life, Sunnyland began to receive some of the recognition due him. At the 1987 Chicago Blues Festival a crowd of over 100,000 cheered as he received the city's Medal of Merit onstage at the Petrillo Bandshell. For months afterward he played gigs proudly wearing the big gold medallion around his neck. That same year he was feted by the

Elder statesman: Sunnyland Slim on the Front Porch Stage, Chicago Blues Festival, June 1991. Photo by Paul Natkin/Photo Reserve

Chicago Academy of the Arts for "bringing fame to [his] art and to the city." In 1988 the National Endowment for the Arts presented him its National Heritage Fellowship Award.

Sunnyland never stopped recording (discographers credit him with up-ward of 250 sides), he never stopped hustling gigs, and—remembering the friendliness of Broonzy and other veterans when he was starting out—he never stopped helping musicians on their way up. Another of his favorite expressions was "you can't have it all," and no one else in Chicago surpassed him in sharing success with others. Junior Wells remembered that Sunnyland and Robert Jr. Lockwood had let him dance and play harp on their shows, and he added that he would sometimes make more in tips than the band was getting paid. Letha Jones, widow of pianist Johnnie Jones, said that Sunnyland got her husband his first gig in Chicago. More recently, vocalists like Bonnie Lee, Zora Young, and Big Time Sarah have publicly acknowledged their debt to him. The late guitarist Jimmy Rogers (Muddy Waters's fabled 1950s partner), harpists Billy Branch and Mad Dog Lester Davenport, and pianists Erwin Helfer and Barrelhouse Chuck—these are only a few who have come forward to affirm his stature as a virtual musical godfather to several generations of Chicago blues artists.

His strength, as well as his generosity, was legendary. Stories abound of his carrying heavy people around rooms, lifting amplifiers onstage after younger men couldn't budge them, and even overpowering microphones with the force of his voice. Some folks swore, in fact, that Sunnyland had guardian angels working for him full time, and anything they couldn't protect him from, his own single-minded determination simply refused to let stop him. That "tender heart" of his was one of the strongest to ever inhabit a human body ("You got a heart like a go-rilla!" he said a doctor once told him), and for a long time it seemed as if it might never stop beating.

Time and again Sunnyland fought back from pneumonia, injuries, and other setbacks with a tenacity that astonished and humbled people fifty years younger. He was stabbed in both arms in 1968, in 1982 his right arm was partially paralyzed in an automobile accident, in 1988 he fractured his hip, he had at least one stroke, and in his later years he was subject to seizures. But even after ill health and the aftereffects of that broken hip had rendered him all but immobile, he would squeeze himself into his old station wagon and drive from his South Side home to clubs like B.L.U.E.S., on North Halsted, where he would play and party himself to near-exhaustion until the wee hours. Then he would struggle painfully back into his car, grab the wheel, and negotiate his sleepy-eyed way back home.

As he entered his mideighties, Sunnyland's mighty frame finally became frail. He spent increasing time in the hospital, and the voice that had once been strong enough to fill a raucous country juke without amplification began to weaken. Even toward the very end, though, he retained his spark. In his performances he would still come up with subtle new variations on venerable piano themes. He would rasp out his sly down-home witticisms: "I was here 'fore God made land"; "I'm ten years older'n the devil"; "If he can sing, a mule can cry." He would uncork his trademark Woody Woodpecker call to the delight of newcomers and longtime admirers alike. Perhaps the most sublime moments eluded many in the audience. During breaks he would remain at the piano and softly play to himself, creating richly melodic stride meditations resonant with both melancholy and affirmation.

Only occasionally did he get the chance to show that side of his art to the public. In 1991, at the Thirteenth Annual Chicago Jazz Festival, Swiss composer George Gruntz included Sunnyland—as well as Billy Branch, Carl Weathersby, Pops Staples, and a host of others from all walks of jazz, blues, and gospel—in a performance of his *Chicago Cantata,* a specially commissioned orchestral tribute to Chicago's African American musical heritage. There, with a good piano in front of him and world-class jazz musicians on all sides, Sunnyland waited patiently until the orchestra's churning group improvisation had subsided and then eased into that seldom-heard stride tenderness. The crowd erupted into a roar after he finished.

Sunnyland's last gig was in January 1995 at Buddy Guy's Legends, where he played a show put together as part of the Jazz Institute of Chicago's annual Jazz Fair. He was thin and very weak by this time; he had to be almost lifted onto the stage. There, hunched over the piano like an ancient question mark, he struggled to summon the remnants of what had once been among the most powerful voices in the blues. According to witnesses, however, as he played he gathered his powers one more time and turned in an impeccable musical performance over the course of two sets. His hands fluttering across the keys looked almost like birds under the stage lights.[7]

Not long afterward he suffered a fall. Soon he was back in the hospital for what drummer and saxophonist Sam Burckhardt, Sunnyland's accompanist for many years and also his unofficially adopted grandson, said they both knew was probably the last time.

Sunnyland was a man of deep faith, and some who were closest to him maintain that he willed himself to live for as long as he knew it was right and then let go. Burckhardt says that when he went to Thorek Hospital to visit Sunnyland one day, he found him unusually agitated and restless. "Come over here and get my shoes," he said. "Little Brother's waiting for me downstairs." About a week later, on Friday, March 17, 1995, Sunnyland did indeed put on his traveling shoes and went to join Little Brother Montgomery, his beloved "best friend," who had passed away ten years earlier.[8]

For a full day, with the golden Medal of Merit draped around his neck, Sunnyland lay in state at the Cage Memorial Chapel, on South Jeffery in Chicago. The following day, March 23, he was memorialized there in an inspirational service. Musicians and ministers alike gave testimonials. Otis Clay infused the

The last performance: Sunnyland Slim onstage at Buddy Guy's Legends, January 1995. Photo by Susan Greenberg

chapel with spiritual fervor through his renderings of "When the Gates Swing Open" and "Sending Up My Timber," and saxophonists Marcus Johnson and Sam Burckhardt played hymns. Alderman Dorothy Tillman read a mayoral proclamation designating June 4, the final day of the 1995 Chicago Blues Festival, as Sunnyland Slim Day in Chicago; she also announced that in the future the Blues Festival would feature an annual Sunnyland Slim Memorial Piano Set.

That night, at the North Side's B.L.U.E.S. Etc., on Belmont Avenue, Burckhardt, guitarist Steve Freund, bassist Bob Stroger, and drummer Robert Covington—the Big Four, Sunnyland's last regular working band—held down the stage for nearly four hours as a stream of colleagues and protégés paid final musical tribute to their friend and mentor. Junior Wells, sassy and dapper as always, joined guitarist John Primer to re-create for a magic instant the sound that used to fill Theresa's Lounge, the fabled South Side juke that introduced generations to the living history of Chicago blues. Pianist Barrelhouse Chuck sent chills down many listeners' spines with an exact replica of Sunnyland's trademark two-handed treble cascade. Fiery young Turks like guitarist Vince Agwada eschewed their usual pyrotechnics to play eloquent, low-key Chicago-style blues in honor of the man who had played such an important role in codifying and defining that sound.

Sunnyland Slim was a man who reveled in the hardscrabble, often profane blues life yet saw—and taught others to see—the handiwork of the divine in people from church sisters to streetwalkers. He once related how he was struggling through a low period when his father passed away in 1959, and he resigned himself to not being able to afford the trip back to Mississippi. But one evening a prostitute he knew helped him out. The woman had "hustled them niggers" out of a lot of money that night, and she remembered Sunnyland as a man who had once done her a favor when she had nowhere else to turn. Returning the goodwill, she provided him the funds for the journey. The moral of the story? That's "how God works."

Sunnyland's deepest personal satisfaction, in fact, came from knowing how many people he had helped and how many cared about him in return. I once saw him reclining in a hospital bed with a telephone receiver to each ear, taking call after call from friends and admirers. "You see how many people love me?" he asked when he finally put the phones down. He wasn't bragging or even smug. He had earned it and he knew it.

During his memorial service I thought of the gifts he had given and of the countless people in whose hearts those gifts still thrived—everyone from musical contemporaries almost as old as he to children like Steve Freund's young son, who used to extend his hands in glee over an imaginary keyboard whenever he heard Sunnyland's name. It occurred to me then that Sunnyland was—and is—what we writers like to call so many but what so few really are: an "immortal." Because Sunnyland Slim did not die. The music lives on, of course, but more important, the pieces of Sunnyland Slim himself—the seeds of wisdom, inspiration, and affirmation he cultivated all his life—will live as long as there is memory.

After the service, as the men lowered Sunnyland's casket into the ground under a gray sky in Mount Vernon Cemetery in the western suburb of Lemont, Illinois, it seemed to me as if the earth herself must be smiling to receive the worldly remains of such a powerful and jubilant spirit. As I left the cemetery that afternoon and looked out over the rolling midwestern countryside, where prairie grass still waves and ripples in the breeze, I thought of the words of Willa Cather, modified only slightly to apply to Sunnyland instead of Alexandra Bergson, Cather's pioneer heroine: "Fortunate country, that is one day to receive hearts like this into its bosom, to give them out again in the yellow wheat, in the rustling corn, in the shining eyes of youth!"[9]

3

Big Walter Horton
"I Mean It from My Heart"

He was tall and lanky. He moved with an off-center, shambling gait, sometimes listing a bit when burdened with his old amplifier or the effects of a few too many pulls from the whiskey bottle. His wrinkled face was angular, with hollow cheeks hanging on regally high cheekbones. In his younger days he had been dubbed "Shakey" and "Tangle Eye," for he was a nervous man whose eyes seemed to bulge out of his head, staring like a chameleon's in different directions below the overhang of a sharp brow. They generally looked mournful and often appeared somewhat distracted.

He used his gap-toothed grin like a benediction and guarded it jealously, saving it for close friends on special, happy occasions. Then he would toss his head back like a horse and laugh, eyes twinkling with a gentle, childlike joy. Most of the time, though, he kept his jaw clenched tight, his lower lip curled askew, maintaining a mask of hardness tempered by the worry he carried knotted up in his brow and by the sorrow that seemed always to swim in the depths of his eyes.

That chameleon image seemed appropriate in other ways as well. He could turn from garrulous to sullen, from generous to miserly, from trusting to suspicious; he was capable of performing heartbreaking acts of simple generosity and crudely insensitive gestures of defiance within seconds of each other. If you saw him on a bus, wrapped in an old gray coat and wearing a Russian-style fur hat, or maybe sharing a half-pint with some buddies in a vacant lot near his home on Thirty-fifth Street on Chicago's South Side, he would look like a thousand other anonymous old men, creased and stooped from too many years of hard living and neglect.

He was, however, one of the greatest American musicians of the twentieth century.

His name was Walter Horton, he played the harmonica, and the sound he made was in turn sweet, supple, harsh, and declamatory—as mercurial as his own personality. When he played "La Cucaracha," it was radiant, like the sparkle in his eyes when he was happy, a child's toy of wonder and delight. Then, on "Trouble in Mind" or "Worried Life Blues," he could mine the depths of a despair few artists have had the courage to explore, recalling what Thomas Pynchon has called "voices whose misery is all the world's night."

Between those two poles Walter played the great boogies and shuffles of Chicago blues in long, swooping lines punctuated with his own patented creation, a rapidly repeated three-note figure usually inserted toward the fifth bar of a twelve-bar form. These blues he played with the abandon of Bacchus himself, only occasionally tempering even the most extroverted solo with a sustained phrase of pristine delicacy, as if to remind us that nothing he ever did could be simple or easily understood.

Walter was born in Horn Lake, Mississippi, on April 6, 1918, but his family moved to Memphis while he was still young. His mother, Emma, was a dominant force in his life and by all reports a formidable figure. Guitarist and vocalist Floyd Jones, an early friend and traveling companion who went on to carve his own niche in Chicago blues history, recalled that as a young boy he occasionally stayed at Walter's house, and some nights they would sneak out and cross the bridge into West Memphis. When they returned, they would fight over who had to sleep on the outside of the bed. They knew that Emma would soon come striding in with a switch, hollering, "I want to see *bare ass!*" before administering her swift and terrible punishment.[1]

According to most accounts, Walter had mastered his chosen instrument by the time he was a teenager. His longtime musical partner Johnny Shines remembered how music consumed Walter even as a boy: "When Walter was about thirteen . . . he would be sitting on the porch, blowing in tin cans, you know, he'd blow tin cans and he'd get sounds out of these things." Shines concluded: "You see, this harmonica blowing is really a mark for Walter, it's not something he picked up, he was born to do it."[2]

Beyond that, little is known about Walter's early years. In Memphis he

Big Walter Horton at ChicagoFest, 1979. Photo by Norman Joss

played on the streets and in W. C. Handy Park with such artists as Frank Stokes, Little Buddy Doyle, and the team of Jack Kelly and Dan Sane. It has been said that he toured with Ma Rainey and the Memphis Jug Band in the 1920s and that he recorded with the Jug Band as well, but these assertions are questionable; it's unlikely that even a prodigy like Walter would have been ready for such a prestigious gig before his tenth birthday. There was apparently a "Shakey Walter" who performed on Rainey's show,[3] and a harpist by that name is credited on a Jug Band session from June 1927, but exactly who this was remains a matter of conjecture.

Details of Walter's activities through most of the 1930s and 1940s are likewise vague. One story that has persisted through the years has him recording with Little Buddy Doyle for Vocalion in 1939, but no documentation of these sessions has been unearthed, although guitarist Homesick James has maintained that both he and Walter played on them. Walter claimed to have been blowing amplified harmonica alongside Honeyboy Edwards on the streets of Jackson, Mississippi, as early as 1940. Indeed, in his landmark 1997 autobiography *The World Don't Owe Me Nothing,* Honeyboy tells of traveling to Jackson with Walter and another harpist, Rice Miller ("Sonny Boy Williamson no. 2"), in the late 1930s. Walter, although barely out of his teens, was already so accomplished that he overshadowed the older Miller, who soon departed.[4]

Walter also sometimes hinted that he escaped conscription during World War II by securing a government-related job, perhaps driving a truck; other versions of the scenario name guitarist Eddie Taylor as the driver, with Walter riding shotgun and keeping an eye on the whiskey supply. Less happily, there is evidence that Walter spent time incarcerated in 1946 and 1947, hauled in on a charge of vagrancy. Of course, in the South during those days, an African American man could be labeled a vagrant if he showed up at the wrong time of day in the wrong part of town.[5] It stands to reason that he would be eager to get out of Dixie; some accounts suggest that he traveled to Chicago for a while in the mid- or late 1940s, perhaps with Floyd Jones.

But he was definitely back in Memphis by 1951. In January of that year he recorded some demos at Sam Phillips's studio on Union Avenue; the next month he returned and cut a series of sides, including "Cotton Patch Hotfoot," "What's the Matter with You," "Now Tell Me Baby," "Little Boy Blue," "Blues in the Morning," and "I'm in Love with You Baby (Walter's Blues)." He recorded another series early that summer: "Black Gal," "Jumpin' Blues," "Go Long Woman," and a jaunty jump-blues version of "Hard Hearted Woman." Taken together, the works in these two sessions constitute a remarkable run that remains, over half a century later, one of the most dramatic documentations ever recorded of a protean blues talent in full bloom.

Working under Phillips's watchful eye and supported by the likes of Joe Hill Louis, Calvin Newborn, and Willie Nix, Walter virtually exploded with inspiration. His melodic imagination seems to have been inexhaustible; his tone was alive with myriad shadings and shifts of timbre as he swooped and sailed over, under, and through his band's accompaniment. Most of these sessions have been reissued on Kent (*Memphis Blues*), Polydor (*Cotton Patch*

Hotfoots), Nighthawk (*Lowdown Memphis Harmonica Jam*), and Ace (*Mouth Harp Maestro*); they're as revelatory today as they were when they were first recorded.

In 1951 Sam Phillips was still leasing material to either Chess in Chicago or to the Los Angeles–based Bihari brothers, who owned the Modern and RPM labels. The Biharis issued a few sides with Walter, whom they dubbed "Mumbles" because of his murky enunciation. By 1952, though, Phillips had initiated Sun Records, which quickly became one of the country's most significant blues, R&B, and gospel labels, a status it retained until 1954, when Phillips released Elvis's first sides and in so doing rewrote the template for a good deal of the later twentieth century's cultural history. Walter's recording of "Sellin' My Whiskey," with Jack Kelly (billed as "Jackie Boy & Little Walter"), would have been the label's debut had it been issued. The sole extant fragment appears on Charly Records' *Sun Box 100,* with Walter's harp barely audible.

It was probably later that same year that Muddy Waters recruited Walter to come to Chicago and play in his band. In an interview published in *Living Blues* magazine in 1985, Muddy recalled that he had obtained Walter's Memphis address from Eddie Taylor and that he sent for him to replace Junior Wells when Junior was drafted.[6] Another version suggests that Muddy dispatched Taylor to Memphis to fetch Walter personally—a cumbersome recruitment strategy by today's standards but more understandable in a milieu where none of the story's principals were literate and telephones were not universal among the poor.[7]

Walter stayed with Muddy for a while, maybe for a few months or maybe, off and on, for the better part of the next year. Nonetheless, whether by temperament or bad luck, he seems never to have been able to hold on to a good thing for long. Popular legend has long held that Muddy fired Walter after he called in sick one night, even though Walter had sent Henry Strong to fill in for him. Muddy recalled, however, that he let Walter go only after learning that he hadn't taken sick at all but instead had found his own gig.[8] For a few low-paid nights in some anonymous Madison Street tavern, Walter apparently lost his chance to remain in the most influential and prestigious blues band in the world. The only recorded evidence of what he sounded like with that band are sides from a January 1953 session that were not released until years later: "Flood," "My Life Is Ruined," two alternate takes of "She's All Right," and "Sad, Sad Day."[9]

That same January Walter recorded with Johnny Shines for J.O.B., but by February or March he was back in Memphis. There, with guitarist Jimmy DeBerry quietly comping behind him, he recorded what would become his most widely acclaimed early masterpiece, "Easy" (Sun 180). "Easy" was a tour de force of raw harmonica power and tonal manipulation based on the melody of Ivory Joe Hunter's "I Almost Lost My Mind." The artists were billed as "Jimmy and Walter"; Walter received three dollars for the session. In fact, according to existing documents, Walter received only fifty-nine dollars the entire time he was with Sam Phillips, and it wasn't even all payment: personal loans accounted for five dollars, and an additional one dollar went toward the cost of a harmonica. Despite the tune's title, life wasn't easy, then or ever.

Throughout his early career Walter often seemed perched on the edge of success. The J.O.B. recordings with Johnny Shines ("Brutal Hearted Woman" and "Evening Sun") recaptured and maybe even surpassed the initial brilliance he had shown recording for Sam Phillips in Memphis. A few years later, having again settled in Chicago after the breakup with Muddy, he cut some sides under his own name for both Cobra and States. Produced by Willie Dixon, these recordings featured riffing horns and jump rhythms.

Characteristically, though, his most historic performance as a sideman came about almost by accident. On October 29, 1956, harpist Charles Edwards (Good Rockin' Charles) failed to show up for a Jimmy Rogers session at Chess. According to Rogers, Walter was working a day job as a house painter. Jimmy went over, "got him off the ladder," and brought him back to the studio. Walter, his clothes smeared with paint, was so self-conscious about his appearance he had to be coaxed to approach the microphone.[10] But when he did, he erupted into glory. His harp break on Rogers's "Walking by Myself," initiated by rapid-fire staccato patterns that billow out into extended, swooping phrases—all delivered in a tone as raucous and full-bodied as any he ever summoned—is arguably his finest recorded moment. It's certainly one of the most thrilling blues harmonica solos ever waxed.

After that, the good times became fewer. As blues gave way to rock 'n' roll, and as the music industry became more conservative and professionalized, blues artists who, like Walter, had come up the old way found themselves left out musically, personally, and even culturally. Walter, never the strongest of men, faded further and further from the mainstream scene, although unlike Johnny Shines and some others, he never gave up music entirely. As late as 1964 he was still trying to break into the dwindling blues market with efforts like "Good Moanin' Blues," produced by Willie Dixon at Chess and released on the Chess subsidiary Argo.

When the so-called blues revival of the 1960s and 1970s got under way, Walter had what looked like a genuine shot at revitalizing his career. He began to work the U.S. college, coffee house, and festival circuits; Willie Dixon included him in his Chicago Blues All-Stars; and he played in Europe. Rereleases of his earlier recordings cemented his reputation as a revolutionary force in blues harmonica, with overdue recognition now given to the Modern/RPM and Sun classics; the masterful J.O.B. sessions with Shines; States and Cobra sides such as "Need My Baby," "Have A Good Time," and an updated version of "Hard-Hearted Woman"; and of course the epic "Walking by Myself."

Walter's activities as a "rediscovered" blues musician also included recording sessions on Vanguard, Testament, Delta, Alligator, and other labels, often alongside old friends such as Johnny Young, Floyd Jones, and Eddie Taylor, as well as protégés like harpist Carey Bell. On many of these, especially some of the outings with Young, Walter demonstrated that he had lost none of his gifts. If anything, the years had added depth to his creative vision. Willie Dixon, who would tell anyone who cared to listen that "Shakey" was by far the finest harmonica player he had ever encountered, used Walter on his *I Am the Blues* LP on Columbia in 1970.

Walter's reunion with Muddy Waters on *I'm Ready* in 1978, although not quite up to the vintage standards of either artist, provided a tantalizing glimpse of what might have been had the two not parted company under such prosaic but final circumstances nearly a quarter-century earlier. At about the same time Walter turned in a solid performance on *Fine Cuts*, a Blind Pig LP that paired him with one of his staunchest young admirers, guitarist John Nicholas. Walter returned the guitarist's affection in his usual hard-bitten fashion: "You're a Greek," he said he once told the young musician in a declaration of brotherhood, "and a Greek ain't nothin' but a nigger turned inside-out."

But always, when the session or the tour was over, Walter returned to his established routine: gigs in small Chicago clubs; Sunday mornings playing for tips in the open-air Maxwell Street Market; and day-to-day life in a series of grim South Side apartments where he attempted to preside over a turbulent, sometimes violent household. As the years wore on, it became rarer and rarer for Walter's muse to elevate him when the audience, the moment, and the money were right. In fact, he sometimes seemed to save his best for the times that could least help him. A chaotic Saturday nightclub date, marred by moodiness and alcohol, would be followed by a flawless performance early the next morning in front of a handful of people on a sidewalk or in a vacant lot near Maxwell Street; an apathetic evening's work would segue into a majestic final set of dreamlike brilliance long after most of the crowd had left. With his turns away from stardom and his twisted excursions down the alleys of self-sabotage and isolation, Walter became the archetypal phantom bluesman even as he recorded with world-famous names and continued, off and on, to perform on the road and at various places around town.

One gets the feeling that Walter's elusiveness, his penchant for great and outrageous lies, and his refusal to be interviewed or even photographed were at least partly a way of refusing to acknowledge—to himself or anyone else—the full magnitude of the setbacks and disappointments in his life. Like Rice Miller, who never revealed much about his childhood beyond saying, "I had it tough, you know, in them days,"[11] Walter constructed for himself a protective covering of legend and self-invention that made him mysterious and unique, even in the blues world.

He would go to almost any lengths to avoid getting caught in a lie or a mistake. When all else failed, he would simply take a stand and brazen his way through. Once, when a companion kidded him for wearing a watch that was at least an hour wrong, Walter matter-of-factly replied that he had set it that way on purpose, since he was going to the coast in a few days and wanted to get used to the change. Then there was the time he grabbed the stick shift of my car in the middle of the northbound lane of Chicago's Lakeshore Drive and proceeded to give me a lesson, at fifty-five miles per hour, on shifting gears as I desperately clamped the clutch to the floor and prayed he wouldn't jam it into reverse.

Walter's greatest lie may have been his Charlie Patton story, a tale he set up so smoothly and then unfurled with such deadpan seriousness that to this day I can't say whether he was conning me or he had actually convinced himself it was true. After repeatedly referring to Patton in the present tense over the course of a conversation, Walter denied my protests that Patton had died in the 1930s. No, he retorted; not only was Patton still alive, but he himself had been surreptitiously caring for the Delta blues legend all this time. "He was a Mason." Walter declared. "They faked his death, and they sent him to live with me. . . . I've been taking care of him ever since. He's up in my apartment right now."

Several blues veterans, including Walter's old partner Johnny Shines, have gleefully recounted how they used to enjoy tweaking the naïveté of earnest white aficionados with outrageous stories, doing so to maintain their dignity and privacy under the invasive scrutiny of patronizing folklorists and dilettantes.[12] Perhaps Walter was doing this when he laid his Charlie Patton tale on me. Walter's inscrutability was, among other things, a carefully honed survival tool, a noncomic trickster's mask, impenetrable and ever-changing. Walter never learned to read or write, and even many of his longtime friends considered him "slow." Honeyboy Edwards, for one, said that as a boy Walter was "half retarded," although he added that "he grew out of a lot of it" as he got older.[13] Walter nonetheless became expert in maneuvering behind his crazy-like-a-fox facade to get what he needed from the fast-moving modern world—a world with which, in many ways, he had only a tangential everyday relationship.

In early December 1981, shortly after returning from a triumphant appearance at the Blues Estafette in Utrecht, Holland—his first European performance in years—Walter either fell or was pushed down some stairs, an incident that resulted in some badly bruised ribs. Not long after that, on December 8, he collapsed in a neighbor's apartment and died. For weeks dark rumors about beatings and family violence circulated among those who knew him. It was easy to believe the stories, as sordid as some of them were. Walter's household consisted of too many people with too many personal problems crowded into too little space, and it was wracked with the social dysfunctions and pathologies that oppress the hard ghetto world of U.S. cities. He was known to stay away from that house for days at a time, nursing scars and bruises that he sometimes claimed were inflicted by robbers. Other times, though, he would admit that they were the result of domestic strife.

But it's also true that Walter took poor care of himself, especially where

Big Walter Horton with guitarist Jimmy Rogers at Blues Estafette, Utrecht, Holland, December 1981. Photo by Bert Van Oortmarssen

alcohol was concerned (the official cause of his death was heart failure due to the effects of "acute alcoholism").[14] When he was exiled from the house, as apparently he had been in the days just before his death, his agony was palpable. He would drink more than ever and sometimes seemed physically convulsed with the psychic pain of being separated from the only home and family he had. It's not hard to imagine that his heart simply gave out under the strain.

Walter's admirers were legion, but he seldom bonded intimately. His affection for most of his younger acquaintances, when he chose to show it, was alternately brusque and playful. He had a repertoire of sayings ("You're *ugly,*" "You're *fired,*" and "Here come the devil") and names ("dummy," "ugly mother-harper," or for women, "Gran'ma" and "you old goat") that he delivered with a playful scowl or mischievous grin. When he really wanted to get a point across—whether in jest, anger, or pleading sincerity—he would proclaim simply, "I mean it from my heart."

Meanwhile he maintained solid, if sometimes tempestuous, relationships with his longtime companions in the music world. Younger harpists like Carey Bell, Billy Branch, and Charlie Musselwhite sought him out as a mentor, and he responded to their overtures with the graciousness of a gruff but kindly elder statesman. The late Little Joe Berson, a harp player who worked with Jimmy Rogers and helped Walter land his brief slot in the movie *The Blues Brothers* (he's in the Maxwell Street scene playing harmonica in John Lee Hooker's band), was among his closest friends in later years. Berson, another complex man with a fiercely guarded personality, was in some ways the perfect soulmate for Walter. They shared secrets, played music together, laughed together, and probably wept together—two hard-bitten souls savoring the rare sanctuary of mutual trust and security. They sometimes wore their friendship like a suit of armor, and it may have been the safest protection either ever had.

For the rest of us, there are fondly remembered moments of comradeship interspersed with the maddeningly inexplicable behavior that made more than one would-be savior shake his or her head and sadly turn away. The scenes were legion. There was Walter on a dangerously cold winter night, huddled into his coat and shivering in the doorway of a nightclub that wouldn't open for at least another hour and then wordlessly climbing into the car of an acquaintance who happened to drive by, accepting a ride to a nearby hotdog stand as if he'd been waiting for it all along. Or there was Walter succumbing to the stupidity of a young follower who had sneaked into his hotel room and got him roaring, sloppy drunk before a Carnegie Hall performance with Sunnyland Slim and others in 1979—yet another splendid opportunity plunged irrevocably into chaos.[15] Or there was Walter hogging solos and quarreling with his bandmates on stage, growling and whooping incoherently into his microphone, and prompting the drummer Playboy Venson to stop playing in disgust or goading bassist Floyd Jones into packing up and leaving midset.

But there were also those moments when everything came together, when that legendary bell-like tone came ringing out, a timbre so angelic one felt it could have come only from a man who, like Walter, had spent most of his life wrestling with demons. He would coax it from his instrument, sometimes one note at a time, his back arched and eyes clenched shut, sweat pouring down his face, those impossibly long, sinewy fingers cupped around his harp. Walter's crusty musical comrades always returned, put up with his eccentricities the best they could, and glowed with delight when it all fell into place and the old brilliance shone again—a brilliance that will remain a standard by which blues harmonica expression is judged for as long as the blues is played.

And the blues, of course, continues to be played. Capable young musicians create new variations on venerable themes, even as veterans like Walter's contemporaries Honeyboy Edwards and pianist Pinetop Perkins continue the legacy of their generation, the generation of blues artists who migrated from the South and created the sound now known worldwide as Chicago blues. None of it is in danger of dying any time soon. Nonetheless, as more of the old guard passes away and as the community-based cultural life they shared and helped cultivate crumbles and implodes under the assault of "urban removal" and corporatization, an empty realm of silence seems to grow ominously in places where there once was music. Standing in abandoned nightclubs and vacant lots, on desolate streets that used to teem with life, you can hear the absence of song.

But the silence may yet be broken. If that long-awaited Judgment Day ever does arrive, and if Gabriel is still in the mood to blow one final, swinging solo before it all comes down, rest assured we'll be hearing a harmonica somewhere in the choir.

And if I know Walter, Gabriel is going to have to share that solo.

Part 2

"We Gon' Pitch a Boogie-Woogie!"

4

Florence's Lounge
Memories of an Urban Juke

I'd been in Chicago for less than six months, if memory serves, when I first went to Florence's Lounge, on Shields Avenue near Fifty-fifth Street. It was about three o'clock on a Sunday afternoon; as usual, I had spent most of the day on Maxwell Street, guzzling warm beer and listening to the rugged sounds of musicians like guitarist Pat Rushing and venerable drummer Tenner "Playboy" Venson, along with their rough-and-ready ensembles. No doubt, then, my head was buzzing and my consciousness primed for revelation long before I arrived at the club.

From the street it looked like any other ghetto gin mill, despite its odd pastel-purple paint job. Then I paid my dollar at the door, went inside, and found myself in a different world. The room was sealed tight except for a rear exit that was open but protected by burglar bars. The entire place probably couldn't have held more than seventy-five people comfortably, but it was so dark you could barely see across the floor. Magic Slim and the Teardrops were playing on a tiny bandstand in a far corner; the air was thick with cigar smoke, the smell of cheap perfume, and a mixture of raw blues, raucous laughter, and conversation that seemed headier and more richly seasoned than the most potent whiskey or exquisitely prepared soul food imaginable.

Through the haze walked a plump, dapper man who looked as if he had just come from church. As he took the microphone into his hands, the band dug into a slow-grinding groove reminiscent of Little Walter's classic ballad "Last Night." The newcomer opened his mouth, and a voice of muscular resonance, shot through with an aching gospel vibrato, filled the room:

> Mmmmmm, it's been so long
> Since I had to shed a tear
> Such a lonely, lonely feeling
> When you lose someone so dear[1]

My eyes filled with tears as I sat in stunned disbelief. I'd recently moved to Chicago from New England, hoping to experience some of the fabled power of the blues on its home turf. Now, in a little neighborhood bar, in front of a crowd of regulars who seemed to take it all in stride, a singer I had never heard of was creating music laced with an emotional power and majesty I hadn't dreamed possible.

As I later learned, the singer was Andrew "B. B." (or "Big Voice") Odom, and he was only one of many who regularly sat in on Slim's Sunday afternoon session. I soon learned, too, that my initial impression of the mood at Florence's had been misguided. True, there wasn't much applause when Odom finished his performance and stepped down; a lot of people hadn't even bothered looking at him while he was singing. But they hadn't been taking his music—or anything else going on there—"in stride." During his set and throughout the afternoon, celebrants affirmed and responded to everything that happened with shouts, gestures, and dance moves that were coordinated to take in not just the bandstand and the musicians but fellow dancers and the entire assembled crowd, affirmations that weren't terribly dissimilar to what many had been using in church just a few hours before.

As I returned over the next few months, my perspective on the blues widened and deepened immeasurably. It became apparent that this music was about more than rhythm, more than notes, more than a twelve-bar structure and a shuffle beat, more even than the lyrics whose evocative folk poetry had originally captivated me. A way of life was being celebrated here, a life rooted in strength, community, and shared experience. More than just a party, it was a ritual of affirmation and—despite the coarseness of the jokes, despite the wine-soaked eyes and slurred conversation, despite the violence and sorrow that occasionally impinged—a ritual of dignity and spiritual regeneration as well.

A bittersweet lode of irony ran through this revelation: the power and determination to prevail that were celebrated and reborn every Sunday on

Shields became increasingly necessary for me as I found myself attending funerals, mourning the loss of friends and companions cut down before their time, and eventually witnessing the demise of Florence's itself. Today most of the other venues I attended during those years are gone as well, yet they are "history" not in the cavalier American vernacular sense of being expunged from consideration but in the deeper, more indigenous sense of being irrevocably and permanently a part of our lives, still vital, still infusing our world with the nourishing life-force of memory.

What follows is the way things felt to me in December 1983, after the music at Florence's was silenced forever.

* * *

Suddenly the only sound was the wind. It kicked up dust and garbage as it swirled across the vacant lot at the corner of Fifty-fifth and Shields and moaned its way through the charred timber and crumbling plaster of the gutted building next door. A few weeks earlier James Cotton had paid a surprise visit to that building and sung to a packed house: "Blow wind, blow wind, blow my baby back to me." But now, as the smell of burned wood lingered in the air and the icy breath of winter drove a solitary pedestrian deeper into his buttoned-up overcoat, that wind was blowing in nothing but silence. Florence's Lounge, one of the last of the legendary South Side blues bars and a mecca for music lovers from around the world, was gone.

You couldn't miss it. The brick building was painted reddish purple with orange trim. A Schlitz malt liquor sign hung in front, and a window of extra-strength bullet-proof glass was built into the masonry. An outdoor dice game attracted a crowd there every Sunday afternoon, their shouts, curses, and deep-throated laughter punctuating the play. Occasionally one of the gamblers would grab a snack from Bob the Pig-Ear Man's custom-made wooden cart, which Bob had hitched to his red Cadillac and parked directly in front of the club. There he dutifully served patrons and held forth with his never-ending stream of talk, the steam from his kettles swirling around him, redolent with the odor of polish sausages, steak sandwiches, and his famous boiled pig ears:

> Now look here. One of these days I'm gonna open me up a club of my own, and ain't *none* of these raggedy-ass motherfuckers gonna get in without payin' full price at the door, *especially* the musicians. You understand? I'm gonna already *have* a band up on the bandstand, and I don't need all these other musicians comin' up in my club and they ain't gonna spend no money. And if my band doesn't show up, I'll hire me a chorus line of about fifteen shake dancers, take my little ol' guitar up there, and play my damn self.

Magic Slim at the 1125 Club, 1972. Photo by Wes Race

If it looked as if you were taking him seriously, he would carry on in that vein for hours, occasionally glancing up at the musicians and hangers-on gathered around his cart, men with names like Baby James, Smiling Bobby, Alabama Junior, and Toothpick Slim. He would embellish his rap with asides—"Ain't I right, Slim?" "Is I'm lyin', James?"—and they would nod and grin in bemused admiration at his apparently inexhaustible supply of words and opinions.

By the time you reached Bob's cart, though, the sounds of the blues would be audible from inside the club, and you were unlikely to hang around on the sidewalk for long. After you paid your dollar and squeezed through the tiny front entrance, you felt transported to a rural Mississippi juke: the paneled walls were bare, the low ceiling sagged ominously and dripped water, and multicolored balloons and streamers from long-forgotten birthday parties and celebrations hung down. There was no spotlight for the band. The singers clustered around a single microphone or passed it among themselves, and the amplifiers crackled, fed back, and faded in and out under the assault of Magic Slim's piercing lead guitar and the relentless, bass-heavy accompaniment of the Teardrops.

The place was also filled with the lively racket of the regular patrons, mostly working people from the neighborhood, many still dressed for church: men in aging but impeccably cleaned and pressed suits and women decked out in white, flaming pink, or purple sequined dresses and sporting flamboyantly plumed hats. It was pretty much the same people who had been gathering there every Sunday since the late 1960s, when the weekly sessions began, or else their sons and daughters.

Back then it was nicknamed "the Bucket of Blood," and the main attraction was slide guitarist Hound Dog Taylor, the ribald juker who would eventually find himself plucked out of the ghetto by Bruce Iglauer to become the first artist on Iglauer's then-fledgling Alligator label. Florence Arnold, who had opened the place in the 1950s, had managed to acquire the only liquor license for blocks around, and disagreements of every description—lovers' quarrels, gambling debts, street-gang feuds—got settled in or near the club. The atmosphere was rowdy and exhilarating, with a constant threat of danger lurking at the fringes of the celebration.

In a way, Hound Dog was the perfect entertainer for the rough-and-tumble little tavern. He was a wiry, intense man, addicted to alcohol and given to violent fluctuations in mood. Onstage he was extroverted, the tireless life of the party, cracking jokes and breaking into peals of laughter. In private, though, he was often brooding and morose, haunted by recurrent nightmares and afraid to sleep alone in the dark. With his spells of magnanimity punctuated by violent outbursts, Taylor was as mercurial as Florence's itself.

Shortly after he began to play there, word of the weekly parties started to spread among white aficionados such as Iglauer, Steve Cushing (now host of the syndicated NPR program *Blues before Sunrise* and a blues drummer), and Jim O'Neal and Amy Van Singel of *Living Blues* magazine. From the beginning, O'Neal recalled, Florence's with Hound Dog at the helm was "a party, always such a party." Cushing, though, remembered the club's darker side:

The second time I ever went to Florence's was the last time Hound Dog ever played there as the featured act. This was in December 1973. I was still a little nervous; it was one of the first times I'd been to a black club, and I hadn't learned how to relax. All of a sudden this gang broke in and started throwing chairs around.

They hit [guitarist] Brewer Phillips; Brewer ducked and they hit Hound Dog, who was sitting down playing. He got up, started rubbing his head and looking around, and one of the gang members shouted, "Everybody get out!" Nobody moved, so he shouted again: "Everybody get out, or we'll start shooting!" Everyone started falling over each other, running for the door.

Once outside, Cushing said, he muttered nervously, "Us white boys ain't used to this shit," to which a regular patron responded, "If you're gonna come down here, you white boys better *get* used to this shit."

About half a year later, on a Sunday afternoon, a gunshot exploded inside the club, and a man who had been sitting in a booth suddenly lurched forward with a bullet in his head. Again Cushing and everyone else bolted for the door, stumbling over the body on their way out. Outside, the dead man's brother stood helplessly in the street, screaming and crying and shaking his fist at the killer's car as it sped away.

Sometimes even the musicians got into the act. After Hound Dog quit the Florence's gig for the better-paying and safer life of touring and recording for Alligator, several bands tried to fill his shoes, but not until Magic Slim and the Teardrops took over did the scene regain its original vitality. Slim is a gigantic man, standing about six feet six and weighing at least 260 pounds. His temperament is affable, but his humor is gruff. As he dominates the stage with his massive body, roaring voice, and aggressive, sometimes violently misogynist lyrics, he shouts out threats to the men in the audience: "Man, it's gonna be a mess in here, I tell you! I'm madder'n a one-eyed Russian and crazier'n a constipated Gypsy!"

Cushing remembered an afternoon when a visiting harmonica player insisted on keeping his amplifier turned up so high nobody could hear Slim's band. Slim was taking a break at the time, but after repeated warnings to the harp man, he finally strode back to the bandstand, pulled himself up to his full height, and ordered the miscreant off. The harp player, who gave away almost a foot of height and well over a hundred pounds to the big man, continued to harangue and taunt Slim as he plugged in and prepared to regain control of his show.

Finally Slim could take no more. Like an enraged bull he charged out into the crowd, spilling tables and drinks, and plunged toward his tormentor, who was now desperately trying to reach the door. Slim's brothers and bandmates, bassist Nick and drummer Lee-Baby—both at least as tall as Slim—grabbed his arms and tried to restrain him, but he reached the terrified harpist with death in his eyes and his knife drawn. At the last minute the smaller man managed to push his way out to safety.

Through the 1970s things mellowed somewhat. The brash young bloods who had caused most of the trouble at Florence's either went to jail or grew older and wiser, and by the early 1980s you could see some of them standing around by Bob's cart, telling their stories with a mixture of fond reminiscence and disbelief that they had survived all that chaos: "Man, I was one crazy motherfucker in those days. I remember I held up a man right in that men's room in there!" They become the unofficial guardians of the tavern, gruffly looking out for the white blues fans, especially the women, who had gotten the word and were now venturing to the South Side. The occasional troublemaker still appeared, but the old "bucket of blood" atmosphere was gone. Remaining, though, was the joyful cacophony of conversation, roaring laughter, and throbbing music that was rapidly making the club famous.

But its fame was special, even in Chicago. Perhaps its side-street location put it just far enough out of the way to make it uninteresting to most tourists; maybe stories from the old days scared some people off; or perhaps the music's uncompromising volume and lack of slickness or the club's lack of physical amenities (a newspaper article once described the bathrooms, very charitably, as "questionable") was too much for the casual observer.[2] Whatever the reason, Florence's never became a trendy must-see, as did the Checkerboard and Theresa's. Of those who made it to Fifty-fifth and Shields, most were either longtime blues fans or in the company of someone who was, and many returned as regulars. The club's black patrons accepted the newcomers with a mixture of amused affection and live-and-let-live tolerance. Aside from casting an occasional suspicious look or hostile glare, the regulars rarely exhibited anything but dignity and respect toward anyone from "outside the neighborhood" (as racial difference was usually and euphemistically designated).

Florence's was no stranger to diversity, anyway. On some days the guest list read like a roll call from a Disney cartoon: Pops, Crazy Daisy, Baby Duck, Godfather, Daddy Rabbit, the Chocolate Kid, and Mr. Pitiful were among the regular patrons, and many were musicians as well. Mr. Pitiful, a bassist who also used the name Dancin' Perkins, was the leader of the original Teardrops when Magic Slim first joined them. Daddy Rabbit—né Coleman Pettis, aka Alabama Junior—was Slim's second guitarist for years before he struck out on his own. Both Godfather and the Chocolate Kid either led bands or sat in regularly at Florence's, with Baby Duck sometimes featured as a singer.

Then there was Mor-Diz, or at least that's how he pronounced it, although he always signed his named "Moridzs, Prod.," on the hastily scrawled posters he hung on the wall near Florence's entrance. Aside from his self-appointed role as Slim's "producer," Mor-Diz claimed variously to have been Hound Dog's manager, a bilingual writer preparing a blues book in either Korean or Japanese, and even a former professional hit man. Short and burly, with piercing eyes, he usually had a gold medallion hung around his neck, and he always carried a battered briefcase containing papers, pluggers for upcoming shows, a notebook, and sometimes a half-pint of whiskey from which he would sneak snorts.

The notebook, though, was his primary occupation. Every Sunday he would position himself directly in front of the stage and painstakingly prepare three columns on the pages. In the first he wrote the title of every song played that day; in the second he made entries in an arcane personal code that he claimed identified each soloist in order of performance; and finally, in the third column, there was the "Japanese," intricately drawn and eagerly described to anyone who asked him what it meant.

The descriptions tended to change to fit the moment. Bruce Iglauer remembered that Mor-Diz claimed to be writing in Korean in the early and mid-1970s; by the time I met him, in 1979, the characters on the page were the same but the language had changed to Japanese. Others were told that the markings were Mor-Diz's personal secret code, used to prevent plagiarists from stealing his ideas before he could put them all together in a book. Still another explanation was that a Japanese blues magazine wanted to chronicle the events at Florence's, and they had chosen him as their point man because he had learned the language in the military.

Other regulars included Pops, whose surname was Hill and who celebrated his ninety-eighth birthday in the club in the early 1970s. He was said to have served in the U.S. Cavalry in Arizona in the nineteenth century. By the time he reached his nineties, he had outlived most of his friends and family; Florence Arnold took him in, gave him a room, and made him a fixture in her club. Iglauer remembered another old man, a dancer whose sensual grace made him a hit with the women despite his age. "He was really incredible," Iglauer asserted. "If I'd been a woman, I'd sure have gone for him in a minute."

Some of the faces at Florence's reflected the strength and durability of "Pops" Hill and the anonymous dance-floor Lothario, but others told stories of tragedy and defeat. This was after all a club in the ghetto, and many troubled people would come to listen to some music, have as many drinks as they could afford, and forget about their lives for a while. Crazy Daisy was a woman of indeterminate age with thick glasses who would spend most of the afternoon

"Moridzs" and Wes Race at Florence's, ca. 1973. Photo courtesy of Wes Race

sitting at the end of the bar, nodding and muttering to herself. Occasionally she would wave her arms and point into the air with a compulsive, almost spastic motion. She drank heavily, but old-timers maintained that wasn't her real problem. She had served in Korea—as a nurse, some said, or maybe a cook—and something had happened there that she had never gotten over.

The eccentrics were treated with a uniform kindness at Florence's; only after they had made an exceptional ruckus would someone kick them out. One woman who looked to be at least in her fifties would show up once every few months in a badly fitting wig, drink herself into incoherence and helpless sobs, and end up sitting on the ground in the vacant lot next door, bawling loudly until a taxi took her away, the wig hanging down one side of her face like a dead poodle.

But the common denominator at Florence's, the thing that drew everyone back again and again, was the music. It was quite simply exhilarating. From the raw whine of Hound Dog Taylor's slide to the searing frenzy of Melvin Taylor (no relation), a fire-on-the-fretboard young blood whose solos sometimes sounded as if there weren't enough notes in the world to palliate his manic energies, blues of every stripe was played at Florence's, and the musicians were almost always at the height of their capacities. Some, like Magic Slim, played better there than they would ever play again.

James Cotton, fresh off the aging-hippie roadhouse circuit, would sometimes drop by when he was in town, often grabbing a pig-ear sandwich from Bob before entering the club, fixing himself up with a half-pint, and filling the room with his leather-lunged harmonica riffs and hoarse vocals. One Sunday around 1980 Florence's was blessed with a surprise appearance by Good Rockin' Charles, an elusive 1950s harpist who had reemerged in the 1970s, recorded an album on the Mr. Blues label, and then virtually dropped out of sight again. The hawklike intensity of his harp tone and the growling urgency of his voice lured Bob away from his cart and into the club—a rarity for that cynical hustler—and for weeks afterward, he raved about what he had heard. Some hoped that this might signal the beginning of a genuine comeback for Charles, but although he landed a few gigs at various North Side venues over the next few years, he never really made it back. His one-afternoon stint at Florence's gave a tantalizing glimpse of the might-have-been for everyone who was lucky enough to see it.

Big Walter Horton would drop by occasionally, before his death in 1981; Sunnyland Slim, sometimes with protégé Big Time Sarah in tow, would come in, stride up to the microphone, and fill the club with his stentorian downhome holler. Louis Myers, the lead guitarist of the legendary Aces, would park in a vacant a lot across the street and sit in his car for hours before finally deigning to get out and amble slowly into the club. Once inside he'd strap on his guitar and engage Magic Slim in head-to-head duels, his jazz-tinged melodicism providing an elegant foil for Slim's furious upper-register arpeggios and serpentine leads.

Some of the local artists who played and sang at Florence's occasionally traveled to Europe on "all-star" Chicago revues, yet they remained virtually unknown in town outside their immediate neighborhoods. Andrew "Big Voice" Odom would mesmerize the crowd with his gospel-drenched vocals, sometimes working himself into such a frenzy that his veins would bulge, his eyes seemed to lose their focus, and it looked as if he was going to start speaking in tongues if he didn't drop dead of a heart attack first. Slide guitarist Joe Carter brandished a vintage Epiphone on which he seared out note-for-note covers of Elmore James classics, including "The Sky Is Crying" and "Dust My Broom." On a good day you could hardly tell his playing from the original. Even some who seldom ventured out of Chicago turned in performances that would probably have earned them standing ovations overseas: Baby James presented an energetic mix of blues and soul hits both venerable and recent; the Chocolate Kid bent strings and wailed B. B. and Albert King standards before departing for his own gig at Morgen's Lounge, about a mile and a half to the southeast.

The caliber of the music is even more remarkable given the financial and managerial problems the club suffered over the years. According to Iglauer, Florence Arnold was in ill health as early as 1968, when she began to book Hound Dog every Sunday. She didn't come into her club very often. Instead she would shout from the window of her second-floor apartment, giving instructions to the musicians and patrons gathered on the sidewalk below. She finally sold the business in the late 1970s. The new proprietor, a matronly woman named Emma, took a more hands-on interest in the place: she tended bar, supervised the door, and maintained complete control of the room.

But Emma had her problems, too. She suffered from diabetes, and neither she nor her husband, Jack, had the physical or financial reserves to keep things running smoothly. When Slim was there he commanded a loyal following, and the club pretty much ran itself. But as his reputation grew, he began to secure more gigs out of town. Emma would book someone else, maybe guitarist John Embry, flanked by Dancin' Perkins and the Chocolate Kid, tired but still game after playing on Maxwell Street from early morning until two o'clock or so. Without Slim's charismatic presence and relentless drive, however, the scene lagged badly. Many was the Sunday when Emma and Jack had just enough money to open up, serve a few drinks, and take cash from the till as it came in, making desperate liquor runs all afternoon to keep the supply up.

The room's physical condition began to deteriorate as well, and sometimes Emma had to close for weeks at a time for repairs. Even when the club was open and Slim was available, the unpredictability began to hurt business. Emma lost weight and look increasingly tired, and in 1982 she closed the club for good.

For nearly a year rumors flew. One of the dice players had made a big score, bought the place, and was planning to reopen it; Bob the Pig-Ear Man was finally going to make good on his longtime promise to open up a blues club, and he had chosen Florence's as his spot; the building was going to be demolished; Slim himself was preparing to purchase it.

Meanwhile, Slim found another musical home. The BTO ("Big Time Operators") Club on Seventy-third Street, a private men's club run by some buddies of his, decided to open their doors to the public on Sunday afternoons and hired him to play. Slim's old followers slowly began to come around. But the room was a converted warehouse, two or three times bigger than Florence's, and the overhead was tremendous. Slim's Sunday sessions, augmented by occasional weekend blues shows or special events like an evening hosted by the "Bad Girls on the Run Social Club," were barely enough to pay the rent and the electric bill.

In late August 1983 the word was out: Florence's had been purchased by a man with plenty of money who had remodeled the room to conform to the building codes, and he had hired guitarist Lefty Dizz to play there. It was inevitable that sooner or later Slim would return, and in September, after the owners of the BTO finally gave up and closed their doors, he stormed back into the little club where he had originally staked out his turf.

Old-timers couldn't believe their eyes when they saw it. The outside was the same—purple with orange trim, with Bob's shiny red Cadillac parked in front, hitched to his food cart with its bright orange awning. But the new owner had sunk a large amount of money into the place—some said upward of thirty-five thousand dollars. Gone were the paneled walls and crumbling ceiling. The entire room had been redone, from the custom-made wooden glass holders behind the new bar to the new booths, where smooth faux-leather seat covers replaced the notorious old cushions that had tended to tilt whenever a heavy person sat down or got up. Wall-to-wall carpeting covered the floor; the bathrooms had been entirely refurbished. A full assortment of liquors and wines beckoned from behind the bar. Previously the room had seemed incongruous, with its down-home atmosphere and southern juke-joint appearance cocooned in a gritty urban neighborhood. Now a newcomer might think he was in a Wisconsin hunting lodge instead of a blues bar in the heart of Chicago's South Side ghetto.

But then Magic Slim stepped onto the carpeted bandstand and began to bellow and signify at the patrons: "I only want *women* to come up here with requests! I ain't gonna play nothin' for no man!" Raucous laughter reverberated through the room, and Slim's female admirers squealed in delight: "Come on, baby! Do it, Slim! Take your t-i-i-i-me!" Mor-Diz reclaimed his post in front of the stage, nodding his head and directing the show with herky-jerky movements, and filed more entries into his endless bilingual blues journal. Crazy Daisy and Toothpick Slim danced their rubber-kneed way across the floor through clouds of smoke before finally falling asleep, side by side, at the end of the bar. The whole pounding, crazy scene at Florence's seemed returned from the dead, and there were smiles on Sunday once more.

It was not to last. On Monday, November 7, 1983, at around four o'clock in the morning, flames tore through the building. Neighborhood rumors spoke of firebombs and "Jewish lightning" (i.e., arson for profit); the fire department classified it as "suspected arson," but no one was apprehended. For a while the shell of the building stood, dark and battered by icy winter winds, but few believed that the owners or anyone else would try to rehabilitate it again.

Eventually a crime of some sort was committed in or near the place—according to one story, a woman was raped there—and it was torn down.

For a while Slim continued to play his evening set at the Missing Link, formerly Louise's South Park Lounge, at the corner of Sixty-ninth and King Drive, across the street from where Sunnyland Slim used to live, but within a few years he gave up his old neighborhood haunts for the North Side, the national roadhouse and college circuit, and European tours. He eventually moved out of Chicago entirely for the more staid environs of Lincoln, Nebraska, where he had been a mainstay at the Zoo Bar for years.

Meanwhile the stories and tall tales about Florence's passed quickly into blues lore. One never knew who would walk in that door. Anyone from a world-famous blues artist to the notorious shake dancer Lady Ann might show up, although the reception they received was likely to be quite different. Lady Ann's act, which she called her "Bad Girl Revue," consisted of grabbing a man from the audience, dragging him to the stage, and doing a full striptease while bending, leaning, lying, and rubbing all over him in front of the crowd. She soon found that her arrival inspired a general male exodus. The musicians, on the other hand, whether local or internationally known, were treated with respect and allowed to show what they could do for at least two songs. It was a weekly apprenticeship, and Florence's Lounge gave more than one bluesman his first taste of performing live with a professional band behind him.

Between sets, at the right time of the evening, one could stand on the sidewalk in front of the club and see the sun setting behind the railroad tracks that run along an embankment, parallel to Shields, about half a block away. It didn't take too much imagination to envision the thousands of miles of rails that have carried the blues and its people from their original home in the South to every part of the country. A few weeks before the fire that shut down Florence's forever, I said as much to Bob the Pig-Ear Man, who was packing up his things and folding the awning over his cart, getting ready to leave before the late afternoon chill got any worse. Without looking up, he launched into a characteristically blunt-edged tirade about music, the blues, and the pitifully naive idealism that he sometimes seemed to think affected everyone in the world except himself. Yeah, these blues guys, they play, go all over the world, all these peoples comin' down here to look at 'em, writers talkin' 'bout how good they all are—and still they ain't makin' no money! "Good?" Who cares about "good"? They ain't makin' no money!

Then he paused, glanced at the sky reddening behind the tracks, and turned his attention to the purple building behind me, from where the sounds of Magic Slim's guitar could again be heard after a leisurely forty-five-minute break. "I don't know," he muttered in a soft voice suddenly leavened with a melancholy I'd never heard from him. "I don't know about this blues thing. It's been goin' on out here for so long, so many of these cats are gone or gave up—I don't think it's gonna be goin' on around here for much longer."

He wasn't talking about Florence's, of course. He was referring to the entire Chicago scene—if not the blues itself—and as usual, he was overstating his case. There's plenty of life left in Chicago blues, and the periodic predictions of doom from various naysayers are typically shrugged off by the blues community as so many aggravating nuisances. But right then, I couldn't help but remember the words I had written after Big Walter Horton's unhappy death in December 1981: "There's a void in Chicago now, an empty space where there once was music. You can hear the absence of song."

That empty space grew ominously more vast and silent when the flames consumed Florence's, and it has grown even more so over the intervening years. The ever-looming specter of loss; the constant reminder that "death don't have no mercy," as Rev. Gary Davis told us, that we had all better grasp and celebrate this life of the living for as long as we're blessed to know it—this, I believe, is what Bob was trying to express on that cold October evening as he got fixed up to leave. "One of these days, it's gonna be gone," he concluded, and the wind was blowing as he said it.

5

Maxwell Street
Last Dance at the
Carnival of the Soul

Even before its official inception in 1912, when the city of Chicago codified what had been going on for years by zoning the area around Maxwell Street to accommodate an open-air market, the neighborhood known locally as "Jewtown" represented the essence of the immigrant dream in America. It was a haven for hustlers and strivers, people who marshaled whatever resources they had to establish a foothold in society, even though that society often seemed bent on tantalizing them with images of mobility and assimilation while simultaneously denying them these things through prejudice and disfranchisement.

Life there was a struggle; there has never been anything romantic about poverty, rats, festering anger, crime, and seventeen-hour workdays, whether in the Mississippi Delta or on the streets of Chicago's Near West Side. But from the beginning it was also a tightly knit ethnic enclave, a place where people not only celebrated and honored their heritage as a people and a community but also depended on that heritage and the strength it represented for survival. The market was a farrago of noises and aromas, and everything had a Jewish accent. Merchants and peddlers hawked their wares with throaty calls and songlike spiels, children laughed and screamed down side streets, and cantors and klezmer musicians provided an ongoing soundtrack. The air was thick with the smells of fish and kosher meats piled high on pushcarts, in makeshift stands, and in store windows—not to mention smells of mud, sweat, excrement, and rotting produce.

By the 1930s and early 1940s the Jewish immigrants who had settled there had begun to move on. Blacks, recently arrived from the South, took their place; the neighborhood metamorphosed from a Jewish ghetto to an African American one. On Sunday mornings some of the racial tension for which Chicago was already infamous receded a bit as veteran Jewish merchants and their customers returned to participate in the lively street life alongside the newcomers. Blues singers, many of whom had performed on southern street corners for tips, now plugged extension chords into whatever outlets they could rent and honed an aggressive new urban-folk style. Preachers collected donations; showmen like the Chicken Man, who trained his bird to dance and do tricks atop his battered old stovepipe hat, entertained onlookers. Vendors sold whatever they could buy, beg, borrow, make, or steal. The accents had changed, but the market remained a classic alternative economy where goods were recycled and money flowed rapidly from hand to hand.

For years the city had its eyes on Maxwell Street. As early as the 1920s, newspapers were reporting that political operatives wanted to shut down the market. The construction of the Dan Ryan Expressway in 1962 sliced off much of the eastern section; a few years later the University of Illinois, with the city's backing, expanded into the area, displacing many of the Italian residents who lived just north of Maxwell and sending shockwaves through the remainder of the community. By the 1980s few people lived there, although the market still sprang to life every Sunday morning like a once-a-week urban Brigadoon.

Finally the university persuaded the city council to accept a deal whereby virtually the entire neighborhood would be seized under the right of eminent domain and used to expand its campus. To give this land grab the appearance of legitimacy, the city slyly cut off services: garbage accumulated, buildings deteriorated further, and streets and sidewalks crumbled. It was only a matter of time.

In 1994, when the city finally closed the market for good, official spokespeople promised that the new, sanitized version being established on Canal Street a few blocks east would carry on the tradition. But old hands knew better. The eternal paradox of the blues—freedom and beauty nurtured amid conditions of oppression and ugliness; joy, even transcendence, arising from lives scarred by struggle and suffering—found its living realization every Sunday morning on Maxwell Street, and this was the one thing that no one, not even the flinty-eyed hustlers at city hall, could repackage and sell. As Krystin

Grenon, an activist in the failed attempt to block the takeover, once told me: "I see a lot of lives picked up here. It's like finding a piece of junk that nobody else sees, and you take it home and fix it up; you wash it, clean it, put it on your stand on Sunday, and you value it. And by taking people's lives who may be considered junk by other people, or who are not valued—I think a lot of people are rehabbed on Maxwell Street. We don't want to lose that."

On August 28, 1994, we did.

* * *

"I hate funerals!"

Tattoo Tom, his muscular arms a filigree of rainbow colors and his hair matted with sweat, gazes morosely over the heads of the Sunday morning Maxwell Street crowd as he takes a pull from his can of Diet Pepsi and rubs a meaty hand over his army fatigue shirt. "This is fuckin' Maxwell Street, for Chrissakes, not some goddamn yuppie farmer's market in the Loop! Today is a funeral, man; a whole way of life's over. What else is there to even bother comin' into the city for anymore?"

Tom operates a tattoo parlor in the western suburbs. He's a massive man whose lips are curled into a perpetual sneer, and he's fond of roaring out outlaw aphorisms like "God works in strange ways—so does Smith and Wesson!" When he's not scouring the market for bargains on items such as antique furniture, hunting knives and other weaponry, or a sterilizer for his tattoo needles, he hangs out with the blues musicians, most of whom are now confined to one or two cramped spaces near Halsted Street because everything else has been fenced off.

He's here along with everyone else for one last Sunday-morning blowout to commemorate the market's closing. Piano C. Red and his band have begun to lay down their grinding all-day blues groove on a plywood stage they've erected in front of a food stand, which is being operated out of a closed shop that bears the legend "Johnny Dollar's." Dancers are already lurching around in wine-soaked circles; the usual conglomeration of hard-core regulars, shoppers, and wide-eyed tourists has begun to gather. But for Tom, the demise of the market means more than the end of an era or an excuse to party. It's enough to make him move out of town.

"Man, I'm sellin' my place and movin' to Kansas or somewhere. Why not? I got it all set up—some guy tried to fuck me on it, but don't worry, I'm gonna fuck him back. Me and my crazy partner might as well just get the hell outta Chicago and go live off the land, just be left alone. There's no place left where people understand life like they do here. It's time to go."

There have been rumors that the city or someone under its auspices was

The market on Sunday morning, ca. 1990. Photo by John Booz

going to hold a tribute to Maxwell Street on this, the Sunday market's last day in the location where, give or take a few blocks to the east or west, it has operated for over 120 years. Most of the regulars were appalled at the cynical opportunism behind the idea. And they are infuriated at the city for acting as if one site is as good as another; one of Tom's buddies has offered to shoot holes in the banners that hang from streetlamps advertising the new market location on Canal Street. But today it's obvious that there was never much danger that any kind of official recognition of the market's passing would take place.

For once, everyone is glad that the city is ignoring Maxwell Street. The usual crowd is out in force, and the market can put on its own jazz funeral with more class than any politically sponsored send-off could ever muster.

* * *

The Peanut Man trudges down Newberry laden with bags of peanuts and wearing a sour expression on his face. Children squeal and scurry underfoot, a few doing cartwheels through the crowd. Music blares from speakers and hand-held radios; hawkers' spiels fill the air; horns honk, bells clang, and the monotonous singsong jingles of ice-cream trucks provide a constant sonic backdrop.

A scruffy peddler strides through the market with an armful of cloth bags: "Laundry bags! Tote bags! Gettin'-put-out-of-the-house bags!" Another sells X-rated videos, which he sometimes calls "X-ray movies" when he's deep into his spiel. A few blocks north a veteran vendor called "Mama" sits behind her table of found household objects. She barks orders at everyone within earshot in a raucous, deep-chested bellow as her husband, a childlike white man with unfocused eyes and a two- or three-day beard, weaves through the crowd in a drunken dance, spilling beer from a flip-top can onto his sunburned arms. His soundtrack is 1960s soul music emanating from a nearby stereo speaker. Around the corner, in front of Nate's Kosher Deli, Killer Joe the jazz deejay spins platters—Bird, Diz, and vocalists such as Billie Holiday and Frank Sinatra—on a heavy-duty turntable. His music melds with the rougher sounds of R&B, hip-hop, and gospel from the stand down the block where they sell eight-track tapes and cassettes.

Through it all, the Peanut Man never looks right or left, never acknowledges the music or the voices with a smile or even a scowl, until someone who wants to buy peanuts meets his steely gaze or taps him on the shoulder. In a world of spielers, rappers, and hucksters, his refusal to participate in the shout is one of the most effective sales techniques going; his cranky dignity seems like an oasis of hard-won tranquility amid the chaos.

When he gets to Fourteenth Street, the Peanut Man decides to turn west, toward Morgan. Meanwhile, a block east on the corner of Fourteenth and Halsted, the Blues Bus conductor sells cassette tapes from a bus rigged with loudspeakers and adorned with brightly painted legends: "Downhome Music," "Heritage Folk Music," and "Mississippi Delta Blues." He sports an engineer's cap, and his conversation is peppered with references to the Delta, reminiscences of the old days in Chicago when there was a blues club on nearly every corner of the South Side, and warnings about the way today's youth are ruining their souls with rap and sex music and should go back to their roots to "learn about real life, not just abusing people and disrespecting themselves." As if on cue, the blues that have been emanating from the bus's loudspeakers above his head suddenly cease; after a second or two of silence, the majestic cadences of Dr. Martin Luther King's oratory swell out and bathe the corner in inspiration.

A bystander asks if anyone has seen the Hat Man lately. No, that guy hasn't been around for . . . man, it must be months now, maybe a year. The Hat Man didn't sell hats. He made them for himself using Christmas tinsel, pinwheels, old lightbulbs, American flags, and anything else he could find that was colorful or might reflect the sunlight. He would add a little more each week, until by autumn the hat was almost half again as tall as he, and the colors that reflected from it would dance along the street as he walked slowly around the market with his head stiffly erect and his creation balanced precariously atop it.

* * *

The city evicted the Hub Cap Guys a couple weeks ago. In a vacant lot on the west side of Halsted, a bunch of enterprising merchants had set up makeshift shanties that they surrounded with wood fences and filled to overflowing with hubcaps and tires. Several of the Hub Cap Guys lived there full-time. Old-timers resented their presence: the shanties and some of the guys were filthy, they attracted dubious drive-by customers, and they furthered the stereotype of the market as a place where stolen goods were recycled.

Just a few years ago, though, that strip was lined with businesses, including convenience stores, an all-night tacqueria, and a pub on the corner of Halsted and Fourteenth where mariachi bands would play on Sunday afternoon. Everyone remembers the day the death knell sounded there: it was when a house imploded and almost took one of the market's most irrepressible residents with it.

In those days the blues bands would play under a tree in another vacant lot, near the area the Hub Cap Guys eventually appropriated. The tree became dubbed "the Blues Tree"; things would get so jubilant there that you could feel the ground shake from the music. A young deaf-mute woman would regularly show up to dance, and the beat beneath her feet was strong enough that she could move to it as easily as her fellow hearing celebrants.

One Sunday the ground began to shake even more than usual. The band stopped playing and turned to stare as behind them dust came billowing out a hole in the roof of an abandoned house. Within a few seconds the building's entire front half had collapsed. A second-floor back door opened and out came Cookie, a young woman who lived in another abandoned building and danced, drank, and hustled around the market until her death a few years later. She descended the back stairs with the regal nonchalance of a slum-dwelling Scarlet O'Hara. When she got to the ground, she looked back over her shoulder and mumbled, "Man, they must be fighting up in there or something—I was taking a leak in the bathroom and the whole house was shaking."

Someone led her around to the front and showed her the pile of wood, shingles, and twisted metal where most of the edifice had been standing only minutes before. A pair of grizzled regulars shook their heads wryly.

"The Lord looks after drunks and fools," one muttered.

"Uh-huh—he be workin' overtime down here!"

* * *

Every Sunday for the last few weeks, a bus has crawled through the market, festooned with posters announcing rallies and workshops to save Maxwell Street. Even today, in the Mexican portion of the market, south of Fifteenth Street, a child hands out bilingual flyers urging organized resistance. Last Thursday a group marched from the market area to Daley Plaza, across the street from city hall, where they planned to hold a mass rally to demand that the mayor stop the deal to sell the neighborhood to the University of Illinois at Chicago. But the organizers didn't know about the farmers' market planned for the plaza that day, so the fifty or so demonstrators who showed up couldn't assemble. Instead, they circled city hall a few times and went home. This week there has been a nightly candlelight vigil—billed as a "novena" by its organizers—on the corner of Maxwell and Halsted. Few people have shown up, and on at least one occasion no one remembered to bring any candles.

In retrospect, though, it probably wouldn't have mattered if Karl Marx, Saul Alinsky, and Moses had returned to organize the masses and lead "Jew-town" into a new century. It's now clear that the issue is not just UIC or even redevelopment per se, although these are obviously important. Nor is the issue the clearly false claim that a city with the resources and geographic space of

Chicago will go broke if it sets aside a few square blocks of otherwise vacant land so that a few thousand people who aren't rich and powerful can make a little money and listen to some free blues once a week.

No, this is something bigger: a corporate-driven urban vision being visited on America in the age of high-tech economic conversion and deindustrialization. It's Ralph Nader's "planned obsolescence" all over again, but this time the entities being deemed obsolete are people, the children and grandchildren of migrants who, lured by promises of wealth, left the Deep South, Eastern Europe, Asia, and Latin America and settled in the urban North, including Chicago. Those people came looking for streets paved with gold and instead found ghetto alleys filled with death, so they created the Maxwell Street Market and similar places to learn the hustle and get a foothold.

Meanwhile they built cities, forged steel, swept streets, butchered cattle, mopped floors in fancy homes and highrises, typed memos and fetched coffee for lawyers and executives, and still found the time and inspiration to breathe life into America's gray-flannel soul. Now "we" can't afford their presence any more because "our" cities have been built. "We" have enough steel, bricks, and mortar, and it's time for "us" to move on to a new economic order so the rich can get richer, the poor can get laid off and try to find jobs flipping McBurgers somewhere, and everyone else can stick their world over on Canal Street.

* * *

A block or two southwest of the Blues Bus, around Fifteenth and Peoria, a drawn-out braying moan cuts through the aural chaos. A young woman strolling down the street cocks her head: "There's a cow over there!"

"No," her companion answers, "It's a goat."

It's neither. A blind man sits on a chair in the middle of the street. He holds a cup and cries out in a sandpapery baritone rasp that seems to travel throughout the entire market: "Help the bli-i-i-i-nd! Please help the bli-i-i-i-i-ind!"

Any venue like Maxwell Street will have its share of beggars, of course, but down here they seem to have a unique role, almost a place of honor. Judge Hightower sits on a chair at the northwest corner of Maxwell and Halsted, rattling the change in his tin cup and holding his white cane erect like a staff, as if he were the market's royally appointed gatekeeper. Part of his duty there is to attract customers to Jim's polish sausage stand. He also sells pencils, and his spiel is one of the first market sounds you hear as you walk down Halsted toward Maxwell:

"Pencils? Get 'em here! Thank you, thank you very much. Porkchop! Polish sausage! Hotdog! Hamburger! Get 'em here—pencils? Thank you very much—double dog! Double polish! Double chop—thank you very much—pencils? Thank you, thank you very much! Double hamburger! Double cheeseburger! Triple dog! Triple polish! Triple porkchop—pencils? Thank you very much—triple hamburger! Triple cheeseburger! Head 'em up, move 'em out!"

An old acquaintance calls out his name, and Hightower faces the man and exults, "Well, I declare—look who I see!" Before the accident that blinded him, he was a golf caddie at, among other places, Palm Beach Country Club (where he caddied for "Miss Rosalyn [Rose] Kennedy") and Hackensack, New Jersey ("one of the toughest country clubs in America"). Now he plays chess, makes macrame planters and other artifacts in his senior citizens' arts and crafts class, and holds forth on life and philosophy from his Sunday morning station by Jim's.

> Y'see, I don't have any eyes, but the Lord, he focused me. You can't be distracted! They tried to shoot a nephew of mine, but you know what the skin did? The skin just closed up on the bullet. His skin was so tight that when the paramedics tried to give him an injection in his arm, they couldn't stick the needle in. The doctors, they said this was something you'd seldom see—very, very rare. You see, in the scheme of life these things is just a distraction. Never let these things get behind you. Just because they see me with no eyes, don't let it fool you. Talk to me; you'll get the drive back!

A young man folds a dollar bill and carefully places it in Hightower's hand. "I make sure I do that every Sunday," he tells his companion as they turn the corner onto Maxwell and walk into the market. "Even if I'm short of money, I give him that dollar. That's my cover charge."

* * *

At Fourteenth and Peoria a man with luxuriant black hair held back in a braid beneath a natty black fedora sits on the ground with Buddha-like serenity. He plays traditional Ecuadoran music on a pipe; spread out for sale in front of him are multicolored hand-woven blankets, sweaters, and wooden panpipes. Behind him rollicking *norteño* music booms up the street from loudspeakers in the Mexican section of the market a block south.

Out of the Mexican market emerges a chunky little guy pushing a handcart full of fruit-flavored ices on sticks. He passes a table where a jet-black man, speaking in the clipped accents of his native Ghana, displays carved wooden artifacts and bronze statuettes. Down the block somber-dressed young African American men hawk copies of the Nation of Islam's *Final Call*.

There's a bit of a roadblock between the Ecuadoran piper, the Nation of

Islam youths, and the Mexican market, for a group of earnest white Revolutionary Communist Party members have spread a banner across Peoria. The banner urges people to join the struggle for Third World revolution and also to save Maxwell Street. The RCPers shout through bullhorns in English and Spanish and distribute revolutionary literature.

A few blocks to the east of the Maoists a pair of Gypsy women, among the last survivors of a previously thriving Maxwell Street Gypsy community, tell fortunes. A vendor's table near Fourteenth and Halsted displays what appears to be voodoo paraphernalia (including a fake skull and a plaster black fist with a stick of incense protruding from between the second and third fingers). There's also a photocopy of the cover of an old edition of *Death of a Salesman* bearing a handwritten inscription: "VOTE TO SAVE MAXWELL: D-DAY 8-28-94 LITTLE HITLER DAY."

* * *

Back at the blues stage Tattoo Tom is sweating more than ever as he works on his second or third diet pop; he's diabetic and can't drink alcohol anymore. He's been joined by the Daves: Crazy Dave and Brother Dave. Crazy Dave, a paunchy man with the chest and arms of a construction worker, has one of those arms stretched out in front of him. In it he's clutching an ax, which he holds upright by the end of its handle. He then slowly lowers the blade toward his brow as he lectures a fascinated bystander on this muscle-toning exercise to "strengthen your punch." Brother Dave (Tom's "crazy partner" and blood brother) sports a scruffy beard and shoulder-length hair but disdains any association with the 1960s: "I ain't no fuckin' hippie," he proclaims. "I'm a beatnik!"

Brother Dave has just returned from the biker rodeo in Peotone ("Man, they had them chicks there ridin' on the back of the bikes, and they had a hot dog hangin' over the racetrack from a fishing pole, and the chicks had to grab it with their teeth, squattin' on the bikes goin' past it—them chicks were chewin' them sausages, man!"). Now he's explaining to anyone who will listen how the convicted mass-murderer and sexual predator Jeffrey Dahmer is going to get messed up "real bad" in prison, even though they have him in solitary confinement.

"There's always a way. I was in DuPage one time, and this Mexican guy who'd been sent down there for molesting some little kid—it was a real big news story, everybody heard about it—he was in solitary, and the cooks in the kitchen found out that he was allergic to some foods, right? Now for the rest of his fuckin' natural life, all he's gonna eat is gonna be nothin' but what makes him sick. Dahmer? Ha! Believe me—there's always a way."

Brother Dave finishes his monologue and calls Tattoo Tom's daughter, Scooter, to his side. He breaks into a grin and begins to tease and play with her like a proud uncle. Scooter's been away for a few weeks. Last Sunday she and her father stayed home to celebrate her graduation from grade school; she graduated near the top of her class. She's a soft-spoken girl with thick, long hair who defers politely to the adults around her, taking in the noise and chaos of the street with serene, attentive eyes. Tom looks over his shoulder approvingly at her and Brother Dave. He gulps another mouthful of pop and growls, "Dave's the only man I know who isn't family that I'd trust alone with my daughter."

* * *

When Eva goes into her routine, even hardened Maxwell Street veterans have to stop whatever it is they're doing and gawk. A compact woman who appears to be at least in her sixties, she's a legend in South Side blues circles. She shows up at tony show lounges like East of the Ryan or Mr. G's decked out in sparkling gold tiaras and lamé dresses, parades out in front of the audience, and goes into her strut: she hoists up her dress and shakes in time to the music, spreading her legs apart and bending over backward until her head is nearly touching the floor, and then she snaps back upright, grabs her hem, and prances around the room like a can-can dancer. Sometimes she even hops onstage and joins the show; she and soul-blues vocalist Bobby Rush have worked out a routine where they pantomime Rush's bawdy anthem "Sue" ("She took the low stool, I took the high stool") to the delight of patrons and fellow entertainers alike.

On Maxwell she's even more uninhibited than she is in the clubs, although recently she has taken to carrying a small baseball bat for protection. She's dressed a little more casually today, wearing a black fishnet blouse over a low-cut black top, white slacks, socks, and tennis shoes. She begins to grind her hips slowly in time to Piano C. Red's dirty boogie groove; pretty soon she's sashaying around in front of the stage, raising her blouse teasingly as far as her midriff, then a bit higher, then higher still, fixing the men around her with a ferocious look-but-don't-touch glare. In a few minutes she's into her spread-eagle routine and the blouse is halfway over her head.

Finally one of the men can't restrain himself any longer. He approaches Eva with his hands outstretched and begins to dip and weave in front of her. Eva stops moving and plants her feet. Her eyes hardening into a steely glint, she tosses her head back and raises her bat menacingly. He quickly backs away, and she relaxes and slinks back into her dance.

Eva (in white hat) and Pearl, another Maxwell Street regular, shake it with vocalist T. J. Johnson (aka "Incense Tony"), ca. 1990. The guitarist is Little Sam Burrows. Photo by John Booz

* * *

Tucker and the Walker have left the blues stage area to share a quick bottle of wine in an alley. The Walker is a tall man of indeterminate age who wears a pained expression and strides in gigantic steps through the market all day, seeing everything and saying nothing. He seldom stops, and when he does, he almost immediately jerks himself away from whatever had grabbed his attention and plunges back into his endless, obsessive journey. He even drinks on the move, downing an entire bottle of Richard's Wild Irish Rose in a swift gurgle between strides. He dresses in filthy rags and communicates only with a handful of hard-core drinking buddies, mostly fellow street people like Tucker, the "professional dancer."

Tucker lives in an abandoned building on Morgan Street along the western border of the market. He dances for tips wherever the blues bands set up. When he's in high gear, he'll belly-flop into a mud puddle, boogie barefoot in running-in-place stutter-steps on a vacant lot strewn with broken glass, or leap into a trash pile and emerge with a toothless grin, clutching a bottle of wine he'd stashed there earlier. His specialty is a routine where he pulls up his trouser cuffs and whips off his shirt to reveal another layer of clothing underneath, then does it again, and sometimes a third time. He carries a photo of himself dancing, his "publicity photo," framed in a recycled cardboard boxtop. On weekdays he hangs it on a bare wall in the room where he sleeps.

It's unclear whether Tucker or the Walker knows that the market is about to be closed, but as the day wears on, they both seem to be carrying on with especially wild abandon. The hot pavement in front of the blues stage takes a harsher toll on Tucker than do the vacant lots where he used to perform, and after a while he disappears. In his absence the Walker occasionally breaks into a lurching dance routine when he passes through the area, at one point cocking his fists and firing imaginary pistols at the people around him, but mostly he stays locked into his ceaseless travels up and down the streets and through the alleys, conducting one final grim survey of the neighborhood he has called home for as long as anyone can remember.

* * *

Down the street from the blues stage, in front of the Johnny Dollar store, guitarist David Lindsey has carved out a space for himself and his band behind some vendors' tables. They're directly across from the old location of the Maxwell Radio Record Company, the record store/recording studio where entrepreneur Bernard Abrams recorded Little Walter and Othum Brown's "Ora Nelle Blues" in the late 1940s, a disc that laid the groundwork for the revolutionary new urban style that would soon blossom into what we now call Chicago blues.

Al Harris, Lindsey's sweet-voiced lead singer, has been alternating most of the day between spoken tributes to the market ("This is the last day—it's raining already, the sky is crying, but we gonna get down; we gon' rock the house!") and standards like "Sweet Home Chicago" with a few timely lyric changes ("C'mon, baby don't you wanna go / c'mon, Jewtown's the place to go / Talkin' bout Maxwell Street, won't be here no mo'!").

Maxwell Street Jimmy Davis approaches the microphone, a borrowed guitar slung over his shoulder. Davis is an elder statesman of Maxwell Street; a veteran of the old southern minstrel shows, he studied under John Lee Hooker in Detroit, hit Chicago around 1953, and almost immediately began to perform in the market. Eventually he opened a restaurant there, the Knotty Pine Grill, and he often played in front of it to attract customers. Although his performances have become erratic over the years, everyone senses that today he'll take his role as the living repository of over forty years of Maxwell Street heritage seriously.

Davis knocks off a couple of warm-up tunes in his usual hyperkinetic fashion and then falls silent. After a few seconds he jerks back into focus and snaps out a long, moaning bass note. An expectant hush falls over the crowd—this is what they've come for. The band kicks into a hypnotic slow groove, and Davis begins to sing in a rich, quivering baritone: "M-m-m-m-o-o-o-o-h-h-h, there's two, two trains runnin'. . . ."

The song, which Davis calls "Two Trains Running," is his personalized combination of "Rolling Stone" and "Still a Fool," Muddy Waters's anthemic updates of the old Delta standard "Catfish Blues." The lyrics are rife with images of midnight trains, jealous lovers, and fate; Davis plays the melody against a single-chord drone punctuated occasionally by searing slides up and down the fretboard.

Everyone's moving now, regulars and tourists alike. Bodies swirl and spin through the street, stopping traffic and pedestrians. Davis's lady friend stands imperiously beside him at the microphone, fixing her gaze on him with an expression of regal adoration. Finally Davis and the band grind down to a conclusion, and for about thirty seconds after the song ends, hardly anyone speaks or even moves.

Slowly the sounds of the market begin to filter back into everyone's awareness; the band gets ready to play another number, and conversations and laughter resume. Both Lindsey and Piano C. Red will keep playing for another hour or two, but right now the street feels like New Orleans's Congo Square, where African slaves used to dance their whirling kalinda dances every Sunday; where the melding of African, Caribbean, and European music and culture that gave rise to jazz first began; and where those in the right frame of mind who sit still long enough may swear that the spirits of the ancestors still dance, drum, and chant, protecting this sacred space.

In New Orleans they turn such places into shrines. In Chicago we turn them into parking lots.

* * *

Ol' Coot's daughter has made an appearance on the street. Coot—Tenner "Playboy" Venson—was a drummer who lived on Fourteenth Street until his death in 1985. His drum set was a perilously fragile contraption with warped rims, torn and taped skins, and cymbals that sounded like pie tins. Set up in front of the tumble-down brownstone apartment building where he lived, it was a Sunday morning fixture for years. His technique was as elemental as his traps. He would lay down a primitive medium-tempo four-four beat no matter what the rest of the band was doing, and he would sometimes quit playing in the middle of a song, light his cigar, and amble around to the front to pound on the bass drum backward through his legs with his sticks, intoning a sardonic commentary in his ancient-sounding, gravelly baritone.

Nonetheless, some legendary blues musicians used to play with Coot—Floyd Jones, Big Walter Horton, Homesick James, and Honeyboy Edwards, among others—and he claimed to have accompanied Muddy Waters on Muddy's infrequent Maxwell Street appearances back in the 1950s. Today his daughter's appearance triggers an epidemic of nostalgia: everyone says hello, including the younger musicians, most of whom cut their teeth on Maxwell with Coot or other departed old-timers, such as John Embry, One-Arm John Wrencher, and Eddie "Porkchop" Hines. They all begin to trade stories of

Under the blues tree: Willie James (L) and second guitarist Randy, ca. 1990. Photo by John Booz

the old days, back when there was a band on almost every corner and they would all show up at eight o'clock in the morning or even earlier to get the jump on one another. Once there, they would play and fill their tip boxes all day long.

"Yeah, them days, there was dedication out here." one veteran remembers. Guitarist Willie James, who got his start playing with guitarist Pat Rushing, kicks in with some memories of his mentor: "Pat, man—he was a monster. He played more blues with that grungy, out-of-tune guitar of his, he played more blues with *one note,* than half these kids who've been through school and everything can play all night up on the North Side somewhere. And party? Whooooh! He was hard core. He was the real thing, Jack. They don't make 'em like that anymore."

Rushing is still alive, although he hasn't been to Maxwell for a while; after decades of the blues life, he finally joined the church a few years ago. Up to that point, though, he was relentless and unstoppable, gigging with a band made up of family members, including child prodigy Rico on bass, Danny on drums, and daughter Waxie ("Miss Peanut Butter") on lead vocals. They might play a gig downstate somewhere on Saturday night, but they'd always get back to Maxwell by seven or eight the next morning, even if it meant driving all night. As the kids grabbed a few precious minutes of sleep in the car, Pat would be outside setting up equipment. For breakfast he would toss down a bag or two of dry pork skins. Then he would grab another half-pint and summon the family, and before nine o'clock or so the vacant lot between Newberry and Peoria was rocking to his blues, a sound that was, as an observer once put it, "funkier than a whorehouse in a fish market."

Shaking off fatigue and drunkenness, Rushing would play as long as there was anyone within hearing distance and sometimes later than that—you could drive up Halsted at six, seven, or eight o'clock in the evening and he and the band would still be there, half-invisible in the shadows, grinding out chorus after chorus of raw back-alley blues to an empty market under a darkening sky, as garbage swirled over vacant lots and the setting sun cast a crimson glow over rooftops, abandoned cars, crumbling buildings, and a solitary straggler or two trudging silently through the streets.

* * *

Every year, it seemed, there would be a "Gift Sunday." Sometimes as late as Halloween, usually weeks after the wind and cold rain of autumn had swept the market clear of all but the most tenacious devotees, it would suddenly all return for a day. The world would explode one last time into crisp Indian summer ferocity, with temperatures in the fifties or sixties, the sky a harsh hospital blue, and everything looking sharply defined and vibrant. It was as if, with winter closing in, the gods, the elements, and the market itself had conspired to bless everyone with one more reminder that "trouble," as the old gospel song promises, "don't last always."

After having been away or at least threatening to leave for weeks, the bands would return. The dancers, too, would come back, draped in shaggy wraps and knee-length coats, as would the more determined winos, trembling a little more intensely than usual in the morning chill. Thick black smoke would billow from bonfires in oil drums as vendors rubbed their hands in the sooty warmth. Occasionally a spark would ignite the stubborn prairie grass growing in one of the vacant lots, and a lone fire truck would come clanging and careering through the crowds, adding yet another riff to the ongoing Maxwell Street jazz symphony. This, more than any other time, was when Maxwell Street felt as if it might go on forever, when it seemed as if the spirit of survival that had gotten us all this far would see us through the gray winter that hovered just beyond the horizon and bless us with yet another warm, welcoming spring, alive with music and celebration—and would continue to do so, the following year and the year after that, for as long into the future as we could imagine.

On a Gift Sunday a few years back, Willie James and Maxwell Blues played as storm clouds gathered to the west. This was the year the house had almost collapsed on Cookie; a little after that, the university had finally publicized its designs on the market. Wreckers and track loaders had begun to lurk through alleys and crawl over vacant lots, and several buildings had already been razed. The sense of impending doom seemed more pervasive every day. And now here we all were, dancing and boogying under the Blues Tree, virtually in the eye of the storm.

Nobody wanted to stop. Three o'clock, four o'clock, maybe later—the sky darkened as the band recycled song after song and Tucker danced and drank himself into exhausted oblivion, only to rise like James Brown with his cape and do it all over again. The air grew chillier, with dirt and debris swirling and peppering the faces of dancers and celebrants. Finally, as lightning began to rip across the western sky, the band brought everything to a climax: a frenzied medley of blues, R&B, and pop hits recent and venerable, with four or five guitars screaming away on the changes and various guest singers coming to the mic to imitate the voices of the masters—James Brown, Jimmy Reed, Muddy, Wolf, Tyrone Davis—with varying degrees of proficiency.

The musicians' eyes were glazed with alcohol and exhaustion while the crowd huddled under blankets or danced furiously to stave off the chill, yet the music went on until it seemed as if it might keep going clear through till

Christmas. Finally Willie James gave the signal, the band hit one more metallic thunder chord, and everything fell silent. Another summer of Maxwell Street blues was over. The last two songs they played that day were the Isleys' "It's Your Thing (Do What You Wanna Do)" and "Thank You (Falettinme Be Mice Elf Agin)" by Sly and the Family Stone.

And then the rains came.

6

"Let's Go, Baby, to the Hole in the Wall"
Clubbing along the Current Chicago Scene

The "golden age" of neighborhood blues in Chicago is long gone. That's the common wisdom among aficionados, at least, and on its face it seems undeniable. Virtually all the legendary venues where the trailblazers played have closed their doors, and the quality of music in what remains can vary greatly from bandstand to bandstand, if not from song to song. When you listen to the stories from the 1960s and even the early 1970s, when the likes of Howlin' Wolf, the Aces, Mighty Joe Young, and Freddie King might be encountered on the South and West Sides on virtually any weekend, the sense of loss can become palpable, even if you weren't fortunate enough to have been there yourself.

Part of this apparent demise is due to the paradox of cultural desegregation and upward mobility. To the extent that blues musicians can now find more lucrative gigs on the North Side and on the road, most will gladly take them. Meanwhile, younger artists tend to be more inspired by hip-hop or contemporary R&B than by blues, soul-blues, or even deep soul and funk. Between the dual pressures of attrition and apathy, it seems obvious that things, as Duke Ellington told us, ain't what they used to be.

But things also aren't always what they seem. A lot of Chicagoans continue to play the blues, and some of the best still ply their trade in predominantly African·American venues on the West and South Sides. And the blues continues to represent much more than merely a musical form, at least in performance: it's the life of the party, the pulse of a ritual of release and regeneration that is both rooted in antiquity and still vital, especially but by no means only in places where the various types of music called "the blues" are played.

Those places themselves continue to differ from one another, and some of that variety is reflected in the venues I've chosen to profile here. In Chicago, as in the South, the blues has often been the entertainment of choice at outdoor events like fish fries and barbecues. Wallace's Catfish Corner carries on that tradition, having inherited it from the even more down-home Delta Fish Market. The Starlite Lounge, by contrast, is a more conventional neighborhood bar; in fact, in many ways it's the prototypical urban juke. Its ambience, as well as much of the music played there, strongly evokes the southern venues in which the music originally developed. When Harmonica Khan took the stage, those roots became even more immediately evident and alive.

East of the Ryan is a show lounge typical of the clubs where the better-established modern soul-blues artists perform. Patrons dress more elegantly there, and although the dancing is· enthusiastic and laced with the same sensuality and patterns of interactive participation that permeate virtually all blues events, it is usually somewhat more refined. The club's determinedly classy atmosphere may sometimes seem at odds with what's emanating from the stage, especially when a risqué signifier like Denise LaSalle is performing, just as the exuberantly danceable cadences of the music at Wallace's and the Starlite can seem to contrast harshly with the life stories and fates of those venues' patrons and even the communities that are their lifeblood. But this in itself manifests an essential component of what the blues conveys: an affirmation of dignity and self-worth in the face of forces that would insist otherwise, inextricably melded with unabashed celebration of carnal pleasure and in-the-moment liberation.

Fish 'n' Blues: From the Delta Fish Market to Wallace's Catfish Corner

On Saturday, May 11, 1991, a group gathered around the makeshift bar at the Delta Fish Market, at the corner of Jackson and Kedzie on Chicago's West Side, and drank to the memory of drummer Kansas City Red. A video screen displayed a tape of Red in performance, and when some of his trademark lyrics rang through the room—"Take out your false teeth, mama / Daddy wanna suck your gums!"—people chuckled and guffawed in appreciation, raised bottles and paper cups, and then leaned in again toward each other to share more memories of the sprightly little man who had been buried just hours before. Unrehearsed and unadvertised, in a grimy room thick with the odor of whiskey, cigars, cigarettes, and fish, that simple moment of commemoration both embodied and revealed a deeply rooted essence of the blues.

The Delta Fish Market seemed to specialize in moments like that. Proprietor Oliver Davis had begun showcasing blues acts there around 1980, and one of his express purposes was to create a venue where people could "feel at home, just like in Mississippi." Visitors from the South, in fact, commented on the down-home feel of the place. On a hot summer day, as people danced and hollered to the raucous music emanating from the brightly painted stage in the parking lot, it was easy to imagine the roar of the city fading away and being replaced by the harsh buzz of cicadas from some far-off cypress grove.

Davis was a veteran hustler with deep contacts in the music world. In fact, he was a pretty decent slide guitarist himself. The list of artists who played at his place reads like a history of the modern Chicago blues: pianist Sunnyland Slim; guitarists Johnny Littlejohn, Hubert Sumlin (one of the architects of Howlin' Wolf's sound), Luther Allison, and Homesick James; harpists Big Walter Horton and Billy Branch; and saxophonist (and former Wolf sideman) Eddie Shaw—and that's merely a fraction of the front line. Then, of course, there were the local celebrities, including guitarists Hip Linkchain, Left Hand Frank, and Boston Blackie; pianist Foots Berry; and drummers Ted Harvey, Ray Scott, and Kansas City Red himself. Finally, there was a legion of Howlin' Wolf imitators whose relentless repetitions of the master's classics once goaded Sunnyland into hollering, "There's too many wolves out here! I'm gonna go home, get my gun, and shoot some of these wolves!"

Again, that list barely scratches the surface, and it doesn't even begin to do justice to what went on in the parking lot itself, where artists who weren't performing often made things almost as exciting as they were onstage. Harmonica George Robinson, aka "Mr. Smellgood" ("How you doin' today, George?" "Ohhh—just tryin' to smell good!"), strolled through the crowd peddling yarn voodoo charms drenched in cheap perfume; he occasionally also pulled a harp from his pocket and blew a few ragged phrases with the band. Maxwell Street Jimmy Davis lurched stiff-legged around the market rasping out crude, hypercharged Wolf imitations, occasionally improvising a few new lyrics ("Have you ever seen a cross-eyed woman cry? The tears roll down her back!") or cutting himself off in midverse to boast about a personal triumph like his appearance in a club at "Buke Island." A glance at the logo on his cap revealed he was talking about Dubuque, Iowa.

Some of the regulars at the Delta Fish Market were almost literally children of the blues. Larry and Tim Taylor, sons of guitarist Eddie Taylor, played there frequently; they're now among the city's most in-demand blues drummers. Barbara Ann,[1] the daughter of another well-known blues musician, lived across the street with her mother in the early 1980s. She became the fish market's sweetheart, a chubby-cheeked little cherub running through the crowd with unrestrained glee who would inevitably find a lap belonging to a veteran bluesman or a family friend, climb up, nestle in, and squirm and bounce in delight as the music swirled around her.

Despite Barbara Ann's bright-eyed innocence, the atmosphere, like the music itself, was usually as rough as a West Side alley or a Mississippi dirt road. The jokes were coarse, the alcohol flowed freely, and the dancers' moves sometimes came as close to shake dancing as it was possible to get without being naked, and when they held each other tight, twisting and writhing in time to the music, it looked like nothing so much as vertical copulation. The dark side of the blues was always at least subliminally present, with the whiff of violence, dangerous erotic tension, dissolution, and death lurking around the edges of the bacchanal.

Davis himself was a big-timer with voracious appetites, and as he began to drink more heavily and spend more time sequestered in his office instead of running his business, the quality of the music dropped off and the tenor of the crowd changed. By the early 1990s the scene had deteriorated badly. Woods' Tavern, across the alley, eventually took up the slack. The owner, Woods, built a stage outside his building, and vocalist Cyrus Hayes began to hold forth there.

The move from the parking lot into what was literally "the alley" was only a matter of a few yards, but it made a profound difference. At night it was darker and more prone to produce claustrophobia; the odor from the port-a-johns and Fish Market dumpsters often choked the air. Despite the professionalism with which Hayes and his wife, vocalist Lady Lee, tried to run their show, any semblance of the family atmosphere Davis had tried to establish in the early days was gone. This was hard-core backstreet *funk* ("I wanna smell some funk!" a noted guitarist once said he told a hooker by way of demanding that she let him perform oral sex on her); it was the raw underbelly of the blues life exemplified. Even longtime regulars looked over their shoulders, stepped more gingerly, and watched their backs.

Early in the morning of Sunday, July 11, 1993, a running feud between

Taking it in the alley: Cyrus Hayes at Woods Tavern, September 3, 1993. Photo by Steve Sharp

Boston Blackie and vocalist James "Tail Dragger" Jones (one of Sunnyland's "wolves") spilled off the fish market property and erupted into violence in front of, or possibly on, Woods' Tavern's outdoor bandstand. Dragger shot Blackie dead, for which he eventually served less than two years in prison (the life of a poor black man in Chicago can still be cheap). Hayes and his band continued on at Woods', and occasionally a ragtag outfit would materialize on the fish market stage itself, but the shroud cast by what became known as "the fish market murder" never entirely lifted, and some patrons never returned.

In the late 1990s the city purchased most of the block on which the Fish Market stood and demolished the buildings, ostensibly so that a nearby public school could put an athletic field there. Woods took the money from the sale and moved back to Mississippi. For a while it was rumored that Oliver Davis was going to buy a tavern and try again, but the years of high living and big spending had taken their toll—he might have done well to heed the advice his old buddy Sunnyland had been prone to giving: "Put all your money in a hair bank, and you won't draw nothin' but a slick check and a wet bill of ladin'!" Soon he had all but disappeared from the scene.

As ingloriously as it may have ended, though, Davis's run of success proved that the blues could still be profitable on the West Side if presented the right way. Within a few years another entrepreneur with both business savvy and street smarts (to say nothing of a ready supply of fish) took up his mantle.

Wallace Davis Jr., who was no relation to Oliver but a longtime friend and admirer, had been an alderman until 1986, when he and several other city officials were convicted of accepting payoffs in an undercover sting known as Operation Incubator.[2] This being Chicago, a city that actually boasts of its civic corruption, he has remained a force in politics, and his son, Wallace Davis III, ran for office in 1995. Davis's fiefdom is centered on the crossroads at Madison and California, where he owns a soul-food restaurant called Wallace's Catfish Corner. He also owns a nearby beauty salon called Wallace's Touch of Class, as well as most of the buildings on the corner adjacent to his catfish headquarters.[3]

One of those buildings used to house the Five Aces Social Club, an after-hours joint that often booked Cyrus Hayes until a shooting occurred there in December 2002. Perhaps not surprisingly, the gunman was never caught. Davis is now rehabbing the place and says he wants to open a legitimate blues club there. There's little danger that anything like the fish market murder will occur on his property, under his watch. The outdoor blues shows he has been putting on at the Catfish Corner since the autumn of 2002 have drawn large, relatively carefree crowds, augmented more recently by the sets that go on during the colder months inside the new room he has added. On a good evening the musical quality can rival what used to go on at Woods' Tavern, if not the Delta Fish Market itself.

The sound, though, is less down-home. Most of the old-timers who held forth at Oliver's have died, retired, or moved away. Cyrus Hayes usually leads the show. He sings in a well-textured but oddly shrill tenor, and only in recent years has he learned to use his falsetto warble as a seasoning rather than an annoying gimmick, so that it can take a while to get used to his vocals, but his band is tight and proficient in a variety of modern blues, soul-blues, and R&B styles. As before, a steady stream of guest artists ranging from nationally known figures like Cicero Blake to such local legends as Lee "Little Howlin' Wolf" Solomon sit in over the course of an evening, and there are usually almost as many well-known faces in the crowd as on the stage.

More than ever, though, it often seems as if the exuberant energies that rise up there every Friday and Saturday represent a last line of defense against the forces of annihilation that threaten the West Side and, for that matter, the entire heritage that the blues and its people represent. Directly to the north and the east investors have begun to snatch up buildings and market them to mostly white "urban pioneers," replicating the pattern that has displaced poor and working-class people throughout the city. Davis seems unlikely to be able to stop the trend, his boosterish posing notwithstanding (rare is the weekend when he doesn't at least once amble to the microphone and proclaim his dedication to keeping the blues alive for what he calls "my people"), and it's questionable whether he really wants to. If he does open a blues club where the Five Aces used to stand, it could easily become a tourist attraction as the neighborhood gentrifies, like the bistros on Beale Street and the upscale "jukes" that are popping up throughout Mississippi in erstwhile blues strongholds like Clarksdale and Greenville.[4]

Meanwhile, nihilism and dissolution continue to take their toll on those left behind. A few summers ago at Wallace's I ran into Barbara Ann. I hadn't seen her in years, although I had heard that she had fallen on hard times after her mother died and was living in a notorious single-room-occupancy hotel a few blocks east of the old Delta Fish Market site. She greeted me with a hug and pointed proudly to her daughter, Eboni,[5] a toddler of about two who was already learning to jump rubber-legged around her stroller in time to the music.

But Barbara Ann seldom smiled, and her eyes had become flinty and hard. We sat on a curb and shared a pop, and she admitted she had been in rehab; Eboni's older brother, who was living in a foster home, had been born with cocaine in his system. But, she said, things were going better now. She was

out of treatment and living in a halfway house, she was thinking about returning to school to get her GED, and she was attending Narcotics Anonymous
meetings regularly. The only problem was that so many of her relatives and
old friends were still mired in street life, and they kept coming around. She
didn't want to be around them, she said, but she didn't really have anyone
else. Maybe I could help her find an apartment on the North Side somewhere,
so she could get a fresh start? She couldn't work yet because she had clinical
depression—she'd been diagnosed in rehab—but she hoped to start feeling
better and find a job before the year was out.

We reminisced for a while about the old days, when I used to bounce her
on my knee while Sunnyland and her famous father shared the fish market
stage. No, she hadn't seen her daddy. She loved him, she said, but she was sick
of his shit, always trying to avoid her, and she was thinking about giving up
even trying to find him. But she asked me for his most recent phone number,
along with mine. I dropped her off at the halfway house and pretended not to
notice when she strolled to the corner, with Eboni in tow and her cell phone
in hand, instead of going inside. I saw her at Wallace's a few more times, and
she phoned me once or twice. One time she left a message asking me to call
back "as soon as possible." When I did, she didn't answer, and after that I
didn't see or hear from her for a long time.

* * *

After many months of silence Barbara Ann has once again gotten in touch with
me, but her story has not become any more hopeful. She continues to struggle
with addiction, and at the time I write this, she is behind bars again. Eboni
has been temporarily placed in a foster home, and it is questionable whether
Barbara Ann will be allowed to have custody of her when she is released.

"Break and Run! Break and Run! Break and Run!"
Harmonica Khan at the Starlite Lounge

If you cross the street from Wallace's to where the Five Aces used to be and
then head southwest on Fifth Avenue, past Kedzie (where the Delta Fish
Market and Woods' Tavern once stood), and keep going to Pulaski Road,
you'll find yourself at the Starlite Lounge. If it's Sunday night, you might
recognize a musician or two hanging out in front, and you'll hear the band
inside even before you park your car.

The Starlite is a cramped, poorly lit space decorated with the usual half-
shredded Christmas tinsel and peeling "Happy Birthday" greetings sagging
from the walls and ceiling. During the week it does most of its business in the

front vestibule, where package goods—mostly cheap wine and half-pints—are sold over the counter. But a regular clientele can usually be found at the bar, and some of the West Side's most prominent blues musicians pass through on a regular basis.

Like most neighborhood clubs, the Starlite books the same band every weekend until someone gets fired or leaves for a better-paying gig elsewhere. For years the featured vocalist on Sundays was Jumpin' Willie Cobbs, a rawboned Arkansas galoot whose cousin, also named Willie Cobbs, wrote and recorded "You Don't Love Me" in 1961 (it was later made famous by the Allman Brothers). Jumpin' Willie, though, doesn't capitalize on the family name; to the best of my knowledge, he has never performed his cousin's song in public.

But then, when Jumpin' Willie works up a head of steam onstage, details like which tune he's singing become somewhat beside the point. He usually kicks off a song in a tempo faster than the original and speeds up from there; pretty soon he's shouting out nearly unintelligible syllables in a stutter-fire style that might be characterized as "blues barking." Drenched in sweat, jumping pogolike or running in place as he sings, he punctuates his vocals with down-home imprecations, shouting out "Gawwd-*dawwwgggggg!*" or "Whoo-eee!" and in general refuses to quit until people have either begun dancing in self-defense or are slumped over, exhausted, in their seats.

Against all odds, the formula seems to work—at the Starlite, anyway—and when Cobbs quit in early 2003, the scene there dwindled for a while as a series of replacements failed to keep the party going at the same rambunctious level. Eventually Willie D., a very different kind of singer, took over.

Willie D. himself was fresh from leaving a long-time gig, this one at the Highway 290 Sport and Juice Bar (all alcohol is stored discretely out of sight), a few blocks to the northeast on Harrison. He prides himself on his versatility, and if you ask him (or sometimes even if you don't—his truculence is as well-known as his musical prowess), he'll make it a point to emphasize that he's actually a rhythm and blues singer. Once, when a busload of white tourists came to the Highway 290 on a "pub crawl" affiliated with the Chicago Blues Festival, he admonished his band to play twelve-bar blues because "that's what these folks want." As soon as they left, he eased back into his usual soul- and funk-tinged repertoire.

Despite his characteristically obstinate insistence on using a hollow-toned microphone ill-suited to his vocal timbre, Willie D.'s renditions of ballads like "The End of the Rainbow," McKinley Mitchell's aching late-1970s paean to loss and redemption, can elevate a club to an almost churchlike ecstasy. On more down-home blues fare—which, despite his demurrals, he performs often and well—he stalks through the room, grinds out a few dirty-dancing moves with a female patron or two, perches on a chair or a barstool for a few minutes, then hits the floor again, all the while goading everyone to get into the scene: "Get up, this is all about a party, we gon' take it in the alley." All the while, his guitarists fire off riffs in a melange of styles that melds the raw aggression of early 1960s West Side blues with the rhythms and harmonies of contemporary soul-blues, garnished with a dash of molten blues-rock lava—an exhilarating and danceable, if somewhat schizoid, stylistic fusion.

Meanwhile, an older man draped in a threadbare overcoat and sporting a gray fedora sits alone at a table, staring moodily into the distance and occasionally muttering to himself. Propped against his chair is a piece of plywood that looks as if it has been broken off a wall or a floor. He reaches into a paper bag and pulls out a harmonica, along with three or four flat oblong plastic strips that he inserts between his fingers. He nods in time to the music, occasionally tapping his heels and toes beneath his seat. Harmonica Khan is warming up for his show.

Willie D. may bring Khan up after a song or two, he may wait until the second set, or he may simply walk away and let guitarist Joe B. take over as emcee when the evening's "guest stars" are deemed ready to make an appearance. But Khan will wait patiently, regardless. As he explained to me one afternoon, sitting in the back room of another West Side tavern and talking about his life, time has come to have a different meaning for him than it has for most people.[6]

Born George Meares in 1934, "on a farm just outside of Whiteville, North Carolina," the man now known as Harmonica Khan grew up enamored of Sonny Terry, the famous Piedmont harpist who interspersed reedy wails and train imitations with vocal whoops that hark back to early work songs and field hollers. He also learned to play the bones, a percussion instrument that originally consisted of actual rib bones, which a player clutched between his or her fingers and clacked together like castanets. (The world's most famous bones performance is "Sweet Georgia Brown" as recorded in the late 1940s by Brother Bones and His Shadows, which the Harlem Globetrotters adopted as their theme song.)

"I'd blow [harp] all the time," Khan reminisced, "walkin' down the railroad tracks blowin'. Different people show me tricks with the bones, give me the wood to put between my fingers, show me how to play. I come up around tap dancers that was *demons*. Eddie Page, he used to travel with shows in the South. Tap dancing, buck-and-wing, soft shoe. I come up with all that."

But if his music and dancing evoked an earlier, more conservative era, his behavior often did not. "I went to school in Whiteville, Whiteville High. I got sixteen, I quit. I was shootin' craps, runnin' with the hos and everything—I'd run away from home and come back, I'd stay gone. I used to stay drunk, stayed in fights. I wasn't brought up thataway; all my family's Christian, brought up in church. I just went other ways. I'm the black sheep of the family."

He did his first stretch of hard time on a road gang in 1953. The following year he married a woman named Emma Henderson, but their domestic stability, such as it was, proved short-lived. "In 1955, in January, she got burned and died. Layin' up in the bed, she might have been smoking; the bed caught on fire. They called me and told me she had been burned. They took her to the hospital. She was messed up."

He continued on with his life, which consisted mostly of day jobs and occasional gigs at parties or community gatherings, interspersed with more stints behind bars ("Violence, that's what I did most of my time for—fightin', cuttin'"). In 1956 he found himself doing harder time again, eleven months at White Lake prison camp in North Carolina. After he got out, he married a woman named Pearline. "She was young, seventeen years old, when I started with her. She came up right behind me when I left in '57, went to my uncle in Camden, New Jersey. We separated in 1965."

In Camden he supported himself working in the Campbell's Soup factory; he also landed occasional gigs, as well as more time in stir ("I got in trouble with a gangbanger in the early sixties, punctured his liver. They didn't give me but a year for that because they knew his reputation. They wanted something to happen to him anyway"). In about 1968, still restless, he moved to Chicago, where he sat in occasionally at venues like the Trocadero on South Indiana and Pepper's on Forty-third. Mostly, though, he hustled, "dealin', loanin' money. Drugs and loan-sharking." Finally, in 1976, he killed a man in a fight in the lobby of the LaSalle Plaza Hotel, downtown just south of the Loop. He was sentenced to twenty-five to seventy-five years in a state prison for first-degree murder.

"I been in and out of jail all my life," he reflected when he told me the story. "Small bits; a year, ninety days, thirty days—I didn't even pay that any attention. When he said twenty-five to seventy-five, that took a different effect on me. I couldn't see no light in the tunnel. I couldn't see no light."

He admits he was wild when he first went in but says that prison changed him:

In 1978 I began to taper off, because I seen the conditions; you either live or you die. Continue on the way you goin', you gonna get killed in this penitentiary. They had more drugs in Stateville Penitentiary than in Chicago. The visiting room was a whorehouse. I know how the police bring the stuff in, workin' with people and all like that. I been through all that.

It's up to you to make the choice. Prison don't rehabilitate nobody; that's a lie they tell. They take credit for that, but you rehabilitate yourself.

So from May—the fifth month and the twenty-second day, 1978—I was in A-Grade [the least restrictive disciplinary classification, for prisoners who've shown good behavior]. I got tickets after that, but it wasn't that I was threatenin' police or stabbin' people or nothin'. See, they were lookin' for me to continue my act that I was doin' in the street—collect your money, stab somebody. And they wasn't gonna let me out. But it didn't work thataway.

Thus motivated, George Meares-El (as he had been calling himself for several years, having joined the Muslim-based Moorish Science Temple after being inspired by Chicago guitarist Eddie El) embarked on a rigorous program of self-improvement. "I played harmonica the whole time," he affirmed. "I read books in the penitentiary that I ain't never read in the street. I took up Spanish. The penitentiary is the World College. You learn things in the penitentiary you don't learn on the street. Out on the street, runnin' with hos and got dope and everything, you don't do no studying. I wasn't going to get no understanding in the street."

He also participated in an inmates' music program run under the auspices of the University of Illinois. The politics of being a prison bandleader could be tricky: "You be playing, everybody wanna control you. Gangbangers wanna control you, so you have to play handicapped—they be the musicians who play behind you."

Nonetheless, he was assertive or diplomatic enough to hold on to his own group, Harmonica Khan's Blues Band. The name reflected his new faith: "Khan—'Sheik,' or 'Ruler,' or 'King'—that's Moorish Science. I claimed my nationality." He and his band were talented enough to win the rare privilege of traveling to Springfield, the state capital, to play on the opening day of the 1982 Illinois State Fair. He still has a copy of the write-up his appearance received in *Perspectives,* a state department of corrections newsletter. It features a photo of Khan in full wail, lying on his back with a harmonica between his lips, a microphone clutched in his left hand and his trusty bones in his right, kicking his feet high into the air. A few years later, in 1985, he and his band appeared on *Jammin' in the Joint,* a limited-issue LP that features several of the program's participants.[7]

Not long after the record came out, the music program was discontinued, but George Meares-El soldiered on. He continued his studies, played harp with buddies or in pick-up bands any time he had the chance, and carefully negotiated his way through the minefield of inmate politics. "Gangbangers," he rasped, "they ran the penitentiary. They'll break you down—they got somethin' for you. But I did enough to realize, 'Don't go back there. I'm goin' farther now.'"

"Going farther" for a long time mostly meant being transferred to institutions with progressively lower security as he racked up hours, days, weeks, months, and years of good behavior. "I got to Stateville December the twenty-third, 1977," he said, reciting from memory like a schoolboy. "I stayed there from '77 to '88. Then I went to Dixon, stayed in Dixon Correctional Center from '88 to '96. Then I left Dixon and went to Danville, from '96 to 2002. I always thought I was gonna be free—that's what kept me going. I was gonna be free. That's faith. 'Cuz if I don't do that, if I don't have faith, then something else would have taken its place."

His faith was finally rewarded on July 15, 2002.

> I didn't know until they told me the day before I come home. They called me to the center one day, they said, "Pops! You goin' home in the mornin', Pops." I froze right there—I said, "Praise God!"
>
> The prison got to find you a place to go if you don't have nowhere to go. My mother passed in '58 after I went to the East Coast; my father passed later, while I was in the state penitentiary. My brother's on the East Coast; my baby brother, he just died from cancer last year [2001]. When I got out of prison, they sent me to New Beginnings, 3450 West Lake.

Fortuitously, the halfway house called New Beginnings was only a few doors away from a tavern that hired blues bands. It didn't take Khan long to start sitting in on weekends, though he was always careful to make it back to his room before curfew. He soon negotiated a more flexible schedule with his parole officer, one that allowed him to alternate between occasional gigs around the West Side, a handful of appearances at North Side bistros, and a lot of free guest slots like the ones he puts in at the Starlite some Sunday evenings.

It's not quite the stardom he had envisioned for himself during his long years of waiting. "I ain't got what I want," he asserts.

> You got different musicians now, different from back in the day. Generation of younger musicians, they're lazy, fightin', jealous. You got so much jealousy goin' 'round, they gonna get behind you and mess you up. I went through that in prison, with the gangbangers. I hear that, I hear threats and intimidation, I don't go.
>
> See, I got three things I can do by myself—I'd like to stress this. I'm a one-man band. Look what kinda backing I have—three things: the harmonica and the bones and the tap shoes. You don't find many people playin' those bones.

Harmonica Khan at Bossman Blues Center, June 2004. Photo by Andrzej Matysik/
Twoj Blues magazine

Indeed, when Khan finally pulls up a chair in front of the band at the
Starlite, lays his plywood board beneath his feet, and goes into his act, the
sound is unlike anything that has been heard in the city's blues clubs for at
least decades, if ever. His clattering tap patterns interweave in multitextured
layers with the percussive rattle of the bones. His harp squalls are primal and
aggressive, and on uptempo numbers he employs trainlike chugging effects
interspersed with hoarse falsetto whoops that make plain the ongoing influence of Sonny Terry.

His showmanship is likewise anachronistic. Bug-eyed and gape-jawed, as
if astonished at his own virtuosity, he spins, shuffles, and even drops to the
floor to play while lying on his back, rotating his feet in the air as if riding a
bicycle. Then he heaves himself back up, sweat dripping from his face, and
begins to trot in a circle, intoning "Break and run! Break and run! Break and

run!" as he clacks out an ongoing bones counterpoint to his tattering taps. Occasionally people snicker or look away in embarrassment, but the relentless intensity of his dedication usually redeems the spectacle from appearing too amateurish or Uncle Tom–like.

Offstage, though, he admits he's haunted by the fear that time might still pass him by before he makes the mark he believes he was born to make on the world. His show takes more out of him than it used to. Sometimes his heavy breathing is audible through the microphone, and to conserve energy he increasingly relies on his long-standing gimmick of tapping while sitting down. "I ain't in the best of health," he admits, "but I refuse to give up. I come out [of prison] with a sound mind; I'm still able to perform—God still blessed me, and keepin' me. I got to go in the studio and put my stuff on record. I *must* get in there; I'm not gettin' any younger."

He insists his faith hasn't wavered and still looks toward the future: "All things are possible. Everybody that's ever been born has a destiny." Nevertheless, he has appeared increasingly weary as the months have dragged on since his release, and the anger that seethed within him most of his life sometimes seems to be coming back closer to the surface. The last time we spoke at length, he suddenly stopped talking, leaned forward in his seat, and with a piercing glare focused on my tape recorder and notebook rasped out an admonition:

> Someone's gettin' paid! Someone's gettin' some money! See, what the system do for one, it don't do for another. I got to buy myself a ride. I need some changing clothes—I ain't got but that one suit you see me perform in. I got to get somethin' for what I do. Lot of people, they don't want me out here. Say, "You a career criminal. You supposed to die and don't never hit the streets." But God don't see things thataway; God saw fit for me to be free. After all the mud that they drug me through, I was able to come out and play my harmonica.
>
> From now on, if you write about me, whenever you use my name, call me Harmonica Khan #1. Not just 'Khan'—Harmonica Khan #1! Not 'Number,' like the word, but, you know, like the tic-tac-toe sign—Harmonic Khan #1. That's what I got to be called.

After his set at the Starlite Harmonica Khan #1 grandly acknowledges what applause there is, blowing kisses and bending at waist, bowing to his public. He then tucks his plywood board under his arm and returns to his seat as Joe B. counts off another number and the band settles back into its usual soul-blues groove. Khan waits for another hour or so; after it has become clear that he won't be called to perform again, he eases out the door and catches a bus back home.

A few months after this appearance at the Starlite, Khan released his long-awaited debut CD, a rough-hewn affair produced by drummer Arnell "Thunderfoot" Powell. It was never distributed to stores, and it's doubtful whether Khan managed to sell many copies; the disc has already become almost impossible to find. But things seemed to be looking up for him. He laid down a couple of tracks for another CD, *Chicago Blues Harmonica Project 2005,* a professionally recorded compilation that showcases six Chicago-based harpists and has been released on the Severn label. He was scheduled to perform along with the others at the 2005 Chicago Blues Festival—certainly the biggest gig of his life up to that point.

Then, on March 11, 2005, his seventy-first birthday, Khan died. The official cause of death was "chronic obstruction of the bowel."[8] I don't think that most of us who had gotten to know him pretty well realized how much we were going to miss him ("You'll never see this again in life!" he would sometimes shout in midperformance, and even his detractors had to concede the point). The indomitability of his spirit was inspiring, even frightening in its intensity. He never came close to realizing his dream of stardom, but he lived long enough to become a free man and have the opportunity to pursue it. That's a lot more than has been granted to the brothers he left behind, still awaiting release.

"Lady in the Street, Freaky in the Bedroom"
Denise LaSalle Headlines a Soul-Blues Revue at East of the Ryan

In the 1970s the motel now called East of the Ryan, on Seventy-ninth Street, was one of the jewels in the crown of the Staples family, Chicago's legendary first family of gospel and soul. Known as Perv's House for Pervis Staples, the son of patriarch Roebuck "Pops" Staples, it was a nexus of South Side social life admired for its amenities, an optimistic symbol of upward mobility and prosperity. But the family eventually sold the business. Today the hallways are dim, and the rooms have been subdivided into small units that consist of little more than a bed and a nightstand. It's the kind of place where, as the deejay told the ballroom audience one night, "You're welcome to stay upstairs—but you gotta have a companion!"

The ballroom itself shows some of the worst signs of wear: the ceiling sags, the wood-paneled walls look faded, and the seating consists mostly of metal chairs lined up at long, cafeteria-style tables. But when there's a blues show there, a remarkable transformation takes place. Music ranging from classic-era R&B to contemporary soul-blues and hip-hop emanates from the deejay's booth; elegantly dressed ladies and their escorts ease in through the door, greeting longtime friends with affectionate hugs and hearty handshakes; and the mellow hum of conversation, punctuated with hearty guffaws and peals of laughter, fills the room. By showtime, as the house lights go dim and sparkles begin to cascade off the disco ball that hangs in front of the bandstand, an indelible meld of sophistication and earthiness has replaced the seedy ghetto-lounge atmosphere that had pervaded the place only an hour or two before.

Visiting celebrities stroll in and take seats. Over the course of the evening most will be recognized from the stage. Among tonight's guests of honor are Artie "Blues Boy" White; Cicero Blake; Ronnie Baker Brooks (Lonnie Brooks's guitar-slinging son); South Side legend Brother Shane, a singer who specializes in a boogity-foot James Brown tribute; and vocalists Nellie "Tiger" Travis and Holly Maxwell. Maxwell distributes flyers advertising her appearance at an upcoming show. Various promoters and club owners also circulate, publicizing their events, and throughout the night musicians and other industry types will gather in clumps at the bar, in a corner, or along the wall to discuss deals and catch up on business.

As the room fills up, a house band begins to pump out a workmanlike set of funk and blues standards. After a half hour or so a series of local singers—mostly absent from the show's promotional material—kick off the evening. A thin, nervous-looking man croons a brief Motown medley in his best Eddie Kendricks/Smokey Robinson warble; others weigh with renditions of contemporary soul-blues hits, delivered mostly in ragged-edged approximations of the originals. The crowd greets these "amateur night" warm-ups with good-natured enthusiasm, because everyone knows that more than one blues, soul, or R&B superstar got his or her start performing at events like this.

The last of the opening acts, a singer known as the Fantastic L-Roy, generates considerably more enthusiasm. L-Roy usually holds down the show at Linda's Lounge, a neighborhood bar on Fifty-first Street, and to watch him in action is to be reminded again that Chicago remains home to undiscovered blues artists of genuine talent. His gravelly baritone and artful stagecraft evoke Kansas City–style jazz shouters (he cites Big Joe Turner as an influence) as well as Lou Rawls, Jerry Butler, and other latter-day soul sophisticates. When he hits the stage, the line between sincerity and showmanship dissolves. Like a canny gospel preacher, he draws on an armamentarium of tricks—lugubrious vibrato; aching, tight-throated ascents; glissandos; dips; and soaring upper-register wails—using them all to accentuate rather than mask his sincerity.

On his version of Latimore's "Let's Straighten It Out," a modern-day soul epic of guilt and repentance, L-Roy first disarms his audience with a wry sermon based on Latimore's own spoken intro: "When you're dealing with the opposite sex, sooner or later something's gonna get crooked." He then plunges into the song itself, his gasps and gargled moans creating a torrid stew of carnal anguish and spiritual fervor. On the good-timey "Mom's Apple Pie" his voice deepens into a full-bodied roar as he dashes from one side of the bandstand to the other, wipes his brow, twirls his towel over his head, and then finally breaks into an inspirational medley, including "This Little Light of Mine" and a Sam Cooke–like "If I Had a Hammer," that has the audience on their feet, waving and testifying.

All of which perfectly sets the scene for tonight's headliner, Denise LaSalle. Like a number of other southern-based soul-blues artists, she has strong links to Chicago. Born Denise Craig in Mississippi in 1939, she moved to the big city when she was in her teens. She sang in a gospel group and wrote songs that she peddled around town in her spare time. In 1967, having caught the ear of veteran bluesman Billy "the Kid" Emerson, she began to record under the surname LaSalle. Within a few years she was enjoying a steady stream of hits on the Westbound label, some of which—"Trapped by a Thing Called Love," "Man Sized Job," "Married, but Not to Each Other"—remain among her most-requested numbers.[9]

Since the mid-1970s she has been based in the South, first in Memphis and then in Jackson, Tennessee, where she has been a leading light in soul music's ongoing evolution into soul-blues. Her repertoire does include a few twelve-bar numbers, most notably her version of Z. Z. Hill's "Down Home Blues," which she transforms from a jubilant ode to roots into a hot-blooded fantasy of erotic vengeance. Nevertheless, most of her material remains, musically at least, pretty close to the 1960s deep soul in which she originally made her mark.

Not her persona, though. Denise LaSalle is unremittingly transgressive even by blues standards. Although one of her most popular numbers has her claiming to be a "lady in the street, freaky in the bedroom," her language and the subject matter of many of her songs seem designed to catapult her boudoir persona to the front and center of the stage, if not into the street itself. ("Bitch Is Bad" and "1-900-Get-Some," both from her 1994 album *Still Bad,* are not atypical titles.) She once introduced her band by remarking, "Do they sound good? They fuck good, too! I auditioned 'em!" For once the blues-seasoned crowd at East of the Ryan was silenced, at least momentarily.

To a considerable extent, of course, such ribaldry is part of the blues heritage. In the African-based cultures that originally gave rise to the blues, carnality did not present an oppositional force against the holy or the good. And of course bluesmen have for years fearlessly challenged the boundaries of propriety in almost every way imaginable (as have blueswomen perhaps even more so; Lucille Bogan's ear-popping "Shave 'Em Dry" retains its power to shock nearly seventy years after it was recorded).

Nonetheless, Denise has come in for her share of criticism, even within the soul-blues world, and perhaps partly for this reason she often couches some of her most profane routines in the context of sisterly solidarity, speaking and singing for women who have been hurt or dissatisfied. Thus she spits out indictments of macho poseurs who think a woman should be glad just to "have a dick in the house" and challenges male complaints about unfaithful women by asserting that "most of the time it's the men who fuck around and step in their own mess." She insists that satisfying a woman—sexually and emotionally—is the first duty of a husband or a lover, and to those whose men aren't doing that, she advises, "Drop that zero, and get yourself a hero." Such proclamations bespeak a powerful ethic—if not exactly a moral center—underlying her rowdy onstage persona; they serve to redeem both the singer and her message. Obscenity or even promiscuity in the defense of justice is no vice.

Few people were prepared, though, for her attempt to transform herself into a gospel singer in the late 1990s. She had been inserting a gospel interlude into her blues shows for some time, which was already a bold move, given the coarse nature of what usually preceded and followed it, but in 1999 she released an entire gospel CD, *God's Got My Back*. Despite her vocal gifts and evident commitment, the CD apparently failed to convince a lot of church folks that bad girl Denise was truly reformed. Although it garnered decent airplay on gospel radio, "the artist was disappointed," as her online bio put it, "that she could not find work in the gospel arena."[10] She soon plunged back into the blues. With characteristic boldness, she announced her return with a CD called *Still the Queen* on which she testifies that, despite her brief hiatus, "the blues is my claim to fame," and any "blues mamas" who thought she was safely tucked away should know that she's back, "kickin' ass and takin' names."

Tonight at East of the Ryan she's got another potential minefield to negotiate. Koko Taylor, Chicago's own undisputed queen of the blues, has walked in with her entourage and taken a seat at a table toward the back. A bit of royal diplomacy is in order. Denise introduces Koko and affirms that Koko is in fact the "queen of the blues." Denise, however, proclaims herself the "queen of soul-blues." With that clarified, she proceeds to sing "Still the Queen" with the appropriate lyric modifications. Pretty soon she forgets herself and starts leaving off the *soul-* prefix, but her point has been made: she has acknowledged Koko's dominion, and she's now free to claim her own regal status on her own terms. By the time the song is over, Koko is on her feet applauding.

Denise's performance more than substantiates her boast. As her band lays down a funk-popping groove, she charges through most of her best-known hits along with a few items from the new CD that show that her feistiness is undiminished. In "You Should Have Kept It in the Bedroom" she discards her sisterly pose and shamelessly steals a girlfriend's man, admonishing her homie that it was her own fault for bragging about his prowess. As for her own bad luck with rivals, "Unloveable Habits" warns an ex that his new girlfriend will never put up with him and then provides a juicily graphic list of reasons (e.g., "the way you snore and bite your nails, the way your funky feet smell").

The man in "What Kind of Man Is This" isn't much of a bargain either—he even calls out another woman's name when he's making love—but he's got her in thrall nonetheless, and she tears into this uncharacteristic woman-as-victim tune with gusto, her voice ranging from a mewling cry to a full-bodied wail. "Freaky Blues Kind of Mood" is a hard-bitten ode to juking; "Cover It Up" warns men to "keep it in [their] pants" and admonishes women to insist that they do just that. Through it all, the women in the room seem galvanized; they rise from their seats, screaming and shouting affirmations for Denise's every assertion—especially her profanity-laced indictments of no-good doggish men and her nonnegotiable demands to the men themselves ("Real women would like you to lick it before you stick it!"). Most of the men, too, are applauding and smiling, if somewhat tightly.

Perhaps most effective, though, are those moments when Denise drops the bad-ass facade and confronts vulnerability, as in the ballad "Why Am I Missing You," a careworn, deeply wounded soul's acknowledgment that even the toughest hearts can break. It's this courage to admit weakness that has always given the blues much of its emotional resonance. Contrary to stereotype, a blues singer who laments is not wallowing in self-pity or masochism but rather proclaiming her determination to prevail in the face of the pain she's unafraid to confront. Especially in recent years, Denise LaSalle has tended to downplay this side of her persona, but when she allows herself to show it, it enriches and deepens her entire presentation.

It also reveals the possibility of a redemptive power more immediate and less dependent on conflicting ideologies and false dualisms than the one she apparently sought by moving into gospel full-time. A singer like Denise, who peppers her onstage comments with more *fucks* than anyone this side

Denise LaSalle at Chicago Blues Festival, June 1987. Photo by Paul Natkin/Photo Reserve

of Andrew Dice Clay and whose celebrations of carnality are laced with an aggression or even a vindictiveness that places them in a very different category from, say, the sexy sass of vintage Etta James or even a modern sex kitten like Millie Jackson, sounds disingenuous at best when she interrupts her hoochie blues mama routine to proclaim, "The blues is just what I do for a living; this is what I really believe" and then offers up a gospel song, as she sometimes did during the early stages of her crossover attempt. If it ain't from the heart, it ain't the blues, and Denise risked losing fans on both sides of the divide if she kept that up.

Better, it seems, to follow the same muse that enlightened Sharon Lewis, another singer of deep faith who spent much of her early life wrestling with the dichotomous paradigm of Western religion before coming to realize that the blues is powerful enough to transcend the very dichotomies that had tormented her for so long. "Read the Song of Solomon," Sharon instructs now. "It talks about life. About the woman's beauty, the beauty of her breasts, her body, that kind of thing. This is a gift from God."[11]

In that spirit, as Denise culminates her set with a raucous rendition of her oddball mid-1980s hit "My Tu-Tu" (a reprise of zydeco vocalist Rockin' Sydney's "My Toot Toot"), and the crowd rises to its feet one more time, testifying and affirming, my mind harks back to a show Solomon Burke did at East of the Ryan back in the early 1990s. Burke is an ordained minister as well as a soul man, so there's usually a powerful undercurrent of spirituality to his appearances. But he remains a suave seducer as well ("Oooh, all we need is a waterbed now!"); like Al Green, he encourages, at least implicitly, the melding of spirit and flesh when he performs. On that particular night he seemed especially inspired: defying curfew, he kept going until well after two o'clock in the morning, as if determined to wring every last bit of energy out of himself, his band, and his audience. When it was finally over (he signed off with, of all things, "Silent Night"), a satisfied-looking woman across the table from me smiled, peered out from under heavy eyelids, and murmured, "I can go home now and not worry about tomorrow. I've already been to church."

Part 3

Torchbearers

7

Jody Williams
Return of a Legend

Everywhere in Jody Williams's house there's music. In the kitchen an electronic musicbox beeps out holiday carols year-round as a string of Christmas lights flashes and twinkles in rhythm along the wall. In the living room and down the hall a collection of clocks both antique and modern tock, tick, chirp, and chime. Gaily colored timepieces line the walls of the children's bedroom, and radios sit atop wooden shelves and cabinets Jody has made by hand, providing an interweaving soundtrack of country music and light jazz.

Recently another sound has been added to that twenty-four-hour-a-day aural farrago. A few years ago Jody retrieved "Red Lightning," his vintage Gibson hollow-body guitar, from under the bed where he had stashed it in the late 1960s after quitting the music business in disgust. These days, when he is not working his day job as an ATM technician, he can usually be found in his den, where the walls are lined with his framed three-dimensional artworks and snapshots of him performing and posing with celebrities like Bo Diddley, Clyde McPhatter, and Howlin' Wolf. He spends most of his free time here running through scales and changes and working out new ideas, reclaiming his mastery of the instrument on which he helped forge Chicago blues and rock 'n' roll history nearly half a century ago.

Blues, R&B, and roots-rock aficionados the world over have heard Jody Williams's music, even if some don't know his name. His combination of linear precision and rough-hewn tonal rawness lent both texture and coherence to some of Howlin' Wolf's most revered early classics; his leads snaked all over Bo Diddley's reverb-drenched chords on Bo's 1956 blast of surrealist machismo, "Who Do You Love." He also appeared on sides by Jimmy Rogers ("I Can't Believe"), Billy Boy Arnold ("Don't Stay out at Night" and "I Ain't Got You"), Floyd Dixon ("Alarm Clock Blues"), and others.

Many of his riffs have passed from his fingers into blues and R&B vernacular. His keen-toned single-string lead patterns on "Billy's Blues," Billy Stewart's 1956 Chess Records debut, were parlayed directly into the Mickey and Sylvia smash "Love Is Strange," released on Groove later that same year. In 1957 Jody recorded "You May," an easy-swinging blues (released on the Chess subsidiary Argo) with a guitar solo that was replicated almost note for note—probably by Otis Rush—on Buddy Guy's 1958 debut for Artistic, "Sit and Cry (the Blues)." As if that weren't enough, the flipside of "You May" was a rugged instrumental romp entitled "Lucky Lou," and a quick listen to that side clearly reveals the origin of the fretboard-long zips, shifting rhumba/shuffle cadences, minor-key chord structure, and solo guitar breaks on Rush's 1958 Cobra classic "All Your Love (I Miss Loving)."

"Back in those days," Jody affirms in a voice that's gentle but hard, "record companies stole. I was young, didn't know any better, didn't know what was going on. They ripped us off royally." This time around, he vows, he's going to do it right.

* * *

Jody Williams, his guitar cradled in his lap, relaxes on a cushioned chair in his den and reminisces about the blues life.

> I was drunk—once! Back in those days, everybody have a seat up there [onstage], look like the pulpit of a church. These women, they're giving me drinks; they give me a drink, I down it, go back to playing my guitar. When it come time to get up and go home, I stood up—that's when it hit me. Somebody had to grab my guitar.
>
> I was drunk for three days. Layin' down, the room spinnin'. I was a member of the South Side Boys' Club; Jesse Owens, the Olympic champion, was running it. I used to fool around with one of his daughters. I went down to the club, drank some water—drunk again. He said, "What's the matter with you, boy?"
>
> "Nothin', sir"—called him "Sir," big man. "Nothin' wrong with me, sir." I staggered back to the house, got back in the bed. I never did that again.

It's probably not the kind of war story and certainly not the kind of conclusion you might expect from a man who played on street corners with Bo Diddley, shared stages with Howlin' Wolf in South Side gin mills, and ended up creating some of the most distinctive and influential guitar lines in blues and rock 'n' roll history. Jody Williams, though, has been defying stereotypes and going his own way almost since the beginning. Born Joseph Leon Williams in Mobile, Alabama, in 1935 ("right in the middle of town—I'm not a country boy!"), he moved with his mother to Chicago when he was about five. Early on he realized he had a flair for artistic expression. "In grammar school I painted," he says. "I was taking an art course from Art Instruction, Inc., in Minneapolis, that Norman Rockwell had something to do with; I still love his work. I had intentions of becoming a commercial artist."

But music won out: "My first instrument was a harmonica. I didn't play blues; my favorite was the Harmonicats—'Peg o' My Heart,' 'September Song,' 'Autumn Leaves.' I did shows in school, played on amateur talent shows. NBC had a talent show every Sunday. That's the first time I saw another instrument, a musical saw. Later, when I had my band, I'd play it occasionally."

It seems difficult to imagine a childhood further removed from the hurly-burly world of Chicago blues. Before he was out of his teens, however, young Jody found himself a charter member of that world courtesy of one of its most flamboyant characters.

"I was doing an amateur show at the old Willard Theatre on Fifty-first and Calumet," he recalls. "Bo Diddley was on the show, just one guitar and a washtub. I'd never heard anything like that. The three of us got backstage, me on the harmonica, they're playing on the tub and the guitar. I said, 'Will you teach me [guitar]?' He said yeah, he'd teach me how to run the bass line while he sang. So I saw a Silvertone guitar in a pawn shop on Forty-seventh Street for thirty-two fifty. My mother was the type of person, she'd back me up in anything I wanted to do—she bought it for me."

According to Jody, Bo was then already using the percussive, syncopated rhythmic pattern he eventually made famous as the Diddley beat. The infectiously danceable pulse was effective for grabbing listeners' attention on the street corners where Bo and his crew often played when they weren't gigging in theaters or clubs:

The week after I got that guitar, all three of us were out on the corners playing—two guitars and a washtub. He lived in the 4700 block on [South] Langley. Got the hat on the ground there, we'd be playing. All over town—West Side, Jewtown [Maxwell Street], Forty-seventh Street, Fifty-fourth Street, everywhere. I saw some of my high school friends out there and I was kinda halfway embarrassed. But I got over it. We made pretty good money. I stopped playing harmonica, concentrated strictly on the guitar. I'd just run the bass line until I learned. I enjoyed the instrument, but I wasn't learning what I wanted to learn. I wanted to improve myself.

Self-improvement through the usual channels, though, was a laborious process. "I went to two different music teachers," Jody recalls. "One semester under the music teacher [Captain Walter Dyett] that . . . [saxophonist] Gene Ammons studied under at DuSable. They weren't teaching me what I wanted to know. They wanted to teach me how to do scales. I said, 'No, what you're teaching me gon' take me years. I wanna play right now—*tonight.*"

Jody's impatience paid off. He left home—"as a professional," he emphasizes—when he was seventeen and moved into an apartment on Forty-eighth and Wabash. The building was managed by Joseph Chess,[1] the father of Chess Records owners Leonard and Phil Chess, and it was full of musicians: Williams remembers pianist Otis Spann, harmonica prodigy Henry "Pot" Strong, singer/guitarist Danny Overbea, and others. "I grew up fast," he admits. "Instead of me running with kids my own age, I was running with older people. I was hungry for knowledge about my instrument. I played with everyone I could, to get that knowledge. I got on-the-job training."

Music wasn't all he learned. If he had ever been tempted to abandon his abstemious ways for the blues life, his early exposure to that life's dark side was enough to keep him on the straight and narrow.

Me, Henry, Otis Spann, we had a flat together [on South Greenwood]. Muddy had just finished at the 708 club. This was in 1954—Muddy had a '54 Holiday Olds, they had kinda like a lightning bolt on the side, and he had a red and green one like that. Henry Strong—everybody called him "Pot"; he got his nickname from smoking reefer—came up to the apartment. This woman went off because a woman at the club had bought him a drink. Pot was in the hall, and she hit him with a knife. Blood was all up and down the hall. Muddy was coming up the stairs to see what was going on. That's when she started at Muddy with the knife. Muddy ran back down, Pot staggered down the stairs, they got to the car, and he took Pot to the hospital. He died on the table. Muddy had to get rid of the car because there was so much blood in it. That taught me a lesson—I see a woman jealous like that, I cut her loose.

I didn't smoke reefers, nothing. Guy looked at me having a conversation outside the Trocadero one night, guy fired up there, passed this reefer around, passed it to me. I said, "Man, I don't smoke that shit." He said, "You don't smoke pot?" I said, "No! Just because I play music, that don't mean I gotta smoke that stuff."

In those days, especially at after-hours jam sessions, artists from different

CHICAGO BLUES

L–R: Washtub player Roosevelt Jackson, Bo Diddley, and Jody Williams, Chicago, ca. 1951. Photo courtesy Jody Williams

genres, including jazz, blues, and R&B, would come together as equals, trading riffs and ideas and forging new sounds. It was a demanding but invaluable workshop for an ambitious youngster like Jody Williams. He and Bo Diddley would play the famous "Midnight Ramble" shows at the Indiana Theatre on Forty-third Street, and entertainers ranging from veteran vocalist Lil Green to Muddy Waters would drop in to perform. Also on the shows were dancers and comedians like the veteran vaudeville troupe Bo Diddley, Coal Dust, and Ash. "They were good," Jody affirms, adding, "I don't know if that's where Bo Diddley got his name from." (Harpist Billy Boy Arnold, who played with Jody in Bo's early band, has said that the musician's name was in fact derived from this comedian's moniker.)[2]

Even smaller neighborhood joints could have their share of famous visitors. Typical of such places was the 708 Club, where the bandstand was set up behind the bar to protect the musicians from the patrons: "Ike Turner, B. B. King, Bobby Bland, all the guys, once they closed at the Regal, they'd come in the 708 and play."

Rapidly honing his proficiency on guitar, Jody had the opportunity to work with West Coast smooth-blues maestro Johnny Moore and his Three Blazers, a band that featured Charles Brown on piano and lead vocals. "I was out on the road with them, that's how I learned. If you hear that recording [pianist] Floyd Dixon made, 'Alarm Clock Blues,' I'm playing Johnny Moore's style on that. I learned the styles and techniques of these people by playing with them."

Sometimes Jody absorbed more than just styles and techniques. His "You May," released on Argo in 1957, is virtually a note-for-note remake, with new lyrics, of Memphis Slim's "Mother Earth," which Slim released on the Premium label in 1951. This doesn't necessarily mean that Jody intentionally ripped off Slim; rather, it exemplifies how blues musicians have long incorporated others' ideas into their own creations and then considered the results to be their own. In any case, Jody has said that Slim gave him permission to use the melody.[3]

But Jody wasn't merely a copyist. He absorbed the melodic elegance of Moore and T-Bone Walker, and he was one of the first Chicagoans to adopt B. B. King's sensual string bends; he also learned from the advanced harmonic construction of King's leads, which King had adapted from jazz musicians like Django Reinhardt. He then added his piercing tone and aggressive attack, which were solidly in the mold of the burgeoning Chicago sound. The result was a personalized blend of sophistication and rawness seasoned with his own improvisational imagination.

Then, in the mid-1950s, he landed a gig with an artist who exemplified urban blues at its most primal and untamed. Most historians believe that the guitarist on Howlin' Wolf's first Chicago session for Chess, in March 1954, was Lee Cooper. But Jody was definitely on hand two months later when Wolf returned to the studio, and he insists he was Wolf's guitarist from the minute the big man hit town.

"I was in the studio when he came in," he maintains. "I could adapt my playing to just about any style, so I adapted myself to his style." Jody brought an adroit fusion of grace and grit to Wolf's crude, Delta-hewn blues sound. His leads wove dexterous filigrees through the band's raucous shuffles and slow-grinding twelve-bar moaners, yet his tone bit with viperlike ferocity.

A gig with Wolf was a far cry from the pulpitlike onstage atmosphere Jody says had prevailed in Chicago clubs just a few years earlier:

> The 708 Club, that's a long bar. Wolf had a long chord on his mike. He would crawl that bar, howlin' and carryin' on. He'd take his handkerchief and put it back in his belt like a tail, singin' and howlin' and playing his harmonica.
>
> In the summertime Wolf would go outside, down to the corner. We're inside playing, he's all out there howlin' and singin' and playing harmonica—police run him back in one night. He put on a show. He'd clown all the while. And Hubert [Sumlin] and I, we'd stand up and we just played. Long as he's out there howlin', we're playing the guitar.

It was during one of the Howlin' Wolf sessions at Chess that Jody met and recorded with one of Wolf's most famous Memphis running buddies.

> We were recording, and I'm playing B. B. King [style]. This guy comes into the studio, watching me. "This dude's trying to steal some of my stuff!" I turned away so he couldn't see my fingers.
>
> We stopped so Chess could play it back. Wolf called me over, said, "Come on over here, Jody. I want you to meet a friend of mine, B. B. King." Aw, man! I felt like goin' through the floor. But he liked what I was doing. You hear all the people messin' all over your stuff, here's somebody can play it just like it's supposed to be—got to admire somebody like that. That same day B. B. King and I recorded "Five Spot" and "It Must Have Been the Devil" with Otis Spann.
>
> I was devoted to Wolf, but certain things happened that I wasn't satisfied with. It was a money thing. I quit the band at Silvio's (on west Lake Street) on a Sunday night, and that Wednesday I opened up in Nashville, with Memphis Slim.

Not long after that Jody resurrected his old partnership with Bo Diddley, who was now a rock 'n' roll star, and parlayed it into a job that expanded his horizons even further. In those days traveling R&B revues crisscrossed

At the 708 Club (L–R): Hubert Sumlin, Howlin' Wolf, pianist Hosea Kennard, un-identified waitress, Jody Williams, ca. 1953. Photo courtesy Jody Williams

the country in buses, bringing teen idols to audiences in urban centers and rural communities alike. Jody joined Bo on a couple of these rolling caravans. Gazing nostalgically at the snapshots clustered on the wall of his den, he remembers:

It was a lot of fun. Two big buses, fill 'em up with entertainers. Bo Diddley, Bill Haley and the Comets, Clyde McPhatter—that's him right there—LaVerne Baker, Big Joe Turner, Frankie Lymon and the Teenagers, Red Prysock and his orchestra, some that I've forgotten about. The Teen Queens—two sisters from California [Betty and Rosie Collins], they had a record out, "Eddie My Love"—I played behind them. I played behind Bo Diddley, I played behind Big Joe Turner and any of the doo-wop groups that need[ed] a guitar, because I was qualified to play behind any of them—Bo Diddley couldn't do that then, and still can't.

But the road also taught some bitter lessons. An integrated horde of rock 'n' rollers descending on a southern town looked rather like the advent of Satan to guardians of the racial status quo. Jody's memories are soured by recollections of the hate he and his comrades sometimes encountered and the horrible sense of impotence they felt facing it: "I remember a time in Montgomery, they had the White Citizens' Council out front with their picket signs. Policemen got in the orchestra pit. We did two performances, one in the afternoon for the white audience, then one at night for the black audience. One place we had whites on the first floor, blacks in the balcony. That's a bad experience. Real bad experience. Another place, the Klan threatened to march, so we did one show and left."

Sometimes it was enough for a southern policeman to simply see a car filled with black faces and sporting northern license plates. Jody remembers another southern swing, this one a blues tour with Otis Rush, pianist Little Brother Montgomery, and bassist Willie Dixon.

We were staying at a hotel in Tampa. One night we played this dance in this town—I can't think of the name of it. Otis was driving a Coupe DeVille Cadillac. We spotted two cars parked in the street; one of 'em was a police car. Otis went and asked 'em could they direct us to a gas station.

"Didn't y'all boys just finish playin' a dance down there at so-and-so place?"

"Yes, sir."

"Where y'all boys from?"

"Chicago."

"We takin' these niggers to jail!"

We get to the police station and the sheriff come down, nightshirt on, barefooted, put his big rusty feet up on the desk. Say they gonna fine us fifty or a hundred dollars or something, because in Florida you're not supposed to be gainfully employed unless you got a Florida license on your car, something to that effect. Somebody said something to the effect of, "What about all the big-time movie stars that come down there in Miami on those shows?"

"Shet up, boy! Ah make the law heah. Ah'm the sheriff! Ah make the law heah!"

Otis came up with the fifty dollars. I always kept some money in my wallet, in my sock, or somewhere. Dixon didn't have any money. So I told Dixon, "Ain't gonna be too good for you to spend the night in this jail and be out on the road gang, like they usually do people down here in the south. I got fifty dollars—all you gotta do is pay me back." So they let him out.

There was plenty of injustice closer to home as well. "People been stealing my music for years," Jody affirms bitterly. "As Howlin' Wolf say, 'It's dog eat dog.' And he said, 'Dog eat cat, too, sometimes.' I'm out there tryin' to survive and not be ate up, and in the meantime, record companies rippin' us off blind."

In late 1956 guitarist Mickey Baker and vocalist Sylvia Vanderpool launched their career as Mickey and Sylvia with "Love Is Strange," a song based on a riff and melody Jody had been playing on shows with Bo Diddley for some time. As mentioned previously, he had also recorded it on singer Billy Stewart's Chess Records debut, "Billy's Blues," earlier that year. According to Jody, Mickey and Sylvia first saw him play the song with Bo's band at the Howard Theater in Washington, D.C. "We oughta stop playing these new songs," he told Bo at the time. "Too many people, certain people, are taking an interest in it." Not long after that, in March 1956, Jody brought Stewart, who had been the Diddley band's valet, to Chess. Jody wrote "Billy's Blues" for Stewart using the melody, rhythm, and sharp-toned, swirling guitar pattern that had attracted Baker's attention in Washington. Jody played that pattern on Stewart's record almost exactly as he had been playing it onstage. The disc didn't chart nationally, but it made enough of an impact around Chicago to kick-start Stewart's career, which continued until his death in an automobile crash in 1970.

A few months after it was released, Jody was back at Chess when Bo Diddley came in. "Bo pulled me over to the side. He said he let Mickey and Sylvia have 'Love Is Strange' and for me not to say anything to Leonard Chess about it. And don't worry about it, I'm gonna get my writer's royalties; they gave him two thousand dollars. Bo Diddley said if I keep my mouth shut, I'm gonna get my money, so I didn't say a thing."

"Love Is Strange," issued on the RCA subsidiary Groove, hit the Billboard pop chart in January 1957 and remained there for fourteen weeks, peaking at number 11; on the R&B chart it reached number 1. It was a big moneymaker from the start. George White quotes Mickey Baker as saying, "RCA sent me a check for $50,000 one day, and $27,000 the next. They told me they had to stop pressing Elvis Presley records to keep up with the orders on mine."[4] Since then, covers by artists ranging from the Everly Brothers, Peaches and Herb, and Chubby Checker to punker Johnny Thunders have earned lucrative royalties for Baker, who was credited as cowriter and whose company, Ben-Ghazi Enterprises, owns the publishing rights.[5]

The similarity between "Love Is Strange" and "Billy's Blues" should be obvious to even a casual listener: the instrumental version of the Stewart song, "Billy's Blues, Part 1," could almost pass as a backing track for the Mickey and Sylvia hit. Recognizing the publishing royalties at stake, Chess sued RCA, but at the time Jody was too wrapped up in the demands of his career to follow it closely. He recorded his now-classic "You May" and "Lucky Lou" for Chess in 1957. He also continued to tour and sit in wherever he could, taking a gladiatorial delight in confounding bandleaders and their regular fretmen with his ability to match them—if not best them—at their own game.

"I first met Bobby Bland," he recalls, "at the old Hollywood Rendezvous on the 3000 block of Indiana. I was playing along with the band; I don't know where his guitar player was. So he comes in and sees a [new] musician in there. I said, 'What you want to play?' He said, 'Further On up the Road.' It surprised the hell out of him when I started playing his song just like the record. That's the type of thing I'd do. If I could hear it, I could figure it out on guitar."

In May 1958 Jody Williams was drafted. He put in two years in an armored artillery and guided missile unit, patrolling the German-Czechoslovakian border; he also played guitar in the service club. On one such occasion he spotted a fellow GI named Elvis sitting in a jeep in front of the club. "I walked over and introduced myself. He knew who I was. I said, 'I don't recall meeting you anyplace.' He said he had seen me perform at the Apollo Theatre and someplace else. He'd go out in disguise, and that's how he caught my act. Somebody was tellin' me they'd seen in *Rolling Stone* about Elvis mentioning my name and that he liked my playing."

When Jody got back home in April 1960, he found that things were different from they way they had been before he left. "Music had changed," he remembers. "The places, the scene had changed. I was driving down the street and I heard music playing. Said, 'I'm gonna go in there and sit in with this band.' I opened the door—no music! Deejays! And before I went into the service you didn't see that."

But one thing hadn't changed: the Chess "Love Is Strange" lawsuit was still dragging on. In 1961 the company asked Jody to testify about his role in creating the song. They enlisted Gene Goodman, Benny Goodman's brother and a savvy industry insider, to help shepherd Willliams through the legal process. But Goodman was also part owner—along with another Goodman brother and the Chess brothers—of Arc Music, the publishing company controlled by Chess. His self-interest was to cut a deal that would be profitable to Arc and Chess, not necessarily one that was profitable to Jody. "I didn't understand all that at the time," Jody admits. "They didn't explain that stuff to us."

> Chess put me on a plane. Gene Goodman was supposed to take care of me in New York, put me up in a hotel and all that. When I went into the courtroom, I saw Sylvia sitting there. They put me in the back, behind the judge's chambers. I must have been back there at least an hour or more, and they finally came back there to get me. There was a jury; they had stereo equipment set up. They had been playing "Billy's Blues," "Love Is Strange," to see the similarities. After I gave my testimony—what I did, who I gave it to, what I recorded, and all that—back in that little room I went. They put me on a plane and sent me back to Chicago.

In November 1961, a few weeks after Jody's testimony, the U.S. Court of Appeals ruled that "Billy's Blues" and "Love Is Strange" are "not substantially or materially similar, and would not sound so to the average listener"[6]—a pretty astonishing verdict, given their similarity. Jody believes a deal was cut: "I heard from somebody that RCA and Chess made an agreement, split the profits, and froze everybody else out."

He also remains bitterly convinced that Bo Diddley, his erstwhile friend and mentor, was the mastermind behind what he sees as a carefully orchestrated rip-off that deprived him of fame and quite possibly millions of dollars. But at this late date it's difficult to discern exactly who was hustling whom at the time. If Bo was trying to claim credit for something that wasn't his, he certainly didn't profit much from it. And Jody seemed more than willing to go along with Bo's scheme until it became apparent that RCA wasn't going to give him what he had been led to believe he had coming.

Bo's own version of the episode, as related in White's book, is ambiguous. On the one hand, he says that the song evolved from one of his own creations: "I was in that 'Love Is Strange' bag at the time. I had a tune called 'Paradise'— which was a instrumental—an' I wrote 'Love Is Strange' from that."[7]

Nonetheless, he acknowledges that the "keen guitar part" on "Love Is Strange" was Jody Williams: "He's the one that came up with that little guitar part. That was a new guitar sound." But according to Bo, Jody himself taught it to Sylvia Vanderpool: "Joe was tryin' to make it with Sylvia. He went in there an' started playin' it for her. He told her it was my tune."[8]

He also insists that he tried to set things right with RCA after Mickey and Sylvia decided to record the song: "I *did not* rip him off! I've never *in my life* took *anythin'* from any one of my musicians that helped me to rise to the point that I have. It hurt me deeply, when I'm the one that taught Joe how to play, that he would think I would do somethin' like that to him. I told 'em, 'Me an' Joe put the tune together, so Joe's gotta get the music, an' I get the lyrics. He is entitled to the music of the song.' They told me: 'We'll take care of Joe.' So I signed a contract for the lyrics, an' I don't know what happened after that."[9]

Such a statement may seem disingenuous today, but at the time few artists had even a rudimentary knowledge of the legal technicalities of copyrights and publishing. Money was something you got for playing a gig or a recording session; cash in hand was better than hypothetical long-term gain, and it wasn't uncommon for songwriters to sell their material outright—sometimes to each other. Jody himself participated in one such transaction: "Junior Wells had a song he did for Chess. As soon as Junior left the studio, Leonard told me, 'If you can get that song away from Junior, I'll let you record it.' I went outside and told Junior what Leonard said. I asked him, 'What you want for the song?' Junior thought about it for a few seconds, and he said, 'Give me twelve dollars.' Twelve dollars was union scale, what sidemen were making for a night. So I gave him twelve dollars and got the song."

He bristles, however, at the suggestion that he taught "Love Is Strange" to Sylvia Vanderpool. "Sylvia wanted me to give her guitar lessons," he concedes, "[but] I never got to teach her anything. I've never been together three minutes alone with that woman. That's a bunch of lies."

As for the mysterious "Paradise," which Mickey Baker, too, cited in a 2000 *Living Blues* interview as the source of "Love Is Strange,"[10] the very word makes Jody furious: "I never heard a song called 'Paradise' in my entire life!" he snaps. "As long as Bo Diddley and I played together, on the corners, the Howard, the Apollo Theatre, all out on the road and everything—I have never played a song named 'Paradise' with Bo Diddley! Never *heard* of a song named 'Paradise'! Oh, they ripped me off, they ripped me off, *they ripped me off!*"

Jody soldiered on for a while with a pop-styled group called the Big Three Trio ("All the hit numbers on the Top 10, on the jukebox, we had the whole thing covered"), but between the "bad taste in [his] mouth" from the "Love Is Strange" case, the day-in and day-out hassles of holding a band together, and his growing desire for stability in his personal life, he became increasingly restless to make a change. In 1962 he met a young woman named Delores Jean Hadenfelt at a club in Calumet City. "Really, I hadn't intended on getting married," he says now. "Matter of fact, I tried to turn her against me, 'cause I knew she could do better."

Delores was white, and even in the North the idea of interracial dating—let alone marriage—caused consternation in some quarters. "People would stare," Jody remembers, "driving down the expressway or something like that. It's the whites that would do that. I said, 'These people just don't know any better.' So I would wave to them, tip my hat. We went together for two years before we got married. We weathered the storm."

Adjusting to his new role as head of household, Jody returned to school to study electronics. "I was still giggin' in the clubs; intermission, I was in my electronics books, either sitting in the booths or up on stage, reading." By 1966 he had recorded his last 45, "Time for a Change," released on the small Yulando label. Not long afterward he decided to pack it in.

> I put my guitar under the bed and forgot about it. Never went into clubs. My wife was running the bar at the Checkerboard, [but] I didn't go in there either. The reason I didn't, somebody spot me and say, 'We got Jody Williams in the house,' first thing they wanna do is throw a guitar in my hand. And I hadn't been playing my instrument; it's been under the bed. I wasn't going up onto anybody's stage sounding like a rank amateur. As good as I was—as good as I thought I was—that's the way I want to be remembered. And that's the way it's been all these years.

After their first son, Joseph Anthony, was born in 1969, the couple purchased a home in the South Side neighborhood of Hyde Park, not far from the University of Chicago. Jody found new ways to stimulate his imagination. He parlayed his electronics expertise into an invention called "the Overseer," designed, ironically, for use in the nightclubs he no longer visited.

> I drew out the schematics: a control system to control the lights, the jukebox. You could plug all this stuff in, and this system would control it, shut everything off at preset times. I had this sign flashing "Last call for alcohol" for a preset amount of time, then that light would go out, it would say "Goodnight folks." Shut the jukebox down, turn off the lights, get people out of there. Hotpoint or Sylvania, one of the two made a nibble at it. But they didn't buy it.
>
> I did a lot of things during my retirement. I got a diploma in AM/FM radio [repair], black-and-white/color television, refrigeration and appliances, air conditioning. I went to school and learned how to wire up IBM equipment, all the control panels and everything; I learned how to keypunch and program the IBM 360 computer. I had my own business for a while, building and installing burglar alarm systems. Somebody reported me to the state. I didn't know you needed a license to install burglar alarms! A lot of people don't want you to get ahead of 'em.

A deeper source of satisfaction was his reacquaintance with his first love, visual art. "Artists can paint only in two dimensions," Jody proclaims, gesturing toward the framed exhibits that line the wall of his den.

> But my art is in three dimensions. It's called paper tole, t-o-l-e. This is done in layers. I cut 'em apart and reposition 'em. You've go to have a pretty good imagination to do something like that, to visualize and figure out who's in front of whom, and how much depth. I use silicone, a pair of tweezers, toothpick, X-Acto knife, and scissors. Those are the simple tools I use to do all this work. And my imagination.
>
> Those clocks on the mantle? They're antiques, worth thousands of dollars. When we first bought this place, I had that grandmother clock in the corner. So just out of curiosity, I said "I'm gonna build me one!" I got the plans and I started building it. It's just about all finished. I envisioned making a clock like I saw in Germany. They've got the life-sized figures that move around and everything. You have to cut the wood, bevel the wood, plane it, sand it down, put it together. It takes time. There's not enough hours in the day for the things I want to do.

Jody and Delores eventually had two more children—a daughter, Sissy (née Yolanda), and another son, Jason—and with his hobbies, his jobs, and his family, it seemed as if Jody had more than enough to keep him busy and happy for the rest of his life. But then, in the late 1990s, after not having set a foot in a nightclub for almost three decades, he finally broke down and went to Buddy Guy's Legends to see an old friend, guitarist Robert Jr. Lockwood. In early 2000, when Lockwood came to the HotHouse, another South Loop club, Jody again came by to check in on his old partner. He still refused to play ("I said, 'I don't want nobody to know who I am'"), but it didn't take him long to realize how much he had missed being around music. "Robert Jr., [guitarist] Homesick James was there, talking about old times. Then they called [harpist] Snooky Pryor. It's been so long since I've seen these people. We were talking on the telephone, then they called somebody else long distance, I forgot who. It was like an old-time reunion up there."

Word got out that he had been seen in public; to his astonishment, he began to get phone calls from bookers and agents as far away as California asking him to perform. At Delores's urging, he returned to HotHouse in June 2000 and played a few numbers at a Chicago Blues Festival after-set that included his old partner Billy Boy Arnold.

> I said, "I'll play no more than about three or four numbers. I just want to see if I still got it." I played four songs. It wasn't my best, my fingers really weren't what they should have been, [but] it was a good feeling. So I said to myself, "I'm going to practice my guitar. I'm gonna get back into it."

The comeback: Jody Williams at the Chicago Blues Festival, 2001. Photo by Paul Natkin/Photo Reserve

I guess it was all over the country then: it was in the magazines, I got all kinds of interviews by different people, and I was called for a booking [at the Blues Estafette] in Holland. Oh, I had a ball over there! The crowd surprised the hell out of me—those people had my old recordings. I autographed a whole lot of 'em. I even autographed "Billy's Blues"! How'd everybody know that was me? That was a big surprise to me; I wasn't expecting it.

Jody began to sit in and do guest spots at various places around Chicago, and he also performed at the University of Chicago Folk Festival. In February 2001 he played at Rosa's Lounge, his first weekend-long engagement as a headliner in over thirty years. That spring he traveled overseas again—this time to Italy with guitarist John Primer—and then returned home for a triumphant appearance at the 2001 Chicago Blues Festival. Articles in the international blues press hailed his resurgence; he entered the studio and began work on a comeback CD, the appropriately titled *Return of a Legend*, for the Evidence label.

Jody has never been one to doubt his own abilities, but he frankly admits he was flabbergasted by the reaction his reemergence generated. "Guitar players lined up in front to watch me," he marvels. "And on the side too. Watching the fingers and everything."

I tell 'em, "Don't watch my fingers. Just *listen* to what I'm playing." My chord construction will be different—tuning is a little different, the same tuning Bo Diddley used, but he can't play what I play. Start watching my fingerwork, you're gonna be in a total state of confusion. People been tryin' to play "Lucky Lou" for years, still can't play it—they play *at* it.

Most of the time I do downstrokes, but every now and then you'll hear me do a backstroke, or rake the strings, to get certain effects. There are some techniques I use, where I use pick and fingers, both of them together. A few techniques that I use to get certain sounds, I will use a backward stroke, just barely touching the nail. Hit a backstroke with a pick, and the string just barely touching my fingernail a little bit, you'll get a different sound.

It was other guitarists watching and copying him, of course, that caused so many problems for Jody Williams in the first place. With that in mind, he gestures toward a pile of papers sitting atop his printer.

You see all those forms up there? Those are copyright forms. That's what I'm working on, doing all my own copyrights. It's not going to happen again. I'll sue everybody out there. I'm going to protect myself.

I made a promise, three things, to myself, when I started back playing my guitar. Number one: I don't compete anymore. There was a time I'd get up there, play all around 'em, all behind my head, between my legs and everything else. I don't do that anymore. Number two: I will never, under any circumstances, perform in public any of my music that's not published. Never! It's going to be published [by Hadenfelt Music, named for his wife] and on record before they hear it. And number three: only time I go into the studio and play on somebody else's session [will be] if I'm not playing my ideas, [if] I'm playing what somebody else wants me to play. That's the only way I'll go into a studio. Those are three promises I'm gonna keep.

Return of a Legend, released in 2002, features remakes of some of Jody's classic recordings—"Lucky Lou," "You May," "Moanin' for Molasses," "Jive Spot" (called "Five Spot" when Otis Spann recorded it, with Jody on guitar, in 1954)—as well as nine new compositions on which Jody sounds as if he has just stepped out of a mid-1950s time warp. But unlike many self-consciously "retro" blues projects, this set is rife with passion and immediacy with no museum-piece reverence to be found. Jody's leads probe and soar above his sidemen's swing-tinged shuffle comping, even as his fierce tone and wrenching, angular lines evoke the deep blues tradition. Only occasionally, as on the caustic "She Found a Fool and Bumped His Head," do his cynicism and sense of betrayal make themselves felt.

At least some of those feelings have begun to dissolve in the wake of the hero's welcome Jody has received since his return. "Over the years, you think you've been forgotten about," he murmurs, his voice thickening into a husky whisper.

When I was in Europe, those people in Holland treated me almost like royalty. It seems like when I come off stage, every time at least one person asks me for a pick. That's why I had new guitar picks made with my name on 'em, for the fans. I've autographed two guitars in the last year. That's a big honor. You probably don't understand how I feel, but really it almost makes me want to cry sometimes. I was trying to figure out—is it hard to accept? Is it hard to understand, or what? Those guys praise me so much, they put me up on a pedestal. I don't know if I deserve to be up there or not.

His voice cracks; he buries his face in his hands and falls silent. "Excuse me for getting a little emotional, but sometimes it just—all that's been stolen from me, that's one thing they haven't stolen. I just hope I can live up to it."

* * *

It's about ten thirty on a Friday night at Rosa's. John Primer and his Real Deal Blues Band have warmed up the crowd with their usual high-energy set.

Now Primer steps to the mike: "Are you ready for star time? It's star time!" Jody, who has been nursing a soft drink at the bar, straps on Red Lightning and makes his way to the stage, unable to hide the triumph in his grin as he gestures toward a line of young men huddled expectantly in the front row. "See? All guitar players," he whispers. "When I get up there, they'll be studying me."

He kicks off his set with a devastating "Lucky Lou" in which his guitar seems to be speaking words as he nimbly zips his fingers along the fretboard. He leads the crowd in a jubilant call-and-response on one of the new songs from *Return of a Legend*, "Wham Bam Thank You Ma'am;" on another new offering, "Brown Eyes and Big Thighs," his bass line rolls and pops like the leering eyes of a street-corner Lothario. But most of his show consists of standards, with an emphasis on the work of sophisticated stylists like Ray Charles ("Unchain My Heart"), Brook Benton ("Kiddio"), and T-Bone Walker ("T-Bone Shuffle").

True to his word, Jody eschews flamboyance, but his guitar seems to strut and preen with its ebullient, brightly sheened tone. Despite the familiarity of much of his material, he makes old ideas sound new: he inserts familiar licks or chords in unexpected places, he comes at them repeatedly but with different tonal attacks, and he tweaks them into unexpected shapes. By slowly rotating his right hand, he evokes the swirling tone of a phase shifter, the result sounding uncannily like a jazz chorus singing bebop scat. At one point he gestures to harpist Steve Bell to take a solo, but Bell seems mesmerized. He stares, motionless, as Jody spins off yet another spiraling run and allows himself a slight smile of satisfaction.

Toward the end of the set Jody eases into T-Bone's slow-rolling classic "Cold, Cold Feeling." For most of the evening he has sung in a grainy baritone croon, his stage presence reflecting an easygoing confidence. But now, as he works his way through "Cold, Cold Feeling," his voice coarsens and his de-meanor becomes more severe. By the final verse he's singing in a declamatory shout: "There's been a change in me, baby," he rasps, "Once I was blind, but now I can see." His eyes harden into a glower, and a tight grin plays around his lips: "I'm gonna put down everybody that ever made a fool of me!"

8

Bonnie Lee

"When I'm up There, I Lets Everything Out"

Like most Chicago blues artists of her generation, vocalist Bonnie Lee migrated to the city at a young age and forged her early career on the neighborhood circuit of clubs, modest show lounges, and private parties. During these years she also recorded for small local labels, most of which paid few if any royalties and at least one of which required her to go out and peddle her product herself after they had cut the sides.

It's no secret that this was a tough life, but Bonnie Lee and other women pursuing it have had particularly daunting obstacles to overcome. Most bluesmen benefited from a mentor who befriended and guided them early on; women have often found it difficult to break into this fraternity on their own terms. "I just really didn't have nobody to take an interest in me," Bonnie has remembered. "I didn't know; I just didn't know how to go about knowing anyone to ask. I think if I'd have taken the chance or had somebody to help me—push me—I would've been gone."

After all, building a "career" was and often remains a complicated and somewhat nebulous concept in the blues world. The demands of life, such as day jobs, families, and children, can make it hard to find the time and energy to keep the music fresh and alive. In addition, the business confronts would-be musicians with labyrinthine intricacies—promotion, contracts, and the precarious balance of nightclub-circuit politics. These can be mysterious and not a little intimidating to artists who, for all their finely honed intelligence and survival skills, have generally not been inculcated in the culture of networking, strategic planning, cut-to-the-chase time management, and other practices necessary to succeed in the modern business world.

For Bonnie Lee, an ambitious yet oddly fearful woman whose thirst for independence has for most of her life been counterbalanced by an equally strong craving for sanctuary and protection, this has meant waiting for the right combination of all the important factors: the time, the music, the money, and above all her confidence and the support of those she could trust. Even in the 1980s, after she had begun to record regularly and embark on overseas tours, she would sometimes retreat home for months or even years, opting not to work until she had again gathered her powers.

Like many others, Bonnie has also maintained a desire to nourish her long-established roots in the community where she got her start. Until recently she occasionally augmented her North Side appearances with gigs at neighborhood venues on the South and West Sides, reaffirming her loyalty to old haunts and old friends and reestablishing her sense of place. These days her local itinerary runs almost entirely north: backed by bassist Willie Kent and his band the Gents, she has a regular slot at B.L.U.E.S. on Halsted and a semiregular one at Blue Chicago in the North Loop. But she still maintains her modest home on a quiet West Side street a few doors from her church—and whenever Kent or someone else comes by to pick her up for a job, she says a prayer of protection before she walks out the door.

A word about what follows: chronology, dates, and names may sometimes be a bit muddled. Bonnie Lee has survived setbacks of many kinds in her life, and along the road some details have been obscured, perhaps mercifully. Aside from the opening vignette, which Bob Koester recounted to me,[1] this is her story as she remembered it in the autumn of 1992, as we sat in the quiet sanctuary of her living room. An open Bible lay on the table, the mantel behind her was laden with trophies and family photos, and LPs and 45s hung on the wall alongside paintings and carved images of Jesus. Relaxed in this atmosphere of cluttered domestic tranquility, Bonnie Lee told her story—a story not merely of survival but of triumph.

* * *

"Mr. Koester?" The young woman clutching an armful of 45s with red labels peered over the cluttered counter at Seymour's Loop Jazz Record Mart on South Wabash. She handed proprietor Bob Koester one of the discs. "I'd like to know if you'd like to buy these so you can sell them." They were blues records featuring a vocalist billed as Bonnie "Bombshell" Lee.

"Who's that?" Koester asked.

The woman smiled and answered, "That's me!"

Bonnie Lee had never met Koester, even though he was one of the few white people in Chicago who frequented the South and West Side clubs where she often sat in as a guest vocalist. But J. Mayo Williams, the producer who had recorded her and then given her the records to distribute, had assured her that Koester was an important figure in the Chicago music business.

It was hard work hustling records all over town, and Bonnie probably hadn't received any money for the session, but she didn't much care. She had arrived in Chicago from Texas only a few years earlier, dreaming of bright lights and fame; this was going to be her big break. She was ready to work for nothing and peddle the product herself if that was what it took.

Koester listened to a side. It was a characteristically crude Williams production, elemental twelve-bar blues with a dash of sketchily conceived jazziness, redeemed from mediocrity by the singer's ebullient power. He told Bonnie he could take a few off her hands, although he might not be able to move very many. "How much you want for 'em?" he asked.

"A dollar apiece."

"But that's what we sell them for. You'll have to come down on your price."

"Well, that's what Mr. Williams wants."

Williams was a powerful and wily music industry veteran whose business acumen had earned him the nickname "Ink." As a newcomer to the business, Bonnie didn't dare go back to him with less money than he had told her to get. She stood silently for a moment. Only a few days earlier she had been thrilled to see her name on a label and hear her voice on record for the first time; now the dream was already starting to crumble. She sadly tucked the records back under her arm and walked out the door. Koester didn't see her again for years.

* * *

Three decades later, her eyes tightly shut and lips twisted in a theatrical sneer, Bonnie Lee bellows out her version of the Jimmy Reed standard "Baby What You Want Me to Do" for a rollicking weeknight crowd at B.L.U.E.S. on North Halsted as Willie Kent and the Gents grind out a tough, loping rhythm behind her. Kent, watching her every move, is locked tightly into drummer Cleo "Bald-Head Pete" Williams's unerring shuffle groove.

Despite the tune's elemental simplicity, Bonnie's interpretation sounds like an aural pastiche of half a century of blues tradition. After singing a couple of introductory choruses in a declamatory wail, she mellows into a croon and starts teasing her phrases into scatlike convolutions. Then she suddenly plunges into a burnished shout reminiscent of the classic women blues singers of Bessie Smith's era. After another verse or two she returns to the stentorian blues holler she started with; she finally signs off with a full-bodied blast of guttural sassiness, waits demurely for the applause to die down, and then eases into another number.

Bonnie Lee with bassist Willie Kent, performing at the Jazz Record Mart in Chicago, June 2004. Photo by Art Schuna

As the stage lights sparkle off her sequined tiara, Bonnie moves hypnoti-cally from side to side and throws her head back to sing. Occasionally she snaps her fingers for a measure or two with a hipster's limp-wristed ease, but for the most part her stage presence is stolid, almost matronly, despite the passion she pours into every syllable. Her new CD is on sale behind the bar; during the break she'll sit at a corner barstool, sip coffee, and autograph copies with a gracious smile. But for now she seems enraptured, oblivious to everything but the music.

Even as a child growing up in Beaumont, Texas, Jessie Lee Frealls knew she wanted to be a singer. Sometimes she would sit on the porch with her feet dangling between the steps and serenade an audience of dolls, playing imaginary piano patterns on the planks as she sang. It was more than just a way of passing the time on lazy Sunday afternoons after coming home from church; it felt more real than anything else she could possibly imagine.

A lot of children in the South might have been chastised for dreaming of such a career. Religious people in those days often insisted on keeping their homes free of "reels," as secular music, especially blues, was sometimes called. But Jessie Lee's mother and stepfather were more lenient. "She paid for my piano lessons, my mother did. I was just learning the notes, the keys, and how to play piano. My mother, she never did stop me. She just said if that's what you want to do, you do it."

Recalling those days nearly fifty years later, Bonnie Lee relaxes on the sofa in the living room of her compact West Side home, eyes softening with memory. (She appeals to business to explain her name change: "I don't use Jessie Lee; I use Bonnie Lee. I figured that Jessie—that wouldn't be a profes-sional name.") She lives on a quiet tree-lined street that feels far removed from the pressures of urban life. Outside on this crisp autumn afternoon, old men sit on front porches and watch children return from school as orange and red leaves swirl around them. It's a scene so tranquil that you have to remind yourself you're only a few blocks from the desolation and harsh cadences of West Madison Street.

As Bonnie tells her story, her voice modulates from a throaty whisper to an exultant squeal of delight. When the recollections are happy, she hunkers down into her seat, lowers her head to coyly look with upturned eyes, and breaks into girlish giggles. Often, though, she falls silent and stares into the middle distance, struggling to find the right words or to remember dates and places. She smiles warmly when recalling her early days growing up in the South—first in Bunkie, Louisiana, and then in Beaumont, where her stepfather labored in the shipyards and her mother worked for the sheriff as a cook. Music resonated through her childhood. "I liked jazz the best—Ella

Fitzgerald, Sarah Vaughan, Dinah Washington. But after I started listening to blues, I got into it."

There wasn't much opportunity for a young girl to practice jazz or blues in Beaumont. Young Jessie Lee instead concentrated on her piano lessons and began to play in church. One appearance on a church program almost resulted in her first road trip. "We went to church every Sunday, Methodist church in Beaumont. The lady who came to my church, her name was Lillian Glenn, and I played behind her.[2] And she did spirituals, and I asked her could I back her up on piano, and she said yes, so I played. And she asked my mother for me. She said, 'Well, can I keep her and take her with me? I will send her to music school, voice lessons, and everything.' My mother said no, I couldn't go. I got disgusted because she wouldn't let me go."

So Jessie Lee stayed home, but she had been bitten: "From right then I said I want to be a singer and leave Texas, go somewhere else and make it. I ain't never been shy in my life, from a kid on up. I loved to sing 'cause I was born with this. When you're born with a gift, God give it to you. I was just born with a voice, that's all."

For a long time, though, it felt like an impossible fantasy. Places like California (where Texas-born blues musicians like T-Bone Walker, Charles Brown, and Lloyd Glenn had migrated) and the northern blues mecca of Chicago seemed inconceivably far away to the dreamy young girl in Beaumont. A young man like Muddy Waters might leave his family behind and catch a train out of the Mississippi Delta to seek his fortune, but a young woman—even an independent-minded, determined one like Jessie Lee—had more constraints on her. She married at fourteen, and although she and her husband separated in less than a year, she remained in her hometown, close to her people.

She also remained as close to music as possible. "A bunch of us girls used to go and hear the blues. The Ravens was about the biggest popular club. That was on Forsythe—B. B. King, different artists like T-Bone Walker. It inspired me because that's what I had in mind that I wanted to be. I didn't know how to go about it. I just would go around and listen at other people sing, and I just said, 'Maybe one day I'll do it.'"

But the only time she got to sing was when one of the visiting celebrities would hold an open session and let her sit in. There were also troubles at home. Despite the affection her mother and stepfather had always shown her, she came to feel alienated because her half-sisters treated her as if she were somehow less than family: "It was whole for them but it wasn't whole for me." Then, when she was about seventeen, her biological father showed up in town.

"That was my first time seeing him," she said. "My uncle, his brother, lived in Beaumont. I knowed I had a father; I had his picture. But I never did think I'd get a chance to see him. And when he came to Beaumont, they called my mother and asked us to come, and we did. I still didn't get used to it. I told him he wasn't my father, because my stepfather had raised me."

Her father's arrival in Beaumont sparked a family reunion of sorts, but it resulted in tragedy for Bonnie, who was raped by a close male relative—though not her father. "It constantly stayed on my mind. How could your own people do that, your own family do that to you? I never told anyone. I just left Texas and went to Alexandria, Louisiana. I had some relatives there. I worked in a shoe shop shining shoes, just did it to earn some money."

Jessie Lee also dropped out of music for a while, but after working for a few years at the shoe store, she joined the Famous Georgia Minstrel Show, a relic from the days when minstrel troupes and patent medicine shows crisscrossed the rural South providing entertainment for country folk and employment for legions of black performers. Touring on such revues could be a terrible grind, for accommodations were often appalling, artists faced the constant threat of racist harassment and humiliation from townspeople, and pay ranged from scant to nonexistent. She left after only a few months. "I just wanted to try something different," she says. "I didn't like the living conditions, living in a tent and things like that. I came back to Texas."

This time Jessie Lee moved to Houston, where she landed a gig working with a female impersonator named Effie Dropbottom. But this was hardly a career-building engagement, and she eventually returned to Beaumont. She found some work singing, including a weekend job with guitarist Erving Charles and his band, and she occasionally sat in with visiting celebrities like Gatemouth Brown. For the most part, however, she supported herself as a waitress.

When Jessie Lee finally had a chance to put Beaumont behind her for good, she grabbed it. She remembers the year as 1958: "I met a fella. I was at the train station to meet *another* fella." She doubles over laughing, still impressed at her audacity after all these years.

I was gonna meet a friend of mine on the train; it was on the Pacific Railroad. He was a cook. And I was only kiddin' with Roy. He was a truck driver for Atlas, so I was just going to pass the time away with Roy until the train come in. I met Roy at the station, and I was just only kidding with him. I said, "I would like to go to Chicago."

So he said, "You really want to go to Chicago?"

I said, "Yeah!"

He said, "Where you live?"

I said, "On the North End."

He said, "Well, get in."

So he went home with me. I got my clothes and everything, and when we got to Liberty, Texas, he said, "Well, I got to go over here and get you some blue jeans and a blue-jean jacket and a cap and put your hair up so they'll think you was a boy." And that's how I come to Chicago, in the truck. I didn't have any idea what it would be like or what it was. I just wanted to go to a big city and see how the big city would look. It hit me. It was fast, it really was.

I didn't run back home; I was determined to make it on my own. A lot of times I didn't have money for food and I was hungry, but I didn't let my parents know that. I didn't have nowhere to stay, and I didn't let my parents know that. I decided I got to do either one—give it up or try to make it.

She eventually landed a job waiting tables in a tavern on South Federal.

It was pretty hard, but I finally met people. I met some friends of mine [from Texas]; everybody used to go over there to the club. Met some lady friends; I just ran up on them. I found my aunt here, and I found out I had sisters and brothers here—that's on my father's side. I didn't even know I had brothers and sisters. I thought I was my father's only child. Where I was working at, I met a girl, and she had an extra room, and all I had to do was come from the apartment and go right across the street to work. The girl told me to come on over here and stay with her. When I got paid, I paid her, and we got along just fine.

In Chicago in the late 1950s and early 1960s, the South and West Sides were peppered with clubs ranging from rough-and-tumble joints like the 708 Club on Forty-seventh Street and Silvio's on West Lake to tonier establishments like the Tay May on Roosevelt Road and the jazz room in the Trocadero Hotel at Forty-seventh and Indiana, just one block north of Theresa's Lounge. But the scene was fiercely competitive. Nobody but the biggest names made much money, and it took shrewd hustling to land even low-paying jobs. Despite her ambition and years of on-again, off-again singing experience, the young newcomer had no idea how to build a career.

Jessie Lee began to do what she had done for so many years in Beaumont: sit in wherever and whenever she could. "When I'd meet people I'd ask them [where the clubs were], and they'd say, 'Come on, we'll take you.' So a lot of the people that I met—entertainers that I met—I would go with them. Then I'd find out how to get around on my own, find out where different places are at. I used to be around the Trocadero; when I'd get tired of hanging around there, I'd just walk down to Theresa's, and when I'd get tired of [that], I'd get back to the Trocadero."

For a while she sang with organist James Reese at "a Mexican club" in nearby Blue Island, Illinois, and he introduced her to J. Mayo Williams. Around 1960 she recorded at least four numbers for Williams—"Fast Life," "My Man's Coming Home," "Black but Beautiful," and "My Rock and Roll Man"—all of which he released on his Ebony label. It was he who billed her as "Bonnie 'Bombshell' Lee," to her displeasure ("Everybody thought I was going to jump out of a cake"). But she received little recognition and less money, for royalties were virtually unknown among struggling blues artists in those days.

Bonnie recalls that at least five years passed before she received any money for singing. Even after landing her first paying gig, at Steve's Chicken Shack in Gary, Indiana, she continued to support herself by waiting tables. Her career consisted mostly of unpaid guest appearances, occasional low-paying engagements, a handful of recording sessions, and long periods of frustrating inactivity.

Adrift in this harsh world, Bonnie avoided doing some things that might have furthered her career because, she says, she felt they would put too much pressure on her. For instance, she did not attempt to form her own band. "I didn't want to deal with it. It's too much of a headache."

In the early 1960s she married a man she had met while singing at the Golden Peacock, on West Madison. This brought her a modicum of financial stability, but she didn't find the professional guidance she needed until several years later. "I really didn't have nobody to take an interest in me," she says, "till I met Cadillac Baby and met Sunnyland." Cadillac Baby (Narvel Eatmon) was a popular blues entrepreneur whose nightclub, Cadillac Baby's Show Lounge, on South Dearborn, was the site of one of Chicago's more impressive stage entrances: to kick off the night's festivities, Eatmon would drive his namesake car onto the stage and emerge from it with a grand, sweeping bow. In 1963, after both his club and his Bea and Baby record label had gone out of business, he opened Cadillac Baby Record and T.V. Repair, complete with a colorful marquee that boasted of "Reverb Sound" and "Change for Sale: 5¢ per Dollar," at 4405 South State Street.[3] The store became a popular hangout among musicians.

Sunnyland Slim, always an imposing figure, caught Bonnie's eye as soon as he came into the shop one day in 1967. "I was at Cadillac's on State Street, and when Sunnyland walked in, I asked Baby, 'Who is that?' He said, 'That's Sunnyland.' So one word led to another. Baby told him I was a singer, and he asked me would I go on the road with him, and I said, 'Yeah.'"

Sunnyland's style, rooted in Delta tradition but with elements of swing and boogie-woogie modernity thrown in, was perfect for Bonnie's meld of blues and jazz influences. "He was the first one took me to Canada," she acknowledges. "He asked me could I drive. I said 'Yeah,' and I drove awhile, he drove awhile. That was my first time even going out of Chicago. And then when I went to Canada, he made me acquainted with the people there."

Although Sunnyland enjoyed a well-earned reputation as a ladies' man, Bonnie insists, "We just worked together; he wasn't my man." In performance her supple vocals and dignified stage presence played well against his gruff Delta exuberance; they toured often, mostly on the predominantly white folk and blues festival circuit, and for a while it seemed as if her dream might finally be coming true. At home, though, things had begun to deteriorate severely. "I was hurt in my marriage. I came home, he used to bring women to the house and things like that. He liked to fight. I couldn't take it."

Yet she stayed with her husband, enduring three miscarriages before finally giving birth to her son, Earl, on July 11, 1968, exactly one month after her thirty-seventh birthday. Shortly after that she ended her marriage. "I got out of it because I didn't want to kill him (her husband); I didn't want to go to jail, wouldn't know where my son is at. We separated after he was born, after I went and got (Earl) out of the hospital. He had to stay in the hospital until he was five and a half pounds, on account of he was premature. I had a fibroid tumor with him; I stayed in Cook County Hospital for quite a while. I think I went and got him about the last of that month; I forgot what month that was."

In the meantime she met Edward Bevely, the man who would become the most important companion of her life until his death in the mid-1990s. A construction worker who shared her passion for jazz, he was a low-key, domestic-minded man who wasn't jealous of her celebrity and who was now willing to step in and take care of little Earl while she recuperated. "I met him, oh my God, I forgot the year. But I know we've been together for years because my son's going on twenty-seven, on the eleventh of July [1992]. I thank God he raised my son. He's a stepfather, just like a father."

Confident that her son was in good hands, she eventually returned to performing, continuing on as Sunnyland's featured guest vocalist. Around 1975 Sunnyland recorded her on his Airway label. She sang "Standing on the Corner" and "Sad and Evil Woman," a song that for a while became a staple of her repertoire, and she contributed a backup vocal on Sunnyland's trademark "Got a Thing Goin' On" and "See My Lawyer." Gigs and opportunities were coming more plentifully now. She also cut sides for Chicago blues deejay Big Bill Collins's Black Beauty label ("Teardrops from My Eyes" and "I Need Your Love So Badly"). The old "Bonnie 'Bombshell'" discs on Ebony began to show up in used-record bins, furthering her reputation among aficionados and collectors.

When Sunnyland took on Big Time Sarah as his new protégée, Bonnie went out on her own. For a while she even led her own band, the Apollos, but another period of stagnation soon set in. The Airway and Black Beauty records, produced locally with minimal advertising or distribution, had little success outside Chicago and didn't get much airplay even in town. Without the guiding hand of Sunnyland to help her, Bonnie again found herself struggling, and her early misgivings about being a bandleader proved accurate. "It didn't go too hot. Some of 'em wanted all the money; I got discouraged. You get some fellows, they don't want to act right, don't want to listen at you."

She kept at it for a little while longer, but eventually the pressure became too much:

> I stopped singing altogether, period, because I took sick. I had a nervous breakdown and I just stopped. Just everything got on my nerves. I'd been through so much alone. I wanted to work and do things, and it just looked like I wasn't getting nowhere. I was trying to take care of my baby. I didn't want him to be in this hand and that hand and the other hand. Because this was the first kid I had ever had.
>
> I was living right there (on the West Side), and I just stayed up in the house, I didn't go nowhere. I didn't go to no clubs. I had money from disability. I was so I couldn't walk. They had to learn me how to walk again; I was just like a baby. I just kept makin' steps just like a baby learnin' how to walk. I didn't even know I had a son in the world, that's how sick I was. There was so much pressure on me . . .

Bonnie's voice trails off and she sinks into a meditative silence. She's in relatively good health today, but she still finds it difficult to talk about those bad years. She credits Bevely with seeing her through the roughest times. "When I was sick, he'd come every day to the hospital, bathe me, put my gown on, wash me, see to the baby. He got me a walker, so I could start to walk again. His family, his mother and them, took care of Earl. It took some pressure off."

She stayed home and rested, slowly "getting [her] mind back together" until the end of the 1970s, when she began feeling restless and ready to try music again. But she still needed assistance: "[I] had to have somebody to help me because I wasn't going to do it alone."

Willie Kent, a West Side veteran who had known Bonnie since her early days in Chicago, was working with guitarist Buster Benton at the time. Kent knew Bonnie hadn't been working for a while; he contacted her and talked her into letting him use her on local jobs and a few out-of-town performances. In Kent she again found someone who could hustle gigs, deal with agents and club owners, and manage the band's finances—all the day-to-day details she had never been able to master.

For once, her timing was perfect. By the late 1970s Chicago saw the emergence of a new generation of women singers, including Zora Young, Big Time Sarah, and the late Valerie Wellington (all young enough to be Bonnie's daughters and all mentored, as she had been, by Sunnyland). Bonnie Lee was welcomed as a kind of elder stateswoman in this circle. Musicians and audiences alike admired her matronly, elegant demeanor and her stylistic flexibility as she spanned years of tradition by fusing blues and jazz with the hard-driving contemporary Chicago style. It was a time of mercurial growth on the Chicago scene, and Bonnie's horizons expanded rapidly.

> I first went to Europe with Zora, Sarah, and [guitarist] Hubert [Sumlin]. I don't know what year that was 'cause I done forgot.[4] I had to go to Texas to see about my father, my father that raised me. Then I came back, and Zora said, "You're going to Paris."
> I said, "What?"
> "You're going to Paris!" So we went to Paris.

While overseas the women recorded *Blues with the Girls* on the Paris label; after returning to the United States, Bonnie continued to gig around Chicago with Kent, Sunnyland, and others. But then, on the verge of success, Bonnie dropped out yet again. She suffered two heart attacks over the next several years and once more found herself housebound.

"I had faith in God," she asserts, "and I had faith in myself. My son used to tell me, 'Mama, you gonna make it; just have faith.'" But again it took Willie Kent to bring her back. By the mid-1980s he had begun working regularly at Blue Chicago, a Near North Side club on State Street with a predominately white clientele. Gino Battaglia, the club's owner, admires women singers and encourages the bands that work for him to hire them wherever possible. Kent began to come by Bonnie's house to encourage her return.

"Kent said, 'You have too good a voice to let it go to waste.' He came by and picked me up, went over to State Street, where he was with Gino, and I did a number. Then Gino called Kent, asked Kent did he know me, and he said, 'Yeah.' He called me and said, 'Gino wants you to work.' I gives him thanks because if it wouldn't be for him, I wouldn't be out here now. I'd still be sittin' up here [in the house]; I wouldn't be happy."

Despite her out-of-state travels with Sunnyland and the international exposure she had garnered from the European tour and LP, Bonnie had never really built her reputation among the North Side audiences in Chicago. Now she began to establish herself at Blue Chicago, B.L.U.E.S., and other trendy blues-themed watering holes. She also recorded two more 45s for Bill Collins, which Collins issued under his Big Boy label: "I'm Good and I Know I'm

Good"/"I Got the Blues about My Baby" (a remake of her earlier "Black but Beautiful" with the lyric "I got the blues about my black man" changed to fit the tenor of the times), and "Got to Let You Go"/"Baby It's Cold Outside." Wolf Records, an Austrian company, came to Chicago in 1987 to record her on an anthology disc that includes two other West Side vocalists, Mary Lane and Barkin' Bill. When Kent went into the hospital for heart surgery in the late 1980s, Bonnie joined forces for a while with guitarist Johnny B. Moore, a musician with tastes as eclectic as her own.

She was most comfortable with Kent, though, and she got back with him as soon as he was well enough to resume playing. Their friendship has been a vital source of stability for her. "There's nothing too good that I wouldn't do [for him]," she says, "'cause I took him and put him in here [she lays a hand on her heart] and that's where he'll stay; right here."

In 1991 Wolf returned to record Bonnie again. After a lifetime of working and waiting ("I'm sixty-one years old and I'm proud!" she proclaimed in 1992), she finally had a full-length album under her own name. She also found a more appropriate moniker than the dreaded "Bombshell"; the liner notes to the Wolf CD refer to her as the "Belle of the Blues."

Entitled *I'm Good*, after her anthemic signature tune, the CD features powerful accompaniment by Kent and members of his band as well as guitarists Magic Slim, Johnny B. Moore, and John Primer. That's an impressive lineup, even though the disc's hardcore Chicago sound doesn't exactly reflect Bonnie's musical self-image ("I'm on a jazzy-bluesy kick; I'm not a really hard, cold blues singer—when you notice me, it's a jazzy blues"). Nonetheless, it provided her with a perfect combination: the structure she needs to stay in the pocket of the beat and the freedom to let her explore vocally. The disc features a reprise of "Sad and Evil Woman" from the Sunnyland Slim days, along with several originals.

Also included was another tune that has become a Bonnie Lee signature, Little Willie John's "Need Your Love So Bad." She had recorded it on *Black Beauty* in 1976 as "I Need Your Love So Badly," but that version was marred by her uncertain timing and theatrical glottal stops on the more emotional passages. This time out she delivered it confidently, in a burnished croon punctuated by hoarse, churchy rasps on the turnarounds. Wolf renamed it "I Need Someone," but these days Bonnie usually refers to it as "I Need Someone's Hand." She says it touches her about as deeply as it's possible for a secular song to do: "That song of Little Willie John's, 'I Need Someone's Hand,' a lot of times they don't know, I be crying. That gets next to me. I don't know why, but it just gets next to me."

More recently, in 1995, Bonnie finally concluded her unfinished business with Bob Koester by signing with Koester's Delmark label and recording *Sweetheart of the Blues*. To add some contemporary urgency to her sound, Delmark augmented Kent and his Gents with a versatile session crew that included saxophonist Hank Ford, keyboardist Ken Saydak, and harpist Billy Branch. The highlight of the disc is Bonnie's rendition of Big Maybelle's "Ocean of Tears," a harrowing portrait of psychic dissolution on which she pushes her voice to its limits of both power and emotional intensity. On some of the other tracks—including a reprise of the Little Willie John song (now titled "I Need Your Love So Bad")—her phrasing and voice seem to have perhaps stiffened a bit with age, but the entire set is seasoned with a feeling of hard-won triumph and worldly power that evokes the deepest essence of blues expression.

But Bonnie did not incorporate "Ocean of Tears" or any of the other fresh material from *Sweetheart of the Blues* into her live act at the time, and she hasn't attempted to do so since. Instead, she keeps her audiences satisfied and her muse at peace by continuing to rely on the same handful of tunes: "Baby What You Want Me to Do," "I'm Good," "I Need Someone's Hand/Need Your Love So Bad," and maybe one or two others, often repeated in the same order several times a night. After a lifetime of dodging the vicissitudes of the unfamiliar, Bonnie Lee seems to have become almost obsessively determined to remain safe within the sanctuary of the tried-and-true. The result, inevitably, is a sameness—even an occasional staleness—to her show that might not make much difference on her occasional whirlwind overseas tours but has probably hurt her over the long term as a local draw in Chicago. Such is her level of commitment, though, that on a good night she's able to summon a feeling of redemptive power that can make even the most worn phrases and ideas sound born anew.

These days, as she looks back on her years of struggle and relishes the success that has come at an age when many singers are considering retirement, Bonnie insists she was never afraid that she might lose her voice or her feel for music, even when it looked as if she might never perform again.

> It just came to me; it never left me. The good Lord gave it to me; I never taken a singing lesson in my life. If you got a good ear to hear, that'll never leave you. Anything, to be successful, you got to put the Lord in front, and you get behind. Without him, you're not going to make it. I'm religious; I put my faith in God. Always have and always will. Because in my life he comes first. Even when he (Kent) comes to pick me up, I say my prayer, I say, "Lord, take care of us 'cause we're going out." When we get off, I say, "Lord, take us back home safe."

Bonnie Lee vamping backstage at the Chicago Blues Festival, June 2003. Photo copyright 2004, Jef Jaisun/jaisunphoto.com

One thing: I'm in the blues field. I don't believe in playing with the Lord. While I'm in this field, I'm going to be in this field. I'll be doing it as long as the good Lord let me and bless me; other than that, this is a living. It's how I make my living. It's how I pay my bills and things.

"I'll tell anybody," she adds, remembering Gatemouth Moore's legendary onstage conversion in 1949 at the Club DeLisa in Chicago, "when the good Lord get ready to change me, he don't care where you're at. You can be up on the stage and he'll change you. And when he change me, I won't look back at no blues."

But if the blues won't bring salvation, redemption might be closer at hand. For all her insistence that performing is just "a living," Bonnie Lee sings with a fervor that approaches the transcendent. Pressed, she will admit that music, both secular and sacred, resonates for her in a way nothing else can.

I'm happy when I'm up on that stage. Most of the time, if you see me, my eyes be closed. I'm in another world. I don't see anybody out there. I put my soul into it; I feel everything that I do. Most times when I'm by myself, I put on a spiritual and I sing along; or either, if I got something on my mind, I get me a jazz record and put it on. Sometimes I put my pillows on the floor and lay down and let jazz relax my mind. And then I don't have to do that, 'cause when you walk in my house I got Bibles open. I get my Bible and read it.

When I was raped, that stayed on my mind. I still keeps that on my mind about the rape. I always think, I hope nobody else don't be like this, so many kids getting raped and things. I think that's what caused me having the heart attack. I kept it to myself; all that just stayed in me. That's a long time to keep something all up in here. I wasn't thinking about it. It was just building up. I have sisters and brothers here, but we don't see one another. The only one I would talk to, I would talk to my doctor about it. I went to a psychiatrist, I didn't even tell him what's going on. I got up and left out of his office.

I don't get too close; once you do me something [wrong], I just back from you. If I'm your friend, I'm your friend; if I like you, I like you. But I'm just afraid I'll be hurt again, and I don't want to get hurt. I hold everything in. I don't care what you do to me, I hold it in, except when I sing. That certain song that I sing ["Need Your Love So Bad"/"I Need Someone's Hand"], it bring tears from my eyes. I feel better when I can let it out through my songs. I'm happy when I'm up there. I lets everything out.

* * *

At B.L.U.E.S., toward the end of her first set, Bonnie pauses silently for a moment with her eyes downturned and then signals Kent and the band; they nod and ease into a slow-rolling gospel intro. Her body stiffens and twists as she begins to sing, and her face contorts into a grimace. For most of the song her eyes are jammed shut, but occasionally they open and her expression softens. She sways in time to the music and delivers the lyrics in a raw growl that occasionally melts into a croon, making her sound both fierce and plaintive at the same time:

I need someone's hand to lead me through the night
I need someone's arms for to hold and squeeze me tight

And when the lights are low, and it's time to go,
'Cause I need your love so bad . . .

I need a soft voice to talk to me at night
Don't worry baby, 'cause I won't fuss and fight
Listen to my plea, bring it on home to me,
'Cause I need your love so bad.[5]

When the song is over, she lets her body relax, and she wipes perspiration from her brow. A woman who's been dancing in convulsive gyrations rushes to the stage and grabs one of Bonnie's hands in both of hers, speaking to the singer in an intense whisper. Bonnie listens politely and then, for the first time since she started her performance, breaks into a radiant smile. After another song or two she steps down and returns to her corner barstool and her coffee cup as the band finishes the set. She's breathing heavily and drenched in perspiration, but the smile is still there, and it remains on her face for the rest of the evening.

9

Billy Branch
"It's the Most Powerful
Music on the Planet"

Billy Branch plays history on his harmonica. In fact, it often sounds as if his harp is not a mere musical instrument
but rather the conduit through which he channels that
history—the voices, the muses, and even the life stories of
his mentors and role models in the blues. These include
such fabled figures as Big Walter Horton, Junior Wells,
and the still-potent James Cotton and Carey Bell, as well
as earlier masters like John Lee "Sonny Boy" Williamson,
and Rice "Sonny Boy Williamson no. 2" Miller.

On a classic like Miller's "Don't Start Me to Talkin',"
he'll kick off a solo with long lines couched in a rounded
saxlike tone borrowed from Little Walter. He then wid-
ens his timbre into a hawk squall like Miller's, playfully
jumping off the beat and then back into the rhythm, and
rolls out his version of Miller's trademark triplet turn-
around. Suddenly he leaps into the upper register and
unfurls a re-creation of Big Walter's personalized buzz
tone and rapid-fire three-note flutter, swooping down to
the middle again for a few funk-flavored riffs borrowed
from Junior Wells's latter-day book of licks. After a liquid
note bend that recalls Jimmy Reed, he snaps out a series
of Carey Bell skitters, even cupping his harp in his palm

like Bell does. Finally he caps it all off with a series of complex descents, enriching both the legacy he has just invoked and the song itself with his own pop-tinged improvisational sensibility.

Billy discovered the blues in the late 1960s as a college student in Chicago, and almost immediately he became consumed with the desire to play the music and carry on the legacy it represented. Nurtured in an academic environment, he gravitated toward teaching, along with performing, as the medium for his mission. In the late 1970s, as he was building his international reputation as a musician, he began what evolved into his lifelong commitment to Blues in the Schools, a Chicago-based educational initiative that Billy has since expanded nationwide.

In both his teaching and in his performances, Billy stresses the universality of the blues ("Everyone gets the blues; doesn't matter what nationality or social status you maintain"). But he's also adamant that the blues are first and foremost living black history and that the musical syntax of the blues must be understood in this historical context and tapped from this source. No matter how funky or rocked-out an arrangement may be, he invokes his mentors' voices in both his harpwork and his grits-and-gravel vocals, although he also throws in enough embellishments—major-scale challenges to blues flats and tonalities as well as extended, rapidly executed multinote patterns—to satisfy both his own exploratory urges and the modernist tendencies of most of his listeners.

Despite the criticism it may get from purists and progressives alike, this searching is where Billy most profoundly exemplifies the blues tradition he has taken on as his own. Since the beginning the blues has represented an existential act of defiance against boundaries, psychic and otherwise, imposed by oppression and poverty and by the despair such conditions can engender. The country boy who fashioned a diddly bow out of a plank and broom wire and nailed it to a wall; the juker who wrung beauty from primal chords hammered out on out-of-tune guitar strings; the modern backstreet poet who invokes prophecy with words and insights considered subversive by arbiters of culture and morality; the musical trickster who elevates a roomful of celebrants by marrying sounds and styles heretofore considered incompatible—these figures are repositories, not denigrations, of the "authentic" blues voice.

Billy Branch plays, sings, and speaks in that voice, both when he is onstage and when he stands in front of a classroom initiating his students into the blues. "You can do anything that you put your mind to," he instructs them, "and don't be afraid to try. We tell 'em from the outset: you don't have to sing perfectly, on pitch—but just try, and you'll be amazed at what you can do."[1]

* * *

"Why are we here?"

"To sing and play the blues!"

"What are the blues?"

"The blues are the facts of life!"

"Why are the blues so important?"

"They're our history, our culture, and the roots of American music!"

An expectant moment of silence follows the call-and-response Blues in the Schools slogan. Then, harmonicas wheezing, voices straining to hit the high notes, the students in the classroom in Seattle's Washington Middle School erupt into a raucous twelve-bar blues shuffle. Billy Branch, who led the chant, nods encouragement and tosses off a few harp riffs as the music builds into a jubilant crescendo around him. He circulates through the room, goading various instrumentalists to blow harder, push higher, and come up with new ideas.

Backstage at the downtown Sheraton Hotel a week or so later, the youngsters, now dubbed the "Blues Biscuits," are afflicted with preshow jitters. A few approach Billy, blow muted harp patterns in his ear, and then stare pleadingly into his face for approval. Once onstage, though, they look and sound remarkably well seasoned. A girl of about fourteen chews gum nonchalantly as she pumps out a steady-rolling electric bass pattern, kicked hard by a fresh-faced young drummer who deftly coordinates multiple rhythmic accents. In the front line about a dozen harpists and singers maintain a side-to-side line-dancing motion as individuals step forward to blow brief solos and sing a few verses into the microphone.

At least one offering, a blues about how it feels to have your bicycle stolen, was written by one of the students. When it's his turn, he gives it the full "star" treatment: he toughens his voice into a growl, twists at the waist, rolls his eyes, and contorts his hands and arms in herky-jerky hip-hop movements as he delivers his song. It doesn't take long for the audience to rise to their feet, and they stay standing for the rest of the show.

Billy and his band, the Sons of Blues, who played a warm-up set, provide additional musical support. After the show, amid shouts of triumph, they circulate backstage, hugging as many Biscuits as they can get their arms around. The Sons were co-instructors along with Billy during this month-long program; it's their last time together with the kids, so the jubilance is tinged with sadness. As everyone packs up to leave, guitarist Carlos Johnson has a final thought he wants to share: "Remember at the beginning, when we got together as a group, I said, 'Now we're family'? Tonight, you all showed it."

Billy adds, "Remember the things we tried you teach you—if you remember 'em, they can take you a long way."[2]

* * *

Billy Branch won't talk much about what life was like before he discovered the blues. "I ain't gonna tell ya!" he once barked at an interviewer who had asked him about his birth date. "I like to keep some shit flyin'."[3]

In fact, he was born in 1951 at the Great Lakes Naval Hospital in Great Lakes, Illinois, just north of Chicago. For a few years he and his family lived on Chicago's South Side. When he was about four, though, his grandmother packed the family into a station wagon, "like the Beverly Hillbillies,"[4] and they headed for Los Angeles, where Billy spent his childhood and most of his adolescence.

"Nothing worth mentioning": that's how he describes those years. "Little kid growin' up, that's all. My grandmother, who raised me, was a classically trained pianist. I didn't know that until after she died; we never had a piano. Her name was Mae Ella Prince. She encouraged me to take piano lessons without a piano."

He practiced those lessons on a little Magnus chord organ that had belonged to his father, who also used to play bass in a jazz combo in the army. Later on he got a bigger keyboard, and when he had the opportunity, he would go to friends' homes and practice on theirs. All in all it was a typical middle-class American childhood, as Billy remembers it. Occasionally Wolfman Jack's exotic blues and R&B programs would come in at night on one of the legendary "outlaw" radio stations in Mexico, but Billy says he barely paid that music any mind. "I listened to Motown and Hendrix, the Doors, the Stones, just like any teenager."

He did, though, become attracted to the harmonica early on. He remembers that he first saw a harp in a window at a Woolworth's, next door to where he and his mother used to go bowling ("I said, I can play that thing'").[5] When he finally got one of his own, however, he didn't think to play blues on it. "Not blues—folk, Christmas carols. It was like destiny, I guess. Because why in the hell would I keep a harmonica from eleven years old, through junior high school, through high school, to college? When one would wear out, I would buy another. It was like I was gettin' prepared for this."

When he was seventeen, Billy returned to Chicago to attend the University of Illinois at the newly constructed Chicago Circle campus, located southwest of the Loop not far from Maxwell Street. He moved in with his father and stepmother several miles away in the Lake Meadows community on the South Side ("a little middle-class enclave—walk three blocks, and you're in the 'hood"), but getting to school from there was a long and lonely commute. "I was in a very introspective state of mind," he told journalist Steven Sharp in 1998. "Kinda isolated. [Circle campus] was the coldest place—even the architecture. The atmosphere was cold. I had the blues because I didn't know anybody."[6]

In late August 1969 the lonely young college student happened to see a newspaper ad about a free concert in Grant Park, on the lakefront east of downtown. The show, billed as the Grant Park Blues Festival and subtitled "Bringing the Blues back Home," included Delta veteran Big Joe Williams, classic blues vocalist and pianist Victoria Spivey, Muddy Waters, Junior Wells, Big Mama Thornton, Earl Hooker, Koko Taylor, Otis Spann, and Willie Dixon with his Chicago Blues All-Stars. It was easily the most impressive array of blues talent ever assembled in Chicago, but it's seldom remembered today.

"I went there on a fluke," Billy recalls. "I just went down there by myself and stayed there all day. That's when I really first saw people actually playing blues harp. Junior, Big Walter—I didn't know who they were at the time, because I hadn't been indoctrinated. I was like, 'Wow! What the hell is *this?*' I was just blown away."

Inspired, he rushed home and grabbed a record by John Mayall and the Bluesbreakers—the only blues record he owned and virtually the only one he had heard up to that point—and tried to play along with it. Not knowing that most harps are tuned to specific keys, however, he didn't get very far. "Ultimately," he remembers, "I found my way into blues record shops, and I was able to start purchasing my own records—Little Walter, Sonny Boy. I'd listen to those and try to practice with 'em."

Billy also began to listen for the blues everywhere he went. He received hands-on training from a street musician named Rashaan, who used to jam with a few buddies in front of a liquor store not far from where Billy was staying. Even more important were some of the friendships he finally began to develop at the university. "My best friend on campus was Lucius Barner. He was Anna Mae's son; Anna Mae was Junior Wells's girlfriend for many years. Some of his [half-]brothers are Junior Wells's sons. So he started taking me down to the clubs—Theresa's, the Checkerboard, Pepper's. We'd go down to Sixty-ninth and King Drive [Louise's South Park Lounge], Florence's, all the spots. And we'd find new clubs. They tease me now, some of my college buddies, say, 'Man, you were crazy!' We'd be ridin' down the street and I'd hear some blues, I'd say, 'Make him stop the car—we goin' in there.'"

When they weren't cruising the South and West Sides, Billy and Lucius would visit North Side hipster hangouts like Alice's Revisited and a coffeehouse run by the Reverend Iberus Hacker, a Baptist minister/community organizer whose Old Country Church in the Appalachian (or "hillbilly") community of Uptown was a center of political and cultural activism. These were venues that offered gigs to older-style blues artists who had retained a more down-home flavor than was popular among mainstream African American listeners. Billy, unencumbered by prejudices about what was or wasn't hip, found himself enthralled. "I remember one magical night," he enthuses, "Big Red and Homesick James, I think it was, just played acoustic guitar. They were goin' at it."

By his own account Billy had been "a little shy and nerdy honor student" for most of his life, but when he got a harmonica in his hand, an amazing transformation took place:

> I would play with any damn body. It could be a country band; it could be a folk band. I would go on a jazz set. That's why all the jazz cats know me to this day. I used to play on the El. I used to play on the street. I even played in the movie theater, during the intermission; I would play on the microphone at Jack-in-the-Box and Burger King. At parties, I would pull out the harmonica. All my sisters, they'd be like, "Billy! Awww—that damn harp!" They would hide my harmonica.
> "Where's my harmonica?"
> "Uh, we don't know." I'd just play, play, play, play.[7]

He thinks the first time he tried to sit in with a blues band was probably at Theresa's, and he still remembers the look he received from Junior Wells, who ran the show there as if it were his private fiefdom ("Junior looked at me like I stole somethin'"). In those days, you didn't go to a bluesman for lessons if you wanted your hand held.

"Cotton used to take me in his Cadillac; he'd take the chromatic: 'Here! You can't do that!' I had to keep coming around before Junior really even gave me [the time of day]. Me and Junior laughed about that. I said, 'You looked at me like I wasn't shit. "Where'd you get this motherfucker?"' But I kept comin' back for more. I was determined, man."

Music wasn't all he learned. Sitting alongside the older bluesmen, he discovered an entire culture unfolding before him, a culture he came to recognize as his own by birthright, even if he had never experienced a lot of it directly.

> I recognized the richness of those guys—not only as musicians, just as people. I loved hanging around with 'em—I'd go to Homesick's house, sometimes I'd hang out with Floyd Jones or Big Red, I'd go to Big Walter's house sometimes. Sunnyland, on occasion; I spent a lot of time with [pianist] Jimmy [Walker].
> I was just so amazed—the musicianship they exhibited, the things they could do. It was very inspiring. This is really amazing music, and to think

that guys not only couldn't read and write music but couldn't read and write [at all]. The accomplishment, the musicianship is just incredible. The subtleties, like when you'd hear Big Walter and his tone, and these licks that he'd play—and Junior, and all of 'em at their prime, their peak performances. And those were the things that I think some of the guys, my generation, missed. And I think that's one of the key differences in me, that great respect that I had—I guess, to some degree, why I'm really steeped in that traditional style, even though I like to play all kinds of styles.

The chronology is a bit vague ("It's hard to remember those years, man—a lot of that's fuzzy"), but in the early or mid-1970s Billy joined forces with Jimmy Walker and a young acoustic guitarist named Pete Crawford. Walker was a veteran keyboardist with a sparse, slow-rolling style who had played around Chicago since at least the 1940s, mostly in small clubs and at private parties. The sound he created with Billy and Pete—and later drummer Steve "Twist Turner" Patterson and bassist Steve Milewski—was an easygoing blend of unadorned folksiness and laid-back urbanity, perfect for the new, predominantly white North Side circuit. It didn't take Billy long, though, to realize that the professed adulation of audiences and club owners on that circuit didn't always translate into a fair deal for the musicians.

"In my association with these great guys," he recalls, "I could see the mistreatment. It was very apparent that they weren't getting paid very much money. I remember fighting, gettin' into it, when they gave Jimmy, maybe it was twenty-five or thirty dollars—I just went off. 'Man, this guy's a legend.' Club full of people! 'How are you gonna pay this guy this?'"

That sense of justice, as well as Billy's appreciation of the deeper cultural and historical meaning of the blues, was heightened immeasurably by his next major musical association. Again, the story began on campus.

This young lady worked as a secretary at one of the offices. Her name was Sarah, and in conversation I found out she did secretarial work for Willie [Dixon]. I kept sayin', "You gotta introduce me to Willie." So finally she said, "Just take the phone number." And I called, and he said, 'C'mon down!' And I came down there [to Dixon's studio], the Blues Factory, 7711 Racine. They were rehearsing "The Last Home Run" with [vocalist] McKinley Mitchell. Carey Bell happened to be out of town, and Willie said, "You got a harp?" I didn't come there expecting to play. I think I had one harp, in this really weird key—F sharp. It happened to be the key of the song. I ended up rehearsing, and Willie said, "You know where Chess Studios is? Well, meet me there tomorrow." That was my first record.

"The Last Home Run" (or "That Last Home Run") was released on at least two of Dixon's labels, Spoonful and Yambo; it has since been reissued on Rhino. Billy sounds supple and relaxed on it, although the song itself is a pretty labored attempt by Dixon to cash in on the publicity that surrounded Hank Aaron's breaking of Babe Ruth's career home-run record in 1974. (It was actually cut before Aaron hit his historic blast on April 8 of that year; according to some reports, Dixon showed up outside Cincinnati's Riverfront Stadium hawking copies the night Aaron tied the record, on April 4.) The flipside, a breezy romp entitled "All-Star Bougee" [sic], features Big Walter Horton at his finest, skittering and swooping above a lithe twelve-bar swing-shuffle.

Billy stayed in touch with Dixon; he also kept gigging around town with the Jimmy Walker Trio, and when he wasn't working with them, he sat in wherever and whenever he could. In early 1975 harpist Little Mack Simmons organized a show he billed as a winner-take-all harp showdown. "It was on the radio," Billy remembers, "WVON."

> "I'm the world's greatest harmonica player! I'll pay anybody five hundred dollars [who] can beat me." Went down there, man, the place was packed. The Green Bunny Lounge, Seventy-ninth and Halsted.
>
> Mack [played] "Rainy Night in Georgia." I had heard it enough on the radio, so I knew it pretty good. I played it, and the crowd said, "Give him the money!"
>
> So then he said, "No, he didn't play it note for note—wait a minute!" Then he played the Four Tops' "Ain't No Woman Like the One I Got." I started playing it, then I stopped the band. I said, "Look, I know I can't play this note for note, but if I can just play something, and then Mack plays what I play . . ." and that's when Mack came out and said, "The boss said it's closing time."
>
> And the whole place went up. It was a full house. All the blues people were there; [Alligator Records'] Bruce Iglauer, Artie "Blues Boy" White told me he was there, [deejay] Mel Collins, Jim O'Neal and Amy O'Neal from Living Blues. Lonnie Brooks was playing in Mack's band. They were amazed, because people didn't really know who I was. [But] I didn't get the money.

So goes the life of the apprentice harp blower. But it was an exciting time nonetheless. The burgeoning "folk" circuit, for all its contradictions, revitalized the careers of quite a few old-timers (or as Stephen Calt uncharitably put it, placed them and their music on "the white respirator").[8] It also created a port of entry for younger bluesmen, like Billy, who might otherwise have been limited to scuffling part-time unless they wanted to conform to the slicker, more pop-tinged sounds (nascent soul-blues) that were popular among most black listeners.

In 1977 then Living Blues magazine coeditor Jim O'Neal was commissioned to put together a group of young Chicago blues musicians to appear with Willie Dixon at the Berlin Jazz Festival. They were billed as "the new generation of Chicago blues." As Billy relates,

> We were, like, the answer to the question, "Are there any young black guys playin' blues?" I think there was thirteen of us, and we comprised about three bands.
> Lucius Barner wrote "Tear Down the Berlin Wall." He said, "I can't go, but I'm gonna go in spirit." He wrote the words, and I kinda put the music to it and arranged it. When we did "Tear Down the Berlin Wall" [at the festival], Willie did a little rap thing over it that went, "If you hear the holler, answer the call / 'cause we gonna tear down the Berlin Wall!" And Willie's got crutches, and he's doin' this little step, and we got behind him, doin' this circle around him.[9]

Intentionally or not, the band had re-created the ring shout, the venerable African ritual of musical and spiritual interaction that lies at the very core of blues expression. In retrospect, it seems appropriate that an ancestral trope like that would be harnessed to proclaim such revolutionary sentiments. And in Billy's case, given the directions he moved in after he returned home, it seems downright prophetic.

"I'd always wanted to work with kids," he affirms. "I have a knack for it, and I relate to kids well. And I came to see the beauty and the power of this music. By listening to the blues you get into the roots, and of course you're going to dig deeper into the history."

He also became consumed with a passion to set right what he came to see as ongoing injustice for and mistreatment of blues musicians and disrespect for the rich cultural legacy they represent. "For me to be befriended by the legends, and to see that these guys were such masters and not getting the recognition, not getting the money—that was a compelling revelation. And I think that during the course of playing I also felt a mission to, in whatever little way I could, try to correct that. It almost compelled me to be a spokesperson for it."[10]

In 1978 Billy received an "Artist in Residency" grant from the Illinois Arts Council, and he began to work at Newberry Elementary School, on the North Side, teaching classes in blues and blues history. He didn't originate the program; drummer and playwright Jimmy Tillman had already been teaching a similar course for about a year. But Billy did the job well: "It was successful, so I got a request to come back."

He enlisted others, too. "I'd bring in guest artists like Sunnyland, Jimmy Walker, Lefty Dizz. I had Lefty Dizz up at eight thirty, nine in the morning, working with kids. He said, 'Billy, only for you.' To get these guys and introduce 'em—and these kids loved it. I mean, they absolutely loved it. [Guitarist] Smokey Smothers was [later] a regular part of Blues in the Schools, with Jimmy Walker. They were there every day. I'd pick 'em up, we'd ride to school."

Within a year or two the scope of the program expanded. "Lurrie Bell and myself, we'd travel statewide to different schools, just guitar and harp, and we'd incorporate the history of the blues within the context of the performance. We'd do those shows, man, and by the time we got to the end of the show and sang 'Got My Mojo Workin',' you'd think you were at a pop concert. Kids—different ages: grammar school, high school—were screamin', just totally into it."

Billy didn't limit his educational activities to the schoolroom. Anywhere and anytime he pulled out his harp, class was in session. After returning from Europe, he had begun gigging around town with Lurrie Bell, Freddie Dixon (Willie's bass-playing son), and some of the other younger musicians who had been on that tour. Billing themselves as the Sons of Blues (or SOBs), they boldly carried the music not just to North Side bistros but to places on the South Side where it hadn't been heard in years.

> At one point it was kind of like I was on a mission—we introduced blues on the South Side in black clubs that didn't have blues. Mother's Lounge, on Seventy-ninth Street, the first place I got, talkin' to the owner, said, "I play blues."
>
> "Ah, you don't play blues!" Went and got my record [probably either volume 3 of Alligator's *Living Chicago Blues* anthology or the SOBs' early 1980s live recording on the German L&R label]. "Oh, man, I think we need to start a night. It'll be great!" We booked this thing, "Monday Night Fish Fry"—free food—and it was packed every Monday. Just on a fluke.
>
> Then somebody saw me [from another club] two blocks down the street; we ended up working two nights there. They already had live entertainment—soul, rhythm and blues, jazz—so when we first came in there, people kinda looked at us like, "Uh-uh." You know, they didn't dig it; they weren't receptive to us at first. But we baptized 'em. After a couple of months they was right there with us. On Monday, Seventy-ninth and Saginaw; Wednesdays, the Raven at Eighty-eighth and Stoney [Island]; then Thursdays and Sundays at Mother's. Four nights, within, like, a three-mile radius. Every club had its own crowd. And it was always a good crowd every week.

As if teaching and fronting the SOBs weren't already enough work, Billy also took over the harp slot in Willie Dixon's Chicago Blues All-Stars after Carey Bell decided to go off on his own. It was rough going at first ("Blowin' so hard, my lips are bleedin' every night—I found out I wasn't as good as I thought I was").[11] Just as when he had chafed under the tutelage of Junior Wells and James Cotton at Theresa's, however, he accepted the struggle as part of the dues and rode it out. He still smiles about the time the All-Stars played a festival in Mexico City and Big Walter Horton, who was also on the show, left him gasping for air.

"Walter was coming behind us," he relates. "And I'm blowin' everything I thought I knew—I know he's in the wings—then I come off the stage. Big Walter says, 'Oh, y'try to hurt the old man, huh?' And he said, 'Now, watch this.' And he got out there, man, played a few tunes, then he jumped into 'La Cucaracha,' started wavin' that one arm, and the crowd went nuts! There I was—got my head cut again."

Willie Dixon, of course, is one of the seminal figures of the postwar era. He had written such songs as "I'm Your Hoochie Coochie Man" and "I'm Ready" for Muddy Waters; "Spoonful," "Back Door Man," "Little Red Rooster," and "Wang Dang Doodle" for Howlin' Wolf (the last tune became Koko Taylor's trademark after she scored a hit with it in 1966); "You Can't Judge a Book by Its Cover" for Bo Diddley; and hundreds of others. He had also been an A&R (artist and repertoire) man for Chess and other labels during the 1950s and 1960s—it was sometimes said that if you wanted to cut a blues record in Chicago, you had to go through Willie first—and he had played bass on some of the most important blues and early rock 'n' roll sides to come out of the city. Known as a savvy marketeer and self-promoter, he reveled in his role as patriarch (he titled a song, an LP, and his autobiography *I Am the Blues*). Nonetheless, he was also sincerely dedicated to furthering awareness of the blues, both as music and as living cultural history. His insights and enthusiasm spurred Billy's own determination to carry the torch.

"Willie was the philosopher of the blues," Billy attests.

I loved the blues already, but I developed a deeper understanding and deeper appreciation—I mean, he lived and breathed it, and he was very proud that this was black folk music, and this was the black people's contribution to America. He wrote a letter to the FCC, and to every member of Congress, stating that there was a conspiracy to keep the blues off the radio. And I remember our conversation, sitting in the Mexico City airport. He said, "You think about it. If it became known that your heritage is just as rich as my heritage, then what basis do I have to put you down?" Willie made the correlation that by keeping the blues hidden, you're keeping history, African American history, hidden. In other words, dig deeper into the history, then you'll find a lot of unknown treasures and accomplishments. Which just blew me away, y'know? A very profound statement.

In the early 1980s, after about six years with the All-Stars, Billy left to devote himself full-time to leading the Sons of Blues. Life on the free-living club and roadhouse circuit was a long way from the cloistered academic atmosphere in which he had spent much of his previous life, and he has admitted that in those days he and his bandmates "were young and crazy, . . . doin' things that young and crazy cats did." But the formidable Dixon, who had worked hard to groom Billy as a successor, took his legacy seriously. He kept as sharp an eye on his rambunctious young protégé as he could. "I'd get a summons," Billy has remembered. "'Hey, Willie wants to see you.' And I'd be like, 'Oh no, not now. Not now!' And I'd go into that dressing room, and usually it'd be some little cold six-by-eight, six-by-six square little box of a dressing room, and [Dixon would say], 'Now, I told you. Just about everybody with me goes on and enjoys a good career. You got a great future. But you can't keep on this way.'"[12]

Billy responded by honing his focus and building the SOBs into an internationally feted unit. Their initial early 1980s sides on Alligator and L&R, solidly rooted in the postwar Chicago style but spiced with R&B, pop, and jazz-fusion flavorings, helped revitalize and sustain the blues as a force in the contemporary musical marketplace. Even the band's stage presence was inspiring: hip and sexy, they oozed urbanity while their music invoked deep roots. This was, of course, pretty much the image bluesmen had purveyed since time immemorial, but it was a revelation to younger fans who had bought into the stereotype of the blues as "folk" music purveyed by Mississippi farmers or sad-eyed old men in backstreet ghetto flats.

Over the years the SOBs have maintained both the sound and the image with remarkable consistency, despite numerous personnel changes. Mose Ruteus, the burly drummer whom Billy has characterized as "the old standby," has held down the percussion chair since the early 1980s. But a host of fretmen—including Lurrie Bell, John Watkins, Carl Weathersby, and Carlos Johnson—have come and gone (and sometimes come back: Carlos, for one, has been in and out several times). Through it all the music has remained raw and raucous in the great juke-joint tradition yet shot through with aggressive improvisational vision. For all his self-characterization as a dedicated roots man, Billy and his band span a wide a range of stylistic influences. Even when they're paying homage, they can blaze new trails. For example, they've worked up a turbo-charged version of Little Walter's "Juke" that retains the original's combination of gutbucket rawness and jump-blues sophistication yet shoots off in postmodernist directions fueled by the band's triplet-sculpted intro, Billy's genre-jumping solo lines, and the multilayered rhythmic impetus provided by Rutues and bassist Nick Charles.

Early SOBs (clockwise): Jeff Ruffin, Jerry Murphy, John Williams, Lurrie Bell, and Billy Branch, ca. 1981. Photo courtesy Billy Branch

"You can't do the lump-de-lump, twelve-bar shuffle all night," Billy offers by way of explanation. "You certainly can't do that today unless you're one of the elders. You have to play to your audience." And the SOBs, in their various incarnations, have always been an eclectic crew of willful musicians from diverse backgrounds, each capable of taking the lead at any given time and each adding his own personal stamp to the overall sound.

But for the most part Billy has not overtly channeled his cultural politics into his music, a tendency that sets him apart from some other contemporary blues artists, such as Alabama's venerable Willie King and younger firebrands like Michael Hill and Chris Thomas King—or for that matter, Willie Dixon, who once mailed copies of his "It Don't Make Sense (You Can't Make Peace)" to every member of Congress. His playing is a living history lesson, however, blending ideas and techniques he learned from role models like Carey Bell, Junior Wells, and Big Walter into shapes both evocative and new. Still, aside from his participation in the "Tear Down the Berlin Wall" ring shout with shaman Dixon, he has tended to eschew overtly political musical statements.

It's in his teaching that Billy's passion for the roots of the music, as well as his fiery insistence that those roots be understood in their historical and cultural context, manifests itself most powerfully. Since his initial success with Blues in the Schools in the late 1970s, he has maintained and expanded the program despite whatever other projects have come his way. Aside from pursuing his ongoing work in Chicago, he has taught month-long classes in Seattle; Charleston, South Carolina; and elsewhere. He also presents an annual minicourse in Helena, Arkansas, to ready a troupe of youngsters for the King Biscuit Blues Festival ("We only have those kids four days, then they're onstage"), and he has done stints in Davenport, Iowa, and other communities.

And it continues to grow. In 2003 Billy launched a project in coordination with Operation PUSH to reach more Chicago-area youngsters. At least two other Chicago-based musicians, Fernando Jones (a former protégé of Billy's) and Fruteland Jackson, have put together their own school-based projects in the wake of Billy's success, and similar initiatives have sprouted up all over the country. Although he's always careful to credit Jimmy Tillman with pioneering the program, Billy is at least as proud of his still-growing legacy as an educator as he is of anything he has achieved onstage or on record.

"I've never had an unsuccessful Blues in the Schools program," he asserts.

I've had thousands of encounters, in classroom and performance situations. A large part is audience participation. I have the kids come up—I still do this—and after they get up there, I tell 'em they're slaves. I have one pickin' cotton, one choppin' wood, one pantomiming playing the guitar, and one pantomiming playing the harp. We trace it, showing the roots of the blues from slavery and bringing it up to date. And the kids love it.

The key with kids is, show them the universality of the blues. Specially when we go into some of the black schools, you can hear, "Aww man, *blues?* I don't wanna!" But after we start playing and going through the whole program, then we got 'em. I say "What gives you the blues?"

"Teachers!"

"Homework!"

"Well, let's write a song about it": "Didn't do my homework today, can't go out and play / I feel so bad, just like a ball game on a rainy day!" Y'know?

And after they get into it, the kids, man, they come up with things, things from their own lives that are really deep. I remember, "I'm gonna kill myself in the broad daylight. . . ." One wrote about the first Gulf War: "We didn't want the war, now it's here / Everybody's livin' in fear / Soldiers fighting on Saudi soil / The military dying over oil." I remember one, at a school in Robert Taylor [Homes], wrote about "gangsters rapin' little girls / what else would they do in this cold, cold world / This world is just like hell / those men should be put in jail."

Mr. Branch and some attentive prodigies: Ft. Smith, Arkansas, early 1990s. Photo courtesy Billy Branch

It's important, man—it's so important. Hip-hop's got the world on a string right now; it's important for kids to know where this music came from. Rap is really nothing new. In some form or another it's been there all the time. It's the "Voice of the Angry Youth." You have a whole community of people who've been neglected, for lack of a better word, and there's a lot of anger. And sometimes, unfortunately, it comes out in a lot of very negative ways. But it reflects—as the blues did—as Willie defines it, "the facts of life." This is the way it is.

Billy is also adamant that students of diverse backgrounds and ethnicities need to learn these facts. "I've always felt that black history shouldn't just be taught to black youngsters. It should be taught as part of American history, which it is. And blues is a very important part of American musical history, and it's important that white youngsters know that, as well."[13]

Yet he continues to maintain just as strongly that the blues is first and foremost "black folk music." In both his conversation and his public statements, he steadfastly champions African Americans as its progenitors and most important torch carriers. This puts him in a somewhat delicate position: he got his start, at least partly, on Chicago's white North Side circuit (a white harpist, Jim Liban, was among the first to welcome him onto a stage), and his first professional band included a white guitarist and later a white drummer and a white bassist. The SOBs themselves arose out of a gig organized for a mostly white European audience; they've been integrated since the 1990s (as of 2004 they included two Japanese members); and despite their weekly gig at a South Side club called Artis', which carries on the tradition Billy began at Mother's back in the 1980s, their audiences remain predominantly white.

At least as far as those audiences are concerned, Billy is delighted with the ever-widening reception the blues has garnered. "Awareness is [still] growing," he exults.

> Any time you have one of the world-renowned motion picture directors [Martin Scorsese] take a major project devoted to just blues, that's lettin' you know something right there. The vision has expanded to that level. Regardless of the critical assessment, whether you liked it [or] you didn't like it, just the fact that he touched it is a statement in itself. You got festivals, a network of festivals, worldwide. It's not played on mainstream radio, it's rarely televised, but yet you have millions of fans, from continent to continent, that support this music.
>
> To me it's the most powerful music on the planet. It's African American folk music, and it's the music of the world. It's the only music [named for an actual] feeling; you can say, "I have this feeling, I have the blues." It's universal—everyone gets the blues. Doesn't matter what nationality or social status you maintain.

Nonetheless, despite the ongoing viability of neighborhood scenes in communities such as Chicago's South and West Sides, there's no doubt that mainstream black listenership is far from the prime supporter of this "music of the world." B. B. King has said that he has gone offstage and cried at the lack of appreciation his blues gets from his own people. Billy must feel a similar sting, but he refuses to admit that things have to be that way.

> At Artis' now, it's a mixed audience. Sometimes you'll have more Japanese than black. But we do get young and older black people, regulars down there, that do come and support us. And we've been there almost twenty years. I was a special guest, a [soul-blues] show at Mr. G's. I did "Help Me"—and the whole damn place got on their feet. You couldn't even see me, 'cuz everybody was on the dance floor. I'm playin' the harp. They loved it!
> If one major station would just program blues one hour a day—not just the soul-blues, I'm talkin' about a mixture—they'd be the number 1 station. If radio would just catch up with the pulse of the people. I mean, think about it—there's thousands of festivals around the world, and everybody's making records, and they're getting bought. There's an audience. But these [major] record companies and radio stations aren't tuned in.

When they do "tune in," though, other problems can arise, many having to do with a trend that seems to be increasingly embraced by "mainstream" (i.e., white) observers (including critics and more than a few musicians): redefining the blues as "just notes" or "just a feeling," devoid of any broader context or implication except, perhaps, the vapidly rebellious stance that has come to be associated with rock 'n' roll. Even when it's acknowledged that the most important blues artists have been African American, that their music evolved from traditions that extended back to slavery and to Africa before that, and that many elements of what might be termed "the blues life" are rooted in conditions experienced by African Americans from the earliest days of bondage into the modern era—that's simply "history." And in America, when we say something is "history," we usually mean it's a dead issue.

Billy isn't the only blues artist to have addressed these considerations, but he has found himself on the front lines of the debate in recent years, even though he has taken pains to emphasize that he begrudges no one the opportunity to participate fully in the music at any level. "I've never questioned anybody's 'right' to be a musician and play whatever music," he insists. "In all honesty, to the credit of some of the white players, they are the ones that are picking up on the old harmonica style. They're the ones that actually play that with authority."

But he has made it clear that he's unhappy with the way the cultural heritage represented by the blues is being obscured—if not aggressively denied—by forces in the industry. In his 1998 *Living Blues* interview with Steve Sharp he addressed the situation:

> There's a discrepancy here in that the fact remains that this is black folk music. And I think that in these days and times that fact has become kind of [ignored] because you find the Stevie Ray Vaughans, the Johnny Winters, and the Eric Claptons . . . but there's not gonna be a white Little Walter, or a white B. B. King, or a white Albert King. There's something in the black experience that defies, probably, definition. And the best of the best of the white players I don't believe can compete with the best of the best of the black players.[14]

He went on to point out how barely postpubescent white prodigies like Jonny Lang can pop up of out nowhere and achieve international acclaim ("Where did these people come from? I been in here close to thirty years and I never heard of 'the legendary so-and-so'"), while veteran black artists have continued to work and die in relative poverty and obscurity, "and these new guys couldn't hold a candle to 'em."[15]

None of which should have been earth-shattering news by 1998, and Billy again tempered his observations by reaffirming that "any musician has a right to play whatever he wants to play, and there are damn good white and other ethnic musicians playing the blues . . . and if they're good, they deserve to be heard."[16] Nevertheless, reaction to his comments was severe: "I got called 'ignorant racist.' . . . I tend to get in trouble when I get into these kinda topics." As a result, he has become leery of reentering those waters. "I don't want to get too deep in this," he demurred when we spoke in 2003, "'cuz I gotta go out here and make a living."

Part of the problem, as Billy tacitly acknowledges, is that it's hard to speak of these things in terms that aren't either maddeningly abstract or futilely rhetorical. On a purely musical level, Billy believes that there are elements of blues expression that anyone who hasn't been deeply touched by the diasporan heritage will find difficult to replicate: "The blues has so many subtleties," he told Sharp. "There are 12 bars and three chord changes. Easy. Anybody can play that shit. But to really play it and make the statement, to create that feeling, you gotta know what the hell you're doin', and it comes from the South. It's a tradition. I was fortunate enough to be around the old timers. I always listened. If they told me to do X, Y, I did it to the best of my ability."[17]

Yet as Billy concedes, white artists have learned to play these styles with facility, and at least in some cases, they've assumed a significant role in keeping them alive. And to complicate matters, Billy isn't entirely thrilled with the direction a lot of black blues players have taken, either: "Guys are playin' the blues, and—I don't know, maybe I'm an old fogy or somethin'—but when those guys like Big Walter and Louis Myers and Sammy Lawhorn would play, I mean, that was classic stuff, man. And again, these guys died unheralded, they died in poverty. And now, the new breed, they're not pickin' up on it, on the nuances, the subtleties. It's almost a lost art."[18].

Even many black performers, of course, play the blues primarily for white audiences these days. And part of what can get lost when the blues crosses that ethnic/culture line is the affirming communal celebration that manifests almost every time music—or, for that matter, any public performance—takes place in an indigenously African American setting. "The whole black experience is an oral culture," Billy affirms. "It's an oral tradition—'Yeah, baby!' 'That's what I'm talkin' 'bout!' 'I hear you!' Even to the point of black folks when they go into the movie theater, commentin' during the movie. It's just a cultural thing."

And it goes beyond the trappings of the ritual itself. In core black culture (to use Gwaltney's term),[19] the public sphere—the church, the classroom, the entertainment venue, "the street"—is also an arena of social solidarity. This sphere constitutes a place where shared consciousness arising from common history and common struggle ("We are the blues," as Amiri Baraka puts it)[20] informs and adds meaning to the activities that take place there. "Black musicians will always say this," Billy affirms. "You can't BS black audiences about playing blues. You can get away with a lot more with white audiences. But them folks, whether they are 100 percent blues lovers or not, they know the blues. Somebody in their family, or one of their relatives—somewhere there's a blues connection. Whether they want to admit it or not. And they may not have to say anything, but they'll let you know. For black audiences, you got to come on with it."

Still, despite the satisfaction Billy reaps from his gig at Artis' and his down-home moments at soul-blues strongholds like Mr. G's, what musicians usually have to "come on with" for black audiences is no longer the blues Billy cherishes as the essence of "African American folk music." When busloads of white tourists hit the West and South Sides on city-sponsored pub crawls, bandleaders sometimes instruct their charges to play the blues—that is, three-chord twelve-bar shuffles—for as long as the visitors are in the house; after things clear out, they return to their usual funk, pop, and soul-blues repertoire.

Billy thus finds himself caught in the middle of a paradoxical and ironic cultural divide. It's evident as well in his long-running campaign to get the blues on the air. "It's got to be played on black radio," he insists, but most black-oriented stations, if they deign to play blues at all, focus primarily on soul-blues. White disc jockeys, meanwhile, still tend toward a traditionalist ideology that often excludes almost anything that sounds influenced by funk, R&B, or any other component of post-1960s pop culture. Billy says he's gone back and forth with deejays about playing the SOBs' records: "'It's too new.' Well, you used to say, 'It's too old!' You gotta make up your mind! We're *here*. We're *making records.*"

As if to throw down yet another, even fiercer challenge to these self-limiting arbiters of the status quo, in 2004 Billy and Louisiana-based guitarist Kenny Neal released *Double Take* (Alligator), a percussionless, all-acoustic CD that masterfully evokes the classic harp-and-guitar duet sound (Billy, as usual, reveled in his mix-and-match homages to role models like Big and Little Walter, Sonny Boy numbers 1 and 2, and Carey Bell); at the same time, however, it also recasts some of the most venerable diasporan themes in a modern context. Reversing the usual migratory imagery, Neal's "Going to the Country" portrays a dissatisfied urbanite returning to the land of his roots ("I don't need burglar bars / Don't have to smell the pollution from all those cars"). Billy addresses similar ideas on "Northern Man Blues" ("I was born in the North, y'all, but my heart was in the South"), while his ballsy machismo on chestnuts like Muddy's "Mannish Boy" serves as a pointed reminder of the direct link between the cocksure strut of earlier bluesmen and the street-tough pose of modern rappers. The pair also deliver a stark reading of Kenny's song "The Son I Never Knew," a wrenching tale of familial discord set to a minor-key contemporary pop-blues framework on which Billy's harp wails, moans, and scurries desperately over the top.

It's that kind of roots-rich exploration—"Ancient to the Future," to use the long-time slogan of Chicago's Association for the Advancement of Creative Musicians—in which Billy most excels, and despite the sometimes strained blend of tradition and modern ideas and influences that increasingly characterizes the SOBs' sound, it's where he seems determined to focus his energies in the long run. Embracing both paradox and irony, he admits that he might someday have to leave home (again) to do it: "I've always had the feeling that I would never leave Chicago," he told Steve Sharp. "But it's changed now. The reason I didn't want to leave is because I couldn't get anywhere else the things that I could get here, and the reason was the old timers. But the old timers are dyin' and you know, it's not the same. . . . Carl (Weathersby) said it right when he said (in *Living Blues*), 'It's a new blues.' It is, which I respect, and which I enjoy playin' to a degree. But the cats are gone."[21]

For now, though, Chicago is both the home and the front line of attack in the good fight to nurture the spirit of the blues as Billy Branch feels, plays,

Billy Branch at the Chicago Blues Festival, 1997. Photo by Paul Natkin/Photo Reserve

and lives it. It's also, of course, the base of his Blues in the Schools activities. "There's a lot of raw talent," he enthuses. "Some of these kids are just exceptional, the talent that they have. I mean writing, as well as playing. It's there—it's like raw material."

The same holds true for the talent on the bandstands, even if some of it is embodied in that new breed who insist on tweaking—and sometimes bludgeoning—the nuances and subtleties of the older styles. "The blues is so open right now," Billy concludes, "and there are so many possibilities. There's a vanguard here in Chicago—Lurrie Bell, Melvin Taylor, Carl Weathersby, Carlos Johnson and, yeah, myself—that's yet to be acknowledged. The power of the blues is manifesting itself. Still, to this day, people, if they can't hear it, they don't know what it is. And I've got a lot of contacts, and it's time [for] what I'm doin'—spreadin' the word, spreadin' the news, spreadin' the blues."

10 Sharon Lewis

"I've Lived through Some Treacherous Times"

> Only the blues can talk to me,
> only the blues knows how I feel

When Sharon Lewis sings "Mother Blues," her voice toughens, smooths into a croon, and then suddenly tears into a knife-edged shriek. Eyes clamped shut, body writhing, she looks and sounds as if she has given herself over to a power both terrifying and redemptive, as if the only source of strength she has left is to surrender, to open herself completely to vicissitude and pain in order to emerge cleansed:

> She stopped by this morning
> and took complete control
> and crawled inside my body
> and began to massage my soul . . .
>
> Only the blues can talk to me,
> only the blues knows how I feel;
> The blues don't take no prisoners,
> Mother Blues just tells it like it is.[1]

As the veteran guitarist Honeyboy Edwards wrote in his autobiography *The World Don't Owe Me Nothing*, the blues is "something that leads you,"[2] a restlessness born of both unhappiness and hope. The dream of freedom—the resolute belief, often against all evidence and odds, that there can even be such a thing as freedom in this world—is one of the most forceful presences in blues lore and lyrics. But the other side of freedom is abandonment; the other side of independence is the pain of isolation. The same Robert Johnson who in "Sweet Home Chicago" boldly proclaimed his refusal to be shackled or tied down ("I'm heavy loaded, baby / I'm booked, I got to go") also sang of being tormented by hellhounds and of being stranded, terrified and alone, at a crossroads at nightfall. It's one of the archetypal blues paradoxes—or for that matter, one of the archetypal paradoxes of the human condition. Sharon Lewis has lived that paradox for most of her life.

Nurtured as a young girl in a loving but strict religious household where the sole purpose of music was to praise the Lord and the sole purpose of life was to serve him, Sharon found herself thrust early on into another world, a world of mistreatment and betrayal in which love itself came laden with treachery. She came to crave sanctuary and yet to distrust it. No shelter—emotional or otherwise—seemed able to hold her, but without it she felt anchorless and alone. It's the story, more or less, of every dispossessed blues traveler who ever hit the road or hopped a freight train, except that in Sharon's case there was no name to give it, no shape to mold her yearnings. In Sharon's world a good Christian girl did not sing the blues; a woman of faith did not even express—let alone sing about—despair, except in penitence or praise.

Sharon, then, was living the blues long before she discovered the music. Today her conversation returns again and again to the revelatory power she felt when she finally got the chance to experience the liberating spirit of celebration, self-worth, and survival represented by the blues as both performance and musical style. Although she didn't come to it until she was grown, by her own account she had been a blues woman, primed and ready, for most of her life.

"When I'm performing," she proclaims, "I feel transformed. I sing, 'Only the blues knows how I feel.' That's the truth for me. Redemption, relief—awareness. What I was searching for in my life for a long time, the blues fill that void. But for a long time I didn't even recognize it. I did not even recognize it."

* * *

The blues was the furthest thing from Sharon Washington's mind when she was a little girl growing up in Ft. Worth, Texas. "I was raised by my grandmother," she remembers.

My mom's mother. My mother, Jessie Mae Washington, died a week before my first birthday. My dad, off and on in my life. I haven't seen him since I was about nine years old.

My grandmother was an incredible woman—probably where I got my strength from. Her name was Maude Anna Odell Childs Bennett. Everybody called her "Sister." She had married Tom Williams; he died, and she married Elmo Bennett. He was a yardman, what people call now a landscaper. I called him "Dad"—he was the love of my life. My fondest memory of him was him coming home, and me kissing him, and he tasted like salt. I will never forget that as long as I live.

My grandmother was very resourceful. She was an old country woman, and she could cook her ass off. She got up every morning and made biscuits. I'd stand there—little girl—and I'd pinch the dough every time she turned her back, and eat it raw. Nothin' like a raw baking powder dough biscuit. I don't eat biscuits to this day 'cuz she don't make 'em.

It was a tight-knit household, nurturing and full of love, but it was also conservative—even repressive—in ways that would resonate for Sharon and eventually haunt her throughout her life:

My grandmother was extremely religious. Fire and brimstone. "This is from the Bible. This is it. It's not to be questioned." And God help you if you did.

We were not allowed to participate in anything in school. I learned to read from the Bible. We couldn't wear short-sleeved blouses; I didn't wear pants until I was nine years old, and that was after she died. Me and my two sisters sang in church; I played a little red tambourine. My grandmother taught us "Will the Circle Be Unbroken." I still remember that song; we get together, we'll sing that song.

Texas in the late 1950s and early 1960s was a hotbed of musical innovation. Jazz-tinged blues artists like T-Bone Walker and Gatemouth Brown, who had codified the swinging, jump-oriented southwestern style, packed tony nightclubs and wide-open country roadhouses alike. Older bluesmen like Houston's redoubtable Lightnin' Hopkins still commanded loyal followings in jukes and cafes; hot-blooded youngsters like Johnny "Guitar" Watson, Albert Collins, and Johnny Copeland were taking their elders' ideas, infusing them with rock 'n' roll energy, and forging revolutionary new sounds. On the white side of town, youths like Buddy Holly and Waylon Jennings borrowed riffs and rhythms from the blues, adding brash rockabilly exuberance to pump up the high lonesome sounds of their C&W forebears, such as the revered and still-potent Ernest Tubb. As if that weren't enough, Clifton Chenier, the Louisiana zydeco king, barnstormed constantly throughout the Gulf Coast region, melding blues, zydeco, R&B, and even country into a tantalizing, forward-looking mix. But for Sharon Washington, safely ensconced in the protective arms of God and Grandma, such music was as remote and unfathomable as the sinful pleasures and dangerous freedoms it foretold.

"From the time I was born until the time I was nine years old," she says, "I have no recollection of music in my life other than church music. We didn't listen to the radio. We weren't allowed to—there was no gospel radio. If it did not glorify the Lord, it was evil. And that stuck. I mean, even to this day I still have to kind of check myself, at fifty years old. That's how it was stuck, just indelible. I think, I believe, I know I've made peace. But it is still there."

Nonetheless, those early years under the stern but loving eye of Maude Anna Bennett remain the most treasured in Sharon's memory. Why? "She took care of me. We didn't have a lot, but we had food, we had shelter, and I remember playing with my sisters and brothers, being together as a family."

That family, along with most of the rest of Sharon's world, was torn apart on October 3, 1961, when her grandmother died, nine years to the day after her mother's death.

After she died, I stayed for a year with my mother's brother. I call it my year from hell. I was physically, mentally, sexually abused. We had no gas, no lights, not a single luxury. They had three other children besides me. For years I didn't eat coconut, because we fought over a box of coconut 'cuz there was nothing in the house to eat.

As it turned out, the lady next door was attentive enough, she saw a change in me over the year that I was there. She had the wherewithal to find my sister. She called and said, "Listen: if you care *anything* about your baby sister, you come get her."

But before her sister could rescue her, Sharon's aunt decided to jettison the little girl herself.

My aunt just abandoned me like a dog. She took me to my uncle's first wife's house, and walked off and left me. She looked at me—I was nine years old—she said, "I'm goin' to California. What are you gonna do?" I remember her very vividly, taking her three children and walking down the street and leaving me standing there.

What am I gonna *do*? I don't know. I had no clue! At nine years old, I don't even know what California *is*. "I'm lost! I'm abandoned!" I'm thinkin'. My mom left me, my grandmother left me—what else can go wrong? My cousin came home, and he looked, and he said, "Sharon?"

I said, "Charles?"

"What are you doin' here?"

"Nora Lee left me."

"What do you mean, she left you?"

I said, "She left me!"

"What?"

"Yeah!"

Cousin Charles was a kindly man, and he did his best to make Sharon feel secure: "He made me a baloney sandwich with two pieces of meat—'You gon' put two pieces of meat on there? Two pieces of baloney? *And* cheese?' I was in heaven." In fact, after all she had been through, his house was a blessed sanctuary. But it wasn't home, and for a while it seemed as if she might never have a place to call home again.

"Finally my sister came and got me. I know there were these hushed discussions—'What are we gonna do with Sharon?' She had two children of her own, she was raising my two sisters, and my second oldest brother lived with her, in a two-bedroom house. She had her hands full. I understand now. I didn't then, 'cuz I wanted to stay with my sister."

They eventually decided to send Sharon to her grandmother's sister Ruby, in Lawton, Oklahoma. She had been to Oklahoma before, to visit her great-grandmother in Chickasaw, but now the thought of moving even farther away from her remaining immediate family was terrifying. It seemed as if the recurring nightmare of flight and abandonment would never end.

"I remember my sisters driving off and leaving me. And I thought, 'I'm not gonna stay here.' I had no clothes, mind you. My aunt, I don't know what she did with 'em; I had no clothes. But I actually liked it. It didn't take long for me to start calling my great-aunt 'Mom.'"

The trauma and fear of the previous few years receded. "I started school in Lawton in the fourth grade. Ahhh! Music could be joyful without going to hell. I was in a choir, I was a cheerleader, I was a majorette, I learned to dance—R&B, Motown Sam and Dave, 'Hold On, I'm Comin'.' Oh my god! There were times when I thought my grandmother was gonna [come back and] touch me on the shoulder."

Although she insists she never got too wild, she admits that "it was a time of release." When she was fifteen, in ninth grade, she got pregnant. She returned to high school after her son, William, was born, but she soon moved out of her great-aunt's house. Despite the responsibilities of motherhood, she was free to pursue life as she chose.

"I saw Tina Turner when I was sixteen," she smiles. "Ike and Tina Turner Revue, at a show at [the] National Guard armory. I met her, in Oklahoma again, in a different venue, at a hall. I used to dance with a friend of mine. They were watching us dance, and we got invited backstage to meet her. She was very nice—'You guys could travel with us. You could open the show!'"

Sharon never seriously considered joining the Revue; among other things,

Ike's mercurial backstage behavior "was too much a reminder of growing up—the yelling and screaming and 'What the hell is going on?'" Instead, she married a soldier from the nearby Ft. Sill army base, a native Chicagoan who was about to ship out to Germany. It wasn't the most romantic union in the world: "He said, 'What we gonna do?' I was like, 'I dunno—we can get married!'" It did bring her north, however, at least for a while. She stayed with his mother in Chicago and began to learn a little about the city, continuing her education at Wendell Phillips High School, the famous South Side school that such luminaries as Nat Cole, Dinah Washington, and Sam Cooke had attended. After her husband returned from overseas, he came north and joined her for a while. But the marriage foundered, and she soon moved back to Oklahoma.

Sharon ended up going to California with a new boyfriend, another soldier, who turned out to be "a straight-up street nigger—pimp, hustler, drug dealer, the whole bit": "He came home crazy as hell one night and put a gun in my head, and he said, 'Bitch, if I can't have you, ain't nobody gonna have you!' I said, 'Okay, I can't take this. I'm just gon' let him have California!'"

She had learned enough about Chicago to feel comfortable in the city. So in 1975, like generations of migrants before her, she headed north, fleeing oppression and mistreatment, determined to build a new life.

Sharon had never had a problem landing a job—even in California, amid all the craziness, she had worked for a prestigious insurance company—so it didn't take her long to get a foothold. When she began dating a CPA named John Lewis, it looked as if her long-deferred dream of stability and emotional sustenance might come to fruition. They married in 1978, and their daughter, Shallon Jonelle—for "Sharon and John"—was born the following year.

It was a good life, at least for a while. John and Sharon sang in a gospel group that appeared at the Chicago Gospel Festival in the early 1980s. She was also beginning to make peace with the formidable, ever-looming spirit of Sister Maude Anna Bennett.

"At this point," Sharon remembers, "I was getting over a lot of my inhibitions about religion and things like that." She and her husband went clubbing around town, taking in the music of artists like Thelma Houston, Peabo Bryson, and the late Phyllis Hyman ("she was a goddess to me"). Once again, however, Sharon's relentless hunger for both independence and intimacy created a tension that began to tighten around her. Inevitably it ruptured, and it took her marriage with it.

"I was in my midthirties. I had a very stressful job, [and] I had started [college] at Loyola, full-time. I couldn't find a babysitter—nobody wanted to keep a black baby. I'd get up at four or five o'clock in the morning, take the bus or the train to work, so I'd have time to study. I wouldn't be home till seven, seven-thirty. I wanted to do things, I wanted to—I wanted to be somebody, goddammit!"

"I ended up leaving," she concludes and then clarifies with a wry laugh: "I put him out."

Regardless of who did the actual leaving, Sharon had already taken flight by the time she and John divorced in 1988. "I was pregnant by someone else. Jesse, my youngest son. My real mother's name was Jessie Mae; his dad's grandfather and uncle were Jessie and Jessie Jr. I was the last of my mother's children; I honored her, even though I didn't know her."

Sharon eventually earned a bachelor's degree in management and industrial psychology, and she found a job at Northwestern University as a faculty assistant. Then, in the early 1990s, she stumbled on the opportunity for which she had unknowingly been searching nearly her entire life—although she didn't recognize it when it first appeared.

"My girlfriend said, 'Let's go holla at the blues.'" She smiles, chuckling as she remembers her initial reaction. "I'm like—'Whaat?' She says, 'There's this blues joint over at Seventy-first and South Chicago—come on!' I'm like, 'Uh, okay. No biggie.' And she took me there."

The blues joint was Lee's Unleaded Blues, a legend among aficionados since the 1970s, when it was known as Queen Bee's and hosted shows by the likes of Junior Wells and guitarist Lefty Dizz. From the mid-1980s through the early 1990s, the house band was led by the late guitarist Buddy Scott, whose wife Pat sang in the featured slot around midnight. Pat Scott was and is a flamboyant entertainer who stalks through the crowd while singing, enticing heated reactions from men and women alike: patrons rise from their seats to stuff folded-up dollar bills into her fist, dance front of her, or just get in her face and shout jubilant responses as she hollers and signifies at them. Her showstopper is her version of Lucille Spann's "Country Girl Returns" ("If you don't put nothin' in / You can't take nothin' out"), a torchy anthem that combines a celebration of body and appetite from a big beautiful woman who demands satisfaction as her due, an in-your-face proclamation of sexual prowess, and a girlfriend-to-girlfriend dish session about no-good men and how to keep them in line. From her first kittenish purr to her final ascending shout, her entire show is a festival of life, an in-the-moment summoning of power and spirit. This was exactly the medicine Sharon Lewis's soul had been craving.

"She took every idea that I had formed about blues," Sharon affirms, "and she *removed* 'em. Oh, she turned my head around. The perception I had of the blues—you know, 'knock my woman down, gon' drag her back home by her hair,' that kinda thing? And here's this *woman* up there—and a very handsome woman, I might add, who seemed to have her shit together—talkin' 'bout what *she's* gonna do. 'Shot my man five times, they left him for dead / I stood over his head, raised my dress / and the man raised his head!' I'm tellin' you! I said, '*Sho' 'nuff.*'"

The atmosphere at the club was almost as much a revelation as Pat Scott's performance was. "It's a party," Sharon marvels, still wide-eyed more than ten years later.

> I was being *entertained*. By *blues*. And the blues artists, they were so easy to get close to—they're sitting right beside you in the club. And it would be this whole row of people sitting there who would get up and sing, and I'd be like, "When is the real band gonna come up?"
> "Honey, you can't pay for this show!"

Enthralled, Sharon became a semiregular at Lee's as well as at another, less formal South Side venue, a hidden cul-de-sac off Fifty-fifth Street known as "the Alley," where bands would set up outside and play as folks barbecued and partied on summer Sunday afternoons. Her head still spinning from these experiences, she then fell into an even more exciting opportunity at work.

"It was a family picnic thing," she remembers.

> I was on the entertainment committee. We were sitting there thinking. I said, "So-and-so plays drums, such-and-such plays guitar, someone else plays bass, someone else plays harmonica—we can be the band."
> I did Tina Turner's "Proud Mary." They called it my magnum opus. I had so many compliments! When I came back to work my e-mail was full. I decided, I'm gonna try doing this. Another turning point in my life. It was a point where I was really seeking, really depressed, didn't know what I needed. And again, you know, there's a Bible thumpin' [she points to her head], and my grandmother's thumb was pressing down on me. I said, "This is a gift from God, and if I don't use it, I'm gonna lose it."

She began to audition around town with various bands, finally settling on Under the Gun, a funk-tinged blues-rock aggregation that showcased original material to offset what Sharon and some others have come to call the "set list from hell," namely, the hoary standards—such as "Sweet Home Chicago," "Got My Mojo Workin'," or "Hoochie Coochie Man/Woman"—considered obligatory on Chicago's touristy North Side circuit. Guitarist Steve Bramer eagerly enlisted the new singer in this cause. "He said, 'The best way to write is to write about things you know.' We wrote this song. It was about my grandmother, and probably me. I came up with these words, 'I've lived through some treacherous times / And I've had some long hills to climb'—and

Under the Gun (L–R): Steve Bramer, Clyde Davis, Sharon Lewis, R. B. Green, and Gordon Patriarcha, 1993. Photo courtesy Sharon Lewis

my grandmother used to say—'I'd better get my house in order / Time's so short, before the sun goes down on me.'"

On May 5, 1993, with Sharon Lewis at the helm, Under the Gun performed at Buddy Guy's Legends in downtown Chicago. "Half of Northwestern was there," she recalls. "Just ran the poor waitress ragged. We were the main attraction. I was shaking so bad before I went on—thought, 'Girl, what are you *doin'* here?' Then they played my theme song to go on. By the time I was halfway through my first number, had people dancing in the aisles—I was on my way."

For a while, though, it seemed as if the sun might go down anyway.

I got laid off at Northwestern. I'd just gone through a bad breakup with Jesse's father. I had all of these obstacles—my two kids, no support, takin' care of my family. And at that point, no job.

Oh, I was deeply depressed. I'd been in the house about a week and a half—not even downstairs to get the mail. Steve would call and say, "Did you go out today?"

"No."

"Well, you need to."

"I know."

"I need for you to come over."

"Nah, I can't sing."

"You can!"

"No."

Half an hour later he talks me into coming. I get up, shower, went down to his house. He said, "Look, I wrote this happy blues song."

"Happy blues song? Yeah, right! There's no such animal." He started playing this song. Somethin' about it just hit me—"Hmm. Happy blues song!" When I heard the words, it just made me kinda jump. The name of the tune was "Everything's Gonna Be Alright."

At this point in our conversation Sharon breaks into a chorus of "Everything's Gonna Be Alright," and within a few bars her face is bathed in radiance, and she's swaying back and forth, oblivious to the stares from people in the restaurant where we've been talking. "Get back on your feet," she lilts. "The end is in sight—hear those gospel chords in there?—When da-a-y-y-ylight comes, always gonna shed some light."

She remained with Under the Gun for about four years. After she and the band "had a little tiff," she continued to gig around town with well-known artists like guitarists Johnny B. Moore and Dave Specter, as well as local celebrities such as South Sider Mervyn "Harmonica" Hinds. Eventually she replaced veteran harpist Little Mack Simmons as front vocalist for the Mojo Kings, a band rooted solidly in the shuffle-based postwar Chicago sound. To keep herself and her kids in groceries during fallow periods, she also held down jobs as an office temp.

She felt as if she was getting closer to realizing her dream, but the pressure of balancing motherhood, music, and day jobs was relentless. In the past, despite occasional bouts of depression, she had always been unafraid to tackle life's travails head-on. But this time, for reasons she still doesn't entirely understand, she began to seek chemical relief. "What brought that on?" she muses, her voice suddenly going soft. "That's a good question—what *did* bring that on? I think back on it now, and I realize I was always terrified of abandonment—of not belonging. I kept telling my sister-in-law, 'I'm tired.' And she kept sayin' to me, 'Why are you so tired?' I said, 'I'm just tired! I'm tired of being everything to everybody, and nobody is anything to me.' And that's exactly what it was."

For a while, she says, she just "dibbled and dabbled," snorting coke with her boyfriend on evenings when she didn't have a gig. The boyfriend cut her loose when she switched from snorting to freebasing ("Tellin' me, 'You chasin' the dragon!' I didn't know what that meant'"). After her apartment was damaged by a fire, she ended up in "a not-so-good building" where she didn't even unpack most of her belongings after moving in. From there, "things really got nasty and ugly": "The more depressed I became, the higher I got; the higher I got, the more depressed I got. I wasn't taking care of my business. My music was suffering."

Nonetheless, in 1998 ("just at the beginning of my demise, as far as my drug use was concerned," she says) she latched onto a European tour with a band called the Next Generation Blues Band, led by guitarist/vocalist Carl Wyatt. Points of call included the Czech Republic, Germany, France, Holland, and Luxembourg. In Luxembourg the band recorded a CD called *Living in Exile* for the Blue Road Records label; Sharon sang lead on three tracks.

Hearing her own voice on record constituted the culmination of yet another dream (a 1995 session for Delmark remains unreleased), but it was also a nagging reminder of what was still wrong in both her life and her career: she was in control of neither. As a sampler CD she culled from the recording shows, *Living in Exile* showcases her wrapping her fervid blues mama shout around songs lifted directly from the dreaded "set list from hell": "Everyday I Have the Blues" and Sonny Boy Williamson's "Help Me." "I was allowing people to dictate my music," she admits now. "I was being led around. Somebody said, 'Oh, learn this'—Hell, I'd learn it. I wanted the opportunity to perform."

When Sharon got home, her demons rose to meet her as soon as she stepped off the plane. "I was lost for three days after being on tour," she reveals.

> I lost my apartment. I lost everything I had. I got evicted—the real eviction, where they put your shit on the street. I wasn't payin' nobody but the dope man. No lights, no gas. 'Bout the only thing I had was my music, and that was slowly becoming a thing of the past.
>
> I remember saying, after I got evicted, "Where do you go when you ain't got no place to go?" I didn't stay with people much; I didn't want 'em to know my situation. Sometimes I'd ride the El, bus. . . . I might meet somebody, they'd go "Let's go to my place." I'd be there for a few days. I had friends who were pretty wealthy. I was a connect—know what I mean? I could get things they couldn't. A lot of 'em didn't want to be seen in them places. These people would pull up, get out of the car [in the ghetto], and walk around with hoods on their head. [One guy] turned out to be crazy and nuts; he threw me through a closet mirror.
>
> There was a rumor for a while that I was dead, because they ain't seen me for a while. I *was* dead, in a sense, because I had no life. That to me is bein' dead. When you have no purpose in life, you might as well be dead. I had been to rehab, I'd been to detox—went and made a call on the dope man on my way home.

Still, whenever a club owner could catch up with her, she would beg, borrow, or steal whatever decent clothes she could and make the gig, already scheming to pay another visit to her connection as soon as the show was over.

Regardless of what I was doing, I'd still put on a show. I played with [guitarist] Melvin Taylor every New Year's Eve. Tony [Mangiullo, proprietor of Rosa's Lounge] would find me or get someone to get in touch with me some kinda way.

"You got money?"

"No."

"Tell me what time you're coming and catch a cab."

By mid-1999 I probably weighed about ninety-six pounds. I was an eyesore. I didn't know which way was up. I was roamin' around in Cabrini-Green [housing projects] for days, weeks, months. I didn't know what to do, didn't know where to go. I'd *never* been in that situation—other than when my aunt said, "Well, what are you gonna do?"

January 20, 2000, I had been with a friend of mine in a hotel for about three or four days, gettin' high. I just turned and looked at him.

"You know what?"

"What?"

"I don't leave here, I'm gonna die." And he had this quizzical look.

"Sharon, how do you think you're gonna die?"

"Because I'm tired, and I'm going to die. *I am going to die.*"

I had been up probably about six days, hadn't eaten in about four days. I think I had drunk a grape pop, and within a matter of twenty minutes I was peein' grape—my body was not able to grasp any nutrition from any intake. I knew I wasn't gonna be long for this world.

She talked her companion into giving her a ride to a detox center on the North Side, near where she had once lived. "We fought to not have this place" in the neighborhood, she recalls. "Isn't that ironic?" She remembers getting a doughnut and a cup of coffee with her last few quarters and then trudging through subzero temperatures to the little storefront office.

I was just beaten down. I hadn't eaten for so long, I couldn't eat. They were like, "Well, just try to get some soup down." I finally fell asleep, and it hurt me to sleep. It actually hurt me to close my eyes. My whole body hurt. You can't imagine what that was like—I hadn't been used to relaxing naturally; I was used to passing out. I was like a zombie for about three days. The mental craving, it's absolutely torture. But it was time, y'know? I knew my youngest son was hurting 'cuz we weren't together, and *I* was hurting. I never thought about leaving.

They sent her to a facility on Fifty-fifth Street, on the South Side; about three or four months later, when she had completed the program there, she moved back north into "a little one-room spot" run by the Chicago Christian Industrial League (CCIL), where her son Jesse could rejoin her.

> Shared the bathroom with the girl next door: We had a bunk bed; I slept on the bottom, he slept on the top. All my clothes were donated. My daughter gave me a few bucks here and there. [Friends] would come by and bring cigarettes and that kind of thing. I gained some humility.
>
> The most torturous thing was not being able to sing. It ate away at me. On weekends, right there in Greektown, there was a bar around the corner. I had to close the window and turn up the TV not to hear the music. We'd sweat to death because there was no air conditioning.

She finally decided to take matters into her own hands—if she couldn't go to the blues, the blues would just have to come to her.

> I wrote a proposal and submitted it to the director, and I put on this show. I titled it "Blues Comes to CCIL."
>
> We put on a hell of a show. I'm tellin' you, a *hell* of a show. Tore the roof off the mutha! Ooohh, it was a catharsis. Absolutely a catharsis. I mean, look at me! [She's aglow—eyes sparkling and cheeks plumped out in a toothy little-girl grin.] It was probably one of the greatest days of my life since the birth of my children. First paid job in over a year. Absolutely incredible. For my share I bought a TV, which I still have in my living room.

In the fall of 2000 ("I don't remember the exact date; I still have some blank spaces left in my memory"), she left CCIL. That same day her brother, George Washington Jr.—named after her biological father—died in Texas, but she had to stay in Chicago and keep focused on her immediate priorities. She moved in with a woman she had met in the program and slowly got her finances together working temp jobs. Her big breakout gig was New Year's Eve 2000, when she did a show with Billy Branch at a club on Lake Street called Rooster Blues—not far from the room where just months before she had been forced to close her window to keep the sounds of the blues from cutting into her heart like a knife.

From there she gradually reclaimed her old position as lead vocalist for the Mojo Kings, who had been carrying on without a regular singer during her absence. "I had lost a lot of self-respect," she admits. "I had lost a lot of respect of musicians, but never completely. I knew I could be somebody in this thing. And I wanted, like the gospel song [says]—'Gotta run on, see what the end's gonna be!' That's why I came back. And I came back strong."

But she also spent much of the next year putting pieces of her life back together.

I had left my stuff in storage; I don't know what happened to it. What hurt me more than anything was my kids' pictures, their hair from their first haircuts, I lost all that. It really hurt me. I mean, I would break down. I had to think about my Jewish friends—you know, Jewish weddings, you can't take pictures of the ceremony, you have to keep it in your heart. And that's how I survived that. I had my children in my heart.

One day I got a call from [guitarist] Moto [Makino]—he'd helped me move when I got evicted. "I have this cardboard box from when you moved." I came over, helped him bring this stuff out to the car. He put this box in my lap. I started looking through it, and there were pictures of my kids. And my mother. Pictures of when I graduated from college, in my cap and gown. A canvas bag with an African motif my mother [i.e., her great-aunt] had given me. A good two, three hundred pictures of my kids and my family. By the time Moto came back, I was just a blithering idiot, crying. . . . I think that was probably the best thing that had happened to me up to that point.

Not all ghosts were laid so easily to rest. Despite her insistence that she never missed a gig during the bad years, the chaos of her life and the rumors that had swirled around her had led some club owners to label her a bad risk. Even now, she says, there are places that hesitate to hire her. "They told me in the program," she muses, "not everybody is going to embrace your newfound sobriety. You've done some things out there that people can still hold against you."

Still—contrary to Bessie Smith's classic admonition—a few people had remained faithful even when she had been most down and out. Acknowledgment had to be paid here as well.

I had to thank [guitarist/vocalist] Charlie [Love] one night. I was crying my eyes out; he said, "What's the matter with you?"

I said, "I never said this to you before—I want to thank you. From the bottom of my heart. For bein' there. I mean, just for that. You didn't down me; you tried to uplift me. You always recognized me no matter what I looked like. Fed me when I was hungry—I hadn't eaten in a few days, I was tired, I had no place to stay, and that plate of chicken wings was like a feast to me. I had to openly thank you, and Billy [Branch]—just for bein' there."

Rejuvenated since getting clean, Sharon now finds the emotional and aesthetic pleasures of her music have been intensified. "Since my senses are all natural," she affirms, "when I can bite into a song and really put it out there—it's a high. I never really got to the meat of the music, or embraced it the way I should have. Now I *feel* the music."

But along with the heightened consciousness of sobriety has come a renewed restlessness to go further, to explore deeper, to move into more meaningful realms of expression. Sharon's church background, her youthful love for R&B artists like Tina Turner, and her eventual introduction, courtesy of Pat Scott, to contemporary soul-blues have combined to give her a determinedly eclectic view of the music she has come to embrace as her own: "It's all blues," she maintains, "if it comes from the heart"—a view shared, to a greater or lesser extent, by most African American listeners and artists. But it's still not widely prevalent among the so-called white mainstream, and it wasn't reflected very strongly on the CD Sharon and the Next Generation Blues Band cut in Europe. She sometimes finds herself battling with critics, club owners, and even some of her own sidemen just for the right to express that attitude onstage (she remembers one club owner telling a musician, "Don't do your own material in here. We want *real* blues").

"We fight a lot," she admits. "I say, 'You blues purists get on my nerves. Thinkin' that if it ain't a one-four-five [chord progression], dump-de-dump, dump-de-dump, that's not blues. Fuck you! That's not *your* blues. You know, I don't have a prejudiced bone in my body, but—who are you to define my blues? Who the *hell* are you to define my blues?'"

The tensions can be evident in her performance, and they've been exacerbated by stylistic conflicts between Sharon and some of the young sidemen she has used. There have been times when she has felt compelled to try to shout down or shriek over the clanging chords and crashing rim shots of accompanists who were playing as if they believed a musician's prowess is measured by how many notes he can pour into a phrase rather than the story he can make those notes tell. She knows, though, that she's at her best when she's in command of her entire timbral and emotional range, when she can ascend in a heartbeat from an intimate near-whisper to a gospel shout and then ease back without having to hesitate so her backing musicians can catch up.

"The first time I did 'God Bless the Child,'" she points out, "I started to improvise."

> Just ad-libbing, with that soft, kind of draw-you-in feeling. When I was in Europe I did that, and the *sound men* were coming to the dressing room, like, "You had me in tears." You should've seen this man at Rosa's. This man had tattoos; I mean, you don't wanna meet him in the alley after midnight. This man cried on my shoulder! I'm like, "Look at you. Here, baby, wait a minute, let me get you some tissue—hold on."
>
> But that's just the way I do. I can sing "Mary Had a Little Lamb" and make you cry. I'm just that kinda girl.

It might seem odd, then, that most of the songs she and Steve Bramer put together for *Everything's Gonna Be Alright,* her long-awaited debut CD issued on Bramer's Sleeping Dog label in 2004, were rooted in the shuffle rhythm and structured primarily in the traditional twelve-bar style. It's easier to write lyrics that way, she explains—and she is, after all, a blues singer. But then she'll agree that, yes, despite her professed allegiance to R&B, Motown, and soul, the venerable call-and-response blues form lends itself to unfettered emotional honesty like nothing else she has ever encountered. Now free to create on her own terms, she finds herself returning to it more and more, especially when she has something particularly heartfelt to communicate—as on "Blues for Jesse," which she says poured out of her in about twenty minutes one evening while she was sitting in a club before a gig:

> You know I love you, baby
> Do anything you want me to do
> But if you don't straighten up
> I'm gonna have to walk away from you.

Hearing "Blues for Jesse" for the first time, many listeners assume that it's directed toward a lover. Actually, Sharon wrote it for her younger son, an A student with an aptitude for math who has nonetheless flirted with the street and was stabbed in a playground altercation a month or two before she wrote the song. His behavior has frightened Sharon, dredging up memories of his older brother, who has been in and out of trouble for much of his life. As the best blues have always done, the song tells a specific story in universal human terms: a "tough love" testimonial to a wayward child, it's also a declaration of independence and self-worth, a line drawn in the sand by a woman of tender heart who refuses to let that heart be broken any more.

The dominant mood of the new recording, though, is celebratory. "Original Girl" is a saucy strut of independence ("I don't wear no funky weave / I don't wear my clothes to tease / I don't want no man to twirl / I am just an original girl"); the title tune, the Steve Bramer song that taught Sharon about "happy blues" in the first place, has been recast as a grinding Texas crunch that sounds more like a weekend warrior's battle cry than a gospel-inspired ode to perseverance. But—especially in live performance—it's on moody, dark-tinged meditations like "Mama's Children" that Sharon shines brightest: her voice broadens into a rich-hued, expansive alto, inviting you into a stark aural landscape that's at once uncompromisingly bleak and vibrant with redemptive power.

Her stage act reflects a similar resiliency. Despite her professed abhorrence of cliché, Sharon feels compelled to make her audiences feel at ease with familiar material, even as she insists on placing her personal stamp on everything she does. Consider, for instance, her take on "Wang Dang Doodle": recalling Pat Scott's flamboyant sassiness, she'll stroll through the room and

Record release party for Sharon Lewis's *Everything's Gonna Be Alright,* Rosa's Lounge, July 2, 2004. Photo by Jennifer Wheeler

single out a male patron for some call-and-response interplay on the chorus ("Can you get it up?" "*All night long!*" "Can you keep it up? "*All night long!*" "Can you satisfy?" "*All night long!*"), offering a bracing dash of participatory celebration for audiences—predominantly white and often from out of town—who may have little experience with these venerable components of blues ritual and expression.

As she looks back on the upward trajectory her life has taken since she has been clean, Sharon admits there are times when the old anxieties come back to haunt her ("It kind of angers me when these Bible thumpings keep me away from something that means a lot to me"). Even when she's not visited by old ghosts, the ongoing stresses of balancing family, a day job, and music can seem insurmountable.

"I was damn unhappy for a while," she admits. "I even told [a troublesome sideman], 'You know, I could be on the verge of a relapse, and you're not important enough in my life for me to do that. If I have to give something up, I'm not gonna give up singing—I'm gonna give *you* up."

But there seems little danger that she'll allow her past demons to resurrect themselves. "The blues fill that void," she affirms. "I knew there was something missing in my life. There were times when I just felt so alone. I didn't think anybody understood anything, what I was going through. With music there was such a catharsis—when I'm performing, it's almost like I feel transformed."

Our conversation is over. We're both a little drained from the emotional intensity of some of the stories she has been reliving for the last hour or so, but as we get up to leave the bistro where we've been talking, she suddenly turns toward me, her face plumped up in that same little-girl-on-Christmas grin she had broken into when remembering her triumphant show at CCIL in 2000.

"Remember, now, we gotta talk again," she enthuses. More memories and vignettes from the old days? "No, no! I mean about *now*, what's coming up—the good stuff!"

11 Lurrie Bell

"God—Give Me Strength to Be Strong"

Dear Lurrie:

I am writing to invite you to perform at a professional meeting of the International Society for Traumatic Stress Studies. . . . I believe that you and your music would be a fantastic part of our meeting. It is really important that people who work with trauma survivors learn about the blues.[1]

Lurrie Bell is not a man who usually thinks in terms of abstractions like irony. The son of harmonica player Carey Bell, he grew up in a musically rich but emotionally chaotic extended family on the South Side of Chicago, enamored of the blues but also haunted by its power. He was mentored by some of the city's best-known blues artists, and before his twentieth birthday he had become a professional guitarist with an international reputation. In those days he seemed to personify the rambunctious, ebulliently confident spirit of the gifted young bluesman ready to conquer the world. Along with fellow guitarist Johnny B. Moore, he was the man to whom aficionados usually pointed as living proof that "Chicago blues is in good hands."

But in the mid-1980s, as he was beginning to reach

his stride as a frontman, he "just snapped,"[2] as his father later put it, and both his life and his career began to spiral downward. A public figure since his teens, he now found he could no more conceal his demons than he could his gifts. For the better part of the next decade, he haunted the Chicago blues world like a living ghost. He would walk the streets for days or weeks and then show up, muttering and disoriented, at some posh North Side club, where he would strap on a borrowed guitar, snap into focus, and astound the room with both his undiminished musical imagination and the near-manic ferocity with which he unfurled it. Then, without a word, he would disappear into the night as mysteriously as he had arrived. It's no wonder that, when he recorded for Delmark in 1995, they titled the disk *Mercurial Son*.

Few in Chicago would have dared predict it, but by the early 2000s, as most of the Western world celebrated the dawn of a new millennium, Lurrie Bell was emerging into a new life. With the support of Susan Greenberg, a Chicago-based photographer who had met him about ten years earlier when she was a waitress at Rosa's Lounge and became his life companion, he began to gather his energies and find an emotional center that had seemed irrevocably lost just a few years before. Even during the bad times he had managed some good recording sessions. Now gigs started to become more plentiful, profiles appeared in the local and international press, and overseas tours and even a movie deal came into the picture. It looked as if, for once, the blues archetype of the doomed young prodigy was going to be faced down and overturned. People were beginning to utter his name and the word *miracle* in the same breath.

But the blues wasn't finished with him yet. In 2003 the couple's twin babies, Elijah and Corrina Bell-Greenberg, both died. Born prematurely the previous November, Elijah passed away in April, and his twin sister succumbed a little over two months later, in June, plunging the grieving parents into a morass of torment and confusion that, by Susan's own account, nearly destroyed both their relationship and her own sanity. It was time for Lurrie to pull off another miracle, and he did. Defying the expectations of nearly everyone who knew him, he summoned his powers, maintained his balance, and became a rock of strength for Susan as she wrestled with her grief and groped her way back into the light. "He is a survivor," she marveled at one point, "and solid—in ways that at times confound me."

So in the autumn of 2003, when he went to meet the University of Illinois professor who had invited him to play for the Society for Trauma Stress Studies, Lurrie Bell didn't bother with wry philosophical observations. He gave the man a hearty handshake, looked him in the eye, and rasped, "I'm a trauma survivor," displaying the ingenuous directness that often explodes from him when he has something especially urgent on his mind.

"When he said that," Susan mused later, "I was thinking in terms of our babies. He was thinking in terms of his life."

* * *

Lurrie Bell breaks into a smile as he sips a Heineken and settles back into an easy chair in the sunny living room of the home he shares with Susan Greenberg on the northwest side of Chicago. We've been reminiscing about Big Walter and some of the catchphrases he used to come up with. "Yeah," Lurrie exclaims. "'I mean it from my heart!' I like that. That's deep to me. That's what it is when I play—I mean it from my heart. Always was like that, every time."

He flashes me a hawk-eyed glance and then looks up at Susan as she comes into the room to quiet down Picasso, the couple's three-month-old poodle, who has started to yip impatiently from beneath the coffee table, where he has been tethered. "Ain't I right, baby?" he asks, his voice suddenly taking on a rough-textured tenderness. "That's right," she affirms. "Always—from the first time I ever heard you play."

The domestic scene is idyllic, if somewhat chaotic: Picasso and Sugar Foot the kitten frolic around and compete for everyone's attention; books are piled everywhere; framed copies of classic paintings and Susan's photographs clutter the shelves; and one wall sports a large calendar with the locations and showtimes of Lurrie's upcoming engagements carefully annotated in bright purple. Lurrie and I begin to share Chicago blues stories. "Yeah, Sunnyland! He was a powerful man, that Sunnyland. He helped me out so much, so many ways. I sure miss that man." Susan retreats to the kitchen to answer the phone; after a pause, her voice wafts softly back into the living room as she asks the caller: "Do you have Elijah's death certificate?"

The offhand casualness with which the specter of tragedy has just darkened our good-timey chat unsettles me, and I stumble over my next few words. But Lurrie doesn't miss a beat. He is caught in a rush of memories of his early days, when the future seemed to hold nothing but promise, and he can't let them go.

Koko Taylor? Between '79 and '85 I worked with her.[3] Her husband found me. Pops Taylor. I was doing a little jamming, sittin' in and stuff, at Theresa's. And Pops, after I got through sittin' in and playing, he asked me did I want to work with Koko, did I want to work with the band? That's when [guitarist] Sammy Lawhorn was living; Sammy was one of the baddest cats out there. Before Sammy died, Sammy was—I just felt good seeing him, seeing Sammy Lawhorn down there.

First time I ever sat in, that was with Willie Dixon. Must've been [pianist] Lafayette Leake and those guys. They did, like, a ski-lodge gig somewhere out of town. My father [Dixon's harp player at the time] took me with him. I had to be around fourteen, fifteen years old. My dad said, "Ladies and gentlemens, we got a surprise for you." I wasn't expecting it—my heart just went down in the bottom of my shoes! But once I got up onstage and played, I was cool. It felt good, I felt comfortable, I felt like I was a part of the blues organization, the blues thing that was going on. And that's when I decided I wanted to play professionally, make a career out of it.

The gruff but affectionate bluesman-dad, coaxing his son the prodigy onto the bandstand to jam with some of the music's most revered living legends—it's a touching scenario. But by then such moments had already become hard-won in Lurrie C. Bell's life. Born in Chicago in 1958, he had spent his childhood surrounded by music and musicians. He remembers first picking up a guitar when he was four or five years old, and he learned about the blues from such legendary figures as guitarist Eddie Taylor, harp maestro Big Walter Horton, and pianist Pinetop Perkins, as well as his father, who, he recalls, also "played slide guitar—he was good."

But Carey Bell had his own demons to contend with. In a fit of madness his mother, Minnie, had burned down the family's sharecroppers' shack in Macon, Mississippi; according to family lore, she was found inside the house, rocking back and forth and laughing, as the flames roared around her. Carey ran away from home when he was about thirteen, and in 1951 he met keyboardist Eddie "Lovie Lee" Watson in Meridian, Mississippi. He so impressed Watson with his harp playing that the pianist, whom Carey always referred to as his "stepfather," took him in and eventually brought him to Chicago. After a couple of difficult years trying to force his way into the cutthroat Chicago blues circuit, young Carey finally established himself playing on the streets and in various local bands, including Lovie Lee's.[4]

Street hardened and given to unpredictable fluctuations in mood when he was drinking, Carey Bell was a respected musician and mentor, but his hardscrabble life had scarcely prepared him for the day-to-day responsibilities of fatherhood. Of the fifteen children he eventually sired, three—including his oldest son, Carey Jr., whom Lurrie considered his "best friend"—died young. Several others have been in and out of institutions for much of their adult lives.

Lurrie can't say for certain how deeply the unsettled family situation affected him as a child, but for most of his life he has been haunted by the feeling that something, at some time, must have gone horribly wrong. His body carries scars he can't explain; he continues to be visited by images from a mysterious several-months' hospital stay he endured as a toddler, recovering from a head injury that might have resulted from a fall or maybe—it has been whispered—from an abusive attack from a drunken adult relative.

"See, I was born on the thirteenth," he offers. "And when I was younger, I was always very superstitious about that. I thought maybe I was gon' be a bad-luck child. Something like that make me feel depressed a lot."

From the beginning, though, "music was everything": "It was like, that was my partner. It was my partner. Music, it's like, 'Wow! I can get on the guitar and express myself. I feel, y'know, pretty good.' I had to be about three, four, five—me and Junior didn't have instruments, used to play like we were playin', with our mouth, y'know? 'Da-dum, da-dum, da-dum. . . .' That ol' hambone shit! I remember when my father used to have bands over his house, used to go down [to] Jewtown, used to take me with 'em. So I remember those guys, way back then."

But the first in a series of unsettling displacements was about to disrupt his life.

I went down south when I was a young kid, around five, six years old.[5] I went to Macon, Mississippi, and after I stayed down there for about two or three years, I went to Lisbon, Alabama [where his mother's family lived]. I don't know—my parents figured I would do better down there than up in the city, for some reason. That's what I think. I was too young to know what was going on. I used to wonder about that a lot—why did I have to go down south and everybody else stay up here?

But when I went down south, there was a church I used to go to, and they would let me play music, play my guitar, in church. I was happy that way. I felt like I was special in a way, coming from the big city, playing in church, playing guitar, and everybody was checking me out. I used to have to dress up, get a haircut every month and a half or so—that part I didn't like. But it was good. I felt like I was doing something right during those days.

And I worked at it. The church people, basically, taught me the songs. Basically uptempo gospel songs, had a blues flavor in 'em: "Precious Lord," "Stand by Me," "Near the Cross," "Can't Nobody Do What My Lord Can Do." My father sent me a guitar, I think it was Christmas—green plastic guitar. And I played that guitar down there in Alabama. The Apostolic Overcoming Holiness Church of God.

The blues, of course, was strictly forbidden. Even when his fast-living older brother came down to join him in Alabama for a while, Lurrie forced himself to stay on the straight and narrow, at least musically. "I knew of a blues club that was on the border, like, in Meridian, Mississippi. Juke joint! I never did go there. Junior went; he used to tell me about, 'Man, they smokin' up there, playin' some real low-down funky blues up there, man.' I used to want to go, but I was this church dude then. They probably would have kicked me out of the church."

That's not to say he avoided all temptations. "I didn't drink down south," he offers and then demurs with a sly smile, "Ahhh, I did. Moonshine. Used to smoke cigarettes and drink moonshine. I'd sneak and do it; I wouldn't let my folks know. They were real church people."

When he was about fourteen, his parents decided it was time to bring him back to Chicago. He lived for a while with his father on the South Side. "That's the time I first met Lovie Lee. He was playing in a club, right on the corner of where we was living at. Called John's Place—right at Fifty-ninth and Honore. A blues club there. And I lived with my father for a little while, and he used to take me to that particular club. I'd sit in and play blues."

But soon—again for reasons that aren't clear to him—he found himself once more apart from his brothers and sisters, living on the West Side with his grandmother. Like most of his other older relatives, Annie Staples was a staunch churchgoer; Lurrie remembers playing guitar in her church "two or three times." Mostly, though, he went to school—first at Marshall High and then at Crane—and continued to develop his secular talents. He played in soul and R&B aggregations with some of his classmates, and sometimes his father would come by and take him to gigs, further enmeshing him in the blues—the music and the life: "Billy Branch was doing a gig with Willie Dixon at a club on the South Side. I forget the name of the club. And my father, he took me there to this place and he introduced me to Billy. And that night I sat in and did two or three numbers with the Willie Dixon band; Billy Branch with Willie Dixon. So that's how we met."

During this period Lurrie was consumed with inspiration and steadfastly focused on his musical development. Despite his youth, he had already codified a personalized guitar style that meshed the Delta-honed harmonic and melodic structures of his father's generation with an incendiary power all his own, heightened by his flair for dazzling displays of virtuosity. In 1977 he made his first forays into a recording studio. He played bass on Eddie C. Campbell's now-legendary *King of the Jungle* LP (Rooster Blues); that same year the blues and R&B mogul Ralph Bass recorded Carey, Lurrie, and a gritty Chicago rhythm section on a straight-ahead blues session that remained unreleased until 1994, when Delmark issued it as *Heartaches and Pain.*

Lurrie was also recruited to play at the 1977 Berlin Jazz Festival, joining Dixon, Branch, and a crew of youngbloods put together by *Living Blues*

Lurrie Bell backstage, early 1980s. Photo courtesy Billy Branch

magazine cofounder Jim O'Neal to showcase "the new generation of Chicago blues." Out of that project arose what eventually became one of the most influential Chicago-based blues aggregations of the era, Billy Branch's Sons of Blues (SOBs). Alligator Records, which had recorded Lurrie playing lead guitar in "Carey Bell's Blues Harp Band" on volume 1 of their *Living Chicago Blues* anthology series in 1978, captured the SOBs at full roar in 1980 on volume 3. Even more exciting was the material that the German L&R label recorded in 1982, songs that combine shuffle-based traditionalism with dollops of hard-edged funk overlaid by Lurrie's high-energy solos.

His versatility on display, Lurrie also played local clubs during this period, performing alongside artists as diverse as Sunnyland Slim, Little Milton, Son Seals, and Big Walter Horton (thus closing the circle that had begun when Horton mentored Carey Bell on harp some twenty-five years earlier). His stint with Koko Taylor brought valuable exposure; he also held down an ongoing job backing up his father, often in a Bell family band waggishly dubbed the Ding Dongs, which included his younger brothers Steve (harmonica), Tyson (bass), and James (drums). "They were little guys," he recalls. Carey would "call up Steve and let him come up and sit in."

Audiences loved to see this crew of fresh-faced prodigies grinding out down-and-dirty Chicago shuffles, but being thrust into that life at such a young age took its toll on all of them. Lurrie had gotten in about three and a half years of high school before quitting to play music full time; his brothers were lucky if they made it that far. One local musician and blues aficionado remembers seeing them in a South Side tavern well after midnight on a weeknight. He asked their father whether that kind of schedule interfered with the youngsters' schooling. According to his account, Carey just shook his head and muttered, "Ah, I'm 'fraid it's too late for that."[6]

The Bell clan recorded together on 1984's *Son of a Gun* (Rooster Blues), and they also put in some time on the road. But despite the sureness with which Lurrie continued to purvey his music, things had already begun to go awry in his life. "He was afraid all the time," his father told *Chicago Tribune* writer Dan Kenning in 2001. "Nobody could communicate with him. He would tell me, 'Dad, I don't know what's wrong with me, but *something* is wrong.'"[7] His growing moodiness and unpredictability eventually cost him his jobs with both the Sons of Blues and his family band. He continued to try to hold down gigs around town for a while, and he still worked on and off with Carey, but by the end of the decade not only did he no longer have a regular band to play with, but he often didn't have a guitar or even a place to stay.

"Ahhh . . . I really don't know," he says today, when asked about those years.

I really can't focus on why that was. That's kinda a hard thing to answer, man, because—I was, like, you know, I felt like—uh—matter of fact, actually, I don't know how I felt back in those days. It felt . . . uhhh—like I was out of place, in some reason, y'know. I was going through a little change where I was getting, like, too sick, or too paranoid, or too—something like that, you know, about being around large crowds of people. I felt like I couldn't fit in, for some way, with the society, and the music industry, and stuff like that. Something happened to me and I just didn't want to pursue my career.

It was like, when you in church, and you say to yourself you're saved, sanctified, stuff like that. I felt like God was tellin' me something, he was telling me, "Look, you need to be in church, you shouldn't play blues," and it got to my head a little bit. I was confused. I thought I needed to be in church and if I backslid, I would go to hell. Shit like that.

I never did go back to church. I never did go back.

Lurrie maintains that he "retired" from performing when things got really bad, but in fact he never entirely lost his ability to find his focus, at least for short periods, when a special opportunity arose. He appeared occasionally, and sometimes brilliantly, at clubs like B.L.U.E.S. or Rosa's Lounge in Chicago; he also summoned the strength to travel overseas a time or two. In 1986, while in England, he and his father recorded the album *Straight Shoot,* backed by a British band, for the Blues South West label. *Dynasty!* and *Everybody Wants to Win,* released on JSP, featured the other Bell brothers as well, along with guitarist Pete Allen.

Increasingly, though, life became a swirling nightmare of paranoia, hallucinations ("They were not good," Susan says he's told her of the voices he heard in his head), and shattered expectations. On several occasions he was barred from clubs in Chicago ("I guess they was scared that I was going to drink too much or something like that, I was going to get up and fuck up the show or something, some kinda shit"). When club owners did take a chance on booking him, he sometimes succumbed to his fears and failed to show up. But even when he wasn't booked anywhere, he clung to music as his one unshakable solace.

"The music never left me," he insists. "I could always depend on that, no matter what happened. It made me feel like I was doing something for myself, and for other people too, at the same time. I would go around to clubs like B.L.U.E.S. on Halsted, Kingston Mines—travel back and forth. I would get a round of applause for what I did, and I could go home and I could sleep a good night's sleep—sleep better when that happened."

When he couldn't get into a club, he simply walked the streets, ragged and mad-eyed, clutching a harmonica that he would blow into the startled faces of passersby. Today he admits that the harp was "like some kind of sanity" that he kept with him at all times. "That wasn't for money. That was just to play some kinda sound, some kinda music. I didn't have a guitar then. I was just roamin' around the streets, off and on living with my mother here and there. And I would borrow harmonicas from different guys, and—'Well, if I can't play the guitar on stage, they won't let me in the blues club, at least I can mess around with the harp a little bit.'"

When he did get his hands on a guitar, the results could still be spellbinding. One Sunday morning he showed up on Maxwell Street, his clothes so filthy it looked as if he might have spent the night in one of the vacant lots there, and talked a guitarist into letting him borrow his instrument. The word *performance* scarcely begins to describe what ensued. As he counted off a slow blues cadence for the band, his eyes brightened and his lips fluttered into a weird half-smile. Then, for the next ten or maybe fifteen minutes, he *inhabited* a version of Buddy Guy's "Man and the Blues" that utterly outstripped the original in both ferocity and anguish. He tore notes from his fretboard like a man ripping chunks out of his own flesh; he screamed Guy's lyrics in a voice that wavered between sobbing plaintiveness and a throat-rending wail that sounded less like a human cry than like an aural travelogue of hell:

The way I feel sometimes
I feel like drinkin' me some gasoline
Strikin' me a match
And blow my fool self up in steam.

Through it all his craftsmanship never flagged. He spun off phrases couched in melodic and harmonic constructions that brought fresh dimensions to the song's standard twelve-bar form, and even at his most intense—as on a terrifying fret-by-fret descent that sounded like a man tumbling down a flight of stairs made of razor blades—he remained as focused on precision and accuracy as on giving free rein to the furies of his imagination. When it was over, he handed the guitar back to its owner, acknowledged people's amazed stares and praises with a muttered "Thank ya!" and a quick smile, and strode away. He didn't show up again for weeks.

Moments like that helped foster his "living legend" status in the city's blues community, but they didn't do much to help him get his life or his career back together. Through the years he had spent chunks of time in various psychiatric institutions; sporadically he found doctors or social workers who tried to diagnose his condition and get him to take the appropriate medication ("I had bad side effects with it—it made me feel bad. I didn't want to eat, didn't want to get up in the morning"). But until Susan Greenberg came into his

Hanging on: Lurrie Bell with harmonica, ca. 1991. Photo by Susan Greenberg

life in the early 1990s, no one seemed able to find the key to the demon box in which he seemed irrevocably trapped.

Even now, over a decade later, Susan is not sure exactly what drew her to him at the beginning. She's adamant, though, that it was not his fame.

"I didn't know he was a musician at the time," she maintains, occasionally looking him in the eye and speaking to him directly as she relates her story.

> He would be [at Rosa's] a lot, sitting at the end of the bar. I knew your name, and I knew you from being there. Then, it was like a scene in a movie. I was cleaning the tables—it was a "West Side Jam" night, [guitarist] Eddie Clearwater [another Bell family relative] was there, Willie Kent—and I hear this guitar, and then I look up, I see Lurrie. I'm sitting there, like, frozen, like—"What?" I was so shocked. No one had told me. It was just some of the best sounds I had ever heard. When you got off, I just—I cried. I complimented you, and you were, like, shy.
>
> I didn't even know he had recorded. I remember once [he] just somehow mentioned, "Oh, I did that recording. . . ." I was like, "You recorded?" I didn't know the history of blues, I didn't know who Carey Bell was, and I didn't know Lurrie's history. I just felt a connection. I felt something from him just because of who he was—a good guy, good person.

In the macho culture of Chicago blues, women who latch on to musicians—especially vulnerable ones like Lurrie—are often greeted with suspicion if not outright hostility. Susan encountered her share of distrust—even today, she says, the gossip can be wounding—although several years passed before they became lovers. In the meantime, she maintains, she didn't take it on herself to try to help him rejuvenate his career until she had become convinced that it was both a possibility and a moral imperative. Then, though, it became almost an obsession.

> Once I knew you were a musician, it was like, "There's something wrong here. Why aren't you working? Why aren't you playing? This is some of the best music I have ever heard." And then when I learned about this history, I had, like, this indignation. "You're supposed to be up there too, and you're supposed to be having gigs, because you have a gift!"
>
> I helped you get that gig with [saxophonist] Eddie Shaw. Then, after that, [the late guitarist] Booba Barnes. I went to Delmark—they knew my photography—I used to bug 'em, "You gotta record Lurrie!" I was always pitching Lurrie.

Steve Cushing, a veteran blues drummer who also hosts the NPR program *Blues before Sunrise*, eventually approached Susan about getting Lurrie into a studio with a set of new songs Cushing had written. That turned out to be the catalyst for a multirecord deal with Delmark, a series that kicked off with

Mercurial Son, an uncompromising blast of Lurrie Bell at his most emotionally raw and musically untamed.

The tension going into the *Mercurial Son* sessions, in December 1995, was palpable. "Nobody really knew what was going to happen," Susan recalls. "The sound engineer and Steve, they kind of gave you the [lyrics], they didn't say much, and—first take! You got what they were looking for. It was like watching Michael Jordan or something. They made high fives; they flipped out."

When the disc came out, some critics were nonplussed by Cushing's lyrics, which had a graphic intensity that sometimes crossed over into unpleasantness ("With your sorry sweet pussy / As well to keep your legs a-crossed")[8] and in general seemed to reflect all too accurately the singer's state of mind at the time. It's been rumored that Lurrie himself demurred at recording some of them. Now, though, he maintains that *Mercurial Son,* with its solid Chicago shuffle grooves and unadorned, stark-sounding production, is his favorite of the four discs he eventually made for the label.

"Some of the words I didn't really agree with," he admits. "But I accepted what he was writing. I like *Mercurial Son*—it's more traditional. It takes me back a little bit, when I first started playing, when Willie Dixon was living and all those guys, and Carey had his band, and Eddie Taylor was living. That was my decision, doing something that would make me relax. Even though I was doing tunes that different guys would write, I put my version into the songs."

Proceeds from his Delmark work kept him housed in the Lawson YMCA, on the near North Side, for a year or two ("Don't give Lurrie cash money," Susan cautioned the company). Reviews, even critical ones, made it clear he was still capable of playing well; promoters and club owners became more willing to take a chance on him. In 1996 he stunned a crowd at the Chicago Blues Festival's daytime Front Porch Stage by turning in over two hours of incendiary fretwork (he played his own set and then stayed to fill in for a guitarist who failed to show), a marathon he capped off with a trademark display of obsessional fury, firing off repeated serpentine codas in a scalding tone as two broken strings dangled from the neck of his guitar.

The following afternoon he came reeling into the performer's tent sporting a new pair of running shoes and babbling incoherently, unable to tell anyone where he had left his instrument. By the next summer he had lost his room at the Y ("I just left; I decided not to go back. I wanted to do something different"). That year he spent most of the Blues Fest wandering through the crowd with his harp. At one point he stood in a torrential downpour, bareheaded and soaked, playing furiously to himself as people around him unfurled umbrellas and ran for cover. He finally fell asleep on the ground, near the stage he had commanded so majestically the year before.

Beneath the surface, though, some good things were finally happening for Lurrie Bell. "The more I played blues," he asserts, "the more I started believin' it's all right to play gospel, it's all right to play blues, too. I just made myself believe that music is great—blues, gospel, whatever I'm doin'. It's still music and it's good for yourself, for your head, mentally."

He continued to record for Delmark, even when he had to come in off the streets and borrow a guitar to make the session. Seldom was there any rehearsal: he would show up at the appointed time and play whatever came to his mind, or maybe do a quick run-though of lyrics someone handed to him in the studio, and then usually nail everything on the first or second take. This ability to summon his powers and put in a coherent performance at a moment's notice, which has confounded observers for years, remains a fierce point of pride for him.

"I like to just come in, do it," he declares.

> Even if I've never seen the words or anything. I kinda focus my mind—get up in the morning, say, "I'm gonna go up in there and do this recording, and that's all [there is] to it. I'm gonna set my mind today." You act like a pro, you get up there, you tune your guitar up, you make sure the musicians are ready, and it happens.
>
> It's a natural talent that I learned when I was at a young age. Good ear for music. And I can use that for an advantage. That was what was happening when I was going though those changes in my life. I don't have to get up there and work on tunes with the band; I can just get up there and play. All the way from the heart! Exactly!

This "from the heart" approach didn't always work perfectly: 1999's *Blues Had a Baby* includes disturbing passages of him rambling semicoherently and thrashing distractedly at his strings on such unlikely fare as "If I Had a Hammer" and a bizarre "Mary Had a Little Lamb." Nevertheless, his overall Delmark output shows him crafting blues of eloquence and originality, apparently mostly in control of both his gifts and himself. Gradually, despite occasional setbacks, his "good" periods began to last longer than his "bad" ones. By 2001, when he released *Cuttin Heads* on the Indiana-based Vypyr label, he had found a manager and was looking forward to another European tour.

The record-release party for *Cuttin Heads,* at Rosa's Lounge on the first weekend in January, represented more than a personal triumph ("I—I—I was a little nervous. But once I got onstage and started playing, I felt good"). It was a public declaration, carefully orchestrated by Susan, that her man was back on the scene to stay. She worked the press; she helped supervise the guest list; and she carefully monitored the hangers-on who assembled before the show, doing her best to stave off anyone who might come bearing dangerous gifts.

Contrary to rumor, Lurrie had never been a hard-core drug addict or alcoholic, even in the worst of times. In fact, his doctor eventually gave him official permission to keep drinking in moderation. Still, part of the reason he was now doing so well was Susan's vigilance in monitoring his intake of chemicals, both prescribed and otherwise ("She made sure, like she's doing today, that I take my medicine, that I don't forget"). This, though, created new challenges. With his mind clear and his emotions at an even keel for the first time in years, he had to learn all over how to summon his inspiration. Many listeners who hadn't heard him for a long time were flabbergasted by his new sound. His craftsmanship was as deft as ever—he had even begun to insert some lines that sounded borrowed from T-Bone Walker's repertoire—but the old manic edge was gone, replaced by something astonishingly close to serenity.

"It felt better," he says. "After I calmed myself down, stopped gettin' high, relaxing on stage. The groove, the music felt better. I felt like I was a part of what was going on. At one time I felt like, 'What am I here for? What am I doing?' It's like I wasn't focused. But once I started focusing—recording first, then going out and playing—I was cool. It took about two years to overcome my shyness and paranoid feelings about being onstage with people—"

Susan interrupts: "It took about ten years, Lurrie! It took us—it took a long time!"

"You think it took a long time? Might've took longer to get the recognition to get back."

Either way, things were looking up as never before. *Cuttin Heads* garnered positive, even raving reviews. Over the next year or so yet another transformation began to take place: the smoothed-out edges that had surprised so many at Rosa's began to roughen; the old emotional directness—uncompromising and brutally honest—began to make its presence known again. But now Lurrie was creating willfully, with the power of his imagination, the splintered aural imagery laced with both ecstasy and dread that had once seemed to erupt uncontrollably out of madness.

Also in 2001 the filmmaker Paul Marcus, in town to work with director Wim Wenders on Wenders's installment of Martin Scorsese's seven-part PBS series *The Blues,* did some shooting at Rosa's. Afterward Susan approached him to pitch Lurrie as a possible subject. After hearing him play and learning more about his still-unfolding saga of reemergence, Marcus decided that the story of Lurrie and Susan was filmworthy in itself, and he began work on the preliminary stages of what eventually became a full-length documentary portrait. Buoyed by their optimism about Lurrie's career and their life together, the couple eventually felt secure enough to consider embarking on a bold, joyously affirmative declaration of faith.

"We didn't have any children," Lurrie muses. "We talked about it. We discussed it. It was nice to know that we could have children. At that particular time it was a good feeling."

"We'd known each other a long time," Susan adds. "We never thought we were ready. But I felt ready; and I felt Lurrie was ready. When he moved in with me this last time, he talked about us getting back together as like having a second heartbeat; he wrote a song called that. When we got pregnant, it signified the fetus's heartbeat. And then we found out we had twins."

On November 16, 2002—over two months before they were due—Elijah and Corrina Bell-Greenberg were born. Elijah was named in memory of Elisha "Eli" Murray, a musician who had played rhythm guitar with the Sons of Blues. Corrina's name came from the folk song "Corrina, Corrina." Their parents settled on the last name of "Bell-Greenberg" instead of "Greenberg-Bell" simply because it rolled off the tongue more easily.

But the babies were frighteningly tiny and weak. "Elijah was not supposed to make it at birth," Susan says. "There was a leak in his water, which made me go into premature labor, probably from an early amnio test. He had lots of needles."

Early on, as the babies lay in isolation with tubes sticking out of their bodies and their lungs connected to a respirator, their father got permission to bring in an acoustic guitar and sing for them. He would croon some of the spirituals he used to sing in church down south—"Stand by Me" and "Precious Lord"—along with Sam Cooke's "Bring It on Home to Me" and, for Corrina, the Temptations' "My Girl."

"Remember that?" Susan turns to him, her eyes going soft. "I remember that first time when you sang to Elijah and he opened his eyes, clearly listening. And you were just, 'Look at that! That's our son!' And you were so happy."

"It was like a miracle," Lurrie affirms. "After all me and Susan been through, we gave birth to kids. And that was like, y'know, that's a blessing from God."

Elijah battled his way through "an up and down course of pneumonia and other infections over four months," Susan continues. "He grew into a big, fat, cute, beautiful baby. Strong beyond belief. One time they had to give him a spinal tap. The nurses told me it took four people to hold him down. Next day, he was fine. The doctor came by and said, 'If he's sick, then I'm dead.'"

But his lungs remained underdeveloped, and eventually they "deteriorated beyond hope." The couple faced the unthinkable on April 9, 2003:

We had to pull support from him. I held him for eight hours straight that day. When the oxygen was pulled, I freaked out and started screaming, "No! No!" crying like a sick animal, stomping on the ground. But I needed to be calm for him, so I started to sing "Bring It on Home": "If you ever change your mind / about leaving me behind." He died in my arms, as Lurrie sang spirituals.

I was freaked out. I was horrified. I couldn't speak the words. I couldn't tell people. We [had his funeral] within two days.

Lurrie continued to gig around town, apparently as focused as ever, and some people wondered whether he was holding back feelings that might someday explode, or whether he had become so emotionally numbed that he was simply unable to react. In fact, though, he kept up his performance schedule not because he wasn't hurting but because he was.

"It was a good thing that I can play," he states, "because that helped me through that whole ordeal. I felt real bad, a lot of grief in my heart about that. It made me want to play more, concentrate more on my music, on performing. It made me want to get in *to* it more. I was, like, going to the music, concentrating on it. It made me concentrate more on that, 'cuz I could."

For the next two months they honed their focus and their faith on caring for their daughter: "We just knew that she was going to survive. Elijah died, but we was gonna have one baby still living."

"She tested out like a superstar," Susan says.

They prepared me that she'd be coming home within a few weeks—"She's going through some things, but at two years old she'll be a happy little girl running around."

To this day I still do not really know why she died; her heart went out. When Corrina was passing, about eight nurses and technicians and doctors were buzzing around her, trying to save her life. I plugged my ears with Kleenex and just focused on her, one arm cradled around her head, the other holding her hand, with my head on the bed, lips to her ear, whispering words of love and comfort . . . while Lurrie stood back in complete shock and paralysis, like a statue, with a blank stare.

"It made everything worse," Lurrie adds, nodding solemnly. "Because Elijah had passed, and when she passed, it was like a big breakdown right there."

Already stretched beyond endurance by the unremitting tension of the previous six months, Susan now found herself dangerously close to falling apart entirely. "I was on the edge," she admits. "Lost, floating, like an alien on a strange planet and I don't speak the language, trying to push myself to just start getting out of bed. . . . Lurrie and I went through great stress. We almost broke up a few times."

But instead of breaking up with her, he ended up becoming the one thing virtually no one—maybe not even Susan herself—could have predicted: her link to sanity. He explains it as a matter of necessity:

> If I hadda fell apart, I don't know what could've happened. 'Cuz Susan needed somebody to be strong and be there for her. Because Susan had a hell of a lot of pain. ["I couldn't do anything," she interjects. "I could barely talk to you; I didn't ask questions. . . ."] We got a little bit closer. Day by day; we kept holding onto each other. That gave us strength.
>
> I was there when both of 'em passed, in the hospital. They suffered a lot when they was here. I asked myself over and over and over again, "Why did this have to happen?" And I finally made myself accept it—that's the Lord's work upstairs, it's nothin' Lurrie or nothin' Susan can do about that. We really loved 'em. And now, after they passed, we think about [how] we did bring 'em into the world. We knew 'em for a short time. In that short time, that was, like, sayin' somethin' to us. It was, like, a message, telling us that we are two very special people in this world.

Eventually, Susan adds, she came to an important realization: "I do want to keep living, reach out and make a good testimony to the lives of my children. If we destroy our lives now, we would be making them testimonies to the devil, not to love and God."

Lurrie, meanwhile, having maintained his equilibrium through the ordeal of the babies' death and its aftermath, continues to move closer toward realizing the promise that so many saw in him in the early days and that Susan steadfastly refused to deny, even during the worst of times. After years of maintaining a tense, on-again, off-again relationship that sometimes threatened to rupture under the pressures of their various personal problems and conflicted histories, Lurrie and his father began to play together again in the early 2000s; as if on cue, in 2004 Alligator Records released *Second Nature,* a set of mostly acoustic sessions the pair had recorded in Finland in 1991. Listening to it—and now hearing the pair re-create those sounds in performance—you would never know anything had ever been wrong. Carey's sharp-toned squeals, lithe runs, and hornlike ululations prod and support Lurrie's gently propulsive chording and fleet leads, rooted deeply in Delta-to-Chicago traditionalism but graced with his characteristically forward-looking melodic and harmonic ideas.

"It's been inspiring to me," Susan murmurs, her eyes darting nervously as if she's almost afraid to contemplate such a thing as good fortune after all she has been through. "Two, three years ago, we might have a gig once a month; we'd be so excited. And now Lurrie works five, six times a week. You look to the universe for signs—it's not all punishing us."

"I'm proud of myself," Lurrie adds in a matter-of-fact tone with no hint of braggadocio, "because we are overcoming the hardships that we've been facing lately."

I got better with myself, and my music, and with faith, and me and Susan together—it's God's way of letting me know that things might get bad but they will, they do get better. I got enough faith and belief that eventually, one of these days, we could probably have another baby. And it would be all right this time. I think we can handle it; we can make a healthy baby. We can be good parents.

But my music is there for me, too. I think it's a gift. You can't explain how you sing and play and go through troubled times in your life and put it into words and music. I started at a young age, playing the blues and—it's like, there's something there for you. And you say to yourself, "Well, I can do this." You get better and better, you get gigs, and people start responding, and—it's a gift. If you can play the blues or even listen to it, it makes you

Lurrie Bell on the Juke Joint Stage, Chicago Blues Festival, June 2003. Photo by Susan Greenberg

feel better in your heart, in your soul. Has a little light; it's some light there no matter how sad the song is. I believe it's a gift from God—music.

* * *

On a crisp Monday evening in October, the yard in front of Lurrie and Susan's apartment is already strewn with fallen leaves. Inside, a Billie Holiday CD plays softly as guests sip wine, munch on barbecued ribs and chicken wings, and greet the host and hostess with affectionate hugs. It's the first time a lot of them have seen either one since before the babies died. Lurrie stalks through the room, sipping a cocktail, obviously savoring his role as head of the household. He carefully introduces people to one another, pours drinks, and makes sure everyone's plate stays full. As he takes a break from his duties to wrap an old friend in a bearlike embrace, his face takes on an expression of wide-eyed wonder: "I'm so glad everyone's here. All the people I love are here. I'm happy—I'm *happy*. I just feel good to be alive, y'know what I mean? I ain't high—well, I got a little bit of a buzz on—but I'm percolatin'. I'm *happy*."

Later, relaxing in his easy chair and stroking Sugar Foot as the kitten purrs contentedly in his lap, he reflects yet again on the faith that he maintains has girded him through the harrowing trajectories his life has taken so far.

> I kinda knew, in the back of my mind, even though at one particular time I was out on the street, I was goin' here and there, didn't have a guitar, if I did get a guitar I would end up pawning it—but I knew in the back of my mind I could get up there and perform, and play guitar, and sing. I kept that in my head. "No matter what, you still can get up there if you want to." If I didn't play for couple, two, three years, I knew I could do that. I had that faith within myself. And it kept me goin'.
>
> It's God's work. I say to myself, "Lurrie, you're here in this world for something. You go through a lot of changes, you can't explain it"—I would praise the Lord and ask God, say, "God, I can't do nothin' about what's goin' on, but give me strength to be strong and go through these changes that I'm goin' through." And somehow or another God blessed me.
>
> I wake up in the morning, I say to myself, "Life ain't over. Life ain't over with now."

* * *

On September 20, 2005, Susan gave birth to a healthy, squalling baby girl whom she and Lurrie have named Aria Avalokiteshvara—"Aria," in honor of music and song; her middle name after the Tibetan Buddhist Bodhisattva of Compassion. "Feels great!" Lurrie said when asked about his new life as a father. "Something to look forward to every day and live for—makes me feel proud to be here."

Part 4

"The Soul Side of Town"

12 Artie White

"It's a God-Gifted Thing"

Artie White is almost as much a fixture in the audiences at blues shows around Chicago as he is onstage. Whenever a big-name blues revue rolls into town to appear at East of the Ryan on Seventy-ninth Street or at Mr. G's Supper Club on Eighty-seventh near South Ashland, you'll probably find Artie there, sitting at the bar or standing in a corner with a group of friends, surveying the scene through heavy-lidded eyes. When the inevitable recognition comes from the stage—"Ladies and gentlemen, we have Artie 'Blues Boy' White in the house tonight!"—he breaks into a smile and acknowledges the applause with a brief wave of offhand, almost regal ease. In his demeanor and his conversation, he seems to epitomize the prototypical big-city blues hipster: affectionate but gruff, a bit profane, signifying and carrying on with his running buddies, a man among men.

His stage act accentuates this image. He sports gold chains and stands loose-limbed at the microphone with a casualness bordering on arrogance, engaging his audience in ribald repartee; his grainy baritone croon is shot through with sinewy machismo. Then there is the lyric content of his songs: "(You Are My) Leanin Tree," his 1977 breakout hit on Altee; subsequent tracks like "Jimmy" (a 1984 reprise of Little Beaver's 1972 hit "Joey");

the more recent "I'm Gonna Marry My Mother-in-Law"; and even "Your Man Is Home Tonight," his 1997 celebration of conjugal bliss—all these seem to confirm his image as a seasoned player, gritty and street tough, wounded by love but still cocky and ready to let the good times roll.

Despite all that, when we spent an afternoon talking in a quiet corner of Chicago's Checkerboard Lounge early in the spring of 2002, the side Artie chose to reveal to me was markedly different. As he nursed a nonalcoholic beer and stared pensively across the room, he spoke with gentle but firm conviction about his religious faith, his pride in having weaned himself from both tobacco and alcohol, and his sorrow over the ravages that casino gambling and other vices have visited on neighborhoods and families from Mississippi to Chicago.

At the time Artie was savoring the reaction he had been receiving for *Can't Get Enough,* his 2001 self-produced disc on his own Achilltown label. His delight at his newfound entrepreneurial success no doubt contributed to the sense of optimism and hard-won inner peace that permeated our conversation. Nonetheless, his low-key but forceful demeanor, hopeful yet leavened with an almost autumnal introspection, seemed mostly the result of a lifetime spent surviving the travails and pitfalls of the blues highway. Artie's life has taught him that a man's inner reserves of faith and determination to prevail constitute his most important assets. His own expression of these views and values showed, yet again, that a bluesman is much more than the image he projects to the public and certainly much more than the stereotypes often invoked, even today, by many mainstream commentators and would-be experts alike.

* * *

Artie White believes he probably came into the world in the city of Vicksburg, Mississippi, but his family was rural, and his earliest memories are of growing up in the country.

> When I was big enough to know, I was back out from Vicksburg, about three, four miles. My father passed, they tell me, when I was like three months old. He was a minister. My mother passed when I was three years old. I remember her vaguely. I was there with my grandmother, my sister, and brother. I was born April 16, 1937. When I turned eleven years old, I got baptized. I started singing gospel with the Harps of David Singers.
>
> I guess God wanted me, helped me, showed me a way to support myself. Because I never was a disobedient child. And I tried to take care of my [family] like they did me. I dropped out of school in Vicksburg, I was thirteen years old. Started driving truck, log truck, lumber truck, to help take care of my grandmother; she got old, and everybody was gone but me.

But see, the Lord blessed me, and he made a way for me to make a living. It's a God-gifted thing; I have been real fortunate. It's a funny thing, now, I tells people all the time, and they don't believe me or they don't pay attention. I say, "You know, I set and wonder some time; I look at kids and I look at their parents. Here one parent can raise seven, eight kids—and seven and eight kids can't take care of one parent?" Think of that, eh? So I tried to do what I could for mine, and that's why the Lord blesses me.

Cast into the adult life of a full-time workingman before his fifteenth birthday, Artie became a fan of blues and R&B early on, despite his gospel singing. His tastes, though, ran more toward sophisticates like B. B. King and Bobby "Blue" Bland—both based in Memphis—than rawer-sounding sons of the Delta like Muddy Waters and Howlin' Wolf: "I remember B. B.'s first record. I used to sing it: 'You know you didn't love me, when you fell down 'cross my bed.'"[1]

But Artie was an ambitious young man, and Mississippi offered little to a black teenager with a grammar-school education who wanted to better himself. Like many others, he looked north. Chicago in those days was a center for gospel as much as it was for blues, and Artie first came to the city in the early 1950s intending to make gospel records. He didn't land a contract, but he kept trying ("Every year, I would leave and go back"); by 1956 he was there to stay.

"I was singing with the Full Gospel Wonders," he recalls. "After I left the Full Gospel Wonders, I started singing with the Sensational True Lights, out of Hopewell Baptist Church at Sixty-fifth and Cottage Grove."

He also made the acquaintance of other young gospel singers, some of whom would eventually make a name for themselves in secular music: "When I came to Chicago, Sam Cooke,[2] Johnnie Taylor, L. C. Cook, Lou Rawls—all them guys, we used to meet up around Ida B. Wells [housing] projects. But I didn't know them, and they didn't know me."

Like many of his contemporaries, young Artie was a worldly man of faith, and in his travels around the city he heard plenty of blues and got to know some of the musicians. "When I came to Chicago in 1956, the hottest artist out here was Bill Doggett—'Honky Tonk' was so big it was ridiculous. Little Willie John, Bobby 'Blue' Bland—them were the hottest artists out here. I always would follow the blues. I'd follow cats that's doing something, and watch 'em."

But in those years he did not cross the stylistic and spiritual Rubicon separating gospel from the blues (or for that matter, gospel from R&B). "They didn't do both at the same time," he remembers. "Once you's in the gospel, you's in the gospel; when you left gospel and went into the blues, you were into the blues. I stayed with gospel until 1966."

An often-told story has a flashy record promoter approaching Artie with a huge sum of money—in some versions, the slickster leaps out of a Cadillac and accosts the young man on the sidewalk—luring him into crossing the line and embarking on a blues career. Artie concedes that it was the lure of lucre and the concomitant fast life that prompted him to make the change. "I'd just watch all the other guys, look like everyone havin' so much fun. [Soul singer] Garland Green, Johnny Edwards—he's with the Spinners now—and all of them was out here having so much fun, I said, 'I'm gonna try to sing blues.'"

As a local singer with little exposure outside Chicago, Artie did not endure the kind of public hostility faced by crossover pioneers like Cooke, whose move to R&B in 1957 sent shock waves through the gospel world from which it has never entirely recovered. Nonetheless, he found it a challenge to master this new musical direction on his own. "I could sing gospel, but I didn't know too much about no blues. I was nothing but amateur. I remember when all the guys used to sing at Peyton Place [at Thirty-ninth and Indiana] and at Bonanza [on South Halsted]. Tyrone [Davis] and I used to stand on the streets. They wouldn't let us sing; said our timing was too bad."

Artie says he recorded his first side, which he remembers as "Don't Jenk Me Around," in 1968.[3] He can't remember the name of the label, but he says it was owned by Bob Lee, a Chicago record man who's probably best known for "I Can't Please You," a torrid soul outing by an otherwise obscure singer named Jimmy Robins, which Lee released on his own Jerhart label in 1966.[4] By Artie's own admission, he was still searching for a style: "I used to sing just like B. B. until a lady really embarrassed me one night, told me, she said, 'Sing, B. B.!' And that was truly embarrassing to me, and that's how I started getting away from that."

His face softens into an expression of almost childlike wonder as he remembers how some of the blues world's biggest celebrities took him under their wings and helped him find his own voice. "Something about them guys," he marvels.

> They taken a liking to me when they seen me. Albert King would come to my house, Bobby Bland would send for my wife, Junior Parker would tell me to come down to where he's at, and Milton and I used to run 'round together.
>
> B. B., every time we meet up, we would sit down and have a conversation. We used to get over in the corner, me and him—"Come on, Artie, let's shoot some dice!" We'd shoot five-dollar dice; it was fun to him,

y'know, something to pass time. Johnnie [Taylor], [Little] Milton, Bobby Bland, B. B., Albert—all of them was a big influence on me.

It was not, for the most part, hands-on musical training. Bluesmen tend to be somewhat Zenlike in their mentoring techniques; usually it was up to Artie himself to absorb what lessons he could simply by immersing himself in the world of his heroes and watching them closely, both on- and offstage.

I was trying to learn how to phrase; I was trying to learn a style. I started to watch what they were doing, watch how they'd carry themselves, and then I would know what to do with myself. And they got to the place where they started calling me on stage.

Really and truly, to be perfectly honest with you, Bobby Bland was the onliest one that set me down in the hotel and showed me how to control my voice and do what I want to do. I was taught by Bobby: "You got to get a style of your own!" So that's where I really started to create a little bit.

Matter of fact, Bobby's the one who gave me the name Blues Boy. We was in Bonanza, and I used to meet Bobby, and I'd sing two blues songs all the time. He said, "I got a name for you." He sat there for a minute, and he said "Artie Blues Boy White!" And he gave me that name. I never will forget it.

Through the years Artie has come under some criticism for having modeled his vocal style too closely after that of the late Little Milton, an important figure in contemporary blues whose run of hits on Checker and Stax in the 1960s and 1970s played a major role in codifying the modern style. He maintains, however, that Milton's influence only helped him refine what he already had.

In 1969 I met Milton. I didn't even know Milton. A guy told me, "Man, there's a guy in St. Louis. You remind me so much of him."

I said, "Who you talkin' about?"

He said, "Little Milton."

I didn't know nothing about no Little Milton—all I knew was Roy Milton. I had my style, and the guy was telling me I sound just like him.

When I got to Milton, we got so close together, and I would watch him do different things. And he would always get on me about learning the song—"Be sure you learn that song." Milton always was going to show me different chords on the guitar; I used to try with the guitar. Back in 1957 or so, bought a Silvertone, $39.95, from Sears and Roebuck— pea green. But I said, "I ain't got time for it. I got to get into this blues [singing]!"

In those days the blues world was an intricately woven, insular network of musicians, managers, club owners, deejays, and various hustlers both big and small time—as it continues to be today. The line between friendships and business relationships was nebulous; it could shift from situation to situation or even from night to night. As a major blues nexus, Chicago was home to some of this world's most important participants, and White was able to insinuate himself into their company.

Another guy that did a lot for me was [WVON deejay] Pervis Spann. 'Cause when I got my little ol' record, he used to carry it into the building and put it on at midnight and play it. He wouldn't take payola. He would not take nary a dime from nobody. He would rather for you to come in and do him a date, something like that. Spann had the Burning Spear [nightclub]. I hung around the Burning Spear, and [emcee/comedian] Carl Wright used to call me on, have me do a few songs.

And things just went on by the grace of God. I carried myself in a way that peoples liked me—I never was sassy and bigoted. All of 'em just took a liking to me. Bobby came to me one night and told me, "Listen. You know, you got a little of me in you, you got a little of Milton in you, you got a little B. B. in you, and you got a little Albert in you. And you got *you* in you. So when you chewin' us all up together, we got some problems."

Artie had been raised in the hard-drinking southern tradition ("I drank since I was nine years old"), so he had no difficulty partying alongside his newfound friends and mentors. But he managed to avoid some of the more ravaging pitfalls of the blues life.

I never, in my life, had the desire for no drugs. Every guy I know that had a thing with drugs, somethin' happened to 'em. I just used to set back and look at all the Temptations—they were the baddest thing out here, all them Temptations. Sly and the Family! Livin' the fast life! I guess they feel you not an entertainer until you use drugs.

I used to was gettin' hooked on the racetrack one time. I lost a hundred and fifty dollars, and an old man—I always would listen to what you say, I wasn't the type of youngster that would talk back, no matter what color you were, I respected you—old Jew told me, "Son, you don't look so good! Look like you lost your money."

I say, "Well, I have."

He says, "Well, I wanna tell you something. Don't get hooked on them horses. Because horses is a rich man's sport. Always been. If you come to this track with two hundred dollars and win six thousand dollars by the sixth race, if you stay until the tenth race you gon' be dead broke." So what I did, I paid attention to what he said.

Artie's early sides included "Gimme Some of Yours"/"Don't Love Him," released on Gamma in 1972, and "She's the One (Pts. 1 and 2)," released in 1975 on harpist Little Mack Simmons's PM label. These cuts showcased him mostly as a raw-edged blues shouter; they made some noise locally but weren't strong enough to put Artie on the road. It wasn't until a couple years later that things really opened up for him. Ironically, at that time many blues artists were finding themselves eclipsed by changing popular tastes.

"Blues was going big in the fifties, sixties," he maintains. "Blues didn't start to turn until around 1976, when the disco came in." Artie, ever optimistic, nonetheless joined forces with Argia B. Collins, a local barbecue mogul who dabbled in the music business on the side, to form a record company called Double A Productions. When singer/producer Andre Williams came onboard, the name was changed to Triple A. Artie released a couple of sides under Collins's Altee imprint that went nowhere, although his vocal technique on them showed marked development from the roughshod holler of his earlier efforts. Then, in 1977, with the help of Chicago-based songwriter Bob Jones, the Triple A team struck pay dirt.

"I was fortunate enough," Artie says. "I had a record come out, 'Leanin Tree.' Bob Jones wrote that, and I was fortunate enough to have a big record. I was number 10 on the [local] charts, number 10 on 'VON. Andre Williams produced it."

"(You Are My) Leanin Tree," graced with a keening guitar solo that ran most of the way through and buoyed by energetic—if tepidly mixed—horns, was easily the most fully realized piece of work Artie had yet achieved. It peaked at number 99 nationally—not a blockbuster, but respectable for a southern-styled blues record in the midst of the disco era. Artie "Blues Boy" White was finally a blues recording star.

Stardom in the blues world, though, often meant little more than scuffling on a slightly higher plane. "I started on the road with 'Leanin Tree.' Really broke me into the opening. I used to play a bunch of joints down there in Vicksburg, Mississippi, out in the field. During this time there were a lotta joints you could play because they were all out in the field. These little joints might hold seventy-five people; bands wasn't gettin' but twenty, twenty-five dollars."

A single hit might carry an artist for several years on that circuit, but even there it takes a track record—and a well-honed musical identity—to really become established. Despite his success with "Leanin Tree," Artie still often sounded as if he was searching for a style. "A Love Like Yours (Is Hard to Find)," his follow-up to "Leanin Tree," uncomfortably grafts his thick Mississippi drawl onto a lurching funk-soul cadence. "Looking for a Good Time," released in 1979 on Cynthia, is an anomalously perky, pop-tinged ode to juking redeemed from mediocrity by a brawny horn arrangement and some of the cleanest production White had yet enjoyed. "Bad Intentions," on the obscure Sky Hero label, is a medium-tempo twelve-bar romp with distinct echoes of Bobby Bland's style (even the arrangements sound patterned after those of Joe Scott, Bland's legendary studio Svengali), but it is marred by a gimmicky stop-time introduction.

In fact, during this period Artie was probably as well known around Chicago for the nightclubs he ran as he was for his records. His first club, Bootsy's Show Lounge, was at 2335 South Cottage Grove, in a building owned by Mack Simmons. "The guys didn't want to rent it to me," he remembers wryly. "They said I was gettin' hold to a pink elephant. But they didn't know I knew the peoples that I know. It was a real popular club. They was all comin' in there."

Within a few years the structure began to deteriorate, and in 1982 he decided to pull out. "When I left, I sold the business back to Little Mack and [veteran South Side club owner] Johnny Pepper. They kept it goin' for a minute or two." Two years later he opened the New Club Bootsy's, at Fifty-fifth and State on the South Side, in a building owned by Pervis Spann. He stayed there until the early 1990s.

Although no study of blues-club demographics is available, Bootsy's and New Bootsy's probably played a significant if unheralded role in exposing contemporary blues styles to a wider audience. By the 1980s many white Chicagoans had gotten used to traveling to the South and West Sides to hear the blues at places like Theresa's, the Checkerboard, Florence's, and Eddie Shaw's 1815 Club (on West Roosevelt Road). These venues, though, show-cased mostly the kind of guitar- and harmonica-heavy twelve-bar shuffles considered passé by most mainstream African American listeners. The new sound on the chitlin circuit, an amalgam of blues, R&B, and deep soul that would eventually be labeled "soul-blues," was an unknown quantity to most fans outside the black community.

Artie, fresh off this circuit himself, booked artists like Little Milton, Otis Clay, Tyrone Davis, and Z. Z. Hill, along with more traditional Chicago-styled bluesmen such as Buddy Guy and Junior Wells. His Cottage Grove location, situated relatively close to downtown, was more accessible to Chicago's whites (most of whom lived on the North Side or in the suburbs) than other soul-blues showcases, such as East of the Ryan and Lonnie's Skyway Lounge, which were farther south. At least some of these new patrons followed Artie when he moved to Fifty-fifth Street. What they saw and heard in his clubs was no doubt a revelation to many of them.

Performing for this audience, though, took some getting used to.

Years ago I used to thought white audiences is one of the hardest audiences to sing for. I was used to black audiences whoopin' and hollerin' and clappin' their hands [during a song]—white audiences didn't do that. They'd wait until you finish a song, then give you what you got comin'.

Now they understand the blues; they is really easy to work for. If I played here [the Checkerboard], this place would be full of white audience. Albert King told me something once, said, "People set like they won't clap their hands, like they don't like the blues." He told me, "Quit lookin' at their hands; look under the table—I bet they're pattin' their feet." And it come out to be true.

The recording end of things was looking up as well. In the mid-1980s Artie secured a contract with Ronn/Jewel, out of Louisiana, and he released his first LP, *Blues Boy*. In 1987 he jumped to Ichiban, where two of his albums—*Tired of Sneaking Around* and *Dark End of the Street*—reached the R&B charts. His Ichiban sides, including "Jodie," "Thangs Gotta Change," and "Tore Up," got good play on blues radio and kept him touring steadily. He finally signed with Malaco in 1993; his output for the Jackson, Mississippi,

The suave soul-blues seducer: Artie White publicity photo from the Malaco/Waldoxy years. Photo courtesy of Artie "Blues Boy" White

soul-blues powerhouse on their Waldoxy subsidiary included the songs he's now probably best known for, "I'm Gonna Marry My Mother-in-Law" and "Your Man Is Home Tonight," and it codified his style as both distinctive and solidly within the framework of the modern soul-blues aesthetic. Backed by a punchy horn section, his vocals are still strongly influenced by gospel, but they're imbued with a grainy aggressiveness that evokes the street more than the pulpit. His range is somewhat limited, but he wrings maximum emotion out of his material with his tremulous vibrato and expressive timbre, which modulates from a guttural gasp to a constricted high-end wail.

In 2001, when it came time to renew his contract with Malaco, Artie decided the time was ripe for him to embark on a new professional path. "I was with them for eight years," he reports. "Really, I never left. My contract was up. I didn't jump up and go sign with nobody else. What I did, while I was waiting on them, I just said, 'I'll do a record on my own.'"

Artie maintains that the same keen powers of observation that had helped him when he was learning the ropes from stars like B. B. King and Little Milton proved even more valuable at this point.

> When I was going along back in the years, I was paying attention to every-thing I was doing and everything everyone else was doing. And I learned to know about quality. If you're gonna do something, try to do your best at it. When I was dealing with Waldoxy, [label owner] Tommy [Crouch] Jr. would always ask me, "Hey Artie, how you feel about it?"
>
> I wouldn't say anything—"Well, you're the producer, I'll let you." Then, "Well," I say, "Tommy, I'm gonna be perfectly honest with you; that ain't soundin' right."
>
> "Well, Artie, you know what you doin'. Why don't you tell 'em what to play?"

Knowing what to play, in fact, represents one of Artie White's greatest sources of personal satisfaction. At Malaco he had access to arguably the most creative and prolific hit factory in modern blues. But he has always relied on outside sources as well, and now that he's on his own, he often finds new songs by continuing to tap this rich network, which includes Travis Haddix, Bob Jones, and Chicago-based keyboardist-songwriter Willie White. He takes his greatest pride less in his success as a singer, which he humbly ascribes mostly to his "God-gifted" voice and his years of workaday perseverance, than in his acumen in identifying a potential blues hit and then polishing it into final form. "What I listen at is the lyrics," he explains.

> If the lyrics make sense, and they're strong lyrics, then it's no problem to arrange it. Like, if you got a blues song sayin', "My woman left me last night"—well, you set and think about it. You got a choice: you can

do it in a ballad, or you can do it in a blues; do it up-tempo, do it slow. So I'll tell the guy, "Get your guitar, man. Give me a B-flat. Give me a A." Then I might hum it to myself [he sings in a high, field-holler type moan], "Mmmmm, my woman left me last night. . . ." Then I say, "No, that ain't right. I don't like this. Let's try it up-tempo" [he sings in a fast shuffle]. "Well, my woman left me, she didn't know what she doin'. . . ." You know, different things.

Certain songs that writers give you, I don't like the arrangement. When I first met [saxophonist and arranger] Willie Henderson, he came out the army, he played on my first session. I always leave about four bars in all of my songs, just in case Willie Henderson come in, say, "I want to start this with the horns"—the intro. If you don't sell a song in the first four to eight bars, you ain't gonna sell it. You ain't gonna sell no song at the end, but you get 'em on the beginning, you got it.

It's more expensive using individual musicians instead of synthesizers and automated rhythm tracks in the studio, but Artie says he's willing to take the risk, even if it means taking longer than he would like to come up with a finished product. "That CD there, I spent—with the production and master, photos, recording, studio time—I spent about eighteen thousand.[5] 'Cuz I made up my mind, I ain't gonna go cheap. Would you believe I started on this CD in April, got through with it in August? Just takin' my time! I would never rush it, because you ain't gonna get the right quality. I would do so much on it, then I go to work and come back, have so much money, put it on it, till I finished the product. When I finished that product, it paid off."

He laughingly suggests, in fact, that he may have become a victim of his own perfectionism. "I take my tracks home and listen at 'em, over and over. You always gon' be able to hear something that you coulda done, or you shoulda done. Some singers hear theyself, it sounds good to theyself, so, 'Hey, that's right'—and it's not. But I set and listen—'This ain't right. I ain't singin' it right.' And sometime it might be right, and I sing it so much I go in and mess it up. That's the way it is about this stuff."

Overall, *Can't Get Enough* pretty much justifies Artie's confidence in himself: he nails Johnnie Taylor's "Not the Same Person" with a knife-edged, keening gospel wail; on Willie White's "I'm Crazy about You Baby," Henderson's behind-the-beat horn arrangement brings a savory whiff of Memphis to Artie's gritty soul-blues treatment; and straight-ahead blues offerings like "My Best Friend" and "I've Been Down So Long" showcase his trademark blend of plaintive vulnerability and street-tough survivor's swagger.

As optimistic as he insists he was going in, Artie was flabbergasted at the disc's success. In fact, it made him wonder why things had been so sluggish during his long-running tenure with other labels. "I don't know what was happening," he says, "if it was the jocks' problem, or goin' through Malaco, or something the jocks didn't like. It don't take much for peoples to don't want to do for you. This CD now have done more than the last, I'd say, seven CDs I had."

But the reaction to his follow-up—*Blues in the Past,* an all-blues project he says he's been wanting to record for a long time—demonstrated all too clearly the unforgiving nature of the business he's in. In general, he comports himself well on it, digging into the heart of chestnuts like Roy Brown's "Hard Luck Blues" and balancing pain, righteous indignation, and sly irony on outings like Haddix's "Woman Lied" ("The truth is not always the answer / but it's so much better than tryin' to get by with a lie"). But despite the steadying hands of Delmark Records veterans Paul Serano and Steve Wagner in the recording booth, the disc shows Artie still growing into his role as a producer: several tracks fade in or out abruptly, and on one song, the old Willie Mabon novelty "I Don't Know," he and the band sound as if they are in different keys—and to make matters worse, he loses the time about halfway through.

In the insular world of the blues, where old-boy networks remain strong and handshake deals often predominate over contracts and formal agreements, it doesn't take much for rumors to start. Word of the new disc's weaknesses began to spread almost as soon as it was released. People who hadn't even heard it began to wonder aloud whether Artie had overextended himself—and given the blurry line between "friendly rivalry" and "professional jealousy," it's safe to say that not all of them were unhappy about the prospect.

For his part, Artie has refused to even comment on the carping. Slow-moving, gazing inscrutably out at the world from beneath heavy, half-shut eyelids, he bears himself like a star, even in casual conversation, even though he still appears more often toward the beginning or middle of a show than in the headline slot, even though none of his singles since "Leanin Tree" has charted nationally. He's adamant that despite his rough-hewn persona and a few mistakes along the way, the same spiritual groundedness that propelled him into gospel has sustained him through the vicissitudes of his secular career. According to his former keyboardist, Sweet Miss Coffy, life on the road with his band in the late 1980s was as memorable for the multiple bus breakdowns they endured as for any financial rewards they attained. But she also remembered him fondly as a gentleman who "didn't try to put the move on" her.[6] It's an observation that jibes perfectly with Artie's self-assessment:

> The Bible tell you, only the strong will survive. The weak ain't gon' make it. And I'm sure I'm strong. I smoked cigarettes from when I was six years old, up to sixteen years ago. I made up my mind to quit, and I quit. I drank, up to two years ago. I used to thought you couldn't go onstage if

you didn't have a drink. Said I wouldn't do nothing—"I ain't got nothin' to drink, I ain't gon' sing!"

The Lord just stopped me and put me in [where] I said, "I either do or die." Me and Milton was on a show together, I went to step up into my van. Missed the running board and knocked a hole in my leg! So there, the Lord is warnin' me—it's time for me to leave that whiskey alone. So I just made up my mind to quit, and I just quit. Now I can go onstage and sing myself to be just as high as the audience.

God been good to me. I've been lucky, the way I used to act when I'd been drinkin'. Now the only thing I might take a drink of, and I ain't gonna have but one or two of them, that's a Morgan [sic] David wine, to stimulate my blood. You know your blood'll get lazy on you; by me used to be a big drinker, kept my blood thin. I haven't even drank a bottle of beer in two years—nothin' but that Shark [Sharp's] and O'Doul's. 'Cuz I got sense enough to know that beer has got alcohol in it. You have to be strong at whatever you gonna do.

Still, keeping it all together remains a struggle. The bus may not break down quite as often as it did before, but road life is enough to wear down even the most resilient of souls: eye-glazing hours of staring out the window, punctuated by bursts of adrenaline-pumped excitement when it's showtime, and then back into the bus at three or four o'clock in the morning with, if you're lucky, something close to the money you've been promised—if the promoter didn't short-change you or run out on you, and if the bass player didn't run up a gambling debt, and if you or someone else didn't get robbed, hustled, shaken down, drunk, or high between the back door of the club and the side door of the bus. On top of all that, nobody has eaten for hours, and nobody's had much sleep for days and it's a ten-hour drive to the next gig, which might be canceled when you get there because ticket sales are slow. . . .

None of which takes into consideration the grinding pressure of staying afloat in a business where you're only as good as your *next* success. A soul-blues artist may coast for years on a single hit, as did J. Blackfoot with "Taxi" or Latimore with "Let's Straighten It Out," but a steady stream of vigorously promoted "product" remains essential to achieve the kind of front-line recognition every performer seeks. Indeed, survival in the music business can depend not just on your talent and dedication but, equally, on a seemingly endless array of uncontrollables: the financial stability of record companies, distributors, and clubs; the economic situation of audiences in your market area; and fickle popular tastes and media-driven cultural upheavals.

It takes its toll. Artie admits that even on his old southern stomping grounds, things aren't what they used to be. "They don't have nightclubs like they used to," he laments. "They used to have them country roadhouses; they don't do that no more. Maybe once in a while you'll have some town got a nightclub."

One thing remains depressingly the same, though: Artie shakes his head and lowers his eyes as he ruminates on how the South and its people, especially the poor, are still being exploited and bled by cynical money men:

What done really hurted us, and hurted a lot more, is the riverboats. Gamblin' really done hurt a lot of peoples. Say you got fifty dollars. So him and his wife want to go somewhere, say, "We got fifty dollars—go see Artie, go see Milton." Now what we do, "Take this fifty dollars to the riverboat and win us some money." *Lose* their money, that's what they doin'. That man ain't put that boat out there, spendin' fifteen, sixteen million dollars, for you to beat them.

What they do, they sew up all the money in this town, then move to the next town. I was in a hotel, I'm standin' there lookin' at 'em when they bringin' three boats into Vicksburg, tryin' to get under the bridge with the boats. Now they tell me they done sent one out of there, because they ain't got enough money now to support it. [On] that boat, they give 'em money on their homes, they give 'em money on their cars—they done lost their cars and their homes! And Vicksburg is my home, you know?

But despite the hard times, the exploitation, and volatile public tastes, Artie invokes both the grit of the bluesman and the faith of the believer in his determination to prevail. "It's very disappointing sometimes," he admits, "and disgusting, if you don't feel like you're makin' progress. But I learnt on down the line, progress comes slow, not fast. If it come fast, it goes fast. Blues, jazz, and gospel will always be around. It just dies down and it comes back. I've had a lot of young audience at my shows. Johnnie Taylor told me, 'Don't let nobody tell you not to sing the blues. You ain't gonna get rich, but you gonna keep eatin'.'"

Like many others, Artie also says he feels the pull of the church more intensely as he grows older. When blues artists claim they're determined to "go back" to the church some time before they die (and after they've made their money), it can be easy to write them off as disingenuous. But there was nothing but sincerity in Artie's expression when he looked me in the eye and affirmed, very quietly, that it's only a matter of time before he returns to his roots.

Another thing about me you don't know, I've been called to preach. I am a Christian man. I belongs to a church. Thing about that, I wouldn't put God behind. If I wanna preach, I'm gon' quit the music. If it's strong enough for me to go, and I see he want me to go, I'll quit the music. The Lord ain't gon' send you out there by yourself. He always say, "You make one step, I'll make two." Like the Good Lord told John, when John was

Still in the game: Artie White performing at his "30th Year in Show Business" celebration at Mr. G's, September 11, 2004. Photo by Jennifer Wheeler

writin' the Book of Revelations, he seen John gon' write everybody's time to die—when you's gon' die, why you's gon' die. And God seen him, he says, "John, close that book. Don't write no more."

Before he makes that final decision, though, Artie is determined to give at least a little bit back to the source of his gifts and his inspiration. "I'm gonna do three gospel songs," he maintains, "but I'm not gonna put that on [a blues] CD."

> They gonna be by theyself, like on a mini-CD. I owe myself that; that's where I started. There's a song that I really love, I'm planning on recording: [Doris Akers and Mahalia Jackson's] "Lord, don't move this mountain, just give me the strength to climb." That's the truth—just give me strength. That's beautiful!
>
> My goal is to try and do another five years, and that's it for me. If the Lord bless me, keep going strong, five years from now I'm out of it. But I wanna tell you something—I love people. The good Lord made me what I am, but the people's hope gave me a lot of support to be where I am today. And I ain't stoppin'—I'm goin' a lot further. Because I love my peoples. I want to help who I can help. God'll bless you if you're right. So I always be grateful and thankful for what the Lord have done for me, and how the peoples responds.
>
> I didn't never thought I'd have as many fans as I got. I be surprised, a lot of times, that the white audience and the black audience know me as well as they do. I'm supposed to be goin' back overseas, two or three places. So I'm gonna see what's happening this year. I'm fixin' to do a lot this year. I think—and God bless—this'll be my year.

13

Cicero Blake

"Give Me What I Have Coming or Give Me Nothing"

Cicero Blake was already a twenty-year veteran of doo-wop, soul, and R&B in the mid-1970s when he wrapped his gritty-sweet tenor voice around "Dip My Dipper," a string-drenched blues ballad fueled by a B. B. King–like guitar lead, and found himself catapulted into the front ranks of the soul-blues world. His crooning delivery made him sound both irresistibly naughty and seductively romantic, and the song remains a modern-day classic of the genre. Although he probably wouldn't have predicted it, his emergence as a latter-day blues celebrity culminated what he had been doing in music almost since the beginning. In his own sweet way, Cicero Blake has always been a dedicated roots man.

As far back as 1952, when he and his buddies at Marshall High School began to meet after classes to blend their voices in sweet a capella harmony, Blake was participating in one of the most significant—if unheralded—folk music developments of the twentieth century: the creation of urban doo-wop. As their southern forebears had done before them, these young men fashioned a new and richly textured art form using the sounds, cadences, and melodies of their world: gospel harmonies, street vendors' cries, the romantic blandishments of pop singers, and even (loath though some may have been to admit it) the charged sensuality and ironic wit of blues musicians and songsters.

This art form, of course, was also a popular music, just as the blues had been and still was and just as soul, funk, and R&B in its various permutations would become. Gifted with the ability to adapt his supple tenor voice to a wide range of musical contexts, Blake maintained an ongoing niche for himself in show business over the next decade or two—first as a doo-wop singer, then as a front man for pianist Sonny Thompson's jazzy show band, and eventually as a pop-soul vocalist leading his own group. He recorded in a variety of styles and performed on all-star revues that drew capacity crowds at theaters and nightclubs in Chicago and beyond.

He was thus primed and ready for success in the developing and at the time unnamed field of "soul-blues" as it evolved from these and other diverse sources in the 1970s and early 1980s. Today, although he still considers himself primarily a soul singer, Blake proudly embraces the title of bluesman. "When it comes to American music," he asserts, "there's only two kinds. And that's gospel and the blues. They can hit the blues in the head with a sledgehammer—it's still going to survive."

* * *

A thin sliver of crimson, fading rapidly to inky black, clings to the horizon behind the slanted roofs and mesalike tenement tops of Chicago's West Side skyline. It has been an uncharacteristically crisp mid-September day; in the parking lot behind Wallace's Catfish Corner, at Madison and California, where a blues band has been performing on a flatbed trailer since about four o'clock in the afternoon, people are pulling sweaters and jackets from the trunks of their cars. Along Madison and up and down the narrow side streets, the air has begun to pulsate with the harsh sounds and cadences of an onrushing Saturday night—the roar of unmuffled engines and the squeal of brakes; percussive, bass-heavy blasts from boom boxes and car stereos; and coarse bellows and shrill yells punctuated by occasional rat-a-tat flurries from what might be either cherry bombs or small-caliber gunfire a few blocks away.

Wallace Davis, the flamboyant former alderman who owns the restaurant and controls most of the adjoining blocks, ambles onto the makeshift stage clutching a long-necked beer bottle. He playfully chastises the crowd for their lack of enthusiasm: "Now y'all don't have to pay nothin' to come out here—you could at least clap!" He then raises his hand:

I told you I was gonna bring y'all something special; now here it is.
This man [he gestures toward a slender figure standing to the side, clad

unobtrusively in a gray sweater and dark blue windbreaker] is famous! Nationwide, worldwide, he's *known*. Y'all've heard his records; y'all been to his shows. Y'all *know* you go to where this man's at, gotta pay twenty-five or thirty dollars to get in. I got him out here, for you, for *free*. 'Cuz he's a friend of mine, we go 'way back, and he believes in what we're doing. So c'mon! Y'gotta give it up for this man. . . ."

The band kicks into the gently swaying intro to "Dip My Dipper," Cicero Blake's signature tune. As the crowd recognizes both song and singer, they drown out Davis's final words in a flurry of shouts and applause.

Blake strolls to the microphone, waits for the verse to come around, and eases into the song. His pleading tenor voice sounds a bit grainy, but it's impeccably on pitch, and it wafts through the chill like a warming benediction—an ironic contrast to the no-good man figured as the song's protagonist, who boasts, "I love to dip my dipper into somebody else's dippin's" and then goes on to draw out, in vivid detail, the joys of being a backdoor Lothario who sneaks in and takes his pleasure while the hard-working man of the house is gone. It's one of the oldest poses in the blues—the night-stalking sexual adventurer with an insatiable appetite and a thrill for danger—but the sixty-seven-year-old Blake's youthful timbre, milky vibrato, and suave delivery strip the image of its usual menace. His timing is imbued with a subtle sense of swing despite the song's slow-rolling cadence. Although stationed several feet above his listeners' heads, he stands at the mic with loose-limbed ease and makes affable eye contact as he sings. After stepping back to allow various soloists to do what they can with the standard twelve-bar changes, he repeats a verse or two and walks off to the most enthusiastic response of the night.

Usually a brief guest appearance like that, even by such an esteemed figure as Cicero Blake, would be relatively unremarkable. Wallace's is the kind of neighborhood blues hangout where celebrities, unknowns, almost-knowns, and used-to-be-knowns hobnob together with unforced ease and where the distinction between star and local name often has more to do with who has been on the radio recently—or who's gigging with whose band on whose show next Saturday—than with any objective measure of fame such as record sales.

But this was special. In 2001 Blake was diagnosed with cancer, and he spent at least a year off the scene recovering from surgery and a debilitating regimen of chemotherapy. More recently, with his health on somewhat firmer ground, he had begun to perform and record again. But in June 2003, after a gig in his hometown of Jackson, Mississippi, and not long after his new CD on the Louisiana-based Mardi Gras label hit the stores, he went to a doctor and discovered that the cancer had returned; he soon embarked on a new round of chemo treatments. So despite the unpretentious surroundings and the apparent casualness with which he tossed off his performance, this informal little appearance at Wallace's was received as something of a hero's triumph, a reminder that Cicero Blake is still in the game, still fighting.

Seated at a table inside the restaurant after his brief set, though, Cicero looks tired and uncharacteristically gaunt as he inspects a bottle of fruit juice for its sugar content ("I'm diabetic; now, since this happened, I gotta watch everything specially close"), and he muses about the frightening turns his life has taken over the past few years. "Lotta folks said I wasn't going to make it," he admits, staring solemnly into the middle distance, "but I never claimed this. I could always say, 'Okay, *you* said that's what I got, but as far as I'm concerned, I don't have it.' I feel that had I claimed it, I would have had happen to me like happens to a lot of people."

Is he empowered by religious faith?

> I don't know. I really don't know. I guess I've always been the type of person that could deal with whatever. One thing I was always taught: you worry about things you can do something about, and things that you can't do anything about, don't worry about. So in this case, I said, "Well, if it's meant for me to not recover, then I won't, whether I worry about it or not." I won't say it's not disheartening—I weighed 198, and when I finished I weighed 138. I could take my hand and put it all the way around my thigh and have a little room left—but I never let it get the best of what I could do.

Cicero Blake does not dwell on the negative. His demeanor both on- and offstage bespeaks a determination to remain resolutely in control of himself and his emotions, even as he admits his vulnerability and negotiates his way through vicissitudes and uncertainties—personal, professional, existential—that might draw another singer into either sanctified shouts or bluesy paroxysms or another man into despair or self-immolation. Such a stance might seem ironic, almost contradictory, in a musical field defined largely by its embrace of unfettered emotional honesty, but for Cicero, it has been a survival tool and, he insists, a carefully honed professional strategy.

"One thing I never did," he reflects, as outside the window the band lurches into an out-of-tune blues lope to bring on yet another guest vocalist, "I never changed my show. Same show I do on the South Side of Chicago, I do on the North Side. But I started out on the West Side and the South Side, and I will always come back here. That's where I got my start. I don't worry about whether or not I've made my big reputation yet. If it's not for me now, maybe it's for me after a while—I'll get my turn."

Cicero Blake at the Chicago Blues Festival, June 2003. Photo by Andrzej Matysik/
Twoj Blues magazine

Even as a boy growing up in Jackson, surrounded by the cadences of gospel and gutbucket blues, Cicero Blake idolized country singers and R&B balladeers like Ivory Joe Hunter. It was their smoothness, he says, that captivated him.

> Just calm, man. Y'know, just lay it out there. As a little kid I was sing-ing gospel, gospel quartet singing. I was a little guy, about six or seven years old, singin' with grown men in church. The gospel thing was an influence; I didn't do a lot of gospel, I didn't adopt the whole sound, but it had some influence on my style. My thing, at that time, was country and western—Red Foley, Little Jimmy Dickens, Hank Williams. I used to listen to the Grand Ole Opry on Saturday nights.
>
> The first song that I ever did in public? In grammar school on Friday afternoons, after everybody had done all their work, we had a program. Everybody who could get up and recite a poem, had a dance they wanted to do, or sing. A little show in the classroom. I decided to do, one Friday, a song by Ivory Joe Hunter, "I Need You So," one of the big records for him back in the early fifties.

It was by his own account a sedate and well-ordered childhood, one that revolved around the axis of church, home, and school—if enlivened, occasion-ally, by a ribald jokefest or night on the town. "Lived right there on what we called 'Fornification' [i.e., Fortification] and Grayson Street," he chuckles.

> It's Lamar Street now. My grandmother and them, I think, were raised somewhere out from Jackson, down around Bolton, about twenty miles south. But my father and mother were always in Jackson. I got some pictures of my mom and dad when they were nightclubbing, and they're sharp, man. Dressed up, mink coats and stuff.
>
> I was raised by my grandmother. She was religious, didn't have a lot of blues records. But I also spent some time with my aunt [he allows himself a mischief-eyed smile]. At one time my aunt had a jukebox in her house; she was bootlegging whiskey. And at one time my father, too. So I would listen to the blues.
>
> One radio station in Jackson played rhythm and blues. A jock named Mike O'Reilly, white guy, name of the show was "Atomic Boogie," and that's the only type of music he played.[1] You could call in a request, whatever you wanted to hear. He came on about three or four o'clock in the evening, after the kids got out of school, stayed on till about seven o'clock.

There was also WLAC, the legendary fifty-thousand-watt Nashville sta-tion that broadcast blues, R&B, and gospel records every night on shows hosted by deejays like Gene Nobles, Herman Grizzard, Hoss Allen, and John R.—jive-talking white hipsters who helped pave the way for the interracial cultural explosion that began to send tremors through the country in the early 1950s. But despite all the music in the air—not to mention his own nascent success singing in church and school—Cicero maintains he never set out to emulate the stars he heard. In fact, he was as surprised as anyone when, after that Friday afternoon talent revue, he became something of a local celebrity: "All I know is that I discovered that I could sing. Kids would say, 'Hey, he can sing! You can sing!' It was just something that, I realized it. I could sing."

Cicero won't say exactly how and why he left Jackson for Chicago in 1952, when he was sixteen ("Well, basically, my mother and father were here"), but he staunchly maintains he felt fully prepared for the move. Unlike many southern-born blues artists of his generation and even younger (and despite his affection for the Opry), he insists he never really considered himself "country" at all.

"Jackson was different from most cities in the South," he insists. "For there, it was a pretty big city. So it was somewhat different. And then you always had relatives or people that you knew who grew up in places like Chicago, St. Louis, Detroit. They'd always come back, and you'd hear the different stories. So you kinda always had the big-city living idea in your head. So when I came, it was not like making an adjustment—it was just leaving Jackson, moving to Chicago."

Nonetheless, he adds, "I had experienced a lot of the prejudice, a lot of the segregation and stuff like that, and I just was like a lot of youngsters at the time. I was ready to move somewhere far away where I thought it would be better. I was just ready to leave the South."

Once in Chicago he adapted himself easily to his new surroundings, attending classes at Marshall High and making friends with other kids like himself who relished the opportunity to grab at a piece of the American dream that had been denied their parents and grandparents. It was a time of optimistic aspirations, especially for the young, who reflected these aspirations in their dress (by the early 1960s kids on the South and West Sides who sported stylish clothes and well-coifed hair were dubbed "Ivy Leaguers"),[2] their language, and—as always—their music.

In fact, cultural stirrings akin to those that would soon convulse white middle-class America were being felt in the burgeoning black communities of the urban North. The midcentury Great Migration actually comprised several migrations: for every ex-fieldhand like Muddy Waters or Chester Burnett who might come north steeped in a rural, blues-and-gospel-rooted cultural framework and then try to adapt those folkways to the new environment ("big-city backwoods people," as Claude Brown scathingly described them in 1965),[3] a forward-looking youth like Cicero Blake arrived as well.

Many of these youngsters developed ideas, values, and aesthetics radically different from those of their more countrified neighbors, even if some of those neighbors were relatives or had ridden up with them on the same train. "Nobody liked the blues," doo-wop veteran Maurice Simpkins boldly assured Chicago music historian Robert Pruter. "We used to laugh at the blues. We were going to school every day, and these blues singers hadn't even gone to grammar school."[4]

That was far from the entire picture, of course. The blues clubs that proliferated in Chicago during the 1950s and early 1960s attracted patrons of all ages, and in fact a good number of Simpkins's musical contemporaries considered themselves bluesmen then and still do. But even those who were more willing to embrace their down-home heritage insisted on doing so on their own terms. Artists like Junior Wells and Magic Sam went on to infuse their blues with elements of R&B, soul, and eventually rock. Bo Diddley updated the folksy tropes of his Mississippi childhood with quick-witted urban signifying, electronic embellishments, and perhaps most important, the hot-blooded declaration "I'm a M. A. N."—providing, among other things, a riposte to elder statesman Big Bill Broonzy's plea, "When Will I Get to Be Called a Man?" Broonzy had written that song in the late 1920s but was still performing it for mostly white audiences in 1955, the same year Bo had his hit (covered by Muddy Waters as "Mannish Boy" a few months later).

Characteristically, Cicero remembers that he kept himself pretty much removed from these nascent culture wars. "I've always liked blues, too," he maintains.

> But I guess I consider myself a soul singer. Sam Cooke, that was another one of my idols, because he was so smooth and classy. When I started high school, word got around that I could sing. Different guys met after school, behind the school, and we finally got to standing up in the bathroom harmonizing. Myself, Howard McClain, John Carter, Teddy Long, and a fellow named James Harper. We named ourselves the Goldentones.
>
> We used to go out and do the talent shows—had our little cute pink caps with a black ball on the top and all that. The Dells, Flamingos, all these guys, we'd go. If you won the show, I think first prize was like five dollars, and most groups had at least five guys in the group. A dollar apiece. Big money! [He chuckles.] It was like a friendly thing—"Okay, you won this time; we gon' get you next week." I think that's why even to this day, a lot of the guys who came along during that time, we're good friends.

As it turned out, the Goldentones went on to make some important musical history in Chicago. "Dee Clark used to come by our rehearsals. And he always had this high falsetto tenor voice. At the time he wasn't wanting to be a singer; he liked to play basketball. Leon Hilliard [the Globetrotter] was his favorite guy. Used to hang out at the gym, always with the basketball in his hand. After I got out of high school, I decided I was going to go into the Air Force. So I told Dee, 'Dee, you should get into the group.' I'm the one who influenced Dee to get in."

Whatever his basketball aspirations may have been, Delecta "Dee" Clark was already something of a show-business veteran by that time.[5] In 1952, when he was about thirteen, he had achieved celebrity as a member of the Hambone Kids, whose novelty hit "Hambone" featured the off-center rhythm Bo Diddley eventually made famous as the "Diddley beat." Clark now introduced his Goldentones bandmates to Herb Kent, the mellow-voiced WGES deejay who went by the nickname "the Cool [or 'Kool'] Gent." Kent took a liking to the group, and after opportunistically rechristening them the Kool Gents, he brought them to Vee-Jay Records in nearby Gary, Indiana. Although most discographies don't credit him, Cicero says he sang on some of the Gents' mid-1950s Vee-Jay releases.

"I came home on leave," he recalls, "and we did 'I Just Can't Help Myself' and 'This Is The Night,' several things. We're switching off leads, Dee Clark and myself, we would switch off lead on songs."

By then, though, Cicero had been lured in a different musical direction. "Once I got into the military in '54, I started traveling with a variety show, like an entertainment group, went to different bases, entertaining troops and stuff. I kinda got used to being a solo artist. After I got out, it just didn't feel right with the group any more. [The record company] had started to venture Dee Clark out as a solo artist, and the group just kind of folded out."

Vee-Jay teamed up a new singer, Pirkle Lee Moses, with the remaining Kool Gents and renamed the group the El Dorados, which had been the moniker of Moses' previous aggregation, one of the most accomplished and influential of all the Chicago doo-wop groups. Clark, meanwhile, went on to achieve considerable success as a soul singer over the next few years with hits like "Nobody but You," "Hey Little Girl," and—perhaps best remembered today—"Raindrops" ("fallin' from my eye-eyes"), all recorded for Vee-Jay or its Abner subsidiary.

Having tasted the pleasures of life as a front-line singer, Cicero decided to keep moving on his own. About a year after returning from the service, he joined pianist Sonny Thompson's band as the featured vocalist. Thompson's aggregation specialized in the kind of good-timey, adult-oriented jump blues—still often called "rhythm and blues"—that remained popular among mainstream black audiences at the time. Cicero remembers that when he was fronting Thompson's band, he sang mostly material by urbane songsmiths like Nat "King" Cole. Professionalism and hip sophistication—"discipline and style," as Johnny Otis has articulated it—were the rule.[6] "When you went out there," Cicero recalls, "you went out there with vests. At the time, the people who would come out to see you, whether it was an auditorium, a club, or whatever, when they came, they put their clothes on."

The band also often worked as the house orchestra on all-star revues featuring eclectic line-ups that may sound impossibly exotic and thrilling to contemporary fans:

> I'd do my thing like an opening act. We did shows with, like, Jackie Wilson, Brook Benton, James Brown; hooked up and did some shows with Dee Clark, who was big then. You'd have Chuck Jackson, you'd have the Temptations, the Miracles, Stevie Wonder, and then you'd have some blues people. Plus a movie; then you'd have comedians—Moms Mabley, Redd Foxx, Pigmeat Markham.
>
> During the time I was working with Sonny, the audience was always mixed—young, old, middle-aged. I think the generation gap, where kids wanted to hear this, old people wanted to hear [that], started when black radio started to go under. They started playing for what they want to call "the young generation." That's when the black audience couldn't hear the blues any more. That's when it started. I never saw that difference—I always admired the older artists.

No doubt partly because of the wide range of music he encountered on these shows, Thompson had an ear for both older blues styles and the growing teen market, despite his own preference for more sophisticated sounds. "At that time," Cicero continues,

> [Sunny] was associated with Federal Records, out of Cincinnati. We'd be on the road, we'd go through Cincinnati, he'd record Freddie King. Sonny kept telling me, "I want to record you. I want to record you." [But] we kept putting it off.
>
> Then I met [producer and label owner] Leo Austell, and he got interested in recording me. So he set up a date, and we went into the studio, and the very first record I recorded was called "Should I Go" [b/w "Could This Be Love"]. I think [guitarist] Lefty Dizz and his group had just come into the Chicago area, and they played the session. Jesse Anderson, saxophone player and singer out of Wichita, was playing in Dizz's band.

The disc was released on the Renee label in 1961. In retrospect, it foreshadowed both the "soft soul" for which Chicago would soon become known and the grittier, more gospel-influenced "deep soul" toward which Cicero eventually gravitated and that eventually led him to cross over into the amorphous modern-day category of "soul-blues." His keening tenor voice, freed from the feathery cushion of doo-wop harmonies, soars into aching realms of adolescent longing as the band lurches forward in a jaunty, neo–New Orleans rhumba cadence, with blaring horn turnarounds and yakkety-sax solo breaks. Dizz, if indeed it is he on guitar, fires off popping single-string rhythm patterns interspersed with aggressive note bends, but there's little evidence of the high-velocity workouts for which he would eventually become famous among latter-day Chicago blues aficionados.

Those early 45s include echoes of Jackie Wilson's sound in both Cicero's fervid tenor ascents and the grandiose instrumentation, but Cicero denies any intentional effort to mold him into a Wilson clone. In fact, he says, these early sides were cut with little planning of any kind: "A lot of sessions then was head sessions—'Just come in and do your thing.' No arrangements. 'You play this; that's what I want you to play,' or whatever. Have to learn the songs. We just went in and did it."

All in all, it was a radical departure from the sophisticated uptown style he had been purveying with Sonny Thompson. Nonetheless, he stayed with Thompson for a few more years, inserting one or two of his pop numbers into his set whenever he could, enjoying life on the road, and expanding his reputation. It was a free-wheeling time ("You weren't thinking too much of 'career'; you just wanted to hear your name called, say, 'I'm on the radio'"), and it was replete with the high jinks and flamboyant hustles that make road stories a staple of blues and R&B folklore.

> There was a singer in Chicago named Billy Valentine. On some shows Sonny used to pass him off as Little Richard. I'll never forget, at Budland [in Chicago's Pershing Hotel], Budland was a place that you'd go down and kinda showcase your new record for all the jocks—Richard Steele, E. Rodney Jones, Don Cornelius. One night—I think at the time [about 1962] I had the record "Don't Do This to Me"—Dee Clark and I was there, and this guy started talking, said "I'm from Detroit. I'm here to promote my new record."
> Dee asked him, "What's your name?"
> Said, "I'm Cicero Blake."
> So Dee looked at him, looked over at me, back at him, said, "What?"
> Said, "I'm Cicero Blake."
> [Dee] said, "Cicero Blake's standing here—that's Cicero Blake!" And the guy just kinda stands up, eased away.

Austell issued Cicero's sides on several different labels over the next few years, but none made much noise until 1964, when a string-sweetened ballad called "Sad Feeling" achieved enough success to embolden the singer to strike out as a solo act. "I had a nice run," he reflects, "between '64 and about, I'd say, three years. I can't remember the names of the guys in the band, but it wasn't hard to [put together a unit], because most of the band guys was used to the type of music that cats were doing at that time. Bands were geared in that direction. I don't think a lot of the bands at that time were playing blues; they were more soul."

Cicero's own ability to blend seamlessly into "the type of music that cats were doing at the time," a trademark of his since the beginning, was probably both a blessing and a curse in the long run. He and his producers seem to have found it increasingly difficult to find material, or even a style, that could make him stand out in the cluttered teen-soul market. By 1968's "Loving You Woman Is Everything," the arrangements had perked up, with punchy horns and throbbing basslines obviously borrowed from Memphis–Muscle Shoals southern soul; Cicero's vocals sounded grittier as well. But between the shallow production, the unimaginative lyrics, and the anachronistically girlish-sounding backing choruses, "Loving You" and most of his other late-1960s sides now sound dated and generic—and probably seemed even more acutely so then.

Cicero admits that by the turn of the decade his career had "dropped off for a minute, just like anything else." Through the years he had usually augmented his musical income with day jobs. He has worked as, among other things, a nurse's assistant for the U.S. Public Health Service, a lab technician, clerk in an insurance company, a Cook County park commissioner, and a coinvestor with blues pianist Lovie Lee in a furniture-upholstering business. As a result, he wasn't in danger of starving if he didn't sell any more records. But having to relegate music to a part-time passion ate at him. Despite the risk it entailed for a nearly middle-aged singer who had never had a real hit, he eventually decided to take the plunge. "In about '72, I just made my mind up: see if I'm gonna make it this way. I just decided, 'What you gonna do, Cicero? You gonna make singing a career or aren't you?'"

By his own admission, it was tough going for a few years. In 1975, though, he latched onto "Your Love Is Like a Boomerang," a song cowritten by veteran soul singer and composer Frederick Knight. Produced by Archie Russell, a partner of Leo Austell's, and released on Capitol, the recording was the most fully realized soul outing Cicero had ever committed to wax. It sold well enough to earn him spots on shows starring the likes of Jerry Butler, Wilson Pickett, and smooth-soul crooner Chuck Jackson—not quite stardom, but an encouraging nudge.

Then came the break every singer dreams of: a song perfectly tailored to his style (although neither he nor his producer knew it at the time), destined not only to become a classic in its field but, even more important, to be forever associated with the artist himself. As Cicero remembers the events, the recording came about almost as an afterthought. "Actually what happened," he says with a smile, "we were in Atlanta, in Clarence Carter's studio. My producer, Bob Riley, who had also been my promotion man at Capital, asked me, 'Can you sing a blues song?' I said, 'Yeah, I can sing it—I just never recorded it.' So he had a thing, just a simple twelve-bar blues. We did one or two takes, that's all we did on it. Up to that point I had never recorded anything similar to that."

The song was "Dip My Dipper." This slow-grinding ode to illicit eros could easily have been an exercise in braying machismo, but Cicero's silken croon, effortless enunciation and phrasing, and overall warmth transformed it into a tender, even yearning testimonial of erotic bliss. It became, in other words, an archetypal blues juxtaposition of an outlaw's pose against a vulnerable lover's plea, updated by Cicero's suave delivery along with Riley's roomy production and the elegant, horn-rich arrangement. Not only did it revitalize his career (almost thirty years later it's still getting airplay in the South, and it's always the first thing audiences request at his shows); in addition, it helped define the fusion of bluesy emotionality, deep-soul vocal style with a contemporary R&B sheen, and playful adult carnality that soon became the hallmark of modern soul-blues.

The record came out in the mid-1970s, and it ended up being reissued at least two more times on different labels over the next few years. Cicero also included it on his 1985 album *Too Hip to Be Happy*, on Valley Vue. By then he had made another breakthrough, this one closer to home. "What really gave me a lot of exposure to the white audience," he declares, "was when I started working at B.L.U.E.S. [on Chicago's North Side]. At that time, you didn't work the North Side unless you played an instrument. Otis Clay and I were the first—I didn't play an instrument, Otis didn't play an instrument—we started doing a different type of music [from that] old lump-de-bump-de-bump 'Sweet Home Chicago' stuff."

Cicero was usually backed on these gigs by Masheen Company, a versatile show band who were as likely to break into a hit by Lionel Ritchie or Culture Club during their stage-warming set as they were to play a blues or even a funk tune. People warned him, he said, that the North Side crowd wasn't ready for that kind of thing, even though such eclecticism had been standard fare in most South and West Side nightclubs for years. "Look at us like we crazy," he says with a laugh. "But I used to tell 'em, 'If you doin' a good job, people will respond—every time—to what you're doing.' Now, pretty much everywhere you go, there's a white audience that knows Cicero Blake's name."

That doesn't necessarily mean that they always understand Cicero Blake's music. Since "Dip My Dipper" broke, he has recorded a series of critically well-received CDs on several labels; he has also toured fairly steadily, especially in the South, although without a follow-up hit to equal the success of "Dipper," he has tended to be a supporting act more often than a headliner. Despite his assurance that Chicago's white blues-club crowd embraced him when he ventured north, though, he has yet to establish his name there as the kind of "authentic" soul man (like, for instance, Otis Clay) who can make the purists forget their three-chord fixation for a while, come out, and have church.

Part of the reason is that Cicero doesn't usually "have church" at all. His mellifluous croon, as seductive as it may be to southern soul sisters, still seems to resonate a bit strangely for fans who associate blues with throat-tearing agony and soul mostly with house-wrecking fervor. (Heated debates continue to rage on Web sites and in fan magazines over whether smooth balladeers like Chuck Jackson, Brook Benton, and even Smokey Robinson qualify as "real" soul singers; Cicero's name has also shown up in these discussions.)

To complicate things further, Cicero has embraced wholeheartedly soul-blues' recent move toward synthesized backing tracks. Today it's a rare soul-blues artist who populates the studio with more than a handful of musicians— probably a guitarist and a keyboardist and maybe a bassist. And increasingly, this sound is being replicated onstage: keyboard synths have replaced horns in most touring bands. To many white fans for whom soul is defined largely by the Stax/Muscle Shoals sound of the 1960s, just as blues has been codified by the twelve-bar guitar-and-harmonica postwar Chicago style, these trends are dangerous signs of homogenization, an abandonment of the eternal quest for the Holy Grail of "authenticity." Cicero, however, insists that in an age when having a recognizable brand is paramount, this trend is an asset, not a detriment.

> Consider the Motown sound. Whatever came out of Motown, you knew it came from Motown, because they had that sound. What's happening, they're developing what they call a southern soul sound. It's beginning to get to the point that if you hear something from the South, you'll say, "That's from the South"—no matter what label it's on. Good thing! If you bring it to some of the stations in the South, you're going to have good outlets. That's why, right now, you concentrate on Mississippi, Alabama, North Carolina, South Carolina, Georgia, Texas, Louisiana, Florida—all that southern area. Lots of good young artists coming out of the South; that's what they're beginning to call southern soul.
>
> I haven't used live musicians [on recordings] since *Too Hip to Be Happy*. I'd rather have synthesizers if it's programmed right. If it's mixed right, it's pretty hard to distinguish what it is. Plus, it's easier—you don't spend as much time in the studio. This last CD, I went down to Jackson on Monday and cut ten tunes; Tuesday night I was on my way back to Chicago.

In performance Cicero still uses a full band, although he generally eschews horns. Nonetheless, his adherence to the modern soul-blues formula of romantic ballads spiced with playful nastiness and light-funk dance workouts has caused problems, at least as far as crossover appear is concerned. His performance on the Petrillo Bandshell's main stage at the 2003 Chicago Blues Festival, his first there in nearly a decade, showcased him at his mellow-toned best as he eased the crowd through his usual set of sweet-soul balladry, jaunty uptempo odes to juking and good times, and his nightstalker-with-a-heart-of-gold testimonial in "Dip My Dipper." But it was clear that some critics, at least, missed the point. The *Chicago Tribune* praised his "feathery trills, gritty warbles, melancholy calls and playful timing" but couldn't resist a dig at "his aptly-named band, Machine [*sic*] Company."[7] The *Chicago Sun-Times* was considerably more acerbic, casting aspersions not only on Cicero's show but, by implication, on the entire cultural and aesthetic milieu represented by contemporary southern soul-blues: "Blake's live shows tend to veer uncomfortably into a chitlin' soaked raunchy direction," sniped writer Jeff Johnson before conceding that "he was on his best behavior at Petrillo, even refraining from the histrionics on his biggest hit, 'Dip My Dipper.'" Johnson also criticized the band for its lack of a horn section and Cicero's show for "dragg[ing] in spots," but he added patronizingly that this was, after all, "one of those career achievement gigs" and that Cicero "did justice" to several of his offerings.[8]

The spectacle of a white critic—a northerner, at that—deriding an African American blues singer for sounding "chitlin' soaked" might be wickedly ironic if it weren't so representative of the cultural obtuseness that still permeates much blues commentary in the United States. Indeed, Cicero prides himself greatly on the classiness of his stage act and his avoidance of "histrionics" ("Just tell the story; all that screamin' and hollerin' ain't goin' on"). He was gallant (or politic) enough to disregard Johnson's not-so-subtly implied ethnic slur, but he remains deeply offended at what he considers to have been not just musical insensitivity but a calculated—and by implication all-too-typical—trivialization of both himself and his art.

"No appreciation at all!" he snaps, a rare bitterness creeping into his voice.

> Plus, I never met him. He could have tried to find out something about me. How can you write about me and you don't know me? I don't want no crumbs; give me the loaf. I want the whole loaf or none of it. Give me what I have coming or give me nothing.
>
> I heard B. B. King tell a young boy at the Blues Festival—the boy came down and he wanted to interview B. B., and he said, "Mr. King, my mother and them are big fans of yours."

Cicero Blake at the Chicago Blues Festival, June 2003. Photo by Paul Natkin/Photo Reserve

So B. B. looked at him and said, "Well, what about you?"

"Well, I don't listen to a lot of blues. . . ."

"Then how can you sit here and interview me?" And he just told him, "Well, this interview is over." It's very seldom you see B. B. telling someone off like that. But he was right—how you gonna [write about] me and you don't know nothin' about me? No! They don't know it.

None of this, however, discourages Cicero in his ongoing determination to expand his base. When we spoke in 2003, he was negotiating with some British fans to set up an overseas tour, optimistically envisioned for a time in the near future when his chemotherapy would be completed and he could again sing with undiminished power ("I figure 'bout March or April. That's when I'm looking to really get back full force"). He was researching the possibility of reissuing his early soul and doo-wop sides on a collectors' label (the label, Grapevine, released the compilation in 2004), and he talked animatedly about a recent gig he had played at a South Loop bistro, which he planned to pick up again soon and which he hoped would attract both black and white young professionals, thus exposing him to yet another new audience. "Thousands of blues lovers in Chicago," he enthused. "Even now, I can still play both sides of town."

But he spoke most emotionally of the reception he had received several years earlier in a nightclub full of longtime fans and admirers, at a benefit held for him during his first bout with cancer. As he talked about it, his voice dropped into a tender murmur that recalled his ballad singing: "The first instance when I really realized was the time when I had the first surgery, and they did the benefit for me. I walked in there—they *walked* me in there; I was so weak I could hardly stand up, but I was determined to be there, and I made it—and when I looked around, the whole club, wasn't a seat nowhere. Folks standing along the walls. And that's when I really realized, 'Cicero, you have an impact on these people in Chicago.'"

But then, as if to avoid any possibility that his musings might be mistaken for autumnal resignation, he quickly broke into a bright-eyed smile and reaffirmed both his physical resilience and his determination to remain true to the professionalism he considers his most enduring asset.

"I feel great," he insisted, despite a hacking cough that occasionally cut him off in midsentence.

I don't hang around; I never did. If you're going to work a club, let's say, Monday night, why you gonna hang around there Tuesday, Wednesday, Thursday, Friday, Saturday, Sunday? That's a thing I feel lowers your standards. So I never did hang out.

I'm supposed to come off [treatment] in February [2004], but they gave me the last two weeks of October and the whole month of November off, to get my strength back. I don't know if they're going to add that to my cutoff date or not. But hopefully they'll say I've had enough for right now. I've been just kind of freelancing. I'm not playing with a band, but I have musicians I can get any time I need 'em. Yeah, I got that. I'm really back, just kind of takin' my time. I'm still an active act, still working. I'm not on the shelf!

14 Little Scotty
"I'm Not Only a Blues Singer—I'm a Motivator"

Clarence "Little Scotty" Scott has spent most of his life challenging boundaries and straddling worlds. Severely disfigured in a fire in his South Carolina home as a boy, he learned early on how to survive as an outsider. He found a haven both in church and in local jukes, where he would sit alone all night at a table, conscious of looking like "somethin' different," and then finally take the stage and astonish people with his commanding, gospel-rich vocals.

Inspired by both the personal acceptance and the financial rewards he found there, young Clarence soon took to the road as an entertainer. Although he insists he never lost his early bedrock grounding in religious faith, he gleefully immersed himself in the fast times and easy money this new life offered; by the time he cut his first records in the 1970s, he remembers, he had already garnered—and lost—a small fortune pimping in New York.

Even then, though, he had his serious side. One of his early 45s appeared on a label affiliated with a Muslim organization with which he had been studying. In New York he also "sat under" such figures as the historian

John Henrik Clarke and the firebrand City College professor Leonard Jeffries; he was eventually certified by several nondenominational churches as an evangelist with preaching privileges. Since moving to Chicago, he has worked for such diverse causes as Jesse Jackson's Operation PUSH, the late Harold Washington's mayoral campaign, Khalid Abdul Muhammad's Million Youth March, anti–death penalty initiatives, and the peace movement. He has also maintained his music career, cutting records in a variety of styles for small labels, performing in neighborhood clubs and show lounges, and occasionally embarking on a modest tour through the South or along his old stomping grounds on the eastern seaboard.

Scotty enjoys near-ubiquity on the South Side blues scene. If he's not gigging or sitting in somewhere, he's probably in the audience, greeting well-wishers, handing out pluggers for his next gig, or peddling his latest self-produced CD. Nevertheless, he is virtually unknown among most of the city's white blues fans. If whites know him at all, it's as the squat, frog-faced little guy with sleepy-looking eyes who waddles around the periphery of demonstrations and other public events decked out with an array of buttons—vintage Harold Washington campaign buttons, portraits of Jesse Jackson and Louis Farrakhan, antiwar and antidrug slogans—engaging passersby in passionate but low-key conversations on the issues of the day. Only in private does the blunt racialism he absorbed from mentors like Jeffries and Muhammad occasionally make itself evident, and even then it's usually tempered by his professed adherence to a philosophy of global brotherhood and peace.

In his everyday presence as a respected if somewhat eccentric public spokesman who lives and works largely beneath the radar of mainstream media recognition, Scotty exemplifies the long-standing and honorable role of the "race man" as an esteemed figure in the African American community. In the ease with which he moves from the jubilant carnality of his blues into the spiritual fervor of his preaching and back again, both onstage and in conversation—to say nothing of the way he brings the quick-minded survival instincts and personal style of the street hustler to all his diverse enterprises and interests—he is also a living testimonial to the unbreakable link between liberation and levity, between solidarity and celebration, which have long been an essential characteristic of ritual black expression.

* * *

It's a warm Sunday night in June.[1] On the 5900 block of South Halsted Street the neighborhood has been plunged into darkness—the streetlights have gone out again. Everything is eerily silent; Chicago's urban roar seems to have receded into a distant soundtrack, bleeding in from another world.

Even Halsted itself, a major north–south thoroughfare, looks deserted. But if you listen carefully, you can hear raucous levity emanating from a clapboard building with sealed windows and no sign in front. Down the block several hooded young men clump together and slouch edgily near a vacant storefront, its boarded-up front door protected by burglar bars. Aside from them, that muted laughter on the west side of the street is virtually the only indication of life—and certainly the only indication of happiness—for blocks around.

Inside the club, which was formerly known as Porter's and is now called the New Excuse Lounge, a Father's Day party is underway. The lights are dim; shredded Christmas tinsel hangs in pieces from the wall behind the bandstand. The pasteboard panels that serve as a ceiling are broken, some dangling precariously a few feet above people's heads. The band is, to put it charitably, raw—the guitars are sour and out of tune, and the drums sound like cardboard. But throaty laughter and high-pitched shouts cut through the smoke-clogged room. In the space in front of the band, where tables and chairs have been cleared away, people dance and grind with exuberant sensual abandon as each in a series of vocalists—Bobby Too Tough, Al Harris, and finally Little Scotty, tonight's headliner—takes his place in front of the rattletrap ensemble and holds forth.

Scotty has been nursing a soft drink at a table for most of the evening. A bit before midnight he finally moves centerstage to perform. He's clad in orange slacks, an orange blazer, and a white turtleneck, with a necklace of wooden beads and a sporty cap to complete the ensemble. As he clutches the microphone and thrusts it to his face to sing, his left hand looks stunted, almost like a flipper; if you look closer, you can see the seared skin stretched tightly over his knuckles and fingers.

Scotty croons the opening lines of "A Change Is Gonna Come" as the band gropes desperately for an appropriate key behind him. He has obviously listened to Otis Redding's 1965 version of the Sam Cooke classic. He gasps, gargles, rasps, and moans out swooping "Oooh! Oooh! Oooh!" imprecations before settling into an almost hypnotic, repeated cadence—"It's gonna come, it's gonna come, it's gonna come"—over his accompanists' halting riffs.

Suddenly he launches into a playfully blustering Father's Day sermon: "We don't take no shit today! Today is our day! We gonna party all night long!" The band obediently extricates itself from its primitive soul groove and grinds into a twelve-bar lope. Scotty in turn takes his cue from the bluesy direction the music has suddenly taken, announcing, "I wanna do a song from my next album called 'I Want to Play with Your Percolator'!"

Raucous guffaws resonate throughout the room as he begins to half-sing, half-preach a series of verses that sound as if he's making them up on the spot: "I called my baby late last night, I thought she was 'sleep, she wasn't right. . . . Crawled in the bed, put my hand down, y'know what I said? 'Let me play wit' that percolator and make it hot! I want to burn it up every time it start! You called me, I called you! Let's don't go to sleep, let's try to do what we got to do.'"

Through it all Scotty comports himself in this dingy little dive as if it were showtime at the Regal. Pudgy and squat, he spins in half-circles, bends at the waist and then snaps up straight, raises his right hand in testimonial, and winks at the women seated nearby. He runs through his full vocal armamentarium of soul-blues and gospel tricks—molasses-thick vibrato, guttural gasps, octave slurs, rich chuckles, and bursts of laughter. He also introduces various friends and "celebrities" in the audience. When he's not singing, his jaw goes slack, his tongue lolls from his mouth, his eyelids droop, and he rocks back and forth in rhythm until the verse he's waiting for comes around.

"Percolator" eventually leads into an unexpurgated version of Clarence Carter's "Strokin'" on which Scotty again alternates between sung verses and spoken improvisations: "I married a woman, weighed nine hundred pounds. . . . When I got in the bed, the damn thing broke down. I fell on the damn floor, she rolled over. . . . She said, 'Kiss me on my thigh.' . . . She said, 'Kiss me further up.' . . . She grabbed me by the ears! She pulled me up to that damn Lord have mercy! . . . Y'know what I did? I started suckin' it! I started wearin' it out!"

The medley finally closes with a cymbal crash and a tepid final chord from the band. Before they can start another song, Scotty suddenly raises his right hand again, palm outward. He begins speaking in an almost conversational tone, but within a minute or two he's hollering and testifying with full gospel fervor:

Let me tell you something—we got to love each other, man. We got to quit killin', stealin', rapin' our women. We got to come together. See, let me explain somethin' to you. I march on City Hall every day for police brutality. I'm out there in the trenches for our young folks. And I'm-a tell you something, young folks. You are the most hated person on the face of th'—black man the most hated person on this earth. A black man! Especially youth!" [People begin to affirm: "Yuh-huh!" Yesss!" "MmmHmmm!"] So we got to pull together. We got to stop killin' each other, man. Y'know? ["Right on!"] That same brother you be killin' may save your life one day, man. Drugs ain't 'bout nothin'! ["Ooooh yeah!"] White man gettin' rich; we gettin' poor! ["That's right!"] We don't even own a graveyard!

His voice sounds anguished as he ascends into a gristle-choked shout:

"We got to wake up, man! So we got to get the young folks, man—give them a standing ovation, man! [Applause and shouts fill the room.] Because those are our youth, man! We got to love our young folks! [The audience responds with more applause.] Ain't no child really bad—the system is bad!"

The band kicks into the opening bars of Tyrone Davis's "Can I Change My Mind." It's difficult to tell whether they've responded to Scotty on cue or whether they're trying to get him off his sermon and back into the music. Either way, he makes the transition seamlessly. With a jaunty "Uh-oh," he executes a brief half-spin toward the musicians and then faces the room to launch into a churchy rendition of the vintage soul hit, complete with impish asides to the women—"She got the holy dance! It got good to her! Shake it, baby! You gon' mess that young boy up!" By the time he concludes with a repeated "Grab that booty! Grab that booty! Grab that booty! Shake it on down!" some people are gyrating and grinding in the middle of the room while others nod, shout, or laugh approvingly from their seats.

Finally the music dwindles to a stop. Scotty is sweating profusely, but he has a few more words to say before he leaves: "I got a new organization I'm puttin' together," he announces.

> The New Black World Order. We can change everything around in the system. We cleanin' our system up, lettin' our women walk the streets without gettin' raped. Put the money back in the community. Young people can open up their own businesses and run their own businesses—they ain't got to sell no drugs. And make 'em respect the elders. Go to college, make something out' themselves. They ain't stickin' up anybody in here; they havin' fun. Let's give 'em a big round of applause again. Now we gon' take a pause for the cause—go outside and smoke a beer!

A few people chuckle appreciatively at that last line and order another drink, but the show is over. Half an hour later the club is as empty as the street outside.

* * *

The roar of jackhammers fills the muggy late-summer air outside the window as Little Scotty, wearing a loose-fitting bathrobe, sits on a cushioned chair in the front room of his modest South Side apartment and ruminates on the power of music. "We can learn from music," he murmurs in his thick South Carolina drawl. "It's a art. You get that feeling, you get that background—it's a beautiful feeling. You be in church, and you got to rev things up with the choir. Everybody get revved up. By the time the minister there, everybody's in the spirit, ready for the Word. It's built around music."

We've been talking about his penchant for mixing the ribald irreverence of his blues act with his earnest commitment to spirituality and social justice. Even by blues standards, Scotty takes some radical chances. It's difficult to think of another performer who would jump, over the course of about five minutes, from a paean to cunnilingus to a sermon on community uplift.

But Scotty insists it's all the Lord's work.

> He said, "Rejoice with a powerful noise—I died to prepare a table before you." This is your table here, that God has given man. He said he would run the heavens, and we would run the earth. This is our mecca of life—we supposed to enjoy ourselves, live every day like it was our last one. Rejoice, let other people rejoice—have a good time! It doesn't bother me when people say, "You straddling the fence, doin' this." My hobby is singing the blues; when I do things for the Lord, my ministry, to help the community—drugs or poverty—I always put God first, before I do anything.

It's a rough-hewn philosophy at best, and it wouldn't be hard to see his protestations as nothing more than the con of a wily trickster who has learned to capitalize on people's immediate reactions to his sleepy-eyed, slow-drawling demeanor (when first encountering Scotty, some folks assume he's "slow" or even mentally retarded). But as you spend more time with him, listening to him unfurl the complex, almost random-seeming web of events and associations that have defined his life, you discover that most of his stories actually check out, give or take a couple years' discrepancy here or an untraceable detail there. By the time he's through, he has you convinced that what might have originally looked like either thick-wittedness or disingenuousness is actually a hard-won albeit funky serenity, that his untutored journey through the perilous and contradictory career of a bluesman/hustler/activist/preacher has brought him to something approximating, if not wisdom, then at least a worldly state of grace.

One thing he's not good on, though, is dates. He came to Chicago, he says, "about twenty-three, twenty-four years" ago: "I don't remember what year." He met his wife, Ada Allen, "not long after" that at a club where he was working. They married "about ten years ago," but he adds, "We was together twenty years."

About the only date he identifies precisely is his birth date: March 24, 1945, in Florence, South Carolina. "Florence, Atlantic coastline—a railroad town. Trains would cross over for the South, change in Florence. [Then] you got Charleston, that's where a lot of old slave ships come in; a lot of history in Charleston. My mother's name was Elizabeth Scott; my father's name was

David Scott. We were sharecroppers: tobacco, cotton, corn. I only had, like, a fourth-year education. I only went to school 'bout four or five years."

Scotty also can't—or at least won't—provide a specific timeline for the most traumatic and defining moment of his life.

> We was deeply involved in the civil rights movement. First black police-man on the force, we was involved in gettin' him there. The Klan threw a firebomb in my mother's house—oh, that had to be about early six-ties, somewhere in there. Severe third-degree burns. Very painful. Very painful. I probably had over ninety operations—blood 'fusions, grafting skin. People used to die, and when they died they cut the skin off 'em, and I got the skin. They used to put worms on me to eat the dead skin off. They had a worm out of Africa—maggots—they'd put it on you and eat the dead skin and drop it on the floor, and I would look at it and just holler, scream like bloody murder. I went through hell, you know, hell and high water—but I made it.

Emerging from this ordeal, Clarence Scott found his world both trans-formed and constricted. "Children was very hateful sometimes," he recalls. "They'd call me [names], 'cuz I wasn't healed like I'm healed now. So I'd escape from the kids; I'd cross over 'cuz I didn't want to hear the names. My father would hold me in because he didn't want me to be going through those kind of things. So I would stay off the street; I would hardly go out."

He did, however, sing in the Savannah Grove Baptist Church choir. At night, when his parents were either asleep or away from the house, he also began to explore the forbidden, exotic nightlife at local jukes. "Bein' the only son," he says, "by myself, on the weekends Mama would go out, sometimes they'd go out and stay a little late, I would sneak down the road. Night-clubs—they were like a hole in the wall."

In those days even big-name blues and R&B artists played "hole in the wall" joints when they toured the South. Scotty saw entertainers like James Brown, Joe Tex, and the Drifters in venues like the Windmill in the nearby town of Darlington. Inspired by the levity and the atmosphere of good-natured acceptance he found there, the lonely young man fought back his self-con-sciousness and began to take the stage himself whenever he could.

> I started singing 'bout maybe sixteen, seventeen. Sometimes people let me sit in; sometimes they didn't. They would see me sittin' there. I was like somethin' different—strange. Say, "He can't do shit! Embarrass the whole joint!" And then, "Give the guy a chance. Let him go up there." Looks is deceiving, I guess. When I go up there, I would turn my back to the audience. Because my hands was burned, I would wrap my hand in a towel or a handkerchief. [Eventually] I started letting myself go—people

loved me the way I am. Tear the whole place up! Get up there, open my mouth, it's a different thing—say, "Oh, man!" Now they want me to do a show. That's really how I got started.

Scotty also meditated deeply on the devastating effects of hate. After what had happened to him, he could easily have succumbed to it himself. Instead, he says, he took inspiration from the courageous and dedicated physician who had tended him through his crisis. "I was very prejudiced at one time," he admits, "because of what the Klans had did to me. I see a white man and go on the other side of the street. But I realized that I had a white doctor. His name was Dr. Jimmy Allen; I never will forget him—one of the greatest white mens I ever lived to see. He's the one that saved me. He stuck right there with me. Through the power of God and him, I'm here now. I don't know if he's still living, but he was my doctor, and he was a great man."

In fact, Dr. Jimmy Allen died on November 1, 1993. His son, Marshall Allen, now an attorney in Charleston, doesn't remember any concerted Klan activity around Florence during the time Scotty says his home was attacked, but he may recall Scotty: "I believe I remember young Clarence Scott . . . while he was still in the burn unit. At the time Scott would have been treated, black rooms were in the basement of the old McLeod Infirmary."

Allen's memories of his father also reflect Scotty's. "From time to time," he recollects, "he would let me go with him on rounds, and inevitably we would end up in the black ward. He was very kind to them. He was never rushed or impatient, and they sensed it, and you could sense how very much they cared for him. Although he never mentioned it, countless others have told me that throughout his entire career he treated blacks [and whites] regardless of their ability to pay. It's his wondrous social conscience that remains my moral compass."

With his confidence buttressed by the reception he received performing, Scotty began "travelin' around, different small shows, one-nighters": "Sometimes you'd do a barn or a field or a National Guard armory. I loved to adventure—I'd just *go*." He eventually settled for a while in Norfolk, Virginia.

> In Norfolk at that time, the clubs would stay packed on the fifteenth and the first, when the soldiers get paid. We had a lot of [shows] where they had a shake dancer and a blues show. You had the girls go out and dance, get the soldiers all riled up, then the guy would come out and sing the blues.
>
> We used to go over there to Portsmouth, Newport News, Suffolk, all through all the beaches, the white beaches and the black beaches, especially Myrtle Beach. The chitlin circuit; these were the places we'd play

at. Sometimes we'd have thirty one-nighters, travel, like Garnet Mimms, Howard Tate, Big Maybelle, Big Mama Thornton, I did shows with those people.

On many of these revues a headliner might take the stage at midnight or later, following a string of opening acts who would sing maybe two songs apiece. An aspiring singer like Scotty was usually somewhere well back in the pack. It was a precarious living—even big-name acts often had trouble collecting their money after a gig—and a lot of entertainers branched out into other areas of the music business. At that time in the blues/R&B world, people moved easily among roles, as they continue to do today: today's performer might be tomorrow's promoter; he might then show up a week or two later at a local radio station with a stack of someone else's records under his arm.

> I was always scufflin'. I started bookin' shows—gospel, blues—pluggin' records, pushing artists. I knowed my way, because I was out there on the road. I had a good name—I wasn't just a nobody. I knowed promotion men for Stax and Ron/Ric Records, and then they hooked me up with Nat Tarnopol [head of Brunswick Records and Jackie Wilson's manager] out of Detroit, and I was good with [deejay] John R. down in Nashville—so I just about knowed everybody in the business. And I was someone to know, too, because I could take a record 'cross the board and get it played.

At this point the chronology gets fuzzy ("I came into Fayetteville, North Carolina, stayed there for a while, left out of Fayetteville, went into New York"), but Scotty definitely reached New York City by the mid-1960s: on the wall of his cluttered home office is a framed certificate from the Mt. Nebo Baptist Church in Brooklyn, dated March 1965, certifying that "Evangelist C. Scott" has been "solemnly and publicly set apart and ordained to the work of Evangelism Ministry."

He's vague about how much preaching he did during this time, but he readily recites a list of theaters and other venues where he performed:

> I went into the New York market—the Apollo Theatre, Smalls Paradise, Cotton Club, I played all those places. I worked back in Richmond; Norfolk; Boston; Washington, D.C.—that was my main area.
>
> I should've been rich in music. A guy called Bobby Robinson [owner of the Fire/Fury label] begged and pleaded me to get on his label. Like I say, I was someone to know. Be around Joe Robinson and Sylvia Robinson, over there in Englewood, New Jersey—All Platinum Records—I was always in the clique. Sylvia liked me—I could've been on that label if I'd wanted to.

He also found time to return to Florence, at least long enough to meet and court Dorothy Downs, a local girl whose horizons had been pretty constricted up to that point ("I think she worked in a sewin' factory"). Her life changed, however, when she returned to New York with her new beau.

"I was a pimp for about ten years," Scotty reveals, breaking into a disarmingly baby-faced smile. "I was the only black guy running a massage parlor in [midtown Manhattan] at that time. I had four or five girls working for me. Sometimes you got a guy come in, want to suck a woman's toes—real strange things. Golden showers! Yeah, they paid big money for this."

He stops short of admitting that he had his wife tricking for him, saying only, "She was runnin' my place" for a while. She gave birth to their sons, Chris and Shawn, in the mid-1970s, but even then, Scotty insists, "It was easy [for the family], 'cuz they had it made. It was exciting to her, coming from a factory, making five-something an hour, then start getting about two, three thousand [a week]. Had a beautiful apartment, Seventeenth and Eighth Avenue, in Chelsea."

But he had finally crossed a line that even his broad vision of spirituality could not encompass; he did not preach during this time. He still insists, though, that if there's any such thing as a pimp with a Christian conscience, it was he. "I still knowed the Word," he avows.

> I wasn't what you call a pimp that beat women. My name was Too Sweet. They used to call me Too Sweet 'cuz I wasn't like the other guys. I didn't make nobody do anything. They loved me for that, because I was someone special. Lot of girls would get out of jail, didn't have nowhere to go, they'd call me, say, "I want to be with you."
>
> "Come on in and go to work!"
>
> I never dressed sharp in the joint; I'd be sitting up in there with a broom, in a jogging suit, so when they ask me, I say, "I'm the clean-up guy." I did very well at it, till I just got tired. I was renting from Jews and Italians—keep a joint six months, all of a sudden it burn down. I was paying [rent] every day, cost me an extra two hundred fifty, three hundred dollars. They'd raid the joint, sometimes twice a week. Between judges, lawyers, police, it's always a payoff.

As he talks about those years, Scotty slowly lowers his eyes and his voice drops to a murmur.

> I was going to write a book on that life, let people know it's not the glamour people think it is. The name of my book was going to be "The Tales of a Clown." You had the Cadillacs built up with the grill on the side, the bubble on the top, these guys with the long hair and the long coats, the canes—it was just a clown outfit. People come from all over the country to come to New York on Broadway to look at these guys. You look back

on some of the pictures, you thought you was clean—great big ol' hat with a feather in it—but you was a clown.

A lot of the old pimps I knew is dead, in the penitentiary, or on drugs, or got so old don't nobody know 'em or want 'em no more. We always got to know: one day, everything plays out.

He had never entirely abandoned his music; he cut his first 45, a midtempo funk outing called "Thinking about My Baby," on the obscure S&J label in the early or mid-1970s. As the player's life lost its luster for him, he began to refocus his energies on performing and, he says, developing his mind and his ministry.

I was studying Islam. I sat under a lot of scholars. Marching and protesting, different parts of town, every weekend we'd have different speakers. Sometimes I hear 'em on Gary Byrd's radio show [on WWRL and WLIB]. John Henrik Clarke—I learned about a Malcolm X, a Nat Turner. Leonard Jeffries—he's a professor. They barred him from City College for teaching black studies.[2] I sat in some of his classes at the university, sat under him for a while. This is what I teach. I go out to colleges and get standing ovations and a lotta people say, what degree, what college did I go to? I tell 'em, "The street college." I had street knowledge, and I had the wisdom from the power of God.

In the late 1970s he recorded the Otis Redding–influenced "Slow That Disco Down" (featuring, according to Scotty, Johnny Copeland on guitar); the recording was made for the Nile label, which was owned by Children of the Nile, a New York–based Muslim organization with whom he had been working. Around that same time he cut a twelve-inch 45, "Going to a Disco Tonight (Pts. 1 and 2)," for the Queen Constance label. He followed that up with a four-track EP called *Shout at the Disco,* which was released on Queen Constance's sister imprint, Sound of New York. *Shout at the Disco* consists mostly of primitively executed but energetic funk workouts, although there is also a bizarre effort called "Acid Freak" on which the onslaught of a fuzz-tone guitar nearly drowns out Scotty's ad-libbed shouts: "We acid freakin' out! Come on, y'all! Freakin' out on acid!"

A few years later Scotty moved to Boston. Dorothy had returned to South Carolina, frustrated, he says, "'cuz I was never home; I was always on the road."[3] The Bluestown label, owned by record-store proprietor Skippy White, reissued "Slow That Disco Down."[4] Scotty had been to the city before; another of his preaching certificates, this one dated 1974, is signed by the Boston-based Rev. S. T. Edmonds. But this time he stayed for a while. "I liked Boston pretty good. I got along with Boston. Kids liked the blues, a lot of college kids

Little Scotty at Lee's Unleaded Blues, April 2004. Photo by Joeff Davis/www.Joeff .com

there, especially over in Cambridge. Then I would go up in New Hampshire and Maine."

Scotty, who never became so righteous that he wouldn't do what needed to be done to keep his niche in the hard-hustling blues world, also remembers "lotta chitlin kinda thing in Boston, too. The Sugar Shack, that was down on the main drag, where all the prostitutes be. [A prominent deejay] was my man—take him some cocaine, and he'll play your records from now on."

Nevertheless, he adds, "I never been to a town so prejudiced like Boston. Any time you come out the house, walk down the streets . . . [he pantomimes looking over his shoulder in fear]. I just didn't stay in Boston. Boston was too slow."

Once again he's vague on specific dates, but some time in the early 1980s he moved to Chicago to further pursue "music and ministry."[5] He sang in local clubs and occasionally on shows with bigger names from out of town;

in 1983 he worked on Harold Washington's historic mayoral campaign. It was around this time that yet another of his public personas—the one many Chicagoans still know best—came to full fruition: "Yeah, I'm the Button Man," he says with a chuckle.

> I used to have buttons of the civil rights movement, Dr. King buttons, and everybody want my buttons. "Man, gimme that button! I'll buy that button!"
>
> "No! I can't afford to part with that button."
>
> Some of 'em offer me ten dollars. I say, "Man, I only paid fifty cents or a dollar for it." So that's how I got into the button business. I was the first one to get Harold money, off buttons. At that time he didn't have no buttons or nothing. We got there and pushed thousands and thousands of buttons. . . . I walked up, gave five hundred dollars. I stayed with Harold up till the end.
>
> I made the first Maxwell Street buttons—"Help save Maxwell Street." The last [African American] guy runnin' for mayor, Rev. Paul Jakes, I did his buttons. Million Man March, I made forty-five hundred dollars in less'n three hours—that money's mine! I did the Million Family March, Million Mom March, the Million Youth March coming up [in the fall of 2003]. I got a march comin' up called Sister I'm Sorry Million Youth March.[6] I'm goin' to get some backings so I get flyers, handbills, advertising—radio stations, newspapers—it's about youth. It's atonement, "I'm sorry," where the black men have walked off from their family, got sisters on drugs, never take care of his kids—atonement to the black woman, things we have done to her.
>
> I want to see my people free of genocide; I want to see my people come out of a depression and learn more about "self" instead of self-hatred. Self-hatred is when you drug yourself to death, drink yourself to death; murder, kill, rob, steal from your people. That's self-hatred among the people. He say, "If you love me, you'll keep my commandments." That's not just the love of God but the love of man, too.

Energized by his own sermon, he gets to his feet, walks over to his stereo console, rummages around in the clutter on top, and lifts out a CD. "I recorded this. I'm thinkin' of puttin' it out now, when the elections are coming up. I think it'd be a good time."

On the cover is a murky photo of Scotty clad in white turtleneck and chartreuse blazer and orating from behind a battered-looking pulpit. Superimposed in yellow are the stenciled words *Voting for Jesus* and *Evangelist C. Scott*. The two-track disc includes a countrified, up-tempo number called "Jesus Is Alright with Me," on which Scotty sounds heavily influenced by Joe Simon, and the title track, a sermon in which the evangelist praises God for giving us "such people as Dr. Martin Luther King, Reverend Jesse Jackson . . . ; such ministers as the Rev. C. L. Franklin . . . ; people like Brother Farrakhan . . . ; people such as the world's greatest gospel singer, Mahalia Jackson . . . ; another great man, Brother Harold Washington." The heart of the sermon returns to his favorite theme of personal and community responsibility in protecting youth from taking the wrong path ("Vote for Jesus, because he knows which way to go").

It's a typical Scotty performance, emphasizing thematic unity over ideological niceties—or perhaps "interpretation" over "text"—but his eclectic list of leaders and "great ministers" raises some of the same questions implied by the confluence of carnality and moral uplift that characterizes some of his blues performances: exactly what *does* Evangelist C. Scott believe?

This is, after all, a man who can preach about "civil rights and human rights," speak (and sell buttons) at rallies for world peace, and then later note, with disarming casualness, "Khalid Abdul Muhammad, they barred him from the Nation of Islam for calling the white man the devil. He was the head of the Million Youth March, and I spoke on some platforms with him." He has also proclaimed that he "marched with [Leonard Jeffries] when the Jews tried to kill him up there" and that he wants to start a community organization in Chicago to "get these ol' A-rabs outta here" (many in Chicago's African American community resent the disproportionate number of grocery stores and convenience stores owned by Middle Easterners, North Africans, and Asians). Does he, in fact, adhere to a form of black nationalist ideology that crosses from solidarity into prejudice?

"No, I don't," he declares firmly.

My friends, my good friends, are white people—through the movement, the [anti-]war movement, the civil rights movement, the death penalty, all of 'em. And my life was saved by a white doctor. It's good and bad in everybody—I always say you have black snakes and you have white snakes. But I say, the dangerous snake is the black snake, because he's there with you every night and every day.

But you know, we've been some of the greatest people in the world; we *are* the greatest people in the world. Not saying the white man was not great; he was too. But he learned a lot of things from us. Our mothers and fathers taught his children, taught him how to farm the land. We give him a spiritual outlook on life; instead of hating, to love—if you go back to the civil rights movement, we was never the peoples that hung people; we never burned people alive, we never give anybody germ warfare. Yet the black man is still is the most hated man on the face of the earth. Everything in the world that's been generated around black folks has been stolen. If you don't know black history, you wouldn't think black folks did anything but act crazy.

Our black boys and girls are getting incarcerated every day because they have no guidance. We got a lot of preachers, but we ain't got no teachers. We must teach each other how to live, first, before we can do anything. This is what I teach. This is a twenty-four-hour job, man—this is deep. I'm not only a blues singer; I'm a motivator. I've seen the power of God and the power of prayer.[7]

Meanwhile, though, being a blues singer continues to take up much of his day-to-day schedule. His first recording after he moved to Chicago took place in 1986, when he appeared on a compilation disk issued on the Beantown label, on which he was credited as coproducer. The record features two twelve-bar blues from Scotty himself ("Play the Blues for Me" and "She Put the Hoo-Doo on the Hoo-Doo Man"); "Down Hearted," a rather chaotic effort from a B. B. King imitator named B. B. Jones; and three pop-soul offerings from the Charley Justice Band.

His recording activity since then has been sporadic, but when Scotty has had the chance to enter a studio, he has done his best to keep up with the times. His early 2000s blues CD, which he has released at least twice under his own Top of the World Records imprint (as *Gimme What You Promised Me* and *Gimme What U Promised*), is in the contemporary soul-blues mold—burbling funk rhythms seasoned with bluesy guitar leads and overlaid by Scotty's gritty, church-inflected singing. *Gimme What U Promised,* billed as being by "Li'l Scotty," includes an extra track: a cover of Aaron Neville's "Tell It Like It Is," which Scotty delivers in a choked sob that recalls his aching deep-soul vocals on "Slow That Disco Down."

Listening to these tracks, as well as to some of his earlier recordings—especially "Slow That Disco Down," on which he wittily inhabits the dual roles of a soul-weary man nursing a wounded heart and a bone-tired dancer nursing sore feet—one wonders why Scotty hasn't achieved more commercial success. He's certainly a seasoned performer: his stage act is slyly crafted to appear unpolished, but it's both flamboyant and intimate in the great tradition, loaded with his time-tested routines and vintage songs, along with more current and original offerings. Despite his years in the business and his association with influential figures, though, he has never managed to ride either their coattails or his own considerable, if quirky, talents to anything more than marginal recognition.

His own demurrals notwithstanding, it probably has at least something to do with the bodily effects of the burning. Unlike other artists with distinctive physical characteristics—blind men like Stevie Wonder or Ray Charles, fat men like Billy Stewart, or waiflike "ugly duckling" figures such as Little Jimmy Scott—Scotty, with his scarred arms and torso and oddly bloated countenance, probably couldn't parlay his appearance into either machismo or vulnerability. There's nothing very sexy about being an object of pity.

But his marginalization also seems at least somewhat self-imposed. After having spent most of his life inventing his career—if not himself—pretty much as he has gone along, he acts in many ways like a man who prefers to stay in a comfort zone once he has found one, even as he extols the virtues of risk-taking and self-reliance. His personality is an odd fusion of hipness and naïveté: though he prides himself on his independence and hustling ability, by his own admission he has sometimes submitted all too willingly to the dictates of the men with the money. Discussing "Acid Freak," from his *Shout at the Disco* EP, he concedes, "The guy that [produced] that, he just said, 'Hey, man, do some rock, man.' And I just started going crazy, just doing stuff. 'That's it! I like it. Don't bother.' I said, 'If that's what you want, man.'"

Raised in the old-school network of record pluggers and dealmakers, Scotty still markets his product almost entirely on his own: he sells CDs out of his briefcase or distributes them to whatever deejay or store owner he thinks might give them a play or a boost. He also designs flyers for his own shows and the various marches and rallies he organizes. Their chaotic, nonlinear design and pasted-on snippets from borrowed sources have made them collectors' items among aficionados of Chicago blues esoterica (he says he learned make the flyers from another indefatigable hustler, X-rated comedian Rudy Ray Moore, aka Dolemite).

"I'm gettin' ready to venture out into the South," he promises. "I still know a lot of people on the blues circuit. Underground, I can get a lot of stuff [sold]. Plus, I can work a lot of mom and pop stores; I know how to put my signs in the stores, work my stuff. Lot of rap artists started out from the back of their cars; now they's multimillionaires. It's what you package! You can sell dog doo-doo—ain't nobody ever heard of it, they wanna know how it smells. I'm serious! Jewish guy told me: 'Long as you got somethin' to sell, somebody gon' buy it.'"

And again his topic segues from his personal ambition to a larger, perhaps equally quixotic vision:

> I want to try to uplift the South Side, if God bless me with the generation of good funds, I want to record some of the blues guys. I want to help a lot of the guys in the blues. I served a lot of 'em—spiritual guidance, they always call me. [Vocalist] Jesse Tolbert, I sung at his funeral; I sung at Buddy [Scott's] funeral, I preached some of 'em's funerals. Some of 'em die with no insurance, have to dig up money to bury 'em. I think it's genocide unto the blues singers: put poor people back in the category where they can't survive. We need to demand a foundation, to help with support and expenses, like funerals for blues musicians.

I'm fifty-seven now, gettin' ready to get all my music back [in distribution], write some new music, producing. All that I've been through in life, my trials and tribulations, it only made me stronger. Everything that happened in life is gettin' ready to pay off now. Sometimes you have to wait upon the Lord and wait for your good days to come.

And indeed, he seems willing to wait and endure for as long as it takes. Whether he has been hardened by suffering or is simply possessed of an unusually unflappable nature, Scotty remains outwardly unruffled by even the most traumatic and painful setbacks. On March 6, 2004, his wife, Ada—a tall, angular woman of deep faith who sang several times a week in the gospel choir at Holy Rock Missionary Baptist Church at Fifty-ninth and Morgan—was brutally murdered in an alley a few blocks from their home. Her funeral, on

Little Scotty serving the people with Rev. Al Sharpton, ca. late 1990s. Photo courtesy Little Scotty

March 15, packed the church with mourners, friends of both Scotty and Ada from all walks of life. Artie "Blues Boy" White and South Side vocalist Shorty Mack sang hymns; fabled Chicago tenor saxophonist Gene "Daddy G" Barge played a resonant, unaccompanied "Amazing Grace." Afterward, at the repast at Lee's Unleaded Blues, Scotty sipped a rare cocktail and greeted well-wishers from behind hooded eyes, exchanging pleasantries with little outward sign of grief or unhappiness. Only weeks later, when I encountered him strolling with a woman friend in the Canal Street Market on a Sunday morning, did he sigh with exhaustion: "I been through a lot, man; I been through a lot."

Not long after that he traveled to Richmond, Virginia, to record a gospel CD produced by August "Mr. Wiggles" Moon, a veteran R&B vocalist and entrepreneur whose hustler's approach toward life and business probably make him a natural partner for Scotty. The disc, *God's Got the Last Word*, features Evangelist C. Scott supported by in-studio instrumental and vocal backing (by "the Babylon Sisters," Tanya, Michelle, and Monica). Especially arresting is the title track, a fervid twenty-minute-plus sermon in which he lays out in harrowing detail the ordeal he suffered after he was burned; by the end he's weeping audibly as an organ billows and swells behind him.

When he played the disk for me in his apartment, Scotty wiped tears from his eyes as he listened; his body trembled, his head lay back, and his mouth lolled open. Then, after it was over, he flashed me that same shy smile he had broken into when he revealed his pimping history, muttering, "That'll be good'n, good seller on the gospel stations." He went into the kitchen to speak to a woman who was busy cleaning—his "housekeeper," he said, adding that she'd been a "street person" until he took her in—and then accepted a ride from me to Forty-seventh Street, where the new Harold Washington Cultural Center was being feted with its official grand opening. On the way he assured me that, contrary to what he had implied in his recorded sermon, he was going to continue on with blues as well as gospel. When we got to the cultural center, he opened the back door of my car and dragged out his briefcase full of buttons, along with another satchel, which he loaded onto a two-wheeled hand truck. He then headed to the corner to do business.

As I watched Scotty, bent under his burden and hitting the streets one more time, I thought of the way he had summed up his attitude toward music, ministry, and life in one of our earlier talks. "There's more than just singing the blues," he told me. "You must carry a message. You have to feel the blues. The blues is something down in your soul; it's like a spiritual thing. It all boils down to love. It's about love among each other. And that's what blues is about. Love."

Coda

"I Was Looking for the Future, but the Blues Was All I Found"

Thoughts on What Was, What Is, and What Might Be in Store

As I write this, it's early 2004. According to legend, precisely 101 years ago W. C. Handy "discovered" the blues as he waited for a train in Tutwiler, Mississippi. A man sat down next to him on the platform and began to sing a plaintive lament about railroad travel—"Goin' where the Southern cross the Dog"—while sliding a knife blade along the strings of a guitar. Handy later remembered it as "the weirdest music [he] had ever heard,"[1] and through the rest of his life he made a fortune creating pop-styled versions of it, including "St. Louis Blues," "Beale Street Blues," and "Yellow Dog Blues." Since then, it seems, there has been at least one prediction about that music's future—or its likely demise—for each year that has passed.

The year 2003 was also the "Year of the Blues," so designated by the U.S. Congress ostensibly in honor of

Handy's moment of epiphany but definitely in convergence with a hype-laden initiative spearheaded by Seattle's Experience Music Project and the Memphis-based Blues Foundation. If you believed the pitch, this official imprimatur and the events surrounding it were going to do for the blues what *American Graffiti* did for Wolfman Jack.

Despite the publicity, however, and despite Martin Scorsese's concurrent seven-part PBS series *The Blues* (which itself was supposed to do for the blues what Ken Burns's *Jazz* project was supposed to have done for jazz), the general consensus among musicians, industry reps, and others in positions to know is that there has been no discernible improvement in any empirical measure of public enthusiasm. In September 2003 *Billboard* magazine calculated that blues represented merely 1 percent of all CDs sold, a figure that hadn't changed for several years.[2] Given today's music marketplace, where record companies are retrenching for their lives and worry about any artist whose CD doesn't go platinum before it even hits the stores, the flatness of these indicators does not bode well. Despite the optimism expressed by most of the people profiled in this book, it's easy to conclude that the future of the blues is bleak indeed.

Why *Don't* They Call It the Blues?

But again, if we're predicting the future of something—or for that matter, analyzing its success in the present—it might help to define the object of our predictions. And this, as I have shown, is an enterprise that leads us into (if you'll pardon the expression) extremely muddy waters. The blues has always been a public-sphere phenomenon—involving performance, performer-audience interaction, and the secularized ritual of ecstatic abandon—at least as much as it has been a consumer trend measurable by variables like record purchases. Moreover, in the African American community the public sphere has traditionally been a venue of deeply felt if not always outwardly expressed solidarity based on common heritage and struggle. According to Johnny Otis,

> The music grew out of the African-American way of life. The way Mama cooked, the Black English grandmother and grandfather spoke, the way daddy disciplined the kids—the emphasis on spiritual values, the way Reverend Jones preached, the way Sister Williams sang in the choir, the way the old brother down the street played the slide guitar and crooned the blues, the very special way the people danced, walked, laughed, cried, joked, got happy, shouted in church . . . ; the trials and tribulations have made their mark on the artistry.[3]

That may seem like yet another obvious point, but I think it, too, is in danger of getting lost. These days arguments against the viability of the blues as a cultural force in the African American community usually focus on data, such as the *Billboard* percentages, that document the paltry amount of "product" sold. Some recent historians have even extended this approach backward into history and implied that the relatively few records sold by early southern blues artists proves that, contrary to legend, many or even most of them were of peripheral importance in their own time.[4] I will return to these points later; for the time being, it suffices to say that the reality is and always has been much more nuanced and complex.

Even on their own terms, though, the sales data raise at least as many

New Orleans Beau at Lee's Unleaded Blues, September 2003. Photo by Joeff Davis/ CitySearch

questions as they answer. For instance, they do not capture most of the styles encompassed by vaguely defined terms like *soul* and *R&B,* even though at least some songs often subsumed under those genres are played on "blues" radio and embraced by the "blues" listenership. They most definitely do not include rap or hip-hop in any of their diverse permutations—an oversight that, at least according to Louisiana bluesman Chris Thomas King, ignores the most authentic blues being played today: "The definition of what the blues is has to be redefined. . . . I was hearing more blues, whatever that's supposed to be, and more what I understand to be the blues—more truth, and honesty—in NWA's earlier records than I was hearing from so-called blues albums. The blues never left these [housing] projects, you know? You don't have to leave the ghetto to find out where the blues is going. It's right there."[5]

For his part, Thomas King has apparently embraced hip-hop as the future of the blues: his label, 21st Century Blues Records, promotes what he has dubbed "dirty South hip-hop blues," which incorporates traditional blues instruments such as guitars and harmonicas into a rap/hip-hop context. Even to those who take a more conservative attitude, however, it seems clear that genre categories such as *Billboard*'s are as arbitrary and limiting as any "purist" insistence on lump-de-lump shuffles and a I–IV–V twelve-bar chord progression. For instance, how might one categorize the music of Mary J. Blige or Erykah Badu? By any objective standards these singers' tales of love, loss, and redemption—often couched in hardscrabble, streetsy imagery—emanate from the same milieu as the rawest of deep blues, even if the music itself sounds smoothed over. (And if that smoothing-over seems problematic, revisit Lonnie Johnson, Leroy Carr, Wynonie Harris, or Dinah Washington, to say nothing of Bessie Smith or pre-"rediscovery" Big Bill Broonzy: heartfelt vocals and gritty lyrics set to stylized pop accompaniments are nothing new in blues.)

But Blige and Badu are marketed as R&B artists, and I doubt that one out of a thousand of their mainstream fans has thought twice about that designation. Meanwhile, though, to use just one example of many, the Detroit-based blues chanteuse Thornetta Davis has made Badu's "Tyrone" a staple of her shows. Her voice is a bit more old-school churchy than Erykah's, but her overall approach to the song is pretty much the same, and after hearing her tackle it, one wonders how "Tyrone" could have ever been considered anything *but* a blues song. The main difference, apparently, is that Thornetta is marketed as a "blues" singer and performs in "blues" venues, while Erykah isn't and doesn't. Conversely, Artie White's "Your Man Is Home Tonight" would probably have been considered a pop or middle-of-the-road song in almost anyone's hands but his.

This leads to a further complication: the data as compiled by *Billboard* tabulate sales of albums (i.e., CDs) rather than measure the success of single songs. So, for instance, the success of R. Kelly's "You Made Me Love You" on black-oriented blues radio will not nudge him into the blues camp, where singers who have had similarly styled releases, such as Sir Charles Jones ("Is Anybody Lonely") or perhaps Willie Clayton ("I Love Me Some You") are firmly ensconced. There weren't any blues album charts in the 1960s, but if there had been, it's a safe bet that twelve-bar "soul" outings like Aretha Franklin's "Dr. Feelgood" and Wilson Pickett's "Mustang Sally" wouldn't have catapulted their respective artists onto them—even though today those songs are so ubiquitous on blues circuits that they've earned the dubious honor of a spot on many singers' "set list from hell." And the 1960s, it should be remembered, are usually cited as the era when the blues as a force in mainstream black culture dwindled to nearly nothing.

This is not to suggest that the putative dearth of interest in blues among contemporary African American listeners is merely a statistical artifact, nor do I mean to imply that if we just fine-tuned a few semantics, blues would suddenly ascend to its rightful place as a recognized cultural presence. There is little doubt, though, that the tension between the universalizing (and ever-shifting) definition of the blues aesthetic among most African American artists and listeners, on the one hand, and the reductionist obsession with categorization and classification among critics, theorists, and industry bean-counters, on the other, has placed both the music and its proponents in a perilous, virtually no-win situation.

It Felt Just Like a Ball and Chain

In Chicago it cuts both ways. A veteran soul man like the late Tyrone Davis may have feared that being pigeonholed into the blues or even the soul-blues niche threatened his hard-earned R&B legitimacy ("It pisses me off real bad when somebody come up to me and says, 'Blues.' . . . How many blues singers you ever seen get a record to sell three million?").[6] Other Chicago musicians, however, insist that the real problem is the opposite: on the local circuit, at least, they feel as if their popular legitimacy is shackled to demands that they style themselves primarily *as* blues (or soul-blues) performers, even though by doing so they consign themselves to the record-sales/radio-play limbo outlined previously.

When I spoke with vocalist Lee Morris and his coproducer Michael J. Mayberry in Mayberry's home studio on Chicago's South Side, both men were adamant about this dilemma and its debilitating effect on young blues-based artists: "A lot of clubs," Mayberry asserted, "you got to do more blues than soul or you won't get the gig. And then you wanna do more soul to be on the radio to make more money than you make doing the blues" (by *soul* Mayberry meant what's usually called "urban contemporary" or "R&B").

As examples, he and Morris pointed to some of Chicago's most prestigious show bands, aggregations that regularly back artists such as Otis Clay and Cicero Blake, as well as serving as house bands for multiact soul-blues revues. None of the musicians themselves would address the issue for the record ("Man, we do it all, and that's called professional" was all one lead guitarist would say),[7] but Morris, a younger-generation singer who has been backed by some of these bands on his own shows, believes that a lot of them would rather be doing other things.

"It's different music they want to play," he maintains. "Can't make it over here, they fall back; lot of 'em say, 'I got to play some blues.' 'Cause a blues band will beat an R&B band any day, 'cause that's what [club audiences] want to hear."

Mayberry elaborated on the point: "Most of these bands are more R&B oriented, and a lot of the bands just stop playing because they can't make it playing R&B—all the other guys converted to playing behind blues artists. What club can you go in right now and do an R&B show, if you ain't no big act? So you got to play behind the blues artists."

"That's the reason people be trying to change," added Morris, "so they can fit [a] format. You might do blues [in your shows], they might not play it on certain stations; but other music—playin' it all the time on there."

Morris and Mayberry's solution to this conundrum has been to make records that cast as wide a net as possible. Morris's best-known disc, *Whip It on U,* released in 2000 on Mayberry's Da Man label, was a complex and somewhat uneasy juxtaposition of tracks alternately couched in hip-hop electronica, soul balladry seasoned with deep-harmony backup vocals, and twelve-bar blues. That, however, creates problems of its own. Such stylistic leaps are guaranteed to make marketers uneasy ("Which rack do we put this in?"), they risk losing critics and listeners with less-than-catholic tastes, and they're difficult to replicate in live performance, especially on the limited budget provided by most clubs. "If you get going making money, you might be able to do it," Morris says, "but right now it's kind of hard. You gotta be working to keep a band with you. So that's why you got to try to get out and get some shows, be working every weekend."

But if so many audiences demand blues and soul-blues from performers, why isn't this reflected in their record-buying habits, and why aren't the companies responding to it? Granted, Chicago is still part of the wide-ranging regional market that reflects the Great Migration and that former Stax Records president Al Bell once affectionately characterized as "Mississippi River culture,"[8] but it's also a cosmopolitan city that has long been at the forefront of popular music. In the 1950s and 1960s it was home to a thriving doo-wop and soul recording industry right alongside its fabled blues activity, and the local gospel and R&B circuits have cultivated such figures as Sam Cooke, Lou Rawls, Curtis Mayfield, Jerry Butler, and Johnnie Taylor (who became considered "soul-blues" toward the end of his career, singing much the same kind of material he had been doing all along). More recently, Chicago spawned house music, and the city is currently the stronghold of several identifiable rap and hip-hop styles.

It's difficult to believe, then, that Chicagoans who attend nightclubs where blues is played are completely anomalous in their musical tastes. Is it possible that record companies and radio stations don't have as accurate an understanding of what "the people" want to hear as they think they do?

Part of the problem is again those damnable definitions. Lee Morris can try to span the stylistic gamut of recent African American pop music, yet with a grits-and-gravy stage act that features spins, twirls, and other dance moves reminiscent of the classic soul revues of the 1960s and backed by a bluesy powerhouse like the Scott Brothers' World Band, he may still be viewed as a "soul-blues" artist. But this virtually disqualifies him for airplay on pop and urban contemporary stations[9]—and if some of the tracks from his disc *did* manage to achieve that kind of mainstream airplay, Morris could conceivably find himself and his entire disc categorized as "R&B," and the blues charts would lose another artist.

That probably wouldn't break Lee's heart: "My biggest challenge, really, is getting a hit record. That's the main thing. Do what you gotta do, get 'em up, make 'em feel good. I can sing blues, I sing soul." In the long run, however, it would exacerbate the crisis faced by artists from neotraditionalists like Billy Branch or even Sharon Lewis to soul-blues stylists such as Morris himself, making it more difficult to keep their music relevant among their core constituency of listeners.

Hey Mister Deejay, Play the Blues for Me

It's always been difficult to get records played on the air, especially for new artists on small or independent labels, but the consensus among industry longtimers is that the corporate consolidation of radio and the accompanying disempowerment of local deejays have made things much worse. The very concept of a "regional market" as a kind of triple-A league in which a song could prove its worth before going national—the way most blues records initially made their marks—has become virtually extinct.

Chicago's Emmett Garner is a bright-eyed, wiry man of about seventy whose conversation is peppered with anecdotes and recollections from the days when he and other record pluggers "broke" records by hustling them personally to deejays, doing whatever it took to get them played. In about 2000 Garner emerged from retirement to try to help a young vocalist named Stan Mosley, a Bobby Womack–influenced singer whose gritty-sweet balladry seemed capable of spanning the stylistic gulfs among blues, soul-blues, and R&B that Lee Morris, Willie Clayton, and others have attempted to negotiate in recent years. But Garner soon became aware of the barriers modern radio has erected to impede the efforts of such artists to get themselves heard and judged on their own terms by mainstream black audiences.

"It's very scary," he said, sitting with Mosley in the spacious living room of Mosley's South Side home. "I'd been out of the business for about fifteen years, so I knew things had changed, but I didn't know it'd changed that much. A deejay don't even know what record's played anymore. He's a token; they tell him what to play. One guy from L.A.—knows nothing about Chicago, don't care about Chicago—sit up there and program the whole [network] across the country. A [deejay] will tell me, 'Emmett, I can't do that unless it's programmed.'"

Add to this the corporate media's obsession with attracting the big-spending, youthful demographic most prized by advertisers, and you have what Garner laments as "almost an impossible venture."

> The radio stations, they're leaning toward teenagers; the record companies are the same way. "How old is he?" First thing they ask. They didn't ask me how good he was, or what he got going. "How old is he?" I went to a station just yesterday, the girl listened to his song, said "You know, I like this—but I gotta be honest with you, it's old." Didn't say it wasn't good. This music relates to older people, and they're not interested in older people.
>
> The only way is to get so popular that they demand to have you. But how can you get popular if they don't want you? It's the craziest thing I've ever seen in my life.

Yet like Billy Branch, Cicero Blake, and almost everyone else who addressed the issue with me, Garner and Mosley were adamant that the public—even the younger public—will embrace and respond to blues if it's given a fair chance on the air. Garner pointed to the still-potent southern market for soul-blues on radio, on record, and in live performance and wondered why it can't translate into broader interest, at least in longtime blues strongholds like Chicago ("How can it be dated here, and not dated over here? How can it be not good here, and good over there? Same kind of format, different city"). Like Branch, Mosley merely related his personal experience as a performer: "They come out, they hear this music—you'd be surprised at the young kids that be at my concerts, I'm talking about kids, now, teenagers—'So how come I can't hear this music on the radio?'"

Indeed, this music is barely represented there. Currently in Chicago only one commercial station, the low-power WSSD, plays black-oriented blues and soul-blues on a consistent basis. A few deejays on college stations contribute a handful of additional hours a week, and elder statesman Pervis Spann continues to host his legendary overnight "Blues Man Show" on WVON, but its wee-hours time slot and Spann's own eccentricities keep it from attracting many young listeners. Niles Frantz, who hosts a Saturday evening blues program on WBEZ, Chicago's public radio station, plays some soul-blues, but NPR's listeners are notoriously white and middle class.

Even with this limited airplay, though, the music manages to get at least somewhat known and liked among African American listeners, a fact that both tantalizes and frustrates its proponents no end. "I did a show at the Regal," noted Mosley, "and when I was singing 'Anybody Seen My Boo' [a song from *Souled Out,* his 2000 Malaco CD], every time I got to the hook, I would see people sitting out there singing. So I said to myself, 'They had to have heard this song.'"

Garner jumped in: "Can you imagine, if we can get this kind of action off of one play, two hours, what would happen if he got played every day?"

There's no guarantee that even daily airplay can make listeners like a record (a point missed by historians who have suggested that the relative success of blues in the 1940s and 1950s was due mostly to payola), and Garner obviously had an interest in pitching the idea of a potential mass market for his singer. But consider an event like the February 29, 2004, soul-blues extravaganza at Chicago's Arie Crown Theater. Publicized primarily through difficult-to-find blues radio programs like those mentioned previously, it nonetheless drew a packed house of over 3,500 who rocked and testified for almost six hours to the music of Willie Clayton, Tyrone Davis, Latimore, Denise LaSalle, and several other soul-blues stars.[10] The Sabre Room, a posh restaurant/show lounge in suburban Hickory Hills, regularly sells out expensive dinner-and-music packages featuring some of the same artists who packed the Arie Crown.

The conclusion seems inescapable: with a fair shake in the open market, the blues—in all its various and evolving forms, blends, and varieties—could stand a solid chance of winning back a significant, multigenerational mainstream listenership in the black community. Garner, for one, asks for little more: "If they just gave us every day for two hours, then I'd be happy. The best man would win then."

Time Has Come Today

But there seems little reason to believe radio will be freed from its corporate shackles any time soon—or that it really wants to be. Garner hinted at but did not explicitly address one of the problems in even thinking about achieving such a transformation, namely, that corporate control spreads beyond just the central office to define virtually the entire marketplace. Mainstream radio's true "customers" are advertisers at least as much as they are listeners. Even if it could be proven that a significant majority of music lovers would gladly tune into blues, soul-blues, or some other "niche" music, it's unlikely that most sponsors would consider them as lucrative a target as the primarily young, fashion-driven listeners who currently tune in and—whatever they think of or do with the music—structure their shopping habits around the commercials they hear. Better to hone one's demographic by reinforcing prejudices based less on the quality of the music than on aggressively marketed stereotypes about what a particular genre is supposed to represent.

This explains Tyrone Davis's concern that labeling him "blues" consigned him to second-tier status, that the very word was enough to discourage mainstream listeners from even giving his music a chance, as if it were a brand name with unsavory connotations. It also explains California-based vocalist E. C. Scott's wry observation about her attempts to ease her way through the ideological thickets of radio programming, even in the putatively blues-friendly South: "When you say you do 'blues,' they say, 'No, we don't play blues on this station.' If you say the full name, 'rhythm and blues'—when you don't abbreviate it—they know you are over forty. When you abbreviate it—'R&B'—you're under thirty!"[11]

In such an atmosphere, is it possible to even envision a stylistic fusion that might allow artists to remain true to themselves, reach as many listeners as possible, and still have at least a fighting chance of getting heard on the air? Despite Cicero Blake's optimism about the development of what he sees as a redeeming and instantly identifiable "southern soul" sound (and for all the disparagement one hears about the white audience's "lump-de-lump" fixation and obligatory "set lists from hell"), much of what's being pumped out by southern soul-blues labels these days is pretty dire as well. Too many CDs on imprints like Ecko, Mardi Gras, and even the once-mighty Malaco have become little more than pastiches of instant cliches, with unimaginative melodies, puerile lyrics, automaton-like rhythm tracks, and backings lifted from previously recorded material—all of which threatens to reduce what was once some of the world's most vital and emotionally riveting music to little more than modestly funky aural wallpaper. It moves enough product within its own sphere to keep the companies afloat, and some truly heartfelt and effective material still gets through, but one wonders how long it will take before soul-blues becomes to "real" soul and blues what Nashville "country-politan" has become to "real" country and western—a tepid mass-produced imitation marketed to listeners who either don't care or don't know where the music came from and what it represented in its heyday.

Meanwhile, it's too early to tell whether alternative-minded initiatives such as Chris Thomas King's attempt to reclaim the word *blues* at least for the hip-hop generation will bear fruit, but in this context the mission he has undertaken is worth noting. Thomas King insists that the very idea of an African American artist daring to play guitar in a hip-hop setting and then calling it "blues" is as radical an act of defiance as his incorporation of drum loops or the presence of a turntablist on his blues shows: "When you hear me rapping and playing guitar, the reason it's hip-hop blues and not hip-hop rock & roll is because black artists aren't allowed to do rap-rock. . . . Do you know of anybody who raps and plays the guitar now?"[12] By challenging both blues and hip-hop purists, he suggests, he's creating a music that's simultaneously rooted and revolutionary. He presents himself as a blues storyteller set in a twenty-first-century context, defying both corporate and critical arbiters of taste by refusing to acknowledge their authority and then daring them to stop him from going even further.

What Thomas King is trying to do, in other words, is to reclaim the iconoclastic *spirit* that has always informed the best blues expression in order to face down the conservative *aesthetic* that has paradoxically often led some of that spirit's most vociferous advocates to insist on a limited vision of what the music itself can be. The results may or may not sound like blues to even the most flexible-minded listeners—if nothing else, the sensual feel of pent-up tension dissolving into release, which has long been associated with the blues, is obscured in much hip-hop, Thomas King's included, which seems often to consist mostly of tension without the release (just as a lot of what's coming out of the soul-blues camp these days sounds like virtually all release and no tension).[13] Nonetheless, it is this spirit—boundary challenging, liberatory, yet unafraid to embrace real-life experience in the here and now—that must be preserved and nurtured if "the blues," by any definition, is to survive.

Blues Hit Big Town

> The blues has this gift of reinventing itself. Blues is alive and well, even
> though it is on the margins, because it is the motherlode—you can't buy
> the chicken that lays the golden eggs; you can buy the eggs. It's always go-
> ing to be on the outside, almost seeming to be bought up and bound down.
> It'll never die.
> —Mighty Mo Rodgers (interview, Jan. 21, 2004)

The concrete pillars supporting the El tracks over Lake Street can make this
major thoroughfare feel almost as narrow and treacherous as a backwoods
dirt road. If you drive west on this street, you can see and hear all too clearly
what Chris Thomas King means when he says the blues never left the ghetto.
Vacant lots, crumbling brownstones, and cavernous warehouses line both
sides of the street. About every five minutes the air is shattered by the roar
of a train overhead, yet a surreal silence pervades the neighborhood. Even in
midday drivers avoid some stretches, and pedestrian traffic consists mostly of
furtive, hooded young men nervously skulking in alleys and around junked
cars alongside gutted buildings. Catastrophe and salvation haunt this world
in equal measure: on the corner of Lake and California the old Tender Trap
Lounge is now the Launch Out into the Deep Christian Center, the bright
red lettering along its facade reading: "IF YOU ARE GOING TO THE JAIL COURT
OR HOSPITAL CALL FOR PRAYER."

It's no surprise, then, that Lake Street has long been home to some of
Chicago's most active blues clubs. The original Silvio's, which showcased
1950s stars like Elmore James, Howlin' Wolf, and Muddy Waters, stood at the
corner of Lake and Oakley Avenue, where the Henry Horner Homes housing
projects are now being demolished to make way for more upscale development. Silvio's later moved farther west, to the corner of Lake and Kedzie.
The name was eventually changed to the Riviera, but the club continued to
book blues bands until it closed in the 1980s. Others have come and gone in
recent years—El Matador, the Sunset Lounge (where I once heard a drunken
drummer bawl a chorus of the venerable "dozens" ditty, "Sittin' on my slop
jar, waitin' for my bowels to move"), harpist Little Arthur Duncan's Artesia
Lounge, a clandestine after-hours joint dubbed Belly's, and a biker hangout
called the Mighty Gun Social Club.

Today, though, most of the music on Lake Street consists of thundering,
bass-heavy hip-hop emanating from cars either cruising the strip or parked on
side streets. If, as has been suggested, the physical terrain of an area informs
the music that's made there,[14] then the uncompromisingly violent, hard-edged

cadences of hip-hop certainly sound like the appropriate folk tonalities for this neighborhood. "All tension, no release," may be a pejorative when it's applied to music, but it accurately describes day-to-day life in the modern ghetto.

In this atmosphere theoretical disputes about abstract notions like musical authenticity seem almost laughably irrelevant—if the oft-repeated manifesto that hip-hop culture is about "keeping it real" isn't enough of a declaration of intent, then further exegesis is worthless. But look a bit further and you still can find other sounds. At the corner of Lake and St. Louis is a club that for years was called, alternately, Mister Tee's and TJ's. Its proprietor, T. J. McNulty, a former drummer in Freddie King's band, booked some of the most dependable blues artists still active on the West Side. McNulty's health began to decline in the 1990s, and he eventually turned the room over to a fast-talking entrepreneur who goes by the name of Bossman. Bossman found backers to help him renovate the place, and he now calls it Bossman Blues Center. He has been trying to market it to white fans—locals and out-of-town-ers alike—hungry for a taste of what he bills as the "gut bucket blues."

Some of the music there actually merits that moniker. When the featured

Lake Street, looking west, October 2004. Photo by Susan Greenberg

act is a venerable journeyman like guitarist Milton Houston (brother of the slain Boston Blackie) or vocalist Lee "Little Howlin' Wolf" Solomon, it's easy to close your eyes and feel as if you've been transported to a 1950s gin mill. But on any given night, anyone from soul-blues singer-guitarist Bobby "Slim" James to young harpist Nuwki Nu and his blues-funk-R&B Nu Blues Groove Band may be presiding over the party. Bossman has occasionally booked nationally known artists like Bobby Rush and Chicago "soft-soul" veteran Garland Green as well. Stereotypes like "gutbucket" primitivism might draw the occasional thrill-seeking tourist, but they don't do justice to the scope or the quality of what goes on there much of the time.

Such stereotypes also tend to both romanticize and obscure the meaning of the music itself. What too many revivalists and roots-music advocates miss, and what well-meaning but ideologically laden efforts like Bossman's "gutbucket" campaign further obscure, is that the blues has already *had* its "roots" movement. In the late 1940s and early 1950s artists like John Lee Hooker, Muddy Waters, and Lightnin' Hopkins breathed new life into tradition by taking it pop, hitting the airwaves and the charts with down-home material delivered in countrified accents and laced with backwoods imagery. (And even then, much of what they put forth in live performance was far more aggressive and contemporary-sounding than their records.) Everything since—not only the so-called West Side blues style, with its emphasis on fervid emotionalism and instrumental virtuosity, which largely paved the way for the white blues-rock of the 1960s, but also R&B, soul, funk, hip-hop and beyond—has represented a further growth and flowering rather than a corruption or dilution of the roots that were recultivated and replanted at that time.

It's not something that usually needs to be proclaimed or even discussed; in fact, to reduce it to words may be to diminish its power. Few people who live on the West Side go out on Saturday night for a history lesson ("What you call nostalgia / really ain't what I'm after," as Gil Scott-Heron pointedly put it in "The Summer of '42"). But whether a song at Bossman's is a postwar Chicago blues classic, a funk-greased cover of a James Brown standard, or a contemporary R&B ballad on the jukebox, what it's called is far less important than the energy it incites and the response it garners. To succeed here, as in most neighborhood clubs, music must be an invocation of life in the present tense, an emotional and often physical call to action—not an artifact. (Bobby "Slim" James's James Brown medley thus includes some inspirational call-and-response preaching: "What we need?" "Soul power!" "We gotta have it!" "Soul power!") Roots are strong only when they nurture something that's alive and growing.

Bossman himself seems to understand this, even if his public proclamations indicate otherwise: on his club's wall, alongside posters proclaiming his gutbucket theme, a "wall of fame" mural portrays Tyrone Davis, B. B. King, Muddy Waters, Bobby Rush, and Leo Graham, a Chicago-based soul songwriter/producer who helped mastermind some of Davis's biggest hits and cowrote the Manhattans' "Shining Star."

This understanding of music as vital and dynamic explains why audiences at Mr. G's Supper Club will dance and respond with equal enthusiasm to the suave soul-blues inducements of Vernon Garrett and the Delta-to-Chicago style of Billy Branch or Willie Kent (with Bonnie Lee on vocals). It explains why teenagers, whose record collections probably consist almost entirely of hip-hop and mainstream R&B, ask Stan Mosley where they can find his records after they hear him in performance. It explains why Mississippi Delta nightspots, as far back as the early 1940s, carried platters by the likes of Count Basie, Louis Jordan, Cab Calloway, and Lil Green on their jukeboxes, even if the featured performers on weekends mostly purveyed sounds that would now be considered traditional or down-home (a phenomenon still evident in jukes and show lounges from Vicksburg to Chicago).[15] And it explains why contemporary radio programmers who insist that blues wouldn't sell even if given a reasonable chance on the air are as short-sighted as the purists (or club owners) who insist that the blues isn't even the blues unless it's drawn directly from the "set list from hell."

Most of all, though, it explains why any discussion of the future (or current or even past) viability of the blues is misguided if it focuses only on record sales and ignores the aesthetic and cultural value of the music in people's everyday lives, especially its essential role in the Saturday night ritual of release and regeneration. This is not to disparage historians who have challenged the romantic stereotype of blues musicians as folk troubadours instead of the professional (or, as Elijah Wald postulates, pop) musicians most were and are. Making records has been indisputably important to blues artists for as long as the option of making them has been available—both for the income they sometimes generate and for the publicity they bring (consider Honeyboy Edwards's anecdote about a woman who asked Robert Johnson to play "Terraplane Blues," a song she knew only from Johnson's recording).[16]

Nonetheless, to rely purely on marketplace criteria for evaluating the success or importance of musicians who play in a cultural context in which public performance, both sacred and secular, is deeply valued is to risk replacing one arbitrary social construct with another. The insistence that enjoying an experience—a party, a dance, a song—must always lead naturally to the desire to purchase a commodity drawn from that experience (i.e., that "culture" and "consumer culture" are always and everywhere synonymous) is laden with assumptions that do not necessarily reflect all times and places. Even in today's world, how many people never bother to purchase a copy of their favorite record on the jukebox in their local tavern or their favorite song performed by the band there, even though they may look forward to hearing it several times every Saturday night?

We Are the Blues

Without getting mired further in debates about what is and isn't folk, then, it's important to reaffirm that informal, community-based enactments of liberation and resistance remain deeply resonant in African American core culture—as they do in the cultures of most groups who have had to summon hope and maintain unity under harsh conditions. As Leonard Cohen has written, "Laughter is a fist in the face of the gods,"[17] and it can fly just as defiantly against a worldly oppressor. An antebellum ballad portrays Gabriel Prosser, the heroic slave rebel, outwitting his captors and returning home to join a "vic'try dance," where he proves himself "the bes' dancer 'mongst them all."[18] Even as Prosser was plotting his insurrection in Virginia in 1800, slave dancers in New Orleans' Congo Square were fusing spiritualist rituals with slyly camouflaged expressions of defiance against their masters (and no doubt the white tourists who came to gawk), summoning the will to prevail by manifesting and inhabiting visions of freedom, if only for a few hours.[19] Over a century later Albert Murray noted that dancers at jazz and jump-blues shows were doing pretty much the same thing. "The Saturday Night Function is a ritual of purification and affirmation," Murray wrote. "The more lowdown, dirty, and mean the music, the more instantaneously and pervasively sensual the dance gestures it engenders. . . . The incantation must be so percussion oriented that it disposes the listeners to bump and bounce, to slow-drag and steady shuffle, to grind, hop, jump, kick, rock, roll, shout, stomp, and otherwise swing the blues away."[20]

This sentiment is echoed in countless blues, soul, R&B, and soul-blues songs extending from their origins to the present (and reprised almost word-for-word in Z. Z. Hill's 1980s hit "Bump and Grind"). And as Mo Rodgers suggests, it's not about to die. More recently Stuart Cosgrove has described the genesis of another of Chicago's gifts to the popular music world, the aggressive fusion of disco, hard-funk, and electronica that in the 1970s and early 1980s came to be known as house music: "Chicago House, a relentless sound designed to take dancers to a new high, has its origins in the gospel and its future in spaced-out simulation (techno). In the mid 1970's, when disco was still an underground phenomenon, sin and salvation were willfully mixed together to create a sound which somehow managed to be decadent and devout . . . , a form of orgasmic gospel, which merged the sweeping strings of Philadelphia dance music with the tortured vocals of soul singers like Loleatta Holloway."[21]

The need for such public-sphere invocations of the spirit of Carnival seems, if anything, to have become more pressing in contemporary American life, and not just in the ghetto—illustrating, again, Billy Branch's observation that for all the cultural and historical specificity in which it is rooted, the blues addresses universal themes. There's little place for Eshu-Eleggua and his raucous band of troublemakers in the boardrooms and suburbs of corporate America, in the empirical universe of science, or in the repressed moral landscape of modern monotheistic fundamentalism. Human beings need an outlet, a place of illumination and release where the suffocating bounds of everyday reality and moral restrictions can be thrown off, even if only for a time. The popularity of elaborately staged events like the annual Burning Man Festival in Nevada's Black Rock Desert illustrates the extent to which people will go in their attempts to create (or re-create) rituals of this nature. This need also explains why the pilgrims who continue to travel America in search of authenticity thrill so deeply to the eros-charged ebullience and fellowship they discover in jukes and on backstreets from Mississippi to Chicago.

But what a pilgrim may see as a mecca the folks next door know merely as the "hole in the wall." The genius of the blues—indeed, of the entire cultural, aesthetic, and musical lineage of which it is a part, from Gabriel Prosser's day to the present—has been its ability to provide people the opportunity to engage in such secular rites of transcendence in the context of their day-to-day lives. "It doesn't matter what you wear, just as long as you are there," Martha Reeves instructed us in 1964, and while that's not always technically true (some clubs do have dress codes), the overlying message—that participants in good standing needn't adhere to any specific cultural (or "countercultural") ideology, be a member of any particular social class, or otherwise represent any ethos or "lifestyle"—expresses yet another vital element of what the blues represents. (When Garland Green played at Bossman's, the audience consisted of workshirt-clad regulars and local businessmen rubbing shoulders with street people, celebrities like ex-boxer Ernie Terrell, demure young women clad incongruously in hoochie-mama chic, and a couple of pimps wielding diamond-studded drinking cups.) It's the accessibility of the experience, the ease with which one can pass through the door of a juke or a show lounge and find oneself thrust into a "ritual of purification and affirmation," that makes that experience all the more profound, because the surroundings and the casualness with which the ritual can be entered seem so quotidian and uncontrived.

Yet I don't want to end on an unrealistically optimistic note. A harrowing array of forces continues to threaten everyday life and even survival, despite the resilient spirit of endurance embodied by the blues. Neighborhoods crumble or get transformed into playgrounds for the wealthy, people die or succumb to dissolution, and hope itself often seems in danger of getting lost. The attrition rate among musicians alone is grim. Lurrie Bell's fellow prodigy Johnny B. Moore suffered what may have been a career-ending stroke in 2003. Willie D. suffered a heart attack in April 2004; he's working again, but it's difficult to watch his hyperactive stage show (to say nothing of his chain-smoking) without a sense of foreboding. Boston Blackie was murdered in 1993; more recently, in July 2002, veteran guitarist Jimmie Lee Robinson, his body wracked with cancer, took his own life.

Ashward Gates, one of the most dependable percussionists on the local scene, suffered a massive stroke on Thanksgiving weekend of 2003, while he was still recovering from a severe beating he had received in a street altercation less than a year earlier. He passed away in late 2004. Al Harris, who sang the jubilant ode to the passing of Maxwell Street on that final Sunday, has looked increasingly frail since falling ill in the early 2000s and now performs in town only sporadically; his guitarist, David Lindsey, also a young man, died from complications of diabetes in the late 1990s. Guitarist Johnny Dollar, an adventurous stylist who emerged to great acclaim in the 1970s and 1980s, has endured a series of mishaps—heart problems, accidents, encounters with street violence, alcoholism—that have left him all but incapacitated as a musician. Some simply give up: despite the promise he showed early on, Lee Morris proved unable to carve out a viable niche for himself on either the local or national circuit, and he has withdrawn from the scene.

Things don't look much better for the community itself. The neighborhood around Wallace's will probably soon be an upscale condominium enclave—good news for "economic indicators" but devastating for the people who have lived there for years and will be forced to vacate their homes. In fact, many urbanologists believe that if current patterns continue, the urban poor—primarily marginalized workers, the long-term unemployed, and their families—will eventually be disfranchised, swept to a peripheral suburban ring largely bereft of human services or even a basic infrastructure, the result mirroring geographic and spatial relations in South Africa under apartheid.[22] And of course the devastating effects of hard drugs, crime, and other pathogens of poverty cast a pall over everyday life that often seems impenetrable.

Nonetheless, the music—and the dance—survives.[23] In the heat of the moment on a Saturday night, even that mechanized soul-blues synth groove pounding out of a jukebox can be almost as compelling a "percussion-oriented incantation" as its antecedents in R&B, funk, soul, and earlier blues. And as Chris Thomas King and Chicago's still-developing Nuwki Nu are proving, the blues continues to "reinvent itself," confounding us by shape-shifting, challenging our preconceived notions about what the music—and we—can be. No doubt such artists will soon be welcomed on festivals and in clubs by the same purists who have belatedly acknowledged the authenticity of performers like the Staples, New Orleans's Neville Brothers, Denise LaSalle, and Artie White—in other words, the blues will yet again reveal itself to be

Johnny Drummer at Lee's Unleaded Blues, April 2004. Photo by Joeff Davis/ CitySearch

a musical language that, once incubated and nurtured in its own cultural milieu, can expand its scope and speak to a universal audience.

Closer to home, clubbers in venues as diverse as Bossman's, Linda's Lounge, East of the Ryan, and the Starlite continue to dance to everyone from John Lee Hooker through Howlin' Wolf to Sir Charles Jones, if they happen to be on the jukebox. They will then respond just as jubilantly to bands whose sets span the gamut from original compositions and bluesified versions of contemporary R&B hits to classics associated with the likes of Muddy Waters, Sonny Boy Williamson, and Elmore James. In other words (Duke Ellington's, as a matter of fact), the blues remains "beyond category"—even, in many ways, beyond name. Until quite recently few if any South or West Side clubs had the word *blues* in their names at all; the word was superfluous. The music was and is simply *there,* the ongoing cadence of the life-dance that's ritually re-created on Saturday night (and redeemed on Sunday morning), the goad that prods us out of our ennui, turns us back around and gets us out the door and into the streets, looking for the place where that rhythm is alive. Because it is, after all, Saturday night—and "I hear some blues downstairs."

Notes

Introduction

1. The direct lineage between African trickster-god myths and the African American folk tradition—including the persona of the blues hero (or antihero) as the Trickster incarnate—has been widely discussed; see, for instance, Gates, *The Signifying Monkey;* Floyd, *Power of Black Music.*

2. All quotations from and information provided by blues artists in this chapter are taken from my interviews with them, as cited in the chapters profiling those artists, unless otherwise noted.

3. "The feeling that the blues are marking time in the city is inescapable; as the older artists die or retire the young ones, hampered by the dictates of changed social and economic pressures, seem unable to make a significant breakthrough to give a cohesion and form to a new style of Chicago blues" (Rowe, *Chicago Blues,* 209).

4. Interview with Cicero Blake, April 17, 2003.

5. I heard Rev. Al Green make these statements in June 1994 when I attended a service at his church, the Full Gospel Tabernacle, 787 Hale Road, Memphis.

6. Guralnick, *Sweet Soul Music,* 286, 290.

7. Interview with Lurrie Bell, September 13, 2003.

8. Interview with Sharon Lewis, June 20, 2003.

9. Interview with Cicero Blake, April 17, 2003.

10. Floyd, *Power of Black Music,* 8. Floyd acknowledges that he adapted this concept from the work of Jason Berry.

11. Davis, *History of the Blues,* 253–54.

12. This topic, too, has been widely addressed. See, for instance, Davidson, *African Genius;* Zahan, *Religion, Spirituality, and Thought.* Valuable works discussing how these holistic perspectives have informed African American (and other American) music and ritual, both secular and sacred, include Dixon, *Digging the Africanist Presence;* Fine, *Soulstepping;* Palmer, *Deep Blues;* Lomax, *Land Where the Blues Began;* and Stuckey, *Slave Culture.* In *The Primal Mind* Highwater focuses primarily on Native American culture, but his meditations on the "indigenous" worldview as posing a direct chal-

lenge to Western dualism are generalizable to this discussion as well ("Primal people have little concern or faith in the materialism that imposes mind/brain and soul/body dichotomies" [150]).

13. For fascinating exegeses of the way this venerable pre-Christian trope has been adapted to Christian theology in the African American church, see Crawford and Troeger, *The Hum;* Mitchell, *Black Preaching.*

14. Guralnick, *Lost Highway,* 323. My suggestion that virtually every active blues artist has a "following" is also adapted from Guralnick, who notes that every artist profiled in *Lost Highway* "has a mass audience—whether of five thousand, fifty thousand, or even half a million" (14). I have expanded—or perhaps contracted—that sentiment to apply it to the local and regional audience enjoyed by artists, whether recorded or not, who ply their trade on the neighborhood, town, or city level. Similar observations, of course, could be made about purveyors of rock 'n' roll, country and western, rap/hip-hop, or any other musical form that reflects the mores and aesthetics of a definable community alongside the further-flung "mainstream" listenership.

15. Calt and Wardlow, *King of the Delta Blues,* 305. Calt, whose slash-and-burn style and penchant for settling personal scores in print have tended to obscure the value of some of his insights, has been particularly relentless in his assault on the romanticized notion of the bluesman as pristine twentieth-century "folk" artist.

16. Qtd. in Davis, *History of the Blues,* 28.

17. Interview with Sharon Lewis, March 7, 2003.

18. E.g., Miller, "I'd Rather Drink Muddy Water."

19. Cox, "Nobody Knows You," as recorded by Bessie Smith, 1929.

20. Even some of the most prescient and knowledgeable commentators on the blues (and the "folk" culture from which it derives) have fallen into the "romantic hero" trap. David Evans's *Big Road Blues* is considered a modern-day classic of blues scholarship. Nevertheless, despite his earnest and informative analyses showing how and why acoustic southern bluesmen composed and performed their material (with a recurring emphasis on concepts like "truth" and "honesty"), he never mentions that most of the "folk" musicians in his case studies performed for money, at least part-time, over the courses of their lives. Even when a musician like string-band veteran Lucius Smith talks about taking requests from dancers (47), or when bluesman Mott Willis recalls performing for "parties and suppers" and adds that he got a lot of "them big plays" [i.e., well-paying gigs] in his heyday (188–89), Evans ignores the obvious and neglects to point out how this income was a welcome and necessary adjunct to the hard-earned money a man received for being a fieldworker or a laborer in the early and mid-twentieth-century South.

In his landmark study *The Land Where the Blues Began,* Alan Lomax waxes almost orgasmic on his discovery of things like "true African turn taking" at a rural church service in the Mississippi Delta (75). In addition, he insistently focuses on the blues as a music of suffering and lament. Of course, this did provide a necessary and at the time radical corrective to generations of racist propaganda claiming, as Lomax puts it, that "blacks were contented with their lot" (16). Nonetheless, Lomax ignores the music's equally important role as a way of making a living for the artist, as well as its social function as an impetus to dancing and celebration. Such an approach also tends to figure the blues singer as lone storyteller instead of a participant in a community ritual of affirmation. Sometimes we do "laugh to keep from crying," but we often laugh simply because we're having a good time.

Ironically, when Lomax does address the good-time aspect of blues expression, he often uses language much like his references to an "unconflicted and happy eroticism" that reflects "the sexually more permissive African cultural tradition" (374). Such archetypes have some basis in truth, but they downplay the spiritualist component of traditional African attitudes toward sexuality and the symbolic nature of the Trickster's [or bluesman's] ritualized transgressions of sexual mores in performance, ceremony, and dance.

21. The active role of the recording industry in perpetuating this "holy primitive" stereotype should not be overlooked. Oxford, Mississippi's Fat Possum label has done a remarkable job in recent years of finding and recording previously under-recognized southern blues artists; several, such as T-Model Ford and the late R. L. Burnside, became internationally known after signing on with the label. But the label's penchant for caricature has drawn criticism, even (or, perhaps, especially) from its artists' admirers. The cover of Burnside's debut Fat Possum disk, 1996's *A Ass Pocket of Whiskey*, was a cartoon that portrayed the bluesman leering at a couple of white girls' derrieres—an image that could have gotten Burnside lynched less than fifty years ago. A Fat Possum publicity release tells us that "old blues men are supposed to be bad people," and boasts that many of the label's stalwarts have "only limited repertoires, [are] unreliable or refus[e] to play standing up. Guys who sometimes have trouble standing up, who are better at falling down. But hey, that's the blues."

22. Mailer, "The White Negro."

23. Van Vechten, *Nigger Heaven;* Mezzrow, *Really the Blues.*

24. Since this was written, the city closed the Checkerboard in an episode that received wide press coverage. It has reopened near the campus of the University of Chicago.

25. Said, *Orientalism,* 1–5.

26. Du Bois, "Review of *Nigger Heaven,*" 81.

27. Holmes, "Philosophy of the Beat Generation," 23.

28. Davis, *History of the Blues,* 21.

Chapter 1: Junior Wells

When Junior died in 1998, I wrote or cowrote several tributes: David Whiteis, "Little Big Man," *Chicago Reader,* March 20, 1998, pp. 26–27; David Whiteis, Billy Boy Arnold, A. C. Reed, and Marty Salzman, "A Tribute to Junior Wells," *Living Blues* 139 (May–June 1998): 46–48; and David Whiteis, "Junior," *Juke Blues* 41 (Summer 1998): 30–34. Portions of these have been rewritten for this chapter.

I never had the opportunity to conduct an in-depth interview with Junior, although I came to know him quite well over the years. Secondary sources were thus important resources for this chapter. O'Neal, "Junior Wells Interview," was especially valuable for its meticulously researched biographical details concerning Junior's life in the South and his early days in Chicago. Discographical data are from Leadbitter, *Blues Records 1943–1970, vol. 2,* and Witburn, *Top R&B Singles.*

1. Told to me by Lena Blakemore during a visit to her home, ca. 1991.

2. O'Neal, "Junior Wells Interview," 11.

3. Related to me personally by Lena Blakemore and substantiated by comments Junior made in O'Neal, "Junior Wells Interview."

4. McGraw-Beauchamp, *Blues Stories,* 15.

5. Ulrey, "Junior," 17; O'Neal, "Junior Wells Interview," 11.

6. O'Neal, "Junior Wells Interview," 15.

7. Rowe, *Chicago Blues,* 117.

8. Tooze, *Muddy Waters,* 106.

9. O'Neal, "Junior Wells Interview," 14.

10. In O'Neal, "Junior Wells Interview," Junior misidentifies this as "Camp Robertson."

11. O'Neal, "Junior Wells Interview," 23.

12. Interview with Jody Williams at his home in Chicago, March 29, 2001.

13. Pruter, *Chicago Soul,* 239–40.

14. Ibid., 239–40, 295.

15. Ibid., 240.

16. Thanks to Jim O'Neal and Robert Pruter for confirming these details.

17. The number varied, but it was almost always over thirty.

18. Per Dick Shurman.

19. Related to me by the late Gail Sacks, who was working the door at the Checkerboard that night.

20. Details of the funeral and burial come from multiple anecdotes related to me by people who were there, as well as Carlozo and Kennedy, "So Long, Hoodoo Man."

Chapter 2: Sunnyland Slim

I interviewed Sunnyland Slim at his home in Chicago on March 25, 1983, for an article that appeared as "A Tender Heart and a Hustler's Soul: Sunnyland Slim's Long Life in the Blues," *Chicago Reader,* April 29, 1983. All quotations and biographical details here are taken from that interview unless otherwise specified. Sections of that article were rewritten and expanded for a tribute to Sunnyland that appeared as "God Can Do It All: Remembering the Life of Sunnyland Slim," *Juke Blues* 36 (Winter 1996–97): 24–28, which has served as a template for this chapter. Discographical data are from Leadbitter and Slavin, *Blues Records 1943–1970,* and Leadbitter, *Blues Records 1943–1970, vol. 2.*

1. The outlines of this story, including the information about Rover Brown, were told to me by Sunnyland. Further details were gleaned from Palmer, *Deep Blues,* 151–52.

2. McIlwaine, *Memphis Down in Dixie,* 22; "March of Events," 362.

3. Palmer, *Deep Blues,* 154.

4. zur Heide, *Deep South Piano,* 33.

5. King and Ritz, *Blues All around Me,* 128.

6. It has long been believed that this tour included the Soviet Union. According to Harold Bremer's liner notes to Sunnyland's mid-1970s Airway album *She Got That Jive,* presumably based on information provided by Sunnyland himself, the song "Levee Camp Moan" was recorded there in 1964. Promoter Horst Lipmann, however, clarified this in Dixon and Snowdon, *I Am the Blues:* "We toured East Germany, Poland, and Czechoslovakia. . . . We recorded all of that session in East Berlin for [the] Amiga [label]. . . . We did not get into Russia in 1964" (136–37).

7. Per photographer Marc PoKempner, who attended the show.

8. This anecdote has been related to me by Burckhardt several times over the years.

9. Cather, *O Pioneers!* 176.

Chapter 3: Big Walter Horton

An earlier version of this chapter appeared as "I Mean It from My Heart: Memories of Big Walter," *Juke Blues* 37 (Spring 1997): 38–43; I thank Cilla Huggins, copublisher of *Juke Blues,* for additional discographical information drawn from her personal record collection and documents. I also thank Jim Themelis, Chicago's number one Big Walter aficionado, for making available his archival material on Walter. All anecdotes are from my own personal experience unless otherwise cited.

Big Walter told many conflicting (and colorful) stories of his life, his origins, and his career. Although I include some recollections of his earlier years that he and his contemporaries shared with me, I have relied primarily on the following sources for biographical and discographical details, unless otherwise specified: Escott and Hawkins, *Sun Records;* Harris, *Blues Who's Who;* Leadbitter and Slavin, *Blues Records 1943–1970;* Leadbitter, *Blues Records 1943–1970,* vol. 2; Oliver, *Story of the Blues;* Rowe, *Chicago Blues;* Santelli, *Big Book of Blues.*

1. Personal conversation with Floyd Jones, ca. 1980.

2. Guralnick, *Feel Like Going Home,* 108.

3. Charters, *Sweet as the Showers,* 18.

4. Edwards, *World Don't Owe Me,* 111, 112.

5. This information is from a Xerox copy of Walter's arrest papers from the Memphis Police Department, dated September 7, 1946, document no. 45621. The document was originally discovered in Memphis by researcher Steve LaVere, who gave a copy to Jim O'Neal, founding coeditor of *Living Blues* magazine. O'Neal gave a copy to Jim Themelis around the early 1980s.

6. O'Neal and Van Singel, "Muddy Waters," 36.

7. Tooze, *Muddy Waters,* 112.

8. O'Neal and Van Singel, "Muddy Waters," 36.

9. Wright and Rothwell, "Muddy Waters Discography."

10. Brisbin, "Jimmy Rogers," 26.

11. Qtd. in Rowe, *Chicago Blues,* 141.

12. "One veteran told me of being on a European tour and listening in disbelief to the lies that the other artists were telling. Not to be outdone, he joined in, and interviewers were subjected to nothing more than a lying contest between musicians as to who could tell the biggest whoppers" (O'Neal, "BluEsoterica"). The writer Lincoln "Chicago Beau" Beauchamp related to me that Johnny Shines informed him of his own participation in such scenarios.

13. Edwards, *World Don't Owe Me,* 61.

14. Cook County Coroner's Office certificate of death for Walter Horton, document no. 625929, December 8, 1981.

15. Related to me by Michael Frank, president of Earwig Records, who booked and promoted the show in conjunction with what eventually became the 1981 Earwig LP *Old Friends,* which included Walter, Sunnyland, Honeyboy Edwards, Floyd Jones, and Kansas City Red.

Chapter 4: Florence's Lounge

All observations and anecdotes are from my own experience unless otherwise noted in the text. The club's former "Bucket of Blood" designation was related to me by Junior Wells, among others. An earlier version of this chapter appeared as "A Farewell to Florence's," *Chicago Reader,* January 6, 1984.

1. Odom and Walker, "Memo Blues."

2. I no longer possess the article in which this description was offered. I originally cited it in the January 6, 1984, piece for the *Chicago Reader* from which this chapter was adapted.

Chapter 5: Maxwell Street

An earlier version of this chapter appeared as "The Last Sunday," *Chicago Reader,* September 2, 1994. The events described here are based on my observations, mostly recorded as notes I wrote as I walked through the market on its last day.

I thank Kenny Tams and Carolyn "the Blues Lady" Alexander for allowing me access to their videotapes of that last Sunday on Maxwell Street; these tapes sharpened my recollections and allowed me to describe scenes such as the Jimmy Davis performance with greater vividness. I myself witnessed both the episode of Cookie and the collapsing building and the final scenario. Historical data about the market itself are taken primarily from Berkow, *Maxwell Street,* and from my own interviews and investigative research into city of Chicago plat maps and historical records conducted in conjunction with another, earlier article that was published in the *Chicago Reader* on Friday, July 27, 1990. The quotation from Krystin Grenon originally appeared in that article.

The term *Gift Sunday* is my own, but longtime Maxwell Street habitués often spoke in almost mystical terms of the idea that every year seemed to bring a final day of good weather after a "false winter" had chased everyone away.

Chapter 6: "Let's Go, Baby, to the Hole in the Wall"

The title of this chapter is taken from Mel Waiters's 1997 soul-blues hit "Hole in the Wall" on the Malaco/Waldoxy label. All observations, quotations, and anecdotes are from my personal experience unless otherwise noted in the text. The opening vignette is modified from my article "'Fish Scent Fill the Air': The Delta Fish Market Brings the Blues Back Home," *Original Chicago Blues Annual* 3 (1991).

1. Not her real name.

2. Information on Operation Incubator from FBI data in "Division History," available at http://chicago.fbi.gov/history.htm.

3. Davis himself told me he owned these buildings and this business.

4. In Clarksdale, the actor Morgan Freeman now owns Ground Zero, a blues bistro that has already garnered international fame. Walnut Street Bait Shop in Greenville attracts touristy crowds, and the 930 Blues Café performs a similar function in Jackson.

5. The identity of "Barbara Ann's" child has been disguised.

6. Biographical details and all quotations from Harmonica Khan are from interviews I conducted with him in October 2002 at Bossman Blues Center, 3500 W. Lake Street, and at his home in Chicago on March 30, 2003.

7. This LP, released on the Delta label, is no longer in print.

8. Per telephone conversation with Arlette Nuñez, Harmonica Khan's widow, in March 2005.

9. Biographical and discographical information on Denise LaSalle from Pruter, *Chicago Soul,* 331–34; and Whitburn, *Top R&B Singles,* 257.

10. "Still the Queen," previously available at www.deniselasalle.com. This Web site is no longer operative.

11. Interview with Sharon Lewis, Chicago, June 7, 2003.

Chapter 7: Jody Williams

I interviewed Jody Williams at his home in Chicago on March 29, 2001, and again on June 21, 2001, for an article that appeared as "Jody Williams: An Unsung Guitar Hero Returns," *Living Blues* 161 (Jan.–Feb. 2000): 10–18, from which portions of this chapter have been adapted. We also had numerous brief conversations and e-mail correspondences to clear up details as I transcribed our interviews. All information and quotations here are from these conversations unless otherwise noted.

I thank Dick Shurman for taping Jody's early sides and sideman sessions for me so I could substantiate the claims that the later Buddy Guy, Otis Rush, and Mickey and Sylvia songs were closely based on melodies and riffs that appeared first on Jody's records. Dick, a longtime friend of Jody's, also provided me with valuable information and insights into Jody's life and career. Further discographical information was derived from Leadbitter, *Blues Records 1943–1970, vol. 2*, and Witburn, *Top R&B Singles*. Dick Shurman's liner notes and annotations from *Howlin' Wolf: The Chess Box* (1991) helped to confirm Jody's work with Wolf.

1. Jody was under the impression that Chess owned the building. Nadine Cohodas, author of *Spinning Blues into Gold: The Chess Brothers and the Legendary Chess Records*, clarified for me that he was the building's manager, not its owner.

2. In Billy Boy's own words: "There was a guy at Indiana Theater, which had Midnight Rambler [*sic*] shows on Saturday night. And his name was Bo Diddley, he was a comedian. . . . The first time I heard the word Bo Diddley, I was playing with [Bo] on the street in 1951. And the bass player said, 'Hey, Ellas, there go Bo Diddley,' talking about this guy that played the Indiana Theater. . . . So we was doing this recording thing . . . ; he was singing, 'Papa gonna buy his babe a diamond ring,' and playing the hambone beat. And I suggested, why don't you say, 'Bo Diddley'? That's how that name came into the picture. . . . When the record came out, to our surprise, the song was 'Bo Diddley,' and to our surprise, [Chess] named the artist Bo Diddley" (qtd. in Unterberger, "Billy Boy Arnold").

3. Shurman, liner notes.

4. White, *Bo Diddley*, 101.

5. A more complete list was available on the Web site www.thecoversproject.com, a site dedicated to documenting cover versions of songs. This Web site is no longer operative.

6. Qtd. in White, *Bo Diddley*, 101–2.

7. Qtd. in ibid., 103.

8. Ibid., 102.

9. Ibid.

10. Dahl, "Mickey Baker," 41.

Chapter 8: Bonnie Lee

I conducted two in-depth interviews with Bonnie Lee—one at her home in Chicago on October 13, 1992, and the other by telephone—for an article that appeared as "I Need Someone's Hand," *Chicago Reader,* February 5, 1993. Numerous follow-up conversations, both in person and by phone, clarified questions and filled in details. All biographical information and quotation here are taken from those interviews, unless otherwise noted. I thank Steve Wisner for confirming details about J. Mayo Williams recordings and for taping some of Bonnie's early sides for me.

1. From a telephone conversation with Koester, ca. November 1992.

2. Bonnie definitely pronounced this woman's name as "Glenn." It is possible, however, that she meant Lillian Glinn, a singer who recorded blues for the Columbia label in the late 1920s. Some of Glinn's sessions were in Dallas.

3. The anecdote about Eatmon bringing his Cadillac onstage was told to me by the host of NPR's *Blues before Sunrise*, Steve Cushing, who interviewed Eatmon for his show. Details about the appearance of Eatmon's store derive from a photo in Rowe, *Chicago Blues*, 186.

4. The year was 1982. This date was confirmed by Jim O'Neal.

5. John, "Need Your Love So Bad."

Chapter 9: Billy Branch

I conducted interviews with Billy Branch on December, 13, 2004; January 10, 2004; and February 7, 2004. All three interviews took place at Rosa's Lounge in Chicago. We also had several follow-up conversations and short interviews over the telephone to clarify details.

Steven Sharp's interview with Billy, "Don't Start Me to Talkin'," which appeared in *Living Blues* (May–June, 1998) and has since been posted in an expanded form on the Web site www.bluesmusicnow.com, was also a valuable resource. In several cases Billy related some of the same information to Sharp that he related to me but did so using more vivid imagery; in other cases (as he explained to me and as I mention in the text), he broached subjects he no longer wishes to revisit, although he is willing to remain on the record as having addressed them in the past. I have thus opted to insert excerpts from the Sharp interview into my narrative when appropriate.

Unless otherwise cited, all quotations, anecdotes, and factual reportage derive from my interviews with Billy and my own observations.

1. *Billy Branch's Blues in the Schools.*

2. Ibid.

3. Sharp, "Don't Start Me to Talkin'," 16–17.

4. Hansen, liner notes.

5. Sharp, "Don't Start Me to Talkin'," www.bluesmusicnow.com.

6. Sharp, "Don't Start Me to Talkin'," 17.

7. Sharp, "Don't Start Me to Talkin'," www.bluesmusicnow.com.

8. Calt, *I'd Rather Be the Devil*, 249.

9. Sharp, "Don't Start Me to Talkin'," www.bluesmusicnow.com.

10. Ibid.

11. Ibid.

12. Ibid.

13. *Billy Branch's Blues in the Schools.*

14. Sharp, "Don't Start Me to Talkin'," 23.

15. Ibid.

16. Ibid., 23–24.

17. Sharp, "Don't Start Me to Talkin'," www.bluesmusicnow.com.

18. Ibid.

19. Gwaltney, *Drylongso*, xxii.

20. Baraka, "Funk Lore," 95–97.

21. Sharp, "Don't Start Me to Talkin'," www.bluesmusicnow.com.

Chapter 10: Sharon Lewis

I conducted primary interviews with Sharon Lewis on March 7, 2003; June 7, 2003; and June 20, 2003. We followed up these three meetings with numerous brief conversations, both in person and over the phone, to clarify details and elaborate on certain points. All biographical data and quotations are from these interviews and conversations.

1. Taylor, "Mother Blues."
2. Edwards, *World Don't Owe Me,* 212.

Chapter 11: Lurrie Bell

I conducted two primary interviews with Lurrie Bell and Susan Greenberg at their home in Chicago, one on September 13, 2003, and the other on October 11, 2003. Follow-up questions were relayed, via phone and e-mail, during the subsequent weeks. I also want to thank Susan for giving me permission to quote from several long and detailed e-mails she wrote me between September and November 2003, in which she related her experiences and feelings surrounding the loss of her babies. All biographical information and quotations in this chapter are from these interviews and correspondences, unless otherwise noted.

1. Letter to Lurrie Bell from Dr. Steve Weine, associate professor of psychiatry at the University of Illinois at Chicago and director of the International Center for Human Responses to Social Catastrophes, August 30, 2003.
2. Qtd. in Kenning, "Mood Music," 19.
3. According to Bruce Iglauer, president of Alligator Records (Koko Taylor's label), Lurrie's tenure with her actually lasted about eighteen months and began sometime in 1978.
4. At other times Lurrie has estimated that he went to Mississippi when he was seven or eight years old.
5. Details of Carey Bell's life are taken from Bell's liner notes to the CD *Carey Bell's Blues Harp,* Delmark DE-622, 1995. Additional Bell family history and anecdotes were related to me by Lurrie and Susan during our second interview and confirmed by Susan via e-mail.
6. Related to me by drummer Kenny Tams.
7. Qtd. in Kenning, "Mood Music," 19.
8. Cushing, "Your Wild Thing."

Chapter 12: Artie White

I interviewed Artie White on May 1, 2002, at the Checkerboard Lounge in Chicago, for a profile that appeared as "Artie 'Blues Boy' White: 'Only the Strong Will Survive'," *Living Blues* 156 (Sept.–Oct. 2002): 12–20. This chapter is derived from that article. I thank Steve Wisner for providing me with tapes of Artie's early and midcareer 45s. Pruter, *Chicago Soul,* was a valuable source of additional biographical and discographical information, as well as details on the Chicago blues and soul scene of the mid-1960s. Whitburn, *Top R&B Singles,* confirmed the status of "Leanin Tree" on the national R&B charts.

1. Artie was mistaken about this being B. B. King's first record. The lyrics are actually from King's "You Didn't Want Me," released on the RPM label in 1952. King's first

release, "Miss Martha King," was recorded in 1949 at the studio of Memphis radio station WDIA, where King worked as a deejay, and released on the Nasvhille-based Bullet label. I thank Brett Bonner, editor of *Living Blues* magazine, for his help in tracking down this information.

2. When Artie met him, Sam Cooke would have still been spelling his name "Cook." He added the *e* in 1957, after crossing over into secular music.

3. I have not been able to uncover any evidence that this record was ever released.

4. Pruter, *Chicago Soul*, 246–47.

5. Despite Artie's apparent awe at how much this project cost, he actually got off pretty cheaply. Vocalist E. C. Scott told me in 2003: "My CD [*The Other Side of Me*, released on her own Black Bud label] is over $30,000—just to do the production, and that's not including putting ads in the paper, paying a publicist, all those things that you need to have a good CD."

6. Nelson, "Sweet Miss Coffy," 53.

Chapter 13: Cicero Blake

I conducted two primary interviews with Cicero Blake: one on April 17, 2003, at his home in Chicago, and one by telephone on October 16, 2003. His appearance at Wallace's Catfish Corner occurred on the weekend of September 19, 2003. Unless otherwise cited, all biographical data and quotations come from these conversations.

Robert Pruter's books *Doowoop* and *Chicago Soul* were valuable sources for background information on Cicero's early career and more generally on the Chicago soul and R&B scenes in the 1950s and 1960s. I took discographical information, too, from these two sources, as well as from records in the collection of Steve Wisner. I thank Wisner for taping these records and sharing the tapes with me.

1. Cicero was unsure of the station's call letters; in conversation he confused it with Chicago's WJJD. Veteran Jackson deejay Bruce Payne told Scott Barretta, former editor of *Living Blues*, that a deejay named Mike O'Reilly had an afternoon show on WJXN in Jackson during the late 1940s and early 1950s. Payne believes that the show was called the Atomic Boogie Hour.

2. Pruter, *Chicago Soul*, 197.

3. Brown, *Manchild in the Promised Land*, 404.

4. Pruter, *Doowop*, 3–4. Simpkins, who nonetheless assured Pruter that he "got to like [blues] for what it was years later," went on to write blues songs for artists such as the late Mighty Joe Young.

5. These and the following details about the Chicago doo-wop scene and the history of Dee Clark, the Goldentones, the Kool Gents, and the El Dorados are drawn from Pruter, *Doowop*, 116; and Pruter, *Chicago Soul*, 28.

6. Otis, *Upside Your Head!* 118.

7. McKeough, "Keyboards," 2.

8. Johnson, "Chicago Blues Festival," 37.

Chapter 14: Little Scotty

I interviewed Little Scotty at his Chicago home on two occasions: August 26, 2003, and September 5, 2003. I would like to thank Scotty for lending me his only copies of his early records and EPs. All biographical information and quotations are from my interviews with Scotty unless otherwise noted.

Scotty's discography is murky because most of the small labels for which he recorded no longer exist. The records themselves generally lack dates or copyright information. I have derived my estimates from the collectors' Web sites www.disco-funk.co.uk and http://members.home.nl/discopatrick/peter.htm, which list some of Scotty's 1970s records on Queen Constance, Sound of New York, and Nile. In personal communication, Skippy White estimated 1979 as the release year of the original "Slow That Disco Down" on Nile and 1980 as the year he reissued it on his Bluestown label.

1. This opening vignette describes a show I attended at the New Excuse Lounge, 5944 South Halsted. Also in attendance was Carolyn "the Blues Lady" Alexander, who videotaped the show. I thank Carolyn for lending me that tape, which helped sharpen my memory and from which I drew the description that opens this chapter.

2. Jeffries, who has claimed that "rich Jews" controlled the slave trade, was removed from his position as head of the Black Studies Department at City University of New York (CUNY) in 1992, at least partly in response to pressure from Jewish advocacy groups. However, he continues to teach at CUNY as a tenured professor.

3. They never did get back together. "We was gonna get another place down there. She had [Chris and Shawn] with her when she went back home. And she got killed there [around 1980]. It's a long story. I heard she got killed in a car accident—a car ran into her on the road. [But] I just left from down there, and I talked to her daughter and her son. The story they told me, she was going with some guy, [and] she'd just had a new baby by another guy. This guy was jealous of her; she got out' the car, she was walking down the road, and he ran her down and killed her. I was [living] in New York, but I was singing in Indianapolis, Indiana, when she got killed."

4. Skippy White believes the original "Slow That Disco Down," on Nile, was probably recorded in about 1979; he acquired the master from Scotty and issued it on his Bluestown label a year or two later. White said it was so popular among mainstream African American buyers and white college students alike that he couldn't keep enough copies in his store to meet the demand. He also remembers Scotty as a popular entertainer in both black and white venues around New England during that time (per telephone conversation with White in October 2003).

5. The Chicago guitarist and vocalist Willie Davis believes that he worked on a few shows with Scotty at a South Side club in the late 1960s, but Scotty maintains he didn't move to Chicago until about 1982. It's possible the club dates Davis remembers were gigs Scotty booked for himself during his 1960s attempts to establish himself as a chitlin circuit entertainer. Scotty is vague about his precise itinerary as a performer during those years, but judging from his comments about having worked with Nat Tarnopol, he did travel to the Midwest early on.

6. To the best of my knowledge, this march never occurred.

7. In September 2003 Scotty had just returned from a sojourn to the East Coast, which included a stopover in his hometown of Florence: "I sung in church. And they knowed my background of civil rights, and so they said, 'Man, we want you to speak on civil rights, speak in front of these boys that just come out of jail; help them out.' It was like a YMCA private organization: when they get out of the prison, get them jobs, clean them up. I laid 'em out, man! They was like in a daze. I was telling 'em how great they really was and that they was born into the world to be kings, maybe a president one day. They want me to come back." He proudly showed me photos taken at the event.

Coda

I interviewed Lee Morris and Michael J. Mayberry at Mayberry's home studio in Chicago on August 5, 2000. I interviewed Stan Mosely and Emmett Garner at Mosley's home in Chicago on August 8, 2000. Quotations from these interviews originally appeared in Whiteis, "Chicago Soul/Blues: Lee Morris and Stan Mosley," *Living Blues* 157 (May–June 2001): 36–43.

1. Handy, *Father of the Blues,* 78.
2. Interview with Geoff Mayfield, director of charts at *Billboard,* April 7, 2004. Mayfield explained that Billboard categorizes musical styles largely in-house and subjectively. Their staff includes individuals with expertise in a wide range of genres, and if a question arises as to whether something should be labeled "blues," "jazz," or otherwise, it is taken to one of those people. In some cases record labels' own preferences for market niches are respected. Occasionally outside experts or the proprietors of record stores will be invited to give their opinions. "With our blues chart," Mayfield said, "we would try to be loyal to traditional blues music. This is a relatively young chart, so we have felt free to [assign] some of these decisions to the labels, [as in the case of blues tribute] albums by Aerosmith, Eric Clapton. [Or] call Bruce Iglauer [of Alligator Records], or call a store that deals with blues. The blues labels really watch this chart like a hawk." He acknowledged that most CDs by artists usually considered "soul-blues" make the chart—for example, Johnnie Taylor or Tyrone Davis—although the established R&B performer Howard Tate, who resurrected his career in the early 2000s with material almost identical to that of a typical modern-day chitlin circuit soul-blues vocalist, got categorized as "Rhythm and Blues."
3. Otis, *Upside Your Head!* 117.
4. Both Calt (*I'd Rather Be the Devil*) and Wald (*Escaping the Delta*) make this argument, albeit in somewhat different contexts.
5. Qtd. in Sinclair, "Chris Thomas King," 33.
6. Nelson, "Tyrone Davis," 16.
7. Personal conversation with Kenneth "Hollywood" Scott, Bossman Blues Center, 3500 W. Lake Street, Chicago, March 6, 2004. Scott plays lead guitar for the band Platinum, one of the groups cited by Mayberry and Morris in this discussion.
8. Qtd. in Bowman, *Soulsville U.S.A.,* 85.
9. Emmett Garner noted that merely recording for a company stereotyped as a blues label can hurt an artist's chances: "Girl [at a radio station] told me, 'I seen his record, but I saw it was on Malaco—I didn't even listen to it. I just put it to the side'" (Emmett Garner interview, August 8, 2000).
10. Attendance figures relayed to me by Bob Jones, Willie Clayton's manager (and longtime Chicago-based blues songwriter), via telephone, April 15, 2004. Jones, who was affiliated with the show's promoters, reported that paid attendance in the 4,000-seat auditorium was between 3,500 and 3,600, with another three or four hundred seats filled by complimentary ticket holders.
11. Interview with E. C. Scott, Evanston, Illinois, August 23, 2003.
12. Qtd. in Sinclair, "Chris Thomas King," 35.
13. I thank Bruce Iglauer for this observation.
14. "It's not too fanciful to imagine [the] dark and dramatic music being torn only from the Delta earth while the sun-scorched barrenness of Texas gave rise to the high, keening voice and intermittently extended guitar lines of the Texas blues. . . . Blues

from Georgia and the Carolinas . . . seem cultivated from a lush and fertile soil" (Rowe, *Chicago Blues,* 12).

15. Wald, *Escaping the Delta,* 278–80.

16. Edwards, *World Don't Owe Me,* 99–100. Edwards also writes that in 1937, when the incident took place, "[Johnson's] songs were on the jukeboxes, and everybody was listening to them"—indicating that the woman who requested "Terraplane" may not have owned a copy of the record herself.

17. Leonard Cohen to "Madeline," ca. March 1962, in Nadel, *Various Positions,* 108.

18. Spalding, *Encyclopedia of Black Folklore,* 236–37.

19. The slave dances of Congo Square were widely noted at the time and have since been cited by historians as representing the crucible of the Africanist-European cultural fusion that eventually gave rise to jazz. An evocative early account—though one tinged with the sort of romanticism that Said disparages among "Orientalists"—can be found in Cable, "Dance in Place Congo," 37–38. For other discussions of the Congo Square rituals as representative of traditional African values and African American cultural practices, see Starr, *Bamboula!* 41; and Berry, Foose, and Jones, *Up from the Cradle,* 207–8.

20. Murray, *Stomping the Blues,* 45, 144.

21. Cosgrove, "History of Chicago House Music."

22. See, for instance, Fainstein and Fainstein, "Restoration and Struggle," 9–20.

23. And when the volatility and vicissitudes of life impede them, the music and the scene simply relocate or rise phoenixlike out of their own ashes. In August 2004, after weeks of rumors and speculation, the owners of the Starlite closed their doors. As if in anticipation, Joe B. and his band had already begun to play on Saturday nights in a vacant lot on Lake Street alongside the boxlike brick building that once housed the Mighty Gun Social Club. When the Starlite closed down, they began to play there on Sundays as well. Within a few weeks musicians from all over the West Side—hard-core bluesmen, funk keyboardists, and aspiring R&B divas—were showing up to enliven the proceedings, and the show eventually moved inside. In late September the Starlite reopened as the V&M Lounge, and Joe B. returned. By then the Lake Street scene had been taken over by the Chi-West Band, a loosely knit aggregation of younger musicians anchored by drummer Arnell "Thunderfoot" Powell. The end result was that more blues was being played on the West Side than would have been the case if the Starlite had remained open—a happy irony that Eshu the Trickster would surely have appreciated.

Works Cited

Baraka, Amiri. "Funk Lore." In *Funk Lore,* by Baraka, 95–97. Los Angeles: Littoral Books, 1996.

Bell, Carey. Liner notes to *Carey Bell's Blues Harp.* Delmark Records DE 622.

Berkow, Ira. *Maxwell Street: Survival in a Bazaar.* New York: Doubleday, 1977.

Berry, Jason, Jonathan Foose, and Tad Jones. *Up from the Cradle of Jazz: New Orleans Music since World War II.* New York: Da Capo, 1992.

Billy Branch's Blues in the Schools: A Summer Pilot Program. Videotape. Prod. Art Kono, Judy Casey, and Claire Beach. Seattle: Technical Assistance Department, Seattle Public Schools, 1997.

Bowman, Robert. *Soulsville U.S.A.: The Story of Stax Records.* New York: Schirmer, 1997.

Brenner, Harold. Liner notes to *Sunnyland Slim: She Got That Jive.* Airway Records 42735.

Brisbin, John Anthony. "Jimmy Rogers." *Living Blues* 135 (Sept.–Oct. 1997): 12–27.

Brown, Claude. *Manchild in the Promised Land.* New York: Signet, 1965.

Brown, Ruth, with Andrew Yule. *Miss Rhythm: The Autobiography of Ruth Brown, Rhythm and Blues Legend.* New York: Penguin, 1996.

Burnside, R. L. *A Ass Pocket of Whiskey.* Fat Possum CD 1026.

Cable, George Washington. "The Dance in Place Congo." In *The Social Implications of Early Negro Music in the United States,* ed. Bernard Katz, 37–38. New York: Arno, 1969.

Calt, Stephen. *I'd Rather Be the Devil: Skip James and the Blues.* New York: Da Capo, 1979.

Calt, Stephen, and Gayle Dean Wardlow. *King of the Delta Blues: The Life and Music of Charlie Patton.* Newton, N.J.: Rock Chapel, 1988.

Carlozo, Lou, and Sheryl Kennedy. "So Long, Hoodoo Man." *Chicago Tribune,* January 24, 1998.

Cather, Willa. *O Pioneers!* New York: Vintage, 1992.

Charters, Samuel. *Sweet as the Showers of Rain.* New York: Oak, 1977.

Cosgrove, Stuart. "History of Chicago House Music." Available at www.globaldarkness.com. Accessed ca. February 2004.

Cox, Jimmy. "Nobody Knows You When You're Down and Out." Recorded by Bessie Smith. *Bessie Smith: The Complete Recordings, Vol. 4.* Columbia Records C2K-52838, 1993 [1929].

Crawford, Evans E., and Thomas H. Troeger. *The Hum: Call and Response in African American Preaching.* Nashville, Tenn.: Abingdon, 1995.

Cushing, Steve. "Your Wild Thing Ain't Wild Enough." Included in *Lurrie Bell: Mercureal Son.* Recording. Delmark Records DE-679, 1995.

Dahl, Bill. "Mickey Baker." *Living Blues* 154 (Nov.–Dec. 2000): 40–48.

Davidson, Basil. *The African Genius: An Introduction to African Cultural and Social History.* Boston: Little, Brown, 1969.

Davis, Francis. *The History of the Blues: The Roots, the Music, the People, from Charley Patton to Robert Cray.* New York: Hyperion, 1995.

"Division History—November 21, 1986." Available at chicago.fbi.gov/history.htm. Accessed ca. November 2003.

Dixon, Brenda. *Digging the Africanist Presence in American Performance: Dance and Other Contexts.* Westport, Conn.: Praeger, 1996.

Dixon, Willie, and Don Snowden. *I Am the Blues: The Willie Dixon Story.* New York: Da Capo, 1989.

Du Bois, W. E. B. Review of *Nigger Heaven. The Crisis,* December 1926, pp. 81–82.

Edwards, David Honeyboy. *The World Don't Owe Me Nothing: The Life and Times of Delta Bluesman Honeyboy Edwards.* Chicago: Chicago Review Press, 1997.

Escott, Collins, and Marin Hawkins. *Sun Records: The Discography.* Vollersode, Germany: Bear Family, 1987.

Evans, David. *Big Road Blues: Tradition and Creativity in the Folk Blues.* Berkeley, Calif.: University of California Press, 1982.

Fainstein, Norman, and Susan Fainstein. "Restoration and Struggle: Urban Policy and Social Forces." In *Urban Policy Under Capitalism.* ed. Fainstein and Fainstein, 9–20. Beverly Hills, Calif.: Sage, 1982.

Fine, Elizabeth C. *Soulstepping: African American Step Shows.* Urbana: University of Illinois Press, 2003.

Floyd, Samuel A. *The Power of Black Music.* New York: Oxford University Press, 1995.

Gates, Henry Louis. *The Signifying Monkey: A Theory of African-American Literary Criticism.* New York: Oxford University Press, 1988.

Guralnick, Peter. *Feels Like Going Home: Portraits in Blues and Rock 'n' Roll.* New York: Harper and Row, 1989.

———. *Lost Highway: Journeys and Arrivals of American Musicians.* New York: Harper and Row: 1979.

———. *Sweet Soul Music: Rhythm and Blues and the Southern Dream of Freedom.* New York: Harper and Row, 1986.

Guy, George "Buddy." "Man and the Blues." Mic Shau Music. Included in *A Man and the Blues.* Recording. Vanguard Records VMD 79272, 1968.

Gwaltney, John Langson. *Drylongso: A Self-Portrait of Black America.* New York: Random House, 1980.

Handy, W. C. *Father of the Blues.* New York: Collier Books, 1970.

Hansen, George, liner notes to *Billy Branch and the Sons of Blues: Live '82.* Reissue. Evidence Records ECD-26049.

Harris, Sheldon. *Blues Who's Who: A Biographical Dictionary of Blues Singers.* New York: Da Capo, 1978.

Highwater, Jamake. *The Primal Mind: Vision and Reality in Indian America.* New York: Meridian, 1981.

Holmes, John Clellon. "The Philosophy of the Beat Generation." In *The Beats,* ed. Seymour Krim, 13–26. New York: Fawcett World Library, 1960.

John, Mertis, Jr., and Willie John. "Need Your Love So Bad." New York: Fort Knox Music/Trio Music, 1955.

Johnson, Jeff. "Chicago Blues Festival Presents Full Spectrum." *Chicago Sun-Times,* June 3, 2003, p. 37.

Johnson, Robert. "Sweet Home Chicago." 1939. Included in *Robert Johnson: The Complete Recordings.* Recording. Columbia Records C2K-46222, 1990.

Kenning, Dan. "Mood Music." *Chicago Tribune Magazine,* June 24, 2001, pp. 19–20.

King, B. B., with David Ritz. *Blues All around Me: The Autobiography of B. B. King.* New York: Avon, 1996.

Leadbitter, Mike. *Blues Records 1943–1970, Vol. 2.* Milford, N.H.: Big Nickel, 1995.

Leadbitter, Mike, and Slavin, Neil. *Blues Records 1943–1970: A Selective Discography, Vol. 1, A–K* Milford, N.H.: Big Nickel, 1987.

Lomax, Alan. *The Land Where the Blues Began.* New York: Delta Books, 1995.

Mailer, Norman. "The White Negro." In *The Portable Beat Reader,* ed. Ann Charters, 582–605. Middlesex, U.K.: Penguin, 1992.

"The March of Events: Murders and Suicides Increase." *World's Work* 48 (Aug. 1924): 362–63.

McGraw-Beauchamp, Lincoln. *Blues Stories.* Chicago: Straight Ahead International, 1992.

McIlwaine, Shields. *Memphis Down in Dixie.* New York: E. P. Dutton, 1948.

McKeough, Kevin. "Keyboards Warm Up Festival Hampered by Blue Weather." *Chicago Tribune,* June 3, 2003, sect. 2, p. 2.

Mezzrow, Milton "Mezz." *Really the Blues.* New York: Citadel Underground, 1990.

Miller, Eddie. "I'd Rather Drink Muddy Water." 1936.

Mitchell, Henry. *Black Preaching.* New York: J. B. Lippincott, 1970.

Murray, Albert. *Stomping the Blues.* New York: Da Capo, 1976.

Nadel, Ira. *Various Positions: A Life of Leonard Cohen.* New York: Pantheon, 1996.

Neff, Robert, and Anthony Conner. *Blues.* Boston: David R. Godine, 1975.

Nelson, David. "Sweet Miss Coffy." *Living Blues* 120 (Mar.–Apr. 1995): 52–55.

———. "Tyrone Davis: I Am Not a Blues Singer." *Living Blues* 105 (Sept.–Oct. 1992): 12–17.

Oates, Stephen B. *Let the Trumpet Sound: A Life of Martin Luther King, Jr.* New York: Harper Perennial, 1984.

Odom, A., and F. Walker. "Memo Blues." Recording. Isabel Records, 1982. Reissued on *Andrew "Big Voice" Odom: Feel So Good.* Evidence Records ECD 26027-2, 1993.

Oliver, Paul. *The Story of the Blues.* Radnor, Pa.: Chilton, 1979.

O'Neal, Jim. "BluEsoterica." *Living Blues* 118 (Dec. 1994): 128.

——— "Junior Wells Interview." *Living Blues* 119 (Feb. 1995): 8–29.

O'Neal, Jim, and Amy Van Singel. "Muddy Waters." *Living Blues* 64 (Mar.–Apr. 1985): 15–40.

Otis, Johnny. *Upside Your Head! Rhythm and Blues on Central Avenue.* Hanover, N.H.: Wesleyan University Press/University Press of New England, 1993.

Palmer, Robert. *Deep Blues.* Middlesex, U.K.: Penguin Books, 1982.

Pruter, Robert. *Chicago Soul.* Urbana: University of Illinois Press, 1991.

——. *Doowop: The Chicago Scene.* Urbana: University of Illinois Press, 1996.

Robinson, Fenton. "I Hear Some Blues Downstairs." Included in *I Hear Some Blues Downstairs.* Recording by Fenton Robinson. Alligator Records AL-4710, 1977.

Rowe, Mike. *Chicago Blues: The City and the Music.* New York: Da Capo, 1982.

Said, Edward. *Orientalism.* New York: Vintage, 1979.

Santelli, Robert. *The Big Book of Blues.* London: Pavilion, 1994.

Saturday Night/Sunday Morning. Film. Dir. Louis Guida. South Burlington, Vt.: California Newsreel, 1992.

Sharp, Steven. "Billy Branch: Don't Start Me to Talkin'." *Living Blues* 139 (May–June 1998): 14–25.

——. "Don't Start Me to Talkin'." Available at www. bluesmusicnow.com/branch80ahtml. Accessed ca. December 2003.

Shurman, Dick. Liner notes to *Howlin' Wolf: The Chess Box,* 16–25. Chess/MCA CH039332.

——. Liner notes to *Jody Williams: Return of a Legend.* Evidence ECD 26120-2.

Sinclair, John. "Chris Thomas King: 21st Century Blues." *Living Blues* 168 (June–Aug. 2003): 26–37.

Spalding, Henry, ed. *Encyclopedia of Black Folklore.* Middle Village, N.Y.: Jonathan David, 1972.

"Still the Queen." Previously available at www.deniselasalle.com. Accessed ca. November 2003.

Starr, Frederick. *Bamboula! The Life and Times of Louis Moreau Gottschalk.* New York: Oxford University Press, 1995.

Stuckey, Sterling. *Slave Culture: Nationalist Theory and the Foundations of Black America.* New York: Oxford University Press, 1987.

Taylor, Sam. "Mother Blues." Islandia, N.Y.: Aradia Music, 1996.

Tooze, Sandra. *Muddy Waters: The Mojo Man.* Toronto: ECW, 1997.

Ulrey, Lois. "Junior." *Magic Blues* 4 (1992): 8–25.

Unterberger, Richie. "Billy Boy Arnold." Available at www.richieunterberger.com/arnold.html. Accessed January 9, 2004.

Van Vechten, Carl. *Nigger Heaven.* New York: Octagon, 1973.

Wald, Elijah. *Escaping the Delta: Robert Johnson and the Invention of the Blues.* New York: Amistad/HarperCollins, 2004.

Whitburn, Joel. *Top R&B Singles, 1942–1999.* Menomonee Falls, Wisc.: Record Research, 2000.

White, George R. *Bo Diddley, Living Legend.* Chessington, U.K.: Castle Communications, 1995.

Wright, Phil, and Fred Rothwell. "Muddy Waters Discography." In *Muddy Waters: The Mojo Man,* by Sandra Tooze, 301–68. Toronto: ECW, 1997.

Zahan, Dominique. *The Religion, Spirituality, and Thought of Traditional Africa.* Chicago: University of Chicago Press, 1979.

zur Heide, Karl Gerte. *Deep South Piano.* London: Studio Vista, 1970.

Index

Page numbers in italics refer to pages on which photographs appear.

sical activities, 102; first marriage, 103; harmonica playing of, 102, 104, 105, 106, 107; joins Moorish Science Temple, 104; participates in inmates' music program in Stateville Penitentiary, 104; performance style of, 104, 106–7; records first CD, 108; released from prison the final time, 105; at the Starlite, 16, 94, 100, 102, 105, 106, 107; tap-dancing of, 102, 105, 106, 107; time spent in jail and prison, 103–5
Harmonicats, the, 119
Harold Washington Cultural Center, 266
Harp Attack, 30
Harper, James, 238
Harris, Al, 87, 251, 284
Harris, Wynonie, 270
Harvey, Ted, 95
"Hat Man, the" (Maxwell Street habitue), 80
"Have a Good Time," 53
Hayes, Cyrus, *3, 96, 98, 99*
Heartaches and Pain, 198
Helena, Arkansas, 166
Helfer, Erwin, 42
"Help Me," 169, 185
Henderson, Emma, 103
Henderson, Willie, 225
Hendrix, Jimi, 156
Henry Horner Homes, 279
"Hey Little Girl," 239
Hickory Hills, Illinois, 275
Higgins, Monk, 27
Hightower, Judge (Maxwell Street vendor), 82–83
Hill, Michael, 166
Hill, "Pops" (patron at Florence's Lounge), 67, 68
Hill, Z. Z., 110, 222, 282
Hilliard, Leon, 239
Hinds, Mervyn "Harmonica," 184
Hines, Eddie "Porkchop," 89
hip-hop, 4, 5, 79, 93, 109, 155, 168, 270, 272, 273, 277, 279, 280, 281, 288n14
Hit Sound (record label), 27
Holiday, Billie, 79, 212
Holloway, Loleatta, 283
Holloway, Red, 40
Holly, Buddy, 177
Hollywood Rendezvous, 127
Holt, Lee-Baby, 66–67
Holt, Morris. *See* Magic Slim
Holt, Nick, 66–67
Homesick James, 50, 89, 95, 131, 158
"Honky Tonk," 217
Honore Street, 198
"Hoodoo Man" (Junior Wells single), 26
Hoodoo Man Blues (Junior Wells LP), 27
Hooker, Earl, 157
Hooker, John Lee, 32, 56, 87, 289, 286
Hopkins, Lightnin', 177, 280
Horton, Big Walter, *49, 55*; appears on Sun-

nyland Slim's Airway label, 40; in *The Blues Brothers* (film), 56; as blues "elder-statesman," 3, 16; as blues "rediscovery," 40; at Carnegie Hall, 56; childhood and youth, 48–49; death of, 55, 74; at the Delta Fish Market, 95; at Florence's Lounge, 70; incarceration of, 50; as influence on Billy Branch, 153, 166; as mentor to younger musicians, 3, 56; mentors Carey Bell, 200; mother (Emma Horton), 48; moves to Chicago, 51; musical style of, 48, 50–51, 52, 53, 57, personality, 47–48, 53–54, 56–57; personal problems of, 55–56; physical appearance of, 47–48; as "rediscovered" bluesman, 52–53; seventies-era recordings, 52–53, 160
—performances and recordings: with Billy Branch on blues festival in Mexico City, 163; early Chicago recordings of, 51–52; early musical activities in Memphis, 48–49; early recordings on Sun label, 50–51, 52; plays in Maxwell Street Market, 53, 56, 89; plays in Muddy Waters' band, 51; records with Muddy Waters, 53; records "Walking By Myself" with Jimmy Rogers, 52; records with Willie Dixon, 53;
—relationships: with David "Honeyboy" Edwards, 50, 54; with Floyd Jones, 50, 53, 57; with John Nicholas, 53; with Little Joe Berson, 56
—remembered by: Billy Branch, 157, 158, 159, 171; Johnny Shines, 48, 54; Lurrie Bell, 195, 196
Horton, Emma (mother of Big Walter Horton), 48
HotHouse, 131
Hot Shot Lounge (Lambert, Mississippi), 36
Houston, Bennie. *See* Boston Blackie
Houston, Milton, 280
Houston, Thelma, 180
Howard Theater, 126, 129
Howlin' Wolf (Chester A. Burnett), 39, 91, 93, 95, *124,* 126, 163, 217, 236, 279, 286; Jody Williams in band of, 118, 119, 123
"Hub Cap Guys, The" (Maxwell Street vendors), 80
Hunter, Ivory Joe, 236
Hyman, Phyllis, 180

"I Ain't Got You," 118
"I Am the Blues" (Willie Dixon composition), 163
I Am the Blues (Willie Dixon autobiography), 163, 290n6
I Am the Blues (Willie Dixon LP), 53, 163, 290–91n6
"I Can't Believe," 118
"I Can't Please You," 218
Ichiban (record label), 223
Ida B. Wells (housing projects), 217

David Whiteis is an internationally published critic and journalist with over twenty-five years of experience writing about blues, jazz, and other music. His articles have appeared in the *Chicago Tribune,* the *Chicago Sun-Times,* the *Chicago Reader, Living Blues, Down Beat, Juke Blues,* and other publications. He is the recipient of the Blues Foundation's 2001 Keeping the Blues Alive Award for Achievement in Journalism.

Music in American Life

The University of Illinois Press
is a founding member of the
Association of American University Presses.

Composed in 10/13.5 Berkeley
with Helvetica Neue display
by Thomson-Shore, Inc.
at the University of Illinois Press
Designed by Paula Newcomb
Manufactured by Thomson-Shore, Inc.

University of Illinois Press
1325 South Oak Street
Champaign, IL 61820-6903
www.press.uillinois.edu